THE RESURGENCE OF CLASS CONFLICT IN WESTERN EUROPE SINCE 1968

Volume 1

Other books by Alessandro Pizzorno

Communità e Razionalizzazione
Political Sociology (editor)
Operaie e Sindacati in Italia 1968–1972 (six volumes) (editor)

Other books by Colin Crouch

The Student Revolt
Stress and Contradiction in Modern Capitalism (editor, with Leon Lindberg *et al.*)
Class Conflict and the Industrial Relations Crisis
British Political Sociology Yearbook: Volume III: Political Participation (editor)

THE RESURGENCE OF CLASS CONFLICT IN WESTERN EUROPE SINCE 1968

VOLUME 1

National Studies

Edited by

COLIN CROUCH
and
ALESSANDRO PIZZORNO

HM HOLMES & MEIER PUBLISHERS, INC.
New York

First published in the United States of America 1978
by Holmes & Meier Publishers, Inc.
101 Fifth Avenue
New York, NY 10003

Printed in Hong Kong

Library of Congress Cataloging in Publication Data
Main entry under title:

The Resurgence of class conflict in western Europe since 1968.

Includes bibliographical references.
CONTENTS: v. 1. National studies —v. 2. Comparative analyses.
1. Strikes and lockouts—Europe—Case studies.
2. Industrial relations—Europe—Case studies.
I. Crouch, Colin. II. Pizzorno, Alessandro.
HD5364.A6R47 331′.094 77–16076
ISBN 0–8419–0355–7 (v. 1)

TO THE MEMORY OF SERGE MALLET

Contents

Preface ix

Acknowledgements xiii

Notes on Contributors xv

List of Abbreviations xix

1 Lies, Damned Lies and Strike Statistics: the Measurement of Trends in Industrial Conflict *Michael Shalev* 1

2 Social Conflicts in Belgium *Michel Molitor* 21

3. The Contradictions of French Trade Unionism *Pierre Dubois, Claude Durand and Sabine Erbès-Seguin* 53

4 Labour Conflicts and Industrial Relations in Italy *Ida Regalia, Marino Regini and Emilio Reyneri* 101

5 From Corporatism to Polarisation: Elements of the Development of Dutch Industrial Relations *Tinie Akkermans and Peter Grootings* 159

6 The Intensification of Industrial Conflict in the United Kingdom *Colin Crouch* 191

7 Economic Development, Labour Conflicts and the Industrial Relations System in West Germany *Walther Müller-Jentsch and Hans-Joachim Sperling* 257

Appendix I Selected Economic and Other Statistical Data 307

Appendix II Problems of Strike Measurement *Michael Shalev* 321

Subject Index 335

Name Index 346

Preface

The most respectable motive leading to sociological research is the desire to understand contemporary events. Unfortunately it is also the most treacherous. Excess may lead to starvation, too much material is available and it is so difficult to put it in order. To make sense out of contemporary events one must forget that they are contemporary and, after noting their relevance and apparent meaning, one must remember not to imagine that they constitute the cradle of the future. In other words, one must not extrapolate from them a curve which starts from very few known points of reference.

The late 1960s were a typical case of an excess of historical stimuli. There were troubles in the universities, generational conflicts, collective resistance to governmental policies (Vietnam, etc.), new intensity and new demands in labour conflicts, new forms of dissent and civil disobedience, generalised questioning of public as well as private authorities, crises in the so-called Protestant work ethic, and finally, the feminist movement. And all – or some – of these were happening not just in one country but in several, more or less at the same time.

Was there a general movement shaking capitalist societies, or merely a random series of occurrences due to national factors? If it was the former, was there some disruption of the economic structure which could account for the whole phenomenon, or should one have looked first to some hidden upset in the moral fabric of society?

The following years showed that the world economy had entered its worst crisis since the war. Might not those 'superstructural' manifestations have resembled the frantic pawing and stamping of horses during the minutes preceding an earthquake? Had not Europe seen many of the same phenomena – labour conflicts and change of union methods and leaders, feminist movements, irrationalism in political thinking, etc. – during the years before 1914?

The ebullience of social scientists followed closely behind that of society itself. A stream of volumes interpreting the course of history and the fate of modern society from the point of view of the late 1960s soon appeared, equivalent (but very different) to the literature of the 1950s and early 1960s, which had predicted a future of happy progress for Western societies. The 'movements', the generational and family crises, the universities, came to be the focus of attention for the new sociological inquiry.

This happened more slowly and cautiously in the labour movement.

Firstly, there was already a well established discipline in the field of industrial relations which had its methods and rules and was rather wary of the new. Then there was the simple fact that the labour movement had a long history. The events of the late 1960s and 1970s were rather new and surprising if compared with what had happened since the Second World War, but much less so if seen in a broader historical perspective (and especially if one took into account the first twenty years of this century). And moreover, information about what was really taking place inside firms, work-groups, or union organizations was not easy to obtain without painstaking research.

On the other hand, after the first shock of events in the areas of education, the family and minority groups, it was becoming increasingly clear that the 'structural' crisis of our society was at least as closely involved with the revolt of labour as with that of youth, women and ethnic groups.

The work published in these two volumes must be seen against this background. The initial idea can be traced back to 1973, when Alessandro Pizzorno was conducting research into changes in the system of labour representation at plant level in Italy.[1] At one of the ISSOCO seminars, during which the first results were discussed, Serge Mallet was also present. He suggested a research project in France, and possibly other countries as well on a comparative basis. The crisis of 1968, which Serge Mallet had personally experienced, had paradoxically both confirmed his earlier ideas about the 'new working class', and initiated a thorough revision of them. Further observation of the kind of industrial action prevalent in France after 1968 had completed that revision. The vanguard of the labour movement was no longer to be found among the 'technical' strata, but rather among the unskilled workers, who were of rural, often immigrant, origin, and although peripheral to the system, were playing a new and crucial role in it.

The experience of the Italian research group seemed to bring new evidence for this hypothesis, but not without qualifications. A difference between the role of the initiators and that of the followers and diffusors was also detected. And a political tradition, or the lack of one, in a certain setting, was felt to be a very central influence.

With these as yet unformed ideas in mind, we established contact with other sociologists working in the same direction. Maurice Chaumont from Louvain, Michael Schumann from Göttingen and Walter Müller-Jentsch and his collaborators from the Frankfurt Institut für Sozialforschung, were the first to join us. Later the Dutch and English contributors were added.

After a few meetings (in Essen, Paris and Brussels) devoted to explaining further organisational possibilities and cultural compatibilities, a first general meeting was held in Milan in May 1973. Three hypotheses were particularly discussed: that the new conflict-proneness and the new forms and contents of industrial action were a function of a new position of unskilled, marginal, migrant workers on the labour market; that lack of a political tradition gave industrial action an explosive and cyclical form (and *vice versa*, long tradition resulting in conflict which was more moderate but more enduring); and that industrial conflicts tended to occur in waves.

Nobody accepted the three hypotheses without reserve. Moreover, it was clear that the participants were motivated to undertake scientific research for at least three reasons. The first was historicist: what trends do contemporary events show? What do current social conflicts tell us about the future of capitalist societies? The second aimed instead at proposing and validating generalisations about the regularities of labour movements and class conflicts. The third was simply directed towards gaining better information and producing better descriptions of the *real facts*, in a field where so much had been written with so little precision.

No particular individuals can be associated with any one of these 'interests', since they were all probably to be found in different degrees in each of us. And they have remained with us throughout the whole project. The reader will judge whether they have hampered or helped our work.

So we decided to proceed. A scientific committee was elected with the following members: M. Chaumont, Cl. Durand, J. Goldthorpe, S. Mallet, W. Müller-Jentsch, A. Pizzorno, M. Schumann, A. Touraine; and A. Pizzorno was elected the co-ordinator of the project. Next month we had a meeting in Brussels. Serge Mallet was not there. He had died in a car accident. More than any of us he had worked for the building of the international group, and he was the main force within it. For some of us he was, above all, an old friend.

The project actually started when the group received a grant from the Ford Foundation (thanks to the mediation of Alessandro Silj), which covered travel expenses and meetings. At the same time Pizzorno had become a Fellow of Nuffield College, Oxford, to which institution the grant was then awarded. Colin Crouch, of the London School of Economics and Political Science, was chosen to help to organise the project, the centre of which had become Nuffield College. In two main meetings, with the participation of several experts external to the group, and in several small meetings of specialised sub-groups, the products of our researches were conceived, discussed and co-ordinated. The initial hypotheses obviously became more complex and more articulated. Comparisons between different national cases immediately helped to dismantle some oversimplified monocausal explanations. The importance of institutional factors, as well as of the *relative* economic position of each particular country, came to the fore.

Moreover the events which occurred during the course of our research not only showed how many processes definitely followed a cyclical pattern, but also how our period was a rather exceptional one, capable of revealing deep and lasting contradictions in the structure of our societies. While to begin with we were chiefly struck by the new types of qualitative demands, we later realised that the jump in wages, experienced everywhere since 1968, had more than a merely *quantitative* significance. Similarly, while at the beginning we were mainly looking for the causes of the movement, some of us later became increasingly interested in its institutional consequences in the reactions of institutions trying to regain their equilibrium, in the kind of compromises reached, the modifications experienced, the contradictions which remained. And finally, whereas to begin with, we concentrated our attention on the individual firm or enterprise, the political system and negotiations between unions and governments came more and more to the centre of our analysis.

This is a brief history of how we started and how we proceeded. It seemed useful to give an indication of it, since for many of us the process was at least as instructive as the substantive results which emerged from it. And the reader, though knowing and judging only the results, might also be interested in looking behind them. Since so many variables are kept constant, the situation could almost be regarded as an experiment by somebody interested in studying how national differences in intellectual style continue to affect the handling of a subject, even within the straitjacket of a comparative framework.

We have divided our material in two volumes. The first, after a statistical assessment of the strikes wave, includes national case studies. These have been prepared following broadly a common scheme, traces of which can be found in the titles of the sections of several of the papers. The second volume will include directly comparative essays on a number of aspects of the phenomenon.

A. P.

NOTE

1 It is published now in A. Pizzorno, ed., *Lotte operaie e sindacati in Italia, 1968–1972*, Vols. I–VI (Il Mulino, Bologna, 1974–6).

Acknowledgements

The editors are grateful to the Ford Foundation, the generosity of whose grant made the project possible, and in particular to Mr Peter Ruof, the officer of the Foundation who administered the grant, for his continued helpfulness.

We are also indebeted to the Warden, Fellows and administrative staff of Nuffield College, Oxford, for providing the base and administrative services for the project and for facilitating our work in many ways. Special thanks are due to Miss Eunice Berry, who did the great bulk of the secretarial work.

Those attending our main seminars included several participants not included among the authors of the papers, and the Oxford seminar in particular was attended by a group of trade union officers. All these people have, through their contributions to the discussion, helped shape our work, and their names are listed below. (Designations are those applicable at the time of the seminars, and in some cases have subsequently changed.)

Tony Banks, head of research, AUEW (Engineering Section), London.
Maurice Chaumont,Centre pour l'Analyse du Changement Social, Université de Louvain.
Ferrucio Clavora, CSC, Brussels.
Alessandro Conte, Istituto di Studi Economici e Sociali, Università degli Studi di Urbino.
Christel Eckart, Institut für Sozialforschung, Frankfurt-am-Main.
Angel Enciso, FGTB, Brussels.
Robert Fraisse, CORDES, Commissariat Général du Plan, Paris.
Gino Giugni, Università degli Studi di Roma.
John Goldthorpe, Nuffield College, Oxford.
Alain Guillerm, Laboratoire de Sociologie de la Connaissance, Université de Paris VII.
Ursula Jaerisch, Institut für Sozialforschung, Frankfurt-am-Main.
Walter Kendall, Centre for Contemporary European Studies, University of Sussex.
Nele Löw-Beer, FRG, IG Metall, Frankfurt-am-Main.
Jean Magniadas, Centre Confédéral d'Etudes Economiques et Sociales, CGT, Paris.
Roberto Massari, Groupe de Sociologie du Travail, Université de Paris VII.
Uwe Neumann, SOFI, Göttingen.
Michael Schumann, SOFI, Göttingen.

Alain Touraine, Centre d'Etudes des Mouvements Sociaux, Paris.
Bruno Trentin, FIOM-CGIL, Rome.
Paul Vercauteren, Centre pour l'Analyse du Changement Social, Université de Louvain.

Translations for papers in this volume were made by: Eddy Slack and Colin Crouch (Belgium); Eddy Slack (France); David Hine, Department of Politics, University of Newcastle upon Tyne, and Marino Regini (Italy); Tine Naburns, Liisa Rasanen, Ans Slegers and Anneke Stuart (Netherlands); Sue Wilcox (W.Germany).

Finally, the editors wish to thank the following for permission to use data in Appendix I: the ILO (tables 1, 5, 6, 7); the OECD (tables 2, 3, 4); CRISP (data on Belgium in table 8); Editrice Sindacale Italiana (data on Italy from *Quaderni di Rassegna Sindacale* in table 8); *BJIR* (data on the UK in table 8).

Notes on Contributors

Tinie Akkermans, D. Phil., is engaged in teaching and research at the Sociologisch Instituut of the Katholieke Universiteit at Nijmegen, Netherlands. He has published articles and collections of documents on industrial conflict and trade union policy.

Colin Crouch, D. Phil., is a lecturer in sociology at the London School of Economics and Political Science. His publications include *The Student Revolt* (1970); (editor, with L. Lindberg *et al.*) *Stress and Contradiction in Modern Capitalism* (1975); *Class Conflict and the Industrial Relations Crisis* (1977); and various articles on class, politics, industrial conflict and education. He is the author of several Fabian Society pamphlets and was chairman of the Fabian Society in 1976.

Pierre Dubois, doctorat en sociologie, is engaged in research with the CNRS Groupe de Sociologie du Travail, Université de Paris VII. His principal publications are *Recours Ouvrier, Evolution Technique, Conjoncture Sociale* (1971); (with C. Durand and S. Erbes-Seguin) *Grèves Revendicatives ou Grèves Politiques?* (1971); *Mort de l'Etat-Patron* (1974); (with C. Durand) *La Grève* (1975); *La Sabotage dans l'Industrie* (1976). He is currently engaged on research into the division of labour in mass-production enterprises and workers' reactions to it.

Claude Durand, doctorat en lettres, is head of research at the CNRS Groupe de Sociologie du Travail, Université de Paris VII. He is the author of several publications on technical change, attitudes to work and trade unions, including *Les Ouvriers de la Sidérurgie et de l'Electrotechnique* (1966); *Conscience Ouvrière et Action Syndical* (1971); (with P. Dubois and S. Erbès-Seguin) *Grèves Revendicatives ou Grèves Politiques?* (1971); *Travail, Salaire, Production: le Contrôle des Cadences* (1972); *De l'OS a l'Ingénieur, Carrière ou Classe Sociale?* (1972); (with P. Dubois), *La Grève* (1975). He is at present engaged in research on Taylorism and the division of labour.

Sabine Erbès-Seguin, doctorat en sociologie, is in charge of research at the CNRS Groupe de Sociologie du Travail, Université de Paris VII. Principal publications include *Démocratie dans les syndicats* (1971); *Memento de sociologies du Travail (1972)*; (with P. Dubois and C. Durand), *Grèves Revendicatives ou*

Grèves Poltitiques? (1971). She is currently working on (1) the economic conditions of industrial conflict; (2) justice and conflicts: the right to employment in the textile industries.

Peter Grootings studies sociology at the Katholieke Universiteit, Nijmegen, Netherlands.

Michel Molitor, doctorat en sociologie, is chargé de cours at the Centre pour l'Analyse du Changement Social, Université de Louvain. He is engaged in research on the sociology of science and of industrial relations, and a member of the editorial committee of *La Revue Nouvelle*.

Walther Müller-Jentsch, Dr rer pol., is a research sociologist with the Institut für Sozialforschung in Frankfurt. Publications include the co-authorship of a study of the development of trade unions in West Germany; since 1972 he has been co-editor of the yearbook *Gewerkschaften und Klassenkampf*.

Alessandro Pizzorno is professor and director of the Institute of Sociology at the Università degli Studi di Milano; he was previously a fellow of Nuffield College, Oxford, and has taught at the Universities of Tehran, Urbino and Harvard. His publications include several works on political sociology, social and labour movements, including *Communita e Razionalizzazione* (1966); (editor) *Political Sociology* (1971); (editor) *Lotte Operaie e Sindacati in Italia, 1968–1972*, six volumes (1974–1976).

Ida Regalia is a sociologist in the Università degli Studi di Milano. Her publications include articles on trade unions and industrial relations. She is currently working on labour relations in the public sector in Italy.

Marino Regini teaches the sociology of work and economic sociology in the universities of Milan and Urbino. He has written articles and books on the labour market, work organisation and trade unions, including (with E. Reyneri), *Lotte Operaie e Organizzazione del Lavoro* (1971). He is currently working on the role of the state in labour markets and in industrial relations in Italy.

Emilio Reyneri is a lecturer in industrial sociology and labour economics at the University of Catania. His main publications include (with M. Regini), *Lotte Operaie e Organizzazione del Lavoro* (1971); *Lotte Operaie e Sindacati in Italia 1968–1972: Innocenti e Marelli* (1974); and articles on automation, work organisation, union membership and democracy. He has just completed a large survey of southern migration and the Italian labour market.

Michael Shalev (formerly Silver) is a doctoral student at the Industrial Relations Research Institute of the University of Wisconsin, Madison; he was formerly a teaching assistant at the Hebrew University of Jersualem. He is the author of articles on strike trends in Britain, and of the forthcoming OECD report *Trends in Labour Disputes*.

Hans-Joachim Sperling, Diplom-Soziologe is engaged in research on industrial sociology and trade unions at the Soziologisches Forschungsinstitut, Göttingen. He was a contributor to *Neue Formen Betrieblicher Arbeitsgestaltung* (1975), and is currently working on collective bargaining over working conditions in the German metal industry.

List of Abbreviations

Belgium

ACEC: Ateliers de Construction Electrique de Charleroi (company).

BSN: Boussois-Souchon-Neuvesel (company).

BSP: Belgische Socialistische Partij (Belgian Socialist Party [in Dutch].

CCSP: Centrale Chrétienne des Services Publics (Centre of Christian [Trade Unions] in Public Services).

CGSLB: Confédération Générale des Syndicats Libéraux de Belgique (General Confederation of Belgian Liberal Trade Unions).

CNPS: Conseil National de la Politique Scientifique (National Council on Science Policy).

CRISP: Centre de Recherche et d'Information Socio-Politique (Centre for Socio-Political Research and Information).

CRECIS: Centre de Recherche sur l'Innovation et la Strategie (Centre for Research on Innovation and Strategy).

CSC: Confédération des Syndicats Chrétiens (Confederation of Christian Trade Unions).

CVP: Christelijke Volks-Partij (Christian People's Party).

FGTB: Fédération Générale du Travail de Belgique (General Federation of Belgian Labour).

IRES: Institut de Recherches Economiques (Institute for Economic Research).

PSB: Parti Socialiste Belge (Belgian Socialist Party [in French].

PSC: Parti Social Chrétien (Christian Social Party).

SGB: Société Générale de Belgique (company).

UCB: Union Chimique Belge (company).

ULB: Université Libre de Bruxelles (Free University of Brussels).

France

CFDT: Confédération Française Démocratique du Travail (French Democratic Confederation of Labour).

CFT: Confédération Française du Travail (French Confederation of Labour).

CFTC: Confédération Française des Travailleurs Chrétiens (French Confederation of Christian Workers).

CGC: Confédération Générale des Cadres (General Confederation of Managerial Staffs).

CGSI: Confédération Générale des Syndicats Indépendents (General Confederation of Independent Trade Unions).

CGT: Confédération Générale du Travail (General Confederation of Labour).

CNPF: Confédération Nationale du Patronat Française (National Confederation of French Employers).

CREDOC: Centre de Recherches et de Documentation (Centre for Research and Documentation).

CRESST: Centre de Recherches en Sciences Sociales du Travail (Centre for Social Science Research on Labour).

FEN Fédération de l'Education Nationale (Federation of National Education [Workers]).

JOC: Jeunesse Ouvrier Catholique (Young Catholic Workers).

ORTF: Office de Radiodiffusion-Télévision Française (Office of French Radio and Television).

OS: Ouvrier Spécialisé (semi-skilled worker).

SMIC: Salaire Minimum Interprofessionel de Croissance (national minimum wage).

UGICT-CGT: Union des Ingénieurs, Cadres, Techniciens de la CGT (Union of Engineers, Managerial Staffs and Technicians affiliated to the CGT).

Italy

ACLI: Associaziona Christiana dei Lavoratori Italiani (Christian Association of Italian Workers).

CGIL: Confederazione Generale Italiana del Lavoro (General Italian Confederation of Labour).

CISL: Confederazione Italiana Sindacati Lavoratori (Italian Confederation of Workers' Unions).

Confagricoltura: Confederazione Generale dell' Agricoltura Italiana (General Confederation of Italian Agriculture).

Confcommercio: Confederazione Generale Italiana del Commercio e del Turismo (General Confederation of Italian Commerce and Tourism).

Confindustria: Confederazione Generale dell' Industria Italiana (General Confederation of Italian Industry).

CUB: Comitato Unitario di Base (rank-and-file committee).
DC: Democrazia Christiana (Christian Democratic [Party]).
Federmeccanica: Federazione Sindacale dell' Industria Metalmeccanica Italiana (Federation of the Italian Engineering Industry [employers]).
FIM-CISL: Federazione Italiana Metalmeccanici-CISL (Italian Engineering [workers] Federation affiliated to CISL).
FIOM-CGIL: Federazione Impiegati Operai Metallurgici – CGIL (Federation of Metal Workers affiliated to CGIL).
Intersind: Associazione Sindacale Intersind (Union of State Industries).
IU: Inquadramento Unico (single-grading system).
PCI: Partito Communista Italiano (Italian Communist Party).
PSIUP: Partito Socialista Italiano di Unità Proletaria (Italian Socialist Party of Proletarian Unity).
UIL: Unione Italiana dei Lavoratori (Italian Union of Labour).
UILM: Unione Italiana Lavoratori Metalmeccanici (Union of Italian Engineering Workers [affiliated to UIL]).

Netherlands

ABVA: Algemene Bond van Ambtenaren (General Union of Civil Servants).
AKZO: AKU-Koninklijke-Zout-Organon (company).
ANBM: Algemene Nederlandse Bedrijfsbond voor de Metallnijverheid en de Elektrotechnische Industrie (General Union of Workers in the Metal and Electrotechnical Industry) (now Industriebond-NVV [q.v.]).
BBA: Buitengewoon Besluit Arbeiderverhoudingen (Extraordinary Decree on Labour Relations).
BVA: Vereniging van Werknemers in Bank en Verzekeringsbedrijt en Administratieve Kantonen (Union of Bank and Insurance Staffs).
c.a.o.: Collectieve arbeidsovereenkomst (collective agreement).
CBS: Central Bureau voor de Statistiek (Central Statistical Office).
CNV: Christelijk Nationaal Vakverbond ([Protestant] Christian National Trade Union Federation).
EVC: Eenheids Vakcentraal (Trade Union Unity Centre).
FME: Federatie Metaal- en Eloktrotechnische Industrie ([Employers'] Federation for the Metal and Electrotechnical industries).
FNV: Federatie Nederlandse Vakbeweging (Confederation of the Dutch Trade Union Movement).

Industriebond-
CNV-NKV,-NVV: Trade Unions for Manufacturing Industry affiliated to the three main federations respectively (q.v.).
ITS: Instituut voor Toegepaste Sociologie (Institute of Applied Sociology).
KAB: Katholieke Arbeidersbeweging (Catholic Workers Movement) (now NKV [q.v.]).
KEN: Kommunistiese Eenheidsbeweging Nederland (Communist Unity Movement of the Netherlands).
KWJ: Katholieke Werkende Jongeren (Young Catholic Workers).
NCW: Nederlandse Christelijke Werkgeversverbond (Federation of Dutch Christian Employers).
NKV: Nederlandse Katholieke Vakverbond (Federation of Dutch Catholic Trade Unions).
NRC: *Nieuwe Rotterdamse Courant* (newspaper).
NVV: Nederlands Verbond van Vakverenigingen (Dutch Federation of Trade Unions).
OWG: Onderlinge Werkgevers Garantieregeling (Regulation of Mutual Guarantee).
PBO: Publiekrechtelijke Bedrifs Organisatie (Industrial Organisation under Public Law).
PvdA: Partij van den Arbeid (Labour Party).
RMHP: Raad van Overleg voor Mediaal en Hoger Personeel (Council of Associations of Middle and Senior Staffs).
SDAP: Sociaal Democratische Arbeiders Partij (Social Democratic Workers Party) (now PvdA [q.v.]).
SER: Sociaal Economische Raad (Social-Economic Council).
SUN: Socialistische Uitgeverij Nijmegen (publishers).
SWOV: Stichting Wetenschappelijk Onderzoek Vakcentrales (Trade Union Research Institute).
Unie BLHP: Unie voor Beambten, Leidingerend en Hoger Personeel (Union of Officials and of Managerial and Senior Staffs).
VNO: Verbond van Nederlandse Ondernemingen (Association of Dutch Enterprises).

United Kingdom
AUEW: Amalgamated Union of Engineering Workers.
BJIR: *British Journal of Industrial Relations*.
CBI: Confederation of British Industry.
CCO: Conservative Central Office.
DATA: Draughtsmen and Allied Technicians' Association.
EEF: Engineering Employers' Federation.
IDS: Income Data Services.
MDW: Measured day work.

NBPI: National Board for Prices and Incomes.
NUBE: National Union of Bank Employees.
NUM: National Union of Mineworkers.
TGWU: Transport and General Workers Union.
TUC: Trades Union Congress.
UCS: Upper Clyde Shipbuilders (company).

West Germany

BDA: Bund Deutscher Arbeitgebersbunden (Federation of German Employers' Associations).
BDI: Bund Deutscher Industrie (Federation of German Industry).
Betr. VG: Betriebsverfassungsgesetz (Works Council Law).
BRD: Bundesrepublik Deutschland (Federal Republic of Germany).
CDU: Christlichedemokratische Union (Christian Democratic Union).
CSU: Christliche Soziale Union (Christian Social Union).
DAG: Deutsche Angestelltengewerkschaft (German Staff Union).
DBB: Deutsche Beamtensbund (German Federation of Civil Servants).
DGB: Deutsche Gewerkschaftsbund (German Federation of Trade Unions).
DKP: Deutsche Kommunistische Partei (German Communist Party).
FDP: Freie Demokratische Partei (Free Democratic Party).
IG Bau-Steine-Erden: Industriegewerkschaft Bau-Steine-Erden (Building and Quarrying Trade Union).
IG Bergbau: Industriegewerkschaft Bergbau und Energie (Mining and Energy Trade Union).
IG Chemie: Industriegewerkschaft Chemie, Papier, Keramik (Chemical, Paper and Ceramics Trade Union).
IG Metall: Industriegewerkschaft Metall (Metal Industry Trade Union).
IMSF: Institut für Marxistische Studien und Forschung (Institute for Marxist Studies and Research).
NPD: Nationalpartei Deutschland (German National Party).
ÖTV: Gewerkschaft Öffentliche Dienste, Transport und Verkehr (Trade Union for the Public Services, Transport and Communications).
SOFI: Soziologisches Forschungsinstitut Göttingen (Sociological Research Institute at Göttingen).
SPD: Sozialdemokratische Partei Deutschland (Social Democratic Party of Germany).

Statistical paper and appendices

EEC: European Economic Community.
ILO: International Labour Office.
IMF: International Monetary Fund.
OECD: Organisation for Economic Co-operation and Development.

1 *Lies, Damned Lies, and Strike Statistics: the Measurement of Trends in Industrial Conflict* *

MICHAEL SHALEV

Overt and collective conflict between labour and management has been a lasting preoccupation of many people ever since strikes and lock-outs appeared on the industrial scene well over a century ago. From the beginning public authorities took great interest in strikes, and were quick to institute the business of counting and classifying them. The statistics they produced were and still are some of the most over-abused and least understood of man's many attempts to freeze and condense richly dynamic social events into static, artificial, and misleadingly accurate arithmetic. And from the first, the indignation or self-satisfaction experienced from looking beyond one's borders and comparing one's own record with those of other countries has been one of the major attractions of stoppage statistics.

In attempting to compare what hardly bears comparison, the perpetrators of many such international comparisons have acted either in ignorance or with downright unscrupulousness. Not surprisingly, however, the grave limitations on the legitimate use of statistics have hardly bothered those whose intention has been to abuse them: there are no rules of evidence in the game of political football. For those whose minds are still open, this paper is designed to offer a sober assessment of the uses and abuses of stoppage statistics and, in particular, to indicate what may and may not be learnt from their use in cross-national comparisons.

*The title of this paper is a corruption of Disraeli's assertion – which the present author fully endorses – that 'There are three kinds of lies: lies, damned lies, and statistics'.

The author gratefully acknowledges his indebtedness to the Social Affairs and Industrial Relations Divisions of OECD, for whom most of the work reported in this paper was carried out. However, neither OECD nor those of its member-governments which co-operated with the author in carrying out the study, are responsible for or necessarily approve what is reported here. Much of the second part of this chapter has been abstracted from the author's much more extensive report to OECD on *Trends in Labour Disputes, 1950–1972* (forthcoming).

Academic opinion differs over the value of the empirical study of strikes to the analysis and understanding of employment relations. One school of thought argues that, as an unusual, even deviant, occurrence, the strike can hardly offer much insight into the overall nature of labour-management relations. Walker, for example, insists that 'the extent and form of conflict are only one aspect of industrial relations', and he cites Dunlop as concurring with his own view that 'Industrial strife is a surface symptom of more fundamental characteristics of rule making and administration in a given industrial relations context' (Walker, 1969: p. 199). Other authors have taken precisely the opposite position, arguing that 'the study of strikes is a particularly useful approach to knowledge of more normal relations' (Kelsall, 1958: p. 1), and some have even considered elevating the strike to the status of 'the most revealing index of the situation and outlook of actual workers' (Stearns, 1974: p. 1). Ironically, although they differ over what ought to be done with strike statistics, there has been little argument between most writers about their rather doubtful value in the first place. The comparative exercise attempted in this paper has been carried out with an awareness of its many handicaps and pitfalls. For a detailed analysis of these, the reader should consult Appendix II to this volume.

It is now necessary to indicate the strategy which has been adopted here to examine statistics pertaining to the six countries of immediate interest. Our aim is to analyse the *process of change* in individual countries, limiting comparisons to the evaluation of unity and diversity in *trends*, rather than directly comparing the statistical characteristics of strikes under different systems of employment relations. The analysis proceeds independently on a country-by-country basis, which means that the indices of strike activity, their industrial coverage, and the periodisation of time series are each determined in accordance with the specific conditions prevailing in the particular country under consideration. Similarly, although the data have in each case been industrially disaggregated in accordance with a standard (15-division) classification, this part of the analysis has been treated as a tool for disentangling the complexities of overall trends in the individual countries – not as a means of identifying industry-specific strike propensities which apply internationally.[1]

Let us begin by considering global trends in their most general sense. It will be obvious from the data presented in the Statistical Supplement (see page 13) that each of the primary stoppage indices[2] has risen sharply in each country in recent years. Indeed, detailed analysis of ILO data on 'Days lost per thousand persons employed in Mining, Manufacturing, Construction and Transport' in seventeen industrialised countries, reveals that the volume at least of strike activity has been rising *throughout* the capitalist world since the late 1960s, reaching a peak first in France (1968) and Italy (1969), and in most other countries in 1970 or 1971 (see Table 1.1). Different countries do, however, vary widely in the extent to which the dimensions of strike activity at the crest of the recent wave constituted a break with earlier experience. Comparing relative volume at the peak with that in the remaining years of the period 1968–72, we find that in France and Germany it rocketed upwards by as much as forty and nearly sixty times respectively, compared with a more 'normal' rise of between three and six times in Belgium, Italy, the Netherlands and the UK. On the other hand, nearly all seventeen countries had experienced at least one strike peak of comparable dimensions at some point during the preceding half a century, and in two-thirds of cases this earlier peak dated back no further than 1950. As chance would have it, however, three of the four countries for which *no* precedent can be found in the ILO series happen to belong to the present sample—France, Italy and the UK.

If the crest of a strike wave has no parallel, this does not of course mean that the dimensions of the wave itself are without precedent, and our own analyses confirm that, in crude quantitative terms, the recent 'resurgence' of conflict is, in a number of countries, precisely that—a *recurrence* of earlier trends. In many cases, the search for coherent sub-periods when analysing trends for the period 1950–73 suggests that history has indeed been repeating itself: that with the ending of the era of 'social peace' which was ushered in towards the end of the 1950s, we have returned to levels of conflict which characterised the earlier, more turbulent epoch following the Second World War. Admittedly, this kind of cyclical pattern does not hold for all the statistical features of strike behaviour (for example, there is no sign of it at all as far as the duration of stoppages is concerned); and it certainly does not tell us much about patterns of *qualitative* change in industrial conflict, such as changes in the identity of strikers, the way in which they strike, their reasons for striking etc. And not all the countries have in fact been through the three 'ideal-typical' phases we have identified.[3] In our present sample, only Belgium, France and Germany conform to this pattern. In Italy, all three standardised indices – Relative Frequency, Involvement and Volume – have been almost *continuously* on the rise since the beginning of the period. This is also true for the UK, except for a brief period of relative calm in the mid-1960s, during which stoppages continued to multiply but involved relatively fewer workers and man-days. The third exception is the Netherlands, in which recorded strikes have been so few and far between that it is hard to make out any clear trends at all, except for a definite overall increase in Relative Involvement and Relative Volume since 1969.

Although stoppage trends are empirically only partially amenable to cyclical analysis, the *conceptualisation* of strike history as a cyclical process is crucial to its understanding. Attempts to impose a linear concept of development on the long-term analysis of employment conflict, highlighting only the evolutionary and not the dynamic and repetitive elements in historical trends, are simply unrealistic. It was due to this essentially philosophical error that Ross and Hartman's famous pronouncement in 1960 about the 'withering away' of strikes has been made a laughing stock by the recent resurgence of conflict. It also looks as if these authors were so blinded by their notion of strike evolution that they perhaps unwittingly moulded their data to fit the hypothesis. In the OECD Report we show that, if analysed with greater objectivity, even the figures for 1900–1956, with which Ross and

Hartman worked, contain very little evidence of any gradual and general decline in strike activity. Ironically enough, it was Arthur Ross himself who, in a later work, most admirably summed up the evidence against what might be called the utopian view of strike history: 'Contrary to the predictions of some scholars, labour-management relations have not been moving towards any single destination . . . Instead there has been a diversity of strike movements, inconvenient to the scholar, but reflecting the great diversity of labour-management relations . . .' (1961: p. 72).

Probably the most interesting comparison for present purposes is that between the contemporary period of high conflictuality and the more peaceful interregnum which preceded it.[4] In this context, perhaps the most impressive change, in all six countries except the Netherlands, is the remarkable upsurge in the number of strikes—what Knowles (1952: p. 145) called 'the prevalence of separate outbreaks of discontent'.[5] This is so even when the figures are 'deflated' in accordance with changes in the size of the labour force. Thus the rise in Relative Frequency (stoppages per million employees) was smallest in Italy – an increase of only 30 per cent – whereas in Britain and France it doubled, and in Belgium it tripled. However, as we have already indicated, because workers cease work more often, it does not necessarily mean that they are more often in conflict with their employers, for the individual stoppage may be merely one of a number of tactical moves dictated by a wider strategy. A single dispute is today more likely than ever to spawn a *multiplicity* of different forms of protest, including those forms which are not covered by stoppage statistics (the go-slow, work-to-rule, etc.). For this reason, a much clearer index of the overall extent of conflict is what we call Relative Involvement – the number of workers involved per 10,000 employees.[6] In Italy, where Relative Involvement has always been much higher in absolute terms than in any other country, its rate of increase has been the slowest, a rise of 'only' about two-thirds; whereas in the other five instances, we note an increase of between 100 per cent and 150 per cent. In other words, in these countries the number of involvements as a proportion of the labour force has risen by between 2 and 2½ times since the late 1960s.

Impressive as these figures are, they cannot of course answer the very important question of how the increases have been distributed. Has worker mobilisation been spreading as industrial conflict rises, or has it become more narrowly confined within traditional centres of conflict? In so far as the spread of dispute activity is indicated by its industrial distribution, then the short answer to this question would strongly suggest the first alternative – namely, that involvement in strikes has been rising over a remarkably broad front, often extending in recent years to branches of the economy where open conflict was previously unknown. Industrially disaggregated analyses of Relative Involvement in thirteen countries for the same periods we have been considering so far strongly suggest that in most countries the industrial scope of strike participation has recently expanded in several directions.[7]

In general, by far the most important proportional increases can be traced to tertiary-sector employees who were previously very far down the strike hierarchy – such as those in commerce, the services and public utilities. Another rather interesting new recruiting-ground for strikers has emerged in certain 'traditional' industries where, due to market constraints, the composition of the labour force or other restraints on militancy, collective conflict tended in the past to be kept to very low levels (examples common to many countries include agriculture and textiles). However, when attention is shifted to alterations in the industrial distribution of strike frequency, in other words the changing composition of the 'strike cake', it is obvious that major inroads have been made into the role played by the traditional industries. In particular, primarily as a result of the secular decline in their numbers,[8] coal miners almost everywhere have experienced a major decline in their share of the number of strikes, which was traditionally disproportionately high. There is also clear evidence of the way in which strike activity has adjusted itself to the changing patterns of Western economies in the almost universal consolidation of the metal-working sector as the leading 'strike centre'. Detailed examination of the component elements of this rather amorphous industrial category reveals certain diversities of trend, yet the overall impression is that the metal and engineering industries account for a large, and in many countries a growing, proportion of strikes.[9]

For the purposes of analysis, then, trends in industrially disaggregated data can be usefully divided between the 'traditional', the 'tertiary' and the 'metal' sectors. In order to get some insight into the nuances underlying the general trends already discussed, and to see how closely they apply to individual cases, we shall now use this framework to review more closely the disaggregated data for four of the countries covered by the present study—Belgium, France, Italy and the UK.

The traditional sector: All four countries have experienced a substantial decline in the relative significance of the mining industry, most dramatically so in Belgium and Britain, where mining strikes had their share of total frequency cut by about 90 per cent and 80 per cent respectively between the years 1950–58 and 1968–73. France, Italy and Britain have also experienced major declines in the proportion of strikes attributable to the construction industry. In addition, Belgium and, to a lesser extent, France saw a decline in the textile industry, while in Italy agriculture may be more clearly singled out. Clearly, the precise make-up of the declining traditional sector is sufficiently variable to require some caution in extending this generalisation too far. Nevertheless, in all countries there are clear signs of a definite shrinkage along some kind of 'traditional' line. In Italy the combined share of agriculture, mining and construction strikes fell from nearly 30 per cent of all stoppages in the 1950s to only 7 per cent in 1970–72. In Belgium the joint share held by the mining and textile industries dropped from over 70 per cent in the 1950s to 20 per cent in the years 1969–72. In Britain the peak for mining and construction together was reached in 1957, when they accounted for 82 per cent of national strike frequency; by 1973 this was down to only 18 per cent.

As was indicated earlier, despite the diminution of their role in national strike activity, the traditional industries have rarely been immune from the overall tendency for a growing proportion of the labour force to participate in strike activity. The most outstanding example in this respect comes from the UK, where the virtual disappearance of the mining *strike* has in recent years been offset by the enormous number of *strikers* involved in just a few major conflicts. A parallel tendency for strikes to become fewer in number but much more broadly based is also discernible in three other 'traditional' British industries – construction, agriculture and textiles. The figures for Belgium's textile industry and Italy's agricultural sector tell the same story. In many cases, a substantially greater propensity on the part of workers in the traditional sector to become involved in strikes has been quite as significant as the general tendency for these industries to account for a diminishing share of the sum total of stoppages.

The tertiary sector: In terms of strike frequency, the increased significance of this sector in the total picture is shown in only two of the four countries analysed here. In Italy, between the years 1950–59, 1960–68, and 1969–72 the combined strike share of transport, the services, commerce and public utilities rose from 21 per cent to 31 per cent to 37 per cent. In France the same group increased its share of total stoppages (outside manufacturing) by half (38 per cent – 56 per cent) between the years 1951–60 and 1961–67, after which no data are available. In Belgium neither of the indices examined (proportion of the strike total and Relative Involvement) suggests any extension of the role of the tertiary sector. But in Britain we find that, while the proportion of total (non-mining) strike frequency attributable to this group of industries has hardly altered, there has been a more or less continuous and very marked tendency throughout the period 1950–73 for their Relative Involvement to increase. Since the end of the 1960s Britain has also experienced a number of massive confrontations involving tertiary employees in the public sector, whose impact on the total volume of strike activity has been outstanding.[10]

The metal sector: We stated earlier that in many countries the already pivotal role played by this sector in the strike scene of the modern economy has recently been further strengthened. However, the detailed picture is somewhat more complex. In two of the four countries under consideration, the metal industries have become increasingly prominent in both absolute and relative terms, while in the other two only absolute increases have been registered. The relevant data for Belgium definitely place it in the former category, with the strike share of the metal sector having risen from 38 per cent to 60 per cent between 1958–68 and 1969–72. In the same period Relative Involvement in this sector rose more than fourfold, and now stands far above the levels recorded for other sectors. A similar finding, although based on much flimsier evidence, may be reported for France. Scores on Volume (the only index available) in the periods 1962–67 and 1969–73 indicate that there has been an increase of one third during this time as far as the metal sector is concerned, while aggregate Volume has risen only slightly. In the British and Italian cases, however, the share of total strike frequency held by the metal sector has remained remarkably stable during the twenty-three year period under analysis. At the same time, during approximately the last five years of the period the Relative Involvement of metal workers has risen substantially, especially in the UK. Nevertheless, in both cases this increase has been no greater than the average rise in Relative Involvement in the economy as a whole (in Italy it was actually lower).

There are clearly risks in generalising about strike behaviour in such a major and diversified sector of the economy as the metal industries. Unfortunately, however, detailed disaggregated data on which a more sophisticated analysis could be based are not usually published. Where such information is available, the results are of considerable interest. Thus in Britain we find that the distinction between modern and traditional industries is once again relevant, in the light of evidence of a decline in the role played by ship-building strikes, and a relative expansion of stoppage activity in the electrical engineering industry. Similarly, in France the data show that despite the increase in Volume in the metal sector as a whole, the traditional mainstay of this sector – the 'production and first transformation of metals' – has experienced an equally significant fall in Volume. The emphasis has thus been shifting away from the primary area of metal-*making*, and towards the more sophisticated metal-*working* industries, with Volume in the transport equipment branch having doubled, and that in the general 'engineering' industries having almost tripled in between the years 1962–7 and 1969–73.

We hope that the preceding survey of industry-specific strike data has shown that this form of analysis is of great value, both for the purpose of forming generalisations about broad changes in the 'location' of employment conflict, and in order to delve in more detail beneath the all too bland surface of aggregate strike data. Nevertheless, it is important to be aware of the limitations of the disaggregated data presently available. One such limitation, of particular significance in the present era, is that the important divisions between groups in terms of their strike propensities are very often those of occupation or of social, economic or ethnic status, rather than branches of economic activity. Thus statistics at the industrial level are of only limited value in trying to answer the major question of how far the recent strike waves have extended to previously 'virginal' sectors of the labour force. For example, the now crucial question of how strikes are distributed between the public and private sectors of employment can certainly not be answered by means of industrial disaggregation; and no country yet makes available statistics specifically addressed to this particular line of demarcation.

There is, however, one final aspect of the relative dispersion of strike activity on which statistics can throw some light—the regional distribution of work stoppages. In Table 1.8 we have brought together some rudimentary data on changes in the degree to which conflict is concentrated in strike-prone geographical enclaves. The data are 'rudimentary' because a full and accurate understanding of inter-regional strike differentials would require simultaneous consideration of both regional and industrial variation, and the comparison of strike shares with employment shares.[11] Nevertheless, the present analysis of changes in the regional concentration of strikes since the 1960s suggests an important trend (except in the UK) – namely, the tendency towards increasing geographical dispersion of the strike movement.

So far we have succeeded in establishing that throughout Western Europe there are now more strikes, and a greater number and variety of workers involved in them, than was the case in earlier years. However, the statistics should be able to tell us not only about changes in the amount and distribution of conflict, but also about innovations in strike forms and techniques. Changes in the typical size and length of stoppages form a major area of interest in this connection. The problem here, however, is defining 'typical'. The mean size of stoppages is conventionally measured by the number of 'strikers per strike', and mean duration by the number of days the average 'striker' spends on strike. These are undoubtedly useful indices, but are both subject to considerable distortion on account of the disproportionate impact of especially long or large strikes on aggregate man-days and involvement. One way of avoiding the undue influence of such 'freak' occurrences is to substitute the median for the mean; yet this may also be problematic. The location of the median is vitally dependent on how we define the unit of conflict – for example, we have already raised the possibility that the typical *stoppage* may change its 'shape', while that of the typical *dispute* remains constant. The median also suffers from inaccuracies because it normally has to be estimated from frequency distributions – a procedure subject to a significant degree of error. In addition, the fact that the median only tells us about the middle of a distribution, and nothing at all about its outer reaches, represents a potentially serious loss of information. In so far as changes in strike shapes actually occur on several fronts, we cannot hope to capture them in a single index.[12] Finally, the fact that the necessary arrays of data are almost always available in the aggregate, means that apparent trends in median size and duration may simply be a product of events in 'deviant' industries.[13]

Bearing in mind these various dangers, what can we learn about the changing shape of strikes from a comparison of the most recent data in the Statistical Supplement with that of the preceding period? We find that in Belgium, and possibly in France as well, both the size and duration of stoppages appear to have remained stable.[14] In Germany the paucity of strikes on the one hand, and their immense diversity of form on the other, make formal analysis of trends impracticable. However, the most important contemporary influence on the size of stoppages has probably been the rise of the large-scale official strike during the last few years (most notably in the metal industry); while the proliferation of brief 'spontaneous' stoppages in recent times represents the most significant development as far as strike duration is concerned.[15] In the three remaining countries – Italy, the Netherlands and the UK – we do have fairly reliable statistical data, and the figures seem to point to an increase in both the size and duration of work stoppages in recent years. At the same time, there is evidence for both Italy and the UK which suggests that the overall increase in size is a result of the growing significance of particularly large-scale disputes, which has occurred at the same time that the vast majority of strikes, which are only local in scope, has undergone no significant alteration in size.[16] We must also express a note of reservation about the apparent increase in duration in all three countries, since in Italy the change was in fact only a very marginal one, while in Holland only the mean, and not the median, length of strikes has increased. Thus, disappointing as it is, we cannot derive from the statistics any clear and consistent generalisations about trends in the shape of strikes in recent years. The availability of more sophisticated statistics, and more detailed analyses of them, would be the minimum conditions necessary to do so – although in all likelihood, greater knowledge would merely reinforce the impression of complexity in the trends already studied.

One of the qualitative characteristics of labour disputes which are sometimes measured statistically is the question of union authorisation – whether strikes are 'official' or 'unofficial'. We have information on authorisation for three countries, which in each case suggests a rather different trend. Kalbitz's study of strikes in Germany between 1949 and 1968 indicates that until the last two years of his period, one strike in every two was 'spontaneous', the proportion in individual years hardly ever diverging from between 40 per cent and 60 per cent (1972: p. 201). Throughout the period 1949–66 we also find that there was a fairly steady decline in the *overall* number of conflicts. In 1967 and 1968, however, this trend was reversed – the number of strikes rose dramatically (from fewer than 15 per year in the preceding 5 years, to more than 60); and this increase was *entirely* the result of a rise in the number of unofficial disputes. This change is even more significant when one realises that it occurred before the waves of spontaneous strikes of 1969 and 1973.

In contrast to Germany, unofficial strikes in the Netherlands seem to have diminished in importance in recent years. By the 1960s, authorised strikes had 'withered away' to the point where there were no more than three each year – compared with an annual average of about forty unauthorised stoppages. The wildcat strike reached its zenith in Holland in 1970, since when union-sponsored conflicts have become prominent. Indeed, if we compare the years 1961–5 with 1966–72 (with the exclusion of 1970), it is clear that unofficial strikes have been diminishing in importance for some time (from 55 per annum to only 17).

Data for Britain on the authorisation of work stoppages are quite different again. Ever since the contemporary collection of figures on the number of strikes 'definitely known to be official' began in 1960, at least 90 per cent of each year's stoppages appear to have been unofficial.[17] Apart from a certain increase in the relative significance of unofficial disputes in the late 1960s, their role underwent little clear change until the present decade, when the ratio of official to unofficial strikes plunged from an average of 1:20 in the years 1960–71, to only 1:13 in 1971–72.[18] However, in subsequent years (1973–4) this ratio returned to more characteristically high levels.

To end our survey, we turn to perhaps the most interesting but questionable series of stoppage data, that which concerns the reasons given for striking. Both the demands of strikers and the underlying causes of strikes (which may, of course, be two different things) are widely believed to have undergone fundamental changes in recent years. Those who expect to find signs of these changes in governmental statistics on strike issues will, however, be disappointed. The author's survey of eleven OECD countries for which such data is furnished, including five of those in the present sample, indicates that wage issues continue to dominate the statistics as much as they did in the past, and that in at least half the nations concerned the dominance of the pay dispute has actually been strengthened in recent years. It is true that non-wage issues in general, and disputes connected with the social and physical working environment in particular, have become increasingly common everywhere – but what is important is that in hardly any instance has their rate of increase exceeded the rise in the frequency of strikes revolving around more conventional issues. Of course, it may well be that the nature of these traditional issues has itself changed, in a way which the conventional categories of strike causation are incapable of indicating.[19]

Indeed, doubts may be cast on whether 'causal' statistics are of any value at all. The strikers' major demand may be simply a unifying rallying-cry, perhaps even no more than an afterthought, a necessary concession to the rules of the game. Motives are in reality far more complex than a simple statistic would suggest; they vary considerably, both between strikers and at different times in the course of a dispute. It must also be recognised that in addition to the strikers' most important explicit demand, they may be acting in accordance with *secondary* motivations and *latent* or *repressed* grievances.[20] Some experts have nevertheless argued that 'The immediate issues in strikes usually seem of a kind that might very well represent to the people concerned grievances which are sufficiently real to explain their stopping work about them' (Turner *et al*, 1967: pp. 58–9). Even if this is so, can it be accepted that the available statistics on strikers' demands are an *accurate* representation of these 'immediate issues'? In the light of what is said in Appendix II about the informational sources of stoppage statistics, this is hardly likely. And even if it were, we should still have to face formidable problems of interpretation. Since questions of pay are on the whole far more 'durable' than those concerning 'qualitative' problems, once demands in the latter area have been met by employers, they may well disappear from the discourse of strikers, in a way that wage claims never can. The true significance of the persistence of pay demands is also blurred by the fact that certain types of seemingly quantitative demands may in fact constitute wholly qualitative innovations (for example, claims for lump-sum, rather than graded, wage increases).

We are therefore obliged to conclude that an answer to the crucial question of workers' motivations cannot be answered by simply referring to strike statistics. The remainder of our quantitative analysis has, however, proved useful in depicting both the type and the order of magnitude of recent changes in the dimensions of the strike movement. To review the most important of these findings:

(a) Analysis of basic trends in a large number of highly industrialised countries suggests that the end of the last decade marked the onset of a major (though not unprecedented) intensification and 'extensification' of industrial conflict which swept like a wave throughout the capitalist world.
(b) In most instances, the recent resurgence of conflict has signalled a sudden end to the decade or so of apparent 'industrial peace' which began approximately in the late 1950s. The major distinguishing feature of the new wave of conflict is that it has made the strike an increasingly common experience for an increasingly broad section of the labour force. Not only are stoppages and involvement in them relatively more common, but the strike experience has extended to sections of the working class which were previously immune from overt collective conflict. At the same time, the industrial composition of the strike movement also reflects how the incidence of conflict has responded to changes in economic structure.
(c) Empirical study of the forms of strike activity – the 'shape' of strikes, their sponsorship and management, and the demands which precipitate them – has proved to be handicapped by the limited availability of data and by severe problems of analysis and interpretation. What strikes the observer most about the characteristics of the recent waves of industrial conflict is their multi-dimensionality; in other words, the fact that the proliferation of strike activity has embraced *all* the major forms of conflict—domestic and nationwide, symbolic and intense, official and unauthorised, inspired by economism and inspired by the deprivations of work itself.

While perhaps none of these conclusions are surprising, it is worth while to have them affirmed and even refined by the intelligent use of work-stoppage statistics. Although they can never serve as substitutes for more reliable research methods, we submit that, for all their deficiencies, these statistics can provide an informative frame of reference for the study of both national and international trends in labour-management conflict.

NOTES

1. Information on the classification used and the data it produced will be found in the author's full report to OECD on *Trends in Labour Disputes* (hereafter referred to as 'The OECD Report').
2. The three 'primary' indices are Frequency, Involvement and Volume (mandays). We prefix these terms with the word 'relative' when standardising the indices by the size of the labour force (number of employees in employment).
3. Of the thirteen countries surveyed in The OECD Report, in four of them the recent period of heightened conflict was not in any sense a repeat performance, at least not of events since 1950.
4. Because data in Germany and the Netherlands do not readily lend themselves to periodisation, the comparison is less rigorous for these countries. In the Netherlands we compare the last five years of the period with averages for all twenty-four years. In Germany we shall try to consider the years 1959–70 – which, as Table 7 shows, were highly unstable in

terms of trend – as a single homogeneous entity.

5. We have no direct evidence that this is also true for Germany in the years since 1968, but common sense suggests that it almost certainly is.
6. Nevertheless, this index also has a serious drawback. In every country except France, an individual worker adds to the total of involvements every time he goes on strike during the year. Hence, overall increases in involvement may be due either to more workers going on strike, or to the same workers striking more often – or, most probably, a bit of both. Furthermore, the number of involvements includes not only those workers who made a 'positive' decision to join a strike, but also persons who, in the classic phrase, were 'thrown out of work' as a consequence of strike action in their place of employment. For most countries we have no way of knowing how the overall increases in involvement divide up between 'direct' and 'indirect' participation in strikes.
7. The detailed analysis, which ended with the year 1972, is contained in The OECD Report. Three of the four countries in which participation had *not* broadened significantly are included in the present sample (Belgium, Germany and the Netherlands). Nevertheless, if more recent events are taken into account, and if consideration is given to 'on-site sanctions' as well as strikes, then conflict may be said to have become more industrially dispersed in all countries except, probably, the Netherlands. However, even there we find evidence of dispersion of a different kind – described in the Dutch report (p. 180) as the extension of strike activity to 'districts and plants where there had been no strikes since the war, or indeed ever.'
8. Miners remain militant (in terms of their Relative Involvement, for example) but there are simply fewer of them left to strike. However, other factors have also been eroding the number of mining strikes. Mechanisation and changes in payment systems have, in some countries, eliminated traditional sources of friction. The steady erosion of the industry's economic viability (until the recent 'energy crisis') was another possible incentive to restraint. Finally, in the British case at least, the decline in strike numbers follows a transformation of the typical *form* of conflict – from unofficial work-place protests to nationwide, union-sponsored trials of strength.
9. In the four countries of the present sample for which data on strike frequency are available at the industry level, 'metal' strikes constituted between a quarter and a third of all stoppages during 1950–72. In the other two countries – France and Germany – this proportion would doubtless have been even higher. Just why this sector should occupy the commanding heights of the strike scene is not entirely clear, but it is notable that the metal-making and metal-working industries have a critical position in the structure of the modern economy, in terms of their financial stature, their links with other sectors, their stocks of capital, and their employment concentration. In addition, the occupational and job content of work in the metal industries is constantly evolving as a result of alterations in the technology of production and the product itself, giving rise to severe problems of adjustment to change.
10. The present author has informally attempted to construct some statistics for the British case insofar as 'broadly-based pay disputes with a volume of at least 250,000 man-days' are concerned. 'Monster' strikes of this variety involving public employees were estimated to account for nearly 40 per cent of total volume in 1969–72 – compared with only 2½ per cent in the years 1960–68.
11. In most countries the requisite data are unavailable, or else nobody has bothered to invest the necessary effort required for such a complex data-analysis. The only example known to this author – now well out of date – is Knowles's construction of industrially-standardised 'strike-proneness ratios' for thirteen regions of the UK (1952: p. 207).
12. For example, it is not inconceivable that in countries where neither the median nor the mean duration of strikes have undergone any alteration in recent years, there has actually been an increase in the prevalence of both very long *and* very short strikes. Only exhaustive checking of the entire range of the frequency distributions could give us definitive answers.
13. A classic example is Belgium where, between the 1950s and the 1960s, the *median* duration for all industries rose by over 40 per cent, while *mean* duration outside mining actually dropped by some 20 per cent. The global median was rising simply because the typically brief mining strikes were rapidly disappearing.
14. Comments on France are necessarily speculative due to difficulties of interpretation

introduced by (a) the recent multiplication of discrete incidents of conflict and (b) the lack of any disaggregated data on frequency and involvement since 1967.

15. The official statistics also indicate a certain decline in duration, in that since 1968 virtually no involvements have been registered for stoppages lasting over twenty-four days.
16. For the evidence for Britain, see Silver (1973: pp. 83–5). The relevant data for Italy, based on the distinction between single-firm, single-industry, and multi-industry strikes, were prepared for the OECD report.
17. Note, however, that government figures on official strikes in Britain have been criticised as being unduly conservative (Silver, 1973: pp. 90–1).
18. These calculations exclude the coal-mining industry, in which the trend of strikes has been at variance with that in other industries. The ratios thus calculated for the individual years from 1960–74 indicate that the number of unofficial strikes exceeded the number of official strikes by the following factor: 16, 20, 15, 21 20, 16, 22, 15, 23, 29, 22, 12, 13, 21, 23.
19. In France, for example, we have some detailed statistics (Durand and Harff, 1973) which indicate that the classic call for a percentage increase in rates of pay constituted less than 20 per cent of the total number of *revendications* put forward by strikers in 1971.
20. For an interesting attempt to operationalise these concepts in a research study, see Durand (1973).

STATISTICAL SUPPLEMENT

EXPLANATORY NOTES

The philosophy behind the preparation of the tables which follow has been intentionally empiricist, the idea being that the figures should tell their own story rather than have it told for them. Thus insofar as it is possible to be objective in such matters, the data have been organised in conformity with their own 'needs' and characteristics, not on the basis of any superimposed framework. As far as the periodisation of the figures is concerned, this has meant that we have been guided solely by changes which appeared obvious from our reading of the numbers themselves. In conformity with our own experience and that of other researchers, where the different strike indices told a different story, we tended to rate their sensitivity to changes in trend highest in the case of Frequency and lowest for Volume. The notes which follow are intended to demonstrate how this method was applied to individual cases.

Table 1.2, Belgium: Trends here were the least ambiguous of any country. All three primary strike indices (for non-mining data) demonstrate a sudden and clear-cut drop dating from 1958, and an equally abrupt and even more impressive change of direction which began in the 1970s.

Table 1.3, France: All three indices were scoring relatively highly until 1958, after which the level of strike activity fell somewhat. During the period 1958–67 the trends become rather ambiguous, with Relative Frequency peaking again between 1961 and 1965, and Relative Involvement and Volume containing no definite indications of trend. Reluctantly therefore we decided to leave this rather heterogeneous period intact. The break in the series in 1968, as well as the obvious enormity of the 'events' themselves, necessitates a further demarcation at this point. In 1971 there was a relative upturn in the level of conflict, which was more or less sustained in the subsequent years, but even so the period following 1968 might have been considered as one were it not that 1971 also saw some innovations in the collection and preparation of the statistics which may have significantly disturbed their continuity.

Table 1.4, Italy: The strong tendency for the level of conflict to escalate with the passing of each successive decade proved difficult to pinpoint. In order to define appropriate boundaries, trends in all three primary indices were examined, but the results can only be considered tentative.

Table 1.5, Netherlands: Trends of any kind have been so lacking that there was no point in attempting to periodise the series. Nevertheless the years since 1970 have been characterised by considerable growth in strike activity (except as far as Frequency is concerned), and to give some indication of the extent of this change figures for the last few years are presented alongside those for the entire period.

Table 1.6, UK: In terms of strike frequency, the periods form in effect four different steps on a staircase of increasing non-mining dispute activity. The same is also true of Involvements and Volume, except for the fact that in these terms the years 1964–7 represent a discernible break with the more general upward trend of conflict.

Table 1.7, West Germany: Periodisation was very difficult because of immense year-to-year fluctuations. After considerable experimentation it was found that the excessively high number of six sub-periods was necessary in order to cater simultaneously for both the indices used. The vast differences between the scores in each time category indicate the necessity for their differentiation. In the case of the Frequency series periodisation was much easier, with the figures in each sub-period being highly homogeneous internally but clearly distinguishable from their neighbours.

TECHNICAL NOTES

1. All period averages are *geometric* means – that is, the arithmetic mean of the data in logarithmic form.
2. Data sources for stoppage statistics were as follows:

Belgium:	*Statistiques Sociales*
France:	*Bilan des Conflits*
Italy:	*Annuario Statistiche del Lavoro*
Netherlands:	*Sociale Maandstatistick* and the Central Bureau of Statistics
UK:	*Department of Employment Gazette*
West Germany:	*Bevölkerung und Kultur: Reihe 6*

3. Data sources for employment statistics were the Ministries of Labour of Germany and the UK, OECD's *Labour Force Statistics* for other countries.
4. For information on the methodology of strike measurement in the six countries, see the discussion in Appendix II (pp. 319–32).

TABLE 1.1: *Trends in Relative Strike Volume* in 17 Industrialised Countries, 1927–1972*

	Rank Order 1948–72	*Recent Peak Year(s)*	*Previous Peak*†	*N of Recent Peak Years (s)*	*Peak Year(s)*	*1968–72 (excl. Peak)*	*1963–7*	*1958–62*	*1953–7*	*1948–52*	*1933–7*	*1927–32*
U.S.A.	1	1970	1959	2,210	170	*100*	70	75	75	125	75	35
Italy	2	1969	None Since 1949	4,160	320	*100*	75	70	40	75	. .	. .
Ireland	3	1969	1937	2,170	335	*100*	170	45	45	150	225	50
Canada	4	1969–70	–	2,360	190	*100*	60	40	55	50	25	10
Australia	5	1970–71	1950	1,160	170	*100*	55	40	80	140	55	150
Japan	6	1971–72	1965	290	155	*100*	100	230	240	470	30	85
France	7	1968	–	10,450‡	3,990	*100*	115	85	160	305	115	160
U.K.	8	1971–72	–	1,530	295	*100*	35	60	45	25	35	80
Belgium	9	1970–71	1957	780	485	*100*	80	105	365	445	345	345§
Finland	10	1971	1950	3,320	1,115	*100*	60	30	60	225	85	. .
New Zealand	11	1970	1951	470	145	*100*	50	30	25	220	40	60
Denmark	12	1970	1965	170	460	*100*	130	245	85	20	620	625
Norway	13	1970	1963	70	320	*100*	180	1,140	2,240	2,280	17,720	36,600
Netherlands	14	1970	1960	140	585	*100*	50	70	130	285	470	1,890
Germany	15	1971	1930	340	5,665	*100*	150	115	1,950	1,015	. .	6,550
Sweden	16	1971	1953	240	2,665	*100*	100	65	265	420	8,590	18,510
Switzerland	17	1971	1963	10	> 200	*100*	> 100	100	> 140	> 340	> 1,360	> 2,700

* Relative Strike Volume defined here as 'Days lost per thousand persons employed in Mining, Manufacturing, Construction and Transport'. Index of 'centred trend': 1968–72 (Excluding the Peak) = 100. Period Averages are Geometric Means.

† The most recent year which previously matched or exceeded the current peak. If there were two peak years, the higher of the two was used for comparison.

‡ Estimated total volume divided by total Wage-Earners and Salaried Employees in non-agricultural industries.

§ 1927–28: Index = 83; 1929–32: Index = 0.5

Source: International Labour Office.

TABLE 1.2 *Belgium*

	1950–7	*1958–69*	*1970–3*
Excluding Mining:			
Stoppages per million employees	27	15	56
Involvements per stoppage (size)	903	454	463
Man-days per involvement (duration)	13.1	10.3	10.7
Involvements per 10,000 employees	243	72	256
Including Mining:			
Man-days per 1,000 employees	319	76	251
Median duration	3.5	4.9	5.1*

* 1970–2 only

TABLE 1.3: *France**

	1950–7	*1958–67*	*1969–70*	*1971–3*
All Industries:				
Stoppages per million employees	179	124	185	235
Man-days per striker† (duration)	–	2.1	1.5	1.5
Strikers per 10,000 employees	–	733	837	1,657
Excluding Mining and Multi-Industry Disputes‡:				
Man-days per 1,000 employees	243	130	117	197

* Stoppage statistics are not available for Agriculture or 'Public Administration' (other than public enterprises and services of an industrial or commercial nature). Employment data exclude agricultural workers.

† Figures on 'strikers' refer to the number of *individual workers* involved in disputes during a year.

‡ Information on the Volume of multi-industry disputes is not available for the years 1954–5 and 1957–9, and therefore could not be deducted from total Volume in these years.

TABLE 1.4: *Italy*

	1950–9	*1960–8*	*1969–73*
Stoppages per million employees	153	263	344
Involvements per stoppage (size)	1,168	876	1,131
Man-days per involvement (duration*)	22	30	32
Involvements per 1,000 employees	1,783	2,306	3,892
Man-days† per 1,000 employees	483	866	1,746

* In hours

† Following ILO practice, man-days are assumed to be of seven hours duration (eight hours prior to 1970)

TABLE 1.5: *Netherlands*

	1950–73	*1970–3*
Stoppages per million employees	14	6
Involvements per stoppage (size)	274	1,599
Median Size*	86	203
Man-days per involvement (duration)	3.8	5.5
Median duration*	1.8	1.6
Involvements per 10,000 employees	37	100
Man-days per 1,000 employees	14	55

* The unit of analysis in the calculation of the median is the number of enterprises affected by strikes, not the stoppages themselves.

TABLE 1.6: *United Kingdom*

	1950–8	*1959–63*	*1964–7*	*1968–73*
Excluding Mining:				
Stoppages per million employees	27	50	67	115
Involvements per stoppage (size)	585	707	426	602
Man-days per involement (duration)	6.1	3.9	3.6	5.4
Involvements per 10,000 employees	159	350	286	697
Including Mining:				
Man-days per 1,000 employees	121	153	110	429
Median size	–	58	80	115
Median duration	1.3	1.5	1.7	2.6

TABLE 1.7: *West Germany (continued on p. 18)*

	*Involvements per 10,000 Employees**		*Man-days per 1,000 Employees**	
1951–8	76		74	
1959–61	11		3	31
1962–3	47		33	
1964–5	3		1	3
1966–70	45	54	4	
1971–4	68		28	

TABLE 1.7: *West Germany (continued)*

	Stoppages† per Million Employees
1950–1	7·4
1952–62	2·5
1963–6	1.1
1967–8	3·4

* Excluding the agricultural and forestry sector, civil service, and the armed forces.

† Unofficial figures compiled by Kalbitz (1972: p. 39).

TABLE 1.8: *The Regional Concentration of Strike Activity in the Six Countries**

	Strike Index †	*(a) No. of Key Regions*	*(b) Total No. of Regions*	*(a) ÷ (b) 1960–3*	*(a) ÷ (b) 1970–3*
Belgium	I	3	9	86%‡	73%§
France	V	3	21	48%‖	41%
Italy	F	5	19	58%	51%
Netherlands	F	1‖	N.A.	31%‡	4%§
UK	I	3	10	51%	57%
West Germany	I	3	10	92%	90%

* Period averages are geometric means.

† F = Frequency; I = Involvements; V = Volume (Man-days).

‡ For the years 1959–62.

§ For the years 1969–72.

‖ For the years 1960–2 and 1964.

‖ 'Key Region' is Amsterdam. Note that for West Holland *as a whole*, if 1973 is ignored, the later years showed *more* concentration than the earlier years (72% *vs.* 53%).

LIST OF WORKS CITED

Durand, C. (1973), *Les Grèves de 1971: Pratiques Revendicatives et Orientations Idéologiques* (Groupe de Sociologie du Travail, Université de Paris, VII).

—— and Harff, Y. (1973), 'Panorama statistique des grèves', *Sociologie du Travail*, 15, 4, 356–75.

Hyman, R. (1972), *Strikes* (London: Fontana/Collins).

Kalbitz, R. (1972), *Die Arbeitskämpfe in der BRD – Ausperrung und Streik 1948–68* (Ph.D Dissertation, Bochum University).

Kelsall, E. P. (1958), 'A theoretical setting for the study and treatment of strikes', *Occupational Psychology*, 32, 1, 1–20.

Knowles, K. G. J. C. (1952), *Strikes – A Study in Industrial Conflict* (Oxford: Blackwell).

Ross, A. M. (1961), 'The prospects for industrial conflict', *Industrial Relations*, 1, 1, 57–74.

—— and Hartmann, P. T. (1960), *Changing Patterns of Industrial Conflict* (New York: Wiley).

Silver, M. (or Shalev, M.) (1973), 'Recent British strike trends: a factual analysis', *British Journal of Industrial Relations*, xi, 1.

Stearns, P. N. (1974), 'Measuring the evolution of strike movements', *International Review of Social History*, 19, 1, 1–27.

Turner, H. A., Clack, G. and Roberts, G. (1967), *Labour Relations in the Motor Industry* (London: Allen and Unwin).

Walker, K. F. (1969), 'Strategic factors in industrial relations systems', *International Institute of Labour Studies Bulletin*, No. 6, 197–209.

2 *Social Conflicts in Belgium*

MICHEL MOLITOR

1 THE SOCIO-ECONOMIC CONTEXT

The development of socio-economic conflict in Belgium in recent years needs to be seen in the context of an economy undergoing transformation. The sources of this transformation are varied, and in several cases relate to factors outside Belgian society. Two factors in particular stand out as important: a change in the relations between the two regions of the country, with the industrialisation and development of Flanders and the structural decline of Wallonia;[1] and the growth of foreign investment and a shift in the control of industry.

Until as late as the mid-1960s Wallonia was the more developed industrial region, while Flanders suffered from under-development and structural unemployment (Verly, 1973). Since then, however, the situation has been reversed. New investment in Flanders has outstripped that in the French-speaking part of the country, particularly in modern technological industries, primarily as a result of foreign investment. Corresponding to this change, employment has declined in Wallonia but increased in both Flanders and the Brussels region. Not only is unemployment now higher in Wallonia, but the population is declining, partly as a result of migration to Brussels.

In the country as a whole, unemployment remained high after the Second World War until 1952–3, when it began to decline until 1964. Since 1965 it has risen again, and apart from a reduction in 1969, it has accelerated rapidly in very recent years. And it is since 1964 that Wallonia has taken over from Flanders as the region with high, structural unemployment.

The growth in foreign investment has been systematically encouraged by successive governments since 1958. By 1968 foreign concerns represented 20 per cent of total employment, 25 per cent of the Gross National Product and 33 per cent of industrial output (Beckers *et al*, 1973). Nearly 90 per cent of this investment has been in manufacturing. Its share of investment has always outstripped its contribution to employment. For example, in 1971 foreign capital provided 78.3 per cent of new investment but only 69.7 per cent of new employment (Verly, 1973). The overall effect of these developments over the years has been the transfer abroad of control over Belgian industry, a factor which has been relevant in the recent closures of firms owned by foreign groups (de Vroey and Carton de Wiart, 1971).

As a result of these changes in regional balance and industrial ownership, Belgium has in recent years witnessed some major shifts in economic power and political relations. These changes have very much affected the crises of the state and of the Wallonian ruling class, although the conflicts engendered by these crises have taken different forms in the two regions. In Flanders, most conflicts have developed in the context of an economy in full expansion, and have concerned conditions of work, wages and the distribution of the fruits of growth – and, eventually, the direction of production. In Wallonia, by contrast, there have been the grave structural conflicts of a region in full recession, concerning initially the protection of employment, and subsequently issues of economic control.

However, these tensions have continued to be masked by the consistently high rates of economic growth and improvement in productivity which the country has experienced since the war. A country of low wages until 1940, Belgium has become a high-wage economy, though since 1969–70 the level of inflation has started to weigh heavily on purchasing power. Similarly, until very recently areas of stagnation have been concentrated in particular localities where a lack of population growth has disguised a reduction in employment. Some statistical details of the development of the Belgian economy will be found in Appendix I.

2 THE SYSTEM OF INDUSTRIAL RELATIONS IN BELGIUM

TRADE UNIONISM

Multi-unionism

In common with several European countries, such as France and Italy, Belgian trade unionism is organised on the basis of more than one industry-wide central body. Two large organisations (the Confédération des Syndicats Chrétiens or CSC, with 965,208 members in 1970, and the Fédération Générale du Travail de Belgique or FGTB, with 836,963 members in the same year) represent the great majority of trade unionists, while alongside these two exist a series of small professionally-orientated unions (such as in public employment) and one minority central organisation (the Centrale Générale des Syndicats Libéraux de Belgique or CGSLB, with 123,210 members in 1970). A further feature is their high membership rates. In 1971, the overall figure was 67.1 per cent of the employed population, which breaks down into a rate of 81.3 per cent among manual workers and 37.3 per cent among white-collar workers (Neuville, 1973).

The three largest organisations (the CSC, FGTB and CGSLB) have ties with the political families' of Catholics, Socialists and Liberals which are the traditional constituents of political affairs in Belgium,[2] and the historical development of the trade unions itself derives from these political families. By the early 1960s the CSC had overtaken the FGTB as the majority organisation. This may be explained by several factors, such as the increasing industrialisation of Flanders and the growth of union membership among groups more readily recruited by the CSC. The CGSLB has developed among white-collar workers, technical and staff grades, and those employed in administration. Although it lacks the organisational structure and political outlook of the two majority unions, it is nevertheless considered 'representative', and may therefore put forward candidates for election to the plant-level committees (the *conseils d'entreprise* and the *comités de sécurité et d'hygiène*). In 1954, when a coalition government was formed made up of Socialists and Liberals, the Liberal Party obtained the recognition of the CGSLB as a 'representative' union (Lorwin, 1975: p. 247). This organisation does not, however, intervene to any great extent in industrial relations activity.

The CSC and FGTB are concentrated in different industries. In the 1971 work-place elections (for the *conseils d'entreprise*), the CSC had a majority in banking and insurance, mining, food, textiles and petroleum, while the FGTB obtained a majority in mass retailing, steel, gas, electricity and glassmaking (Neuville, 1974). However, these figures do not provide the best of indicators, since whatever majority is obtained is based upon a limited overall total of votes. If we look at the figures for union membership according to employment category (i.e. manual workers, white-collar workers, administrative employees, etc), it is noticeable that FGTB membership is very evenly balanced across the sectors: figures for 1965 show that it covers between 39.7 and 41 per cent of the total number belonging to a union in each category (Claeys, 1973: p. 134). The CSC is more important in private sector employment than the FGTB, while the latter is the majority union in public employment (*ibid*).

It is however in regional distribution (which does not correspond exactly to distribution by industry) that the differences between the CSC and the FGTB are most apparent:

TABLE 2.1 *Regional distribution of the CSC in 1974 and the FGTB in 1973 (in numbers of members).*

	CSC	*FGTB*
Flanders	780,001	412,781
Wallonia	206,902	405,760
Brussels	108,308	150,049
Total	1,095,211	
+ other regions	43,850	
Overall total	1,139,061	968,590

The CSC has a higher membership in Flanders (with 65.2 per cent of the members of both organisations in this region), while the FGTB has more members in the Walloon region of Southern Belgium (with 70.1 per cent of the members of both organisations). Within the organisations themselves, members of Flemish origin outnumber other groups in both cases (73 per cent in the CSC and 45 per cent in the FGTB).

This situation leads to problems of two kinds. Each organisation develops a form of regional monopoly (the CSC in Flanders and the FGTB in the Walloon region); and this in turn expresses itself in a certain amount of rigidity in trade union practice, some tendency towards bureaucratism and a sceptical attitude towards new forms of conflict, while there may be some determination to keep a watchful eye on more radical actions or even to stamp them out altogether. Moreover, the existence of a Flemish-speaking majority within both organisations has led to some stress, which was brought to light in 1960 by an FGTB leader of Walloon origin, A. Renard. Renard showed that although the Walloon FGTB was the majority union in the region, it suffered from being in a minority situation twice over, first of all with respect to the Flemish FGTB and then due to the fact that the FGTB in Flanders was outnumbered by the Flemish CSC. The end result was that even though the overall tendency of the Walloon FGTB was more radical, it was forced to align itself with the positions held by the Flemish CSC, a faction with an appreciably more reformist outlook. Such stresses manifested themselves to a considerable extent in the 1960s, and they are at present appearing once again within the trade union organisations, though to varying degrees and in differing forms. The same is also true of certain political parties.

In practice, the existence of separate central trade union bodies has not prevented the CSC and the FGTB from combining forces within a union *front commun* which, though still accepting that each retains full autonomy, allows co-ordinated action in a certain number of areas. The *front commun* originated back in 1962, the year in which two unions of public employees (the Centrale Générale des Services Publics of FGTB and Centrale Chrétienne des Services Publics or CCSP) joined forces in presenting their demands to the government (*ibid*: p. 164). In October 1965, the CSC and the FGTB drew up a joint series of demands, and joint agreements were established at various levels. Moreover, the preparation and negotiation of industry-wide national agreements on social measures (*programmation sociale*) are undertaken jointly by both unions. Nevertheless, a relatively limited number of spheres still exist in which the unions have not been able to reach agreement and where no common front has been set up.

Organisational Characteristics

Both the CSC and the FGTB are highly structured organisations at national, regional, occupational and industry level. The CSC is made up of 19 central (i.e. national) occupational unions and 34 regional industry-wide sub-divisions. The FGTB has 18 central occupational bodies and 24 regional organisations. It is evident that the weight of a central or regional union body may vary considerably. Within the CSC, the engineers (covering 17.6 per cent of overall CSC membership), the building and wood industries (17.7 per cent), textile workers (12.2 per cent) and the white-collar union (11.8 per cent) are the largest. In the FGTB, the public employees (23.5 per cent of all

FGTB members), the general workers union (22.5 per cent), the engineers (20.3 per cent) and the white-collar workers (12 per cent) dominate.

The union organisations have fairly well developed facilities at their disposal, with, among other things, their own press and research and training departments. The machinery at regional and occupational level gravitates distinctly towards the centre, though this trend is more marked in the CSC than in the FGTB; CSC strike funds are organised at national level. Such centralised tendencies are further emphasised by the continuity and irremovable nature of the leadership; in theory, unions leaders are office-holders with a mandate, but in practice they are nominated with a life tenure.

Several factors combine to explain the development of the union machinery and its tendency towards rigid forms of organisation. As unionism evolved from being trade-orientated towards having an industry basis, the organisations came to combine two spheres of activity, namely a unionism based on class orientation and one based on the provision of mutual aid, and these distinctive areas exist nowadays under various forms. Trade unions supply a certain number of services such as the payment of unemployment benefit, which is 'delegated' to the unions by the state, enabling them to obtain undoubted credit in the eyes of their membership. This 'service' outlook also reinforces a particular form of institutionalisation and strengthens links of a certain kind with the rest of society. Furthermore, where a high level of membership results from this kind of activity it does not provide much basis for militancy. There are no formal compulsory closed shop provisions in Belgium, though certain practices do come close to this in that, for example, members have particular advantages reserved solely to them, and the check-off system is established practice. A form of 'union membership bonus' appeared in the sixties, through which employers undertook to contribute a certain percentage of the wage bill to a fund that was redistributed to the unions in the form of grants or other sorts of benefit, such funds constituting a guarantee in case of breach of collective agreements van Outrive, 1974: p. 7). Lastly, the extent to which links are established between the unions and other types of organisation in society (friendly societies, insurance companies, savings banks and cooperative societies), as well as participation in numerous administrative bodies, sheds light on the way union machinery has evolved and diversified.

Political Orientations and Links with Party Organisations

Ideologically the FGTB affirms a class-based orientation. The CSC, which was originally created to compete with, and indeed directly to oppose, socialist trade unionism, has long rejected the principle of the class struggle, and it is this basic position which underlines a certain number of ideological tensions within Christian trade unionism at the present time. The doctrinal outlook of either organisation does not, however, provide much of an indicator, as in both cases they have largely been introduced by the external political groups and parties with which the unions are associated.

The socio-economic objectives propounded by both the CSC and the

FGTB are somewhat similar: workers' control for the FGTB and ultimate self-management (*autogestion*) *via* workers' control for the CSC. In actual practice both the CSC and the FGTB adopt a reformist and pragmatic approach (due possibly to a high degree of participation in national administration), even if they diverge over certain particular points, with the FGTB preferring nationalisation and structural reforms and the CSC opting for direct control. Finally, both organisations have similar positions with respect to public employment. Here, as in other areas for that matter, there is less difference between the FGTB and the CSC themselves than between their Flemish and Walloon wings. In Flanders the CSC has a noticeably populist tendency, while in the French-speaking region, both the CSC and the FGTB share a markedly class-orientated outlook.

As has been stated, the main union organisations originated in and developed from two great socialist and Christian political families, within which are to be found the established political parties: the Socialist Party (the PSB – Parti Socialiste Belge) and the Christian Social Party (the PSC – Parti Social Chrétien).[3] The PSC is predominant in Flanders and the PSB in Wallonia and hence the same overall state of affairs exists as regards regional implantation as it does for the union organisations. It is, however, difficult to determine the pattern of the workers' vote. What can be said is that a high percentage of the working class votes for the PSB. The PSC also obtains a proportion of the workers' vote in Flanders, especially in those areas where it represents a populist tendency, fairly close to certain trends within the CSC. In Wallonia a fraction of the PSC, the Christian Democrats, also has a share of the working class vote.

The links which exist between the trade unions and the political parties are therefore of a varied nature, although they are real enough, and such relations are facilitated, for the FGTB and the PSB in any case, by the fact that their membership or electorate are drawn from the same sections of the population (*ibid*: p. 167). With the PSC and the CSC as well, there are certain bonds which derive more from cultural similarities and a common clientele than any shared political aims. It remains nevertheless true that the nature of union-party relationships is relatively diverse. Each organisation may be complementary with the other or may compete directly against it. It may also happen that neither side is concerned in any way with particular issues.

There is in fact a dual trade union strategy with regard to political affairs as such. Firstly,there is a strategy of an indirect kind, in that political parties provide access to certain areas of negotiation or debate: several MPs of both parties have links with worker-based organisations of some form or another (Debuyst, 1967: p. 150). Secondly, in terms of direct strategy, these unions have direct access to government. It has been argued by Lorwin in a study of relations between unions and parties in Belgium (1975) that the former are increasingly taking the place of the political parties. For example, the unions (together with the employers' associations) are replacing the traditional parties as agents of national unity, and their increasing influence on the political scene is in direct proportion to the decline in political parties. In

October 1975, the Government's economic recovery plan was discussed first by the unions and employers' associations before being presented to Parliament. Those measures that had not obtained agreement from the unions, such as incomes policy, were neither submitted to Parliament, nor were they the subject of talks by the parties.

General economic and social trends (with the effect of the economic crisis and the unstable regional relations) create a certain number of repercussions of a real political kind within the union organisations, and these find expression in terms of internal tensions which in turn affect relations with the political parties. As Lorwin has shown (*ibid*: p. 260) the Flemish wing of both the CSC and the FGTB is both more highly structured and has closer ties with other social bodies and the political parties. Debuyst has also noted (1967: p. 218) that the percentage of Flemish Members of Parliament who participated in the administration of workers' organisations was higher than that of their French-speaking counterparts. It was added that, in the case of the PSB, this could be explained by the fact that 'the links between the party and the other branches of "Action Commune" is a less well-established fact in Flanders than in the Walloon region,' and that in the Flemish-speaking part 'leaders within social bodies are at the same time party officials' (*ibid*: p. 218–9).

The conservatism of both Flemish regional union organisations has led to some measure of strain with the political parties. In Wallonia the PSB and, *a fortiori*, the PSC are to the right of the trade unions. During the 1974 parliamentary elections, the FGTB (and in particular the Liège branch), together with the left wing of the PSB, forced socialist party leaders to take a more radical stand in the Walloon area (Lorwin, 1975: p. 263). Within the CSC, an increasing number of militants no longer recognises the PSC as a channel of political expression, and their radicalism finds expression in political actions at the union level (during plant shutdowns, for example) and in increased participation in 'progressive' movements. Such trends have engendered a more radical outlook among a certain number of Walloon CSC leaders, and this has inevitably strained relations with national-level bodies.

INDUSTRIAL RELATIONS

Means and Levels of Intervention

Trade unions in Belgium act and intervene at three different levels; in the individual plant, at the industrial or regional level and on a national, industry-wide scale.

At plant level, three kinds of institutions exist to administer labour relations; the *conseil d'entreprise*, the *comité de sécurité et d'hygiène* and the *délégation syndicale* (union representatives). The two former bodies are bipartite institutions that are more concerned with administration than pursuing demands, which is the province of the *délégation syndicale*. It is, however, at the level of sector or branch of industry that collective agreements are traditionally negotiated, and these cover areas such as wages, working hours and conditions. Bipartite commissions, which play an important part in the regulation of labour relations, also function at this level. Finally, industrial relations activity at the national and industry-wide (*interprofessionnel*) level has developed considerably over the past twenty years or so. Union action here takes two forms, with the negotiation of industry-wide national labour agreements (referred to as *programmation sociale*) and participation either in a consultative capacity or as a fully deliberating partner within a whole series of institutionalised bodies, such as the Conseil National du Travail, the Conseil Général de l'Economie or the Comité National d'Expansion Economique. The unions also participate in deliberations of varying importance, such as the Conférence Nationale de l'Emploi or the various economic and social conferences. These latter are not permanent standing bodies, but are called either by the government or the social *interlocuteurs* (i.e. the employers and the unions) on an *ad hoc* basis. Lastly, the unions play an even more direct part (under various forms) in the management of different economic or social bodies (*ibid*; see also Laloire, 1971; Molitor, 1971; van Outrive, 1974; Claeys, 1973). They sit on joint management or supervisory committees in a series of industries (steel, electricity, gas, petroleum) and certain economic institutions (the Banque Nationale and public investment and regional development companies), while playing an even more active part in running welfare and social security organisations (the Office National de l'Emploi and the Office de Sécurité Sociale). It should be noted on this point that their role is of greater importance in the administration of more exclusively social problems than of economic affairs (Lorwin, 1975). As far as economic matters are concerned, they have a supervisory rather than a decision-making function.

These links between the various levels of intervention by the unions and the development (or otherwise) of trade union action within one or other of these spheres need to be taken into account in interpreting any variation in the balance of power between the employers and the union organisations, as well as any evolution in social conflicts. Developments in bargaining at the three different levels may be divided into three periods (Vandewalle, 1975):

(a) A period in which negotiation and agreements developed on an industry and national level (1944–60);
(b) A period of decline with respect to certain forms of national overall agreement, and the drift of negotiations towards industry and plant level (1960–70);
(c) A period of increased state intervention, with an important number of agreements being concluded on a nation-wide level at the same time as negotiations were being pursued at plant and industry level (1970–5).

The post-war system of bargaining relations between the two sides of industry dates back to the 'social solidarity pact' of 1944 between the employers and the trade union organisations. This agreement, which was important in that it was to govern occupational relations over subsequent years, is subject to two distinct interpretations. According to the first of these, it illustrated and gave concrete form to an overall climate of solidarity within society which had evolved during the Resistance and eventually directed itself to aims of national reconstruction. According to the second interpretation, the employers at that time found themselves in an inferior situation with respect to a trade union movement which had taken a more radical turn (Communist Party strength had developed to a substantial degree), and it was essential for them to control a highly uncertain situation.

Entente on a social level was thus an apparent concession, though in fact it enabled the employers to organise the mobilisation of human resources within society which a revival in production required. Vandewalle notes that the 'ambivalent and dichotomous nature of this project . . . provides an understanding of the way bargaining relations (*la concertation sociale*) developed in future years' (*ibid*: p. 1).

The 'social solidarity pact' introduced a period during which the 'collective orientation of working conditions' at the national, industry-wide level was to have pride of place. This initial period in fact saw wage levels tied to the price index (in 1950); an overall national agreement on union representation, the *délégation syndicale* (in 1947); the installation of a system linking wages to skill levels; and the joint declaration on productivity. In this period also the Government intervened to define the area of collective agreements, fix statutory wage levels and social security matters, define working conditions, and establish the *conseils d'entreprise* and the *conseils professionnels* (both in 1948). The high point was reached on 11 May 1960, with the first national industry-wide agreement within the framework of *programmation sociale*. As Vandewalle shows, this agreement, which was supposed to reinforce the national level as the one at which negotiations and the organisation of labour relations were to take place, in fact ushered in a steady decline.

The wholesale effects of the May 1960 agreement were not to be achieved due to widespread strikes during the winter of 1960–1; future agreements were of much less consequence,[4] and this period was to end in a deteriorating social climate, the final note being struck by the economic and social conference of March 1970. In point of fact, there was to be a continual movement throughout this period towards bargaining activity at industry and plant level. This dual trend—the growth of the industry-wide *interprofessionnel* formula combined with the declining influence of bargaining at this level—may be explained by several factors. The policy of national-level 'social programming' manifestly provided an answer to a problem of internal structure within the unions. Through the practices engendered by bargaining relations, they became increasingly involved in administration, and this inevitably influenced union objectives, leading to changes in direction (*ibid*: p. 5). Furthermore, national-level negotiations were also used by the central confederations to exercise some authority over unions on an occupational level.[5]

However, this policy became difficult to apply as the various sectors became increasingly different in character, with strong sectors developing and the declining sectors becoming much weaker. The occupational union organisations were reluctant to accept central control of their affairs, and this led to a widespread reaction on the part of occupational groups within the unions. An additional factor working against national industry-wide bargaining was the appearance inside the unions of currents of opinion which were opposed to permanent union/management concerted bargaining tactics. These tendencies developed towards the end of the sixties and were reinforced by disputes over 'social programming' measures and their 'social peace' (no-strike) provisions.

The third period has been that of a slow revival in national-level bargaining since 1970, as revealed by the greater substance given to 'social programming' agreements.[6] Vandewalle sees these agreements as the culmination of years of favourable economic conditions, and as indicating desire on the part of employers to reach agreements covering wider issues so as to limit the possibilities of conflict at industry level during the course of the economic crisis. The strong revival in industry-wide agreements has nevertheless been accompanied by other kinds of negotiation at industry, plant and regional level. Overall national agreements deriving from the 'social programming' concept itself—as well as those which result from talks within the *conférence nationale de l'emploi* or a *conférence économique et sociale*—have thus been more important in the 1970s than during the 1960s. It is none the less true that bargaining at this level is still often considered by the unions as a means by which those in less privileged situations can 'catch up', and it is this which limits thoroughgoing exchanges at industry level and, by extension, at plant level as well. Furthermore, no liaison exists between the various different levels of bargaining.

In 1975, as the economic crisis became more acute and the rate of unemployment still more serious, it was possible to suggest that the various levels of bargaining were increasingly autonomous from one another. Occurring as they do at different levels, confusion is liable to arise between disputes whose aims and scope may vary and which may have no more than slight links between each other. Towards the end of the year the employers started an offensive, the aim of which was to cut back on 'social programming' measures and the effects of other labour agreements. Union organisations reacted to this in various different ways (in particular by advocating increased solidarity between low- and high-strength areas of membership), but it is difficult to predict what their ultimate attitude will be.

If they accept, in one way or another, that the employers are going to place these measures in cold storage for a time, this is liable to lead to divisions between the rank-and-file and the union itself. On the other hand, any hardening of attitudes on the part of the unions over keeping up with the 'rules of the game' can do no more than weigh heavily upon labour relations and worsen the crisis. Paradoxically, those elements which underlay the situation in 1944 are to be found once again in 1975: the power relationship is out of balance, and the aims of disputes are less and less clear cut. In other words, the traditional patterns governing the operation of industrial relations may become increasingly unsuited to dealing with issues as they are raised.

Union Participation in Administration

Trade unionism has a very influential role in Belgian politics, important to which is its nature as a mass organisation. Belgian trade unionism is based upon a strong working-class tradition, and it possesses efficient machinery and an effective full-time officer system. Along with the employers' associations, the unions are the only institutions whose sole terms of reference are those of industrial society. Other institutions in the political sphere define themselves to varying extents in terms of cultural or philosophical distinctions, or such distinctions combined with socio-economic tensions.

Union participation in administrative affairs may be explained in several ways. First, there is the absence of proper worker-based parties. The PSC has a multi-class following, while the PSB, though representing a fair proportion of the working class, also covers other classes and social groups according to the different regions. The socialist electorate is based as much on regional traditions as on social stratification, while the Communist Party is weak, obtaining less than 5 per cent of the votes cast in parliamentary elections. Furthermore, the unions themselves have an innate professionalist tendency that pushes them beyond dealing solely with the interests of a particular group (through their role as self-help organisations) to involve themselves in the affairs of society as a whole—a tendency which has naturally accelerated as the facilities available to the unions have developed. Finally, new institutions have been created in which the unions participate often in response to rank-and-file unrest. Examples of this have been the creation of control committees in the electricity supply industry and the Bureau de Programmation, later the Bureau du Plan.

The fact that the unions have such a firm position makes them effective in both demand and participation activities, though the participation principle sometimes tends to gain the upper hand. The power and influence of Belgian trade unionism, together with the kind of society within which it operates, make it primarily administrative in tendency. Such a definition is real from two distinct points of view. In a narrow sense, Belgian unionism has a purely administrative role, in that it occupies positions which it has succeeded in attaining, while in a wider sense it is a highly influential actor on the social scene, and although not possessing considerable decision-making authority, it does have substantial powers of sanction.

Changes in the Character of Trade Union Action

Union activity at the present time is two-sided in that it is becoming increasingly technical in its approach, and increasingly reflects attitudes and techniques familiar from the political sphere. The preference for a more 'technical' approach may be explained by changes in the points at issue and by the desire to act in an efficient manner, which is clearly apparent in the wide variety of services offered and the increase in the number of full-time officers.

All this has a number of consequences. The technical approach tends to break issues down into sub-issues, which are then dealt with individually. It thus becomes more difficult to pursue an overall objective, since in order to achieve any aim it will be split up into several elements. This leads to an even wider divergence between the overall objective (which comes within the realm of the rhetorical) and those actions which are actually undertaken (which take on a pragmatic turn, adapting themselves as they do to contingent situations). Furthermore, as the technical approach develops, negotiations become fragmented at the expense of those more traditional forms of action which involve all the members of the organisation acting together to achieve them.

Beyond this technical dimension, union action tends to take on certain features peculiar to the social context within which it is carried out. Political practice in Belgium is such that reaching compromise and easing tension are the order of the day (Molitor, 1973), and the same is also true of industrial relations. The very dynamics of bargaining mean that negotiations revolve less around what is at the heart of an issue than the manner in which it is to be resolved.

There are two major reasons why political practice rubs off on union action. First, as has been said previoulsly, the unions occupy an increasingly central place within society. It is therefore very difficult for them to avoid being influenced by the 'rules of the game' and to carry on their activities independently from what happens at other levels. Furthermore, the unions have become involved in an increasing number of what are in fact political issues, and in this respect they take up the lead given by the political parties: they come to be seen as the representatives of society as a whole in certain situations. This gives rise to certain paradoxes, since those organisations which are sometimes accused of being the instruments of consensus politics are at the same time invested with political aims of the most radical kind. The unions are expected to be both a power in society (controlling the interests of the working class) and a countervailing power within that same society, seeking to transform it.

The Institutionalisation of Labour Relations

An examination of the organisational and political characteristics of Belgian unions, their levels of action and the ways in which such action is carried out, has revealed how highly institutionalised labour relations are in Belgium. We may even speak in terms of 'over-institutionalisation' (Lorwin, 1975: p. 257). This can be explained as follows. The Belgian working class is highly organised, as is revealed by the level of union membership. However, this does not so much express a high degree of militancy among the workers as constitute both the cause and effect of the level of institutionalisation. As a cause, it means that the unions are organisations of an increasingly representative nature, and that they are led to play a greater part in the way in which society is run; and as an effect, it originates in the rules defined by the trade unions and employers' associations in bargaining (by which, for example, only union members benefit from whatever advantages are obtained).

A further factor is that the machines of the both the unions and the employers' associations are highly organised and powerfui;[7] each has its own political antennae and means of intervening in social matters. This powerful influence explains the extent to which the machinery of trade unions and employers' associations has penetrated the administrative and decision-making processes inside Belgian society. The unions therefore have a fully-fledged 'political' role, not because they operate by organising social affairs but simply because they have taken over responsibility for a whole range of problems which have normally been the province of the political parties.

The institutionalisation of labour relations as such takes on particular forms, namely the collective labour agreements (the *conventions collectives* and *programmation sociale*), conciliation or mediation procedures for disputes, and the involvement of unions and employers' associations in political, social or economic decision-making. Almost the whole field of labour relations is governed by those 'contractual' relationships which exist between bargaining parties.

From the union point of view, extreme institutionalisation has a series of consequences, whereby the unions have a fairly high level of control over policy matters and decision-making, and they make greater use of this capability in organising what may properly be called social demands (such as over the redistribution of national growth, and welfare and social security questions) than in economic affairs. As regards the latter area, Lorwin has put forward an interesting 'measure' of trade union activity in evaluating the extent to which the 1954 and 1956 FGTB programme was fulfilled (Lorwin, 1975: p. 259).

First, planning practice was only partially achieved. A planning bureau was indeed set up during the sixties, but it tended to deal with economic and social forecasting, and whatever programmes it did develop did not directly concern private investment matters. The FGTB was also in favour of nationalising the energy industry, and the electricity producers agreed to the creation of control committees that had real power, in particular over electricity price levels.[8] Public control of holding companies (or financial groups) has never been achieved. It was only at the 1973 Conférence Nationale de l'Emploi that financial groups were invited to take part in a negotiated investment programme. This measure was to be of no more than slight consequence; as has been stated, Belgian industry is increasingly under the control of foreign-based concerns, so that the major part of investment is not affected by these measures.

To conclude on this particular point, it may be maintained that the unions have been driven by the machinery of institutionalisation to accept that a temporary phase in the balance of power should continue, and that they experience very considerable difficulty in extricating themselves from it. In other words, in a number of instances they end by adapting their behaviour to the norms they were supposed to be regulating. Yet they still retain a substantial amount of influence, especially in 'social' matters, derived as much from their controlling capability as from the possibility of their exercising some form of veto.

The limited possibilities which the trade unions have for undertaking action, due to their established bargaining relationships with other groups, mean that in the final analysis they take very little initiative. The system of negotiation brings together the actors, groups or organisations at the relevant level. Progressively over time the parties to negotiation tend mutually to accept a particular approach to bargaining which is based on compromise. During the course of the bargaining interaction the actual means by which bargaining takes place triumphs over the confrontation of expectations: the logic of mutual understanding, of maintaining a balance, prevails over the logic of expectations or opposing forces (Molitor, 1971: p. 49).

As far as the bargaining parties themselves are concerned, this situation has two different consequences, resulting from the dissociation of 'political' aims or expectations from the practice of compromise. On the one hand, certain of these aims and expectations may take on an ideological slant, and in extreme cases may become utopian in outlook. On the other hand, the day-to-day actions of either party to negotiations will gradually adjust themselves to 'realities' and the various groups come to adapt themselves to whatever situation is prevailing at the time. This two-sided process (the 'rise', an ideological tendency, and the 'fall', an acceptance of reality) results in an increasing divergence between aims and means, and it is this which lies behind both an increasingly bureaucratic approach to negotiations and the radical attitudes taken up in support of negotiations, as the case may be.

On a political level, economic and social problems become depoliticised in favour of a more pragmatic outlook. Hard disputes are avoided lest they give rise to an overt trial of strength and undermine the balance which exists between the various groups. Political confrontation is reduced to its formal attributes and interaction between social groups limits itself to questions for discussion between the various sides. Within such a context, even though the unions do in fact have a great deal of power, they find it extremely difficult to enter into discussion on the economic problems confronting a modern industrial society. This also explains another paradoxical situation, whereby the unions, whose traditional role has always been one of taking action in the economic and social sphere, participate more and more in discussions on socio-cultural and even community questions. Any analysis of problems at an economic and technological level is in fact systematically diverted by the institutional set-up. This places the problems on the level of general debate, thus making them devoid of any political content.

The Role of the State

In the context of industrial relations in Belgium, the state is less involved as a participant than in providing an *area* in which negotiations take place, and in having a *stake* in disputes and the balance of power. Though with considerable means at its disposal (the state budget rose in 1976 to 36 per cent of the Gross National Product) the state has never had a particularly great part to play in industrial relations. It would be more accurate to say that it is involved in the system of relations and disputes on a social, ideological and community level and plays a dual role: an instrumental one (redistribution, investment, control, and so on) and a legitimatory one.

Any analysis of conflicts between political and/or socio-economic groups in Belgium largely involves studying their strategies towards the intervention and control of the state. An illustration of this is the conflict between the Flemish and French-speaking communities, which has evolved around questions of state control and investment. Disputes based on ideological or philosophical lines manifested themselves over education during the *guerre scolaire* of between 1950 and 1958, which centred round state subsidies for Church schools.[9] The same goes for industrial relations: the state is used as an instrument for redistributing the products of economic activity (through welfare and social security measures) or of investment (through public investment or aids to private investment) or even as an agent of enterprise in industry.

The state is not therefore simply placed on a par with the ruling class, but is subject to permanent conflict over the uses which should be made of it rather than over its basic guiding principles. It also provides an area within which bargaining takes place. Over a long period, the employers and the unions concentrated on bipartite relations. This situation changed about fifteen years ago by a transition to tripartite relations, with the state not so much acting as an arbitrator, but as the underwriter of the actual result of negotiation, recording and implementing the compromise achieved.

The extent to which the union organisations, as well as other political groups, have penetrated the state, is one of the basic facts behind the institutionalisation of labour relations, and also sheds light on the level and manner in which the unions participate in running society.

3 SOCIAL CONFLICTS SINCE 1969: A RESURGENCE OF WORKERS' MILITANCY?

From the end of 1969 social conflicts reappeared in Belgium with force and in various forms; there was considerable growth in the number and size of strikes, an increase in unofficial strikes, and the appearance of new forms of conflict (see figure 2.1).

From the general strike of the winter of 1960–1 until the end of the 1960s, the level of strike activity was considerably lower than in the preceding twenty-five years (de Ronge and Molitor, 1975). With the exception of 1966 and, to a lesser extent, 1968 when there were sectoral conflicts in the coal industry, there was little social conflict. This relative stability can be traced to two causes: the failure of the general strike, and the development of large sectoral and national agreements under *programmation sociale*. It is in this context that the early 1970s appear as exceptional years, even though the level of conflict did not reach that of 1950 or 1957. Strikes took place in mining, metals, iron and textiles, though a characteristic of the development

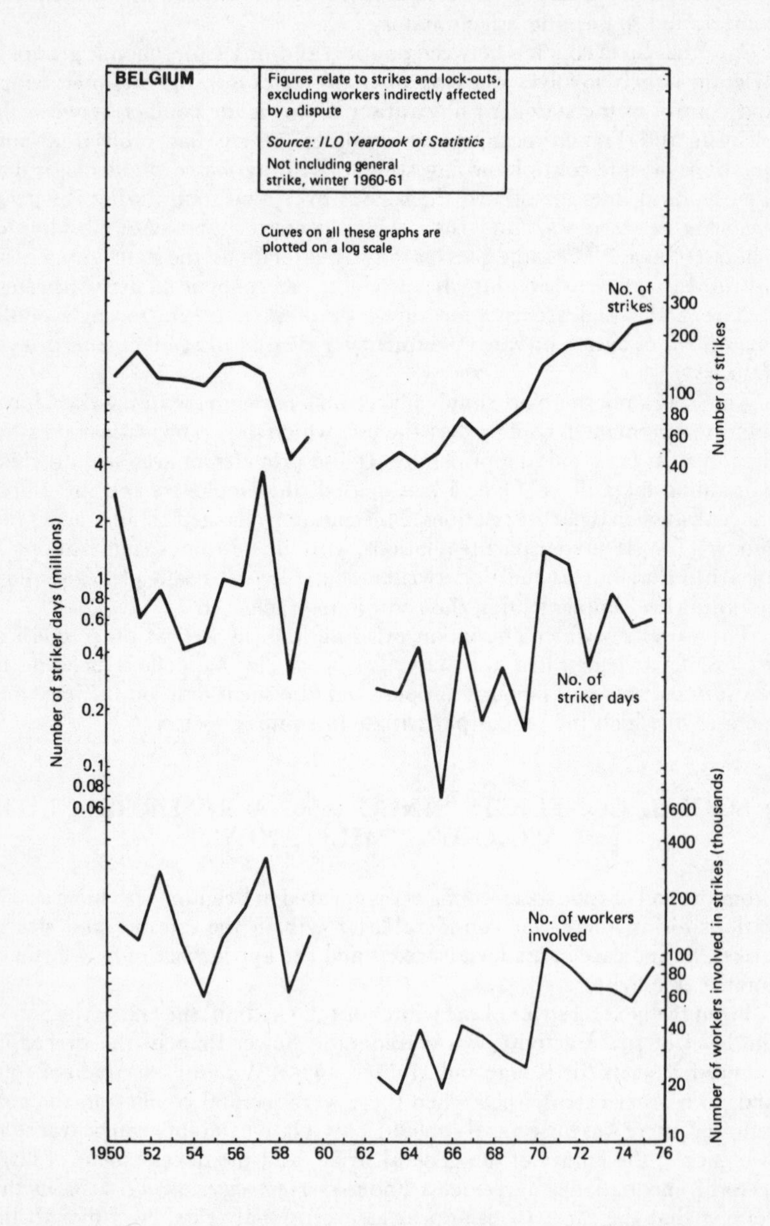

FIGURE 2.1: Industrial conflict in Belgium, 1950–75 (log scales)

was that strikes took place in individual firms irrespective of sectoral developments.

STRIKES IN THEIR CONTEXT

The strikes of the early 1970s took place in a variety of contexts – including the major differences between the economic situations in Flanders and Wallonia – and in some cases, in contradictory situations.

Strikes against Programmation Sociale

From the end of 1964 to 1966 there were several conflicts over *programmation sociale*, reversing the previous tendency for strikes at the sectoral level to decline. As van de Kerckhove has emphasised, the regional and structural agreements of the 1961–70 period concerned general issues and neglected problems emerging at the enterprise level (van de Kerckhove, 1973: p. 341). The conflicts which now appeared concerned three kinds of issue: the difficulty of revising agreements reached during periods of recession, the rigidity of union attitudes, and the limitations placed on working conditions by the agreements.

Collective agreements and economic conjuncture: Agreements signed during the period of recession (1967 and 1969) stressed security of employment at the expense of material improvements. Similarly, the national agreement of April 1969 was preoccupied with employment and reducing the hours of work. Subsequently there was dissatisfaction over the contrast between the growing level of economic activity and the poor rate of pay increases. Several strikes were directed at improving these 'agreements of poverty'.

Rigidity of union attitudes: These demands for new pay increases rapidly became strikes against *programmation sociale* and its no-strike clauses. In some important instances the rigid insistence of union representatives on keeping to the letter of the agreements provoked unofficial strikes. The unions faced a crisis of credibility with both the employers and the membership. In most cases they chose a middle path: not taking up the workers' demands as such, but raising procedural issues and adopting elements of the new demands in their own policy for the next round of bargaining. This was, for example, what happened after the Limbourg mining strike of 1970 (de Bakker, 1970).

The no-strike clauses were reviewed and in the next agreements (which were of shorter duration) provision was made for 'conjunctural' revision clauses. Strictly speaking, the national-level agreements did not contain a peace obligation. At most some, such as those of 1970, were limited to certain recommendations – for example, that sectoral agreements could not exceed those at national level.

In certain cases, as the unions appeared as mediators of conflict rather than as representatives of the workers, the *délégués syndicaux* were sandwiched between the union apparatus and the base. Since 1973 the number of *délégués* dismissed from work for 'serious fault' (i.e. striking in breach of peace obligations) has increased.

'Programmation sociale' and the rigidity of work: Programmation sociale is primarily concerned with calculable factors – pay, material advantages, grading, hours of work – which the employer can take into account when calculating the cost of production. For the duration of an agreement the position of the workers is narrowly circumscribed, while several devices are available to the employer to compensate him for the cost of the agreement. He can elaborate and apply a series of rationalisations and major modifications affecting the work situation, covering grading, output, the volume of production, systems and so forth. This deterioration in working conditions is a further factor to be considered alongside strikes. This point has been well analysed by Piret (1971: p. 7), who has shown that the agreements affected power relations only temporarily and did not mark any permanent shift.

Strikes and the Closure of Firms

Since 1970 many conflicts have concerned the closures of firms. These have occurred in two quite different contexts. In those cases where a whole sector of industry is in decline, the workers' demands have been purely defensive and have developed no political content. For example, the dispute in the coal mines in 1970–1, although superficially over wages, needs to be understood in the context of uncertainty over the future of the industry and the associated relative decline in wages (de Bakker, 1970: p. 24; Molitor, 1971: p. 48). However, there have also been conflicts over the demise of an individual company for reasons unconnected with sectoral or regional developments: for conjunctural reasons, through bad management or (in the case of multinational companies) through rationalisation. In these cases a radical critique of private ownership has developed, involving occupations and demands for nationalisation or workers' control; though often these demands have in practice amounted to a plea for better private management. Because of the political nature of conflicts over employment, this issue is one for which extensive consultative institutions have been developed; the recent closures revealed the limitations of these bodies, which explains the unofficial and frequent anti-union nature of many of these strikes.

Strikes and Multi-national Companies

These companies have been involved in three kinds of dispute: over union rights, working conditions and rationalisation.

Union rights: There have in recent years been notable strikes over union rights (Spitaels, 1969). A study of the consequences of foreign investment in Belgium (Beckers *et al*, 1973: p. 82) has shown that their acceptance of the rules and norms of industrial relations, and the speed with which they conform to them, depends heavily on the degree to which they are integrated into the region in which they are situated (e.g. concentration of firms, level of representation of socio-economic groups), relations between the companies and the unions being difficult in poorly integrated regions. The same research has shown that the level of unionisation in these firms is lower than that in small and medium-sized companies and in newly established enterprises (p. 59). By contrast, the level of unionisation is very high in firms which were originally Belgian-owned but have been taken over by foreign companies.

In some cases the companies have taken steps to restrict the growth of unions, such as recruiting young, unqualified workers (who then receive their qualifications from the company) or immigrant workers; putting workers on monthly payment systems, thereby securing their transfer to a new occupational category; and making the unions' activity more difficult by anticipating workers' demands through unilateral improvements on collective agreements.[10]

Conditions of work: A number of strikes (at Ford, General Motors, Bell, ITT, Citroen) has revealed the considerable differences in working conditions between multi-national and Belgian firms, especially as US companies have transposed to Belgium their systems of controls over work organisation and their organisational hierarchies.

Rationalisation: In decisions over reductions in investment, multi-nationals have not respected the same constraints as Belgian companies. This problem, which is closely related to that discussed above under closures, has been involved in several conflicts (Ampex, Glaverbal, BSN).

Strikes against Inflation and High Cost of Living

Since 1970, and especially since 1974, there have been many conflicts over the declining purchasing power of money. The employers are now seeking a policy of ending all mechanisms for indexing pay rises to the cost of living and a freeze in collective negotiations over pay issues. The unions reject this and are instead studying the possibility of discontinuing collective bargaining in favour of making pay rises totally dependent on indexation.

Strikes of 'New' Groups

Certain new groups – women, white-collar workers and immigrants – have in recent years figured in industrial conflict for the first time.

The female proportion of the labour force is quite large: 33.6 per cent overall, with women in the majority in some sectors. Women tend to be in the less qualified occupations and to be paid at lower rates than men in the same skill group. In some cases, for example the electronics industry, employers recruit an essentially female labour force from specific training establishments (for example, in hairdressing) but do not formally recognise the qualification. Within the unions women are under-represented, usually being represented by men even in firms where there is a majority of female workers. These situations have given rise to certain spectacular conflicts, including demands for 'equal pay for equal work', though women are now also found participating in more conventional strikes. In all these conflicts questions of pay and work have become involved with the politico-cultural phenomena of the women's movement.

Strikes among white-collar workers, who were previously considered to be allied with the employers, have been notable in the recent past: in 1971 in iron, in 1972 in the oil industry and in a general strike of bank employees, in 1973–4 in several industries. One factor in this has been the process of dequalification through mechanisation and the fragmentation of jobs, which had similarly affected manual workers in the 1920s. One indicator of this is the decline of white-collar pay in relation to that of manual workers. These developments have broken the traditional alliance of this group with bourgeois interests, as seen in their increasing level of unionisation and in the alignment of their demands with those of the workers. Although their level of unionisation remains below that of manual workers, the following table indicates its remarkable rate of growth:

TABLE 2.2

	Growth in total number of white-collar workers (index)	*Growth in number of white-collar workers in union membership (index)*
1960	100	100
1965	125	143
1970	157	182

Conflicts which involve a common strategy between manual and non-manual workers have become more frequent, though concerted actions in which one or the other group takes the lead remain quite rare. However, in some strikes in the iron industry the white-collar workers struck in alternate groups so that, while they were able to stop the production of the firm, they did not put manual workers out of work.

Apart from certain conflicts over employment in the mining industry in which they were involved alongside other workers, immigrants have mainly been concerned with strikes over their own particular problems: sub-contracting, dangerous work, the temporary nature of their labour. Some of these strikes have been strongly political (Michelin and Citroen in Brussels), and several have drawn attention to difficulties in certain firms in relations between Belgian and immigrant workers. In the majority of firms with an immigrant work force, the unskilled are almost exclusively immigrant workers, while the skilled and the management are Belgian. Similarly, while the immigrants are in any case less strongly unionised than the native workers, within the unions they are usually represented by Belgians. This situation has changed since 1970, but it has been at the root of certain unofficial strikes which have expressed the double alienation of immigrant workers—as workers and as immigrants.

Conclusions

The diversity of contexts shows clearly that it is difficult to determine a common denominator among the conflicts of recent years. Meanwhile, several major characteristics do emerge:

(a) Belgian society has been affected by structural changes which are modifying the forms and modes of control of production. These transformations have led to the development of a series of conflicts concerned mainly with unemployment and, to a lesser extent, control of the productive apparatus.

(b) The unions have repeatedly shown their incapacity to deal with certain 'new problems' such as demands for equality and control over the conditions of work.

(c) There is an over-institutionalisation of industrial relations at several different levels.

These themes reappear when unofficial strikes are considered, and it is to these that we now turn.

THE DEVELOPMENT OF UNOFFICIAL STRIKES

After the growth in the overall total of strikes, the rise in unofficial actions is the most striking characteristic of the years since 1969. In Belgium there has long been a tradition of strikes beginning as unofficial and being subsequently recognised by the unions, and this tendency is growing; it has been estimated that 70 per cent of official strikes start unofficially. A different matter are strikes which remain outside the union framework. The most important has been the six-week strike by 17,000 miners at Limbourg in 1970, but this was only the first of a series of similar conflicts, such as the eight-week unofficial dock strike in 1973, and the strike in the iron industry in the autumn of 1973. These strikes have had several common characteristics: the pursuit of several objectives apart from the original pay claim; the adoption of a very marked hostility towards the unions (especially in the strikes over *programmation sociale*); the development of new forms of action (such as occupations); and the emergence of new demands.

Characteristics

It is necessary to distinguish two types of unofficial conflict: short, minor stoppages of, say, one hour a day involving few workers and dealing with issues of work organisation and hierarchy; and more important stoppages which immobilise a factory or group of factories for a period of time.

The shorter strikes are quite frequent in Belgium, and their frequency has increased in the past few years. They seem to grow out of the experience of work and the growing contemporary rejection of certain forms of organisation and authority relations. While the expressive character of these strikes makes them very interesting, we shall concentrate here on the second type, which involve a degree of strike organisation, structure and movement.

(a) While the short spontaneous strikes tend to be found in advanced technological industries, the more important unofficial strikes are encountered more frequently in archaic sectors or those involved in rationalisation or reconversion. There is a relationship between the context of a conflict, its unofficial character and the occasion of its origin. For example, in the Limbourg mines there was a clear relationship between the decline of a sector (in employment and pay as much as in security), the pretext for the strike (the demand for a pay rise of 15 per cent) and its anti-union orientation. The unions, having refused to sanction the demand or the strike, were seen as part of the economic and social system against which the workers were struggling. There was some objective basis for this suspicion, since the unions eventually appeared as mediators between the workers on strike and the employers (Molitor, 1971: p. 52).

(b) Young and immigrant workers have often been the important and highly militant actors in these conflicts. To a certain extent one may interpret their radicalism as the product of weakness and neglect. They were rarely involved directly in negotiations, others negotiating on their behalf, and their conflicts rapidly became global. One characteristic explains the other: since the demand which initiated the conflict did not culminate in a negotiation, it slid rapidly from one issue to another until it had become universal.

(c) Important unofficial strikes are rare in factories with a strong union tradition. This phrase does not refer to the level of unionisation, but to the quality of representation and the strength of organisation. The level of membership at Limbourg was high, but the quality of union officials was poor. A similar situation can be found in recently established factories within new industrial estates, though an important exception to the pattern was the strike in autumn 1973 in Cockerill in the iron industry which was the result of a violent internal political conflict within a union.

(d) Unofficial strikes pursue a range of objectives (working conditions, pace of work, hierarchy, pay), pay being far less prominent than among official strikes. Further, demands tend to shift during a conflict (e.g. at Michelin, 1969–70). There are several interpretations of this, of which the following are important:
—as discussed in connection with the role of young and immigrant workers, the shift can result from the impossibility of concentrating the conflict on a point capable of resolution;
—there may be a growth of consciousness developing during the strike which produces new demands;
—finally, a shift towards a pay demand could signify a desire to bring the conflict to a negotiable issue.

At the same time it should be noted that when the unions have intervened in a mediating role they have often been able to end a strike by putting the emphasis on a pay demand. This indicates the tendency for the unions to choose those problems which can be dealt with through the formal channels, and to regard a strike as 'over' when satisfaction has been gained on a pay demand.

(e) In 1970–1 a large number of strikes was conducted against *programmation sociale*. These made demands going beyond existing agreements, frequently developing as an existing agreement drew near its end. These demands were concerned with procedural as well as substantive issues, such as the duration of the agreement and the existence of no-strike clauses.

(f) A significant number of strikes saw the establishment of strike committees or workers' committees to replace union representation which was criticised for its pusillanimity. It is in this context that one should place the development of marked hostility to the unions on the grounds of their 'integration', their negotiating practices, the absence of internal democracy and their modes of consulting members. The workers' committees took two forms: genuinely representative groups which took charge of the organisation of conflict; and minority groups which exercised pressure on the movement without controlling it. Their relations with the unions varied widely, from direct confrontation to taking over the union's own activity through the replacement of existing *délégués*.

New Demands

The new demands which emerged in the course of these conflicts have been discussed at various points above. In summary, they included: demands aimed at the policies of the unions themselves; egalitarian demands; demands for equal pay for equal work; political demands, such as workers' control, control over public investment or for state intervention in industry, usually starting from immediate demands for the protection of employment or improvement of working conditions. It is important to note that egalitarian demands were much in a minority.

Some of these demands were taken up by the unions – especially the egalitarian demands and those for internal union democracy, though they were very divided on those issues. The introduction of these new demands to the union apparatus provoked an important organisational and political crisis.

The Involvement of Groups External to the Working Class

Several left-wing groups outside the working class became involved in the unofficial strikes, especially the Flemish students movement. These groups were almost never involved in the origins of a strike: their intervention generally occurred in the early period of the conflict. Their role was almost exclusively one of assistance: helping with the formulation of demands, assembling facts, distributing information. Their activity was more substantial in four cases: when either the unions were unsympathetic or where there was very little information; when the *délégués* defended the agreements and condemned the movement; when the *délégués syndicaux* were in conflict with the union; and when the objectives formulated by the external groups corresponded to the demands of a section of the work-force.

DEVELOPMENT OF NEW FORMS OF CONFLICT

Apart from isolated incidents during general strikes (1950, 60, 61) factory occupations had been very rarely used in Belgium until 1967–8. But from that time they developed rapidly into a systematic strategy. Initially used in unofficial strikes, occupations were eventually used by the unions (for example, at Grès de Bouffioulx, Glaverbel, Marchand, Ampex, Val Saint Lambert). After 1973 there were a few cases of occupations being linked with appropriation of goods produced or with continuation of production under the control of the workers themselves. (Significantly, the law was never used against workers carrying on this last strategy). These 'active' occupations were usually carried on in firms threatened with closure, and the object was to demonstrate the viability of the enterprise. Only rarely did they lead to the development of demands for workers' control; in most cases the workers simply wanted private owners to accept their responsibilities.

However, the strategy of 'active' occupation became associated with a reappearance of the theme of workers' control, not in the participative sense which had been the policy of the unions for many years, but as a demand for workers to take full control of work organisation. It is nevertheless significant that this demand has usually appeared in connection with closures or rationalisations. The demand for workers' control and the accompanying ideology is again hesitant and full of contradictions. The demands have not been organised into a true union strategy.

CONCLUSIONS

The labour conflicts of recent years have provided evidence of two types of radicalisation: that of the strong and that of the weak. The former concerns workers in a relatively privileged position, largely as a result of their skills, working in the advanced sectors of capitalism such as oil or electricity. These workers were involved in several hard conflicts in 1971 and 1973, mainly over precise demands. In oil, for example, workers secured a job classification controlled by their unions and salaries payable until death. Demands of this kind have not raised global issues, but they have led to important improvements in conditions.

The radicalisation of the weak is that of unskilled workers (such as immigrants) or those in declining sectors (mining) who have not always enjoyed the support of their unions in their conflicts. These struggles have often involved a global level of confrontation. As noted above, this process is open to two complementary interpretations: one demand shifts to another because the workers never become involved in a true negotiating situation; and the union refuses to take over the demand in the terms in which it is formulated.

Finally, it is necessary to note that if the content of demands has remained relatively traditional, the form of conflict has changed and has shown considerable innovation, mainly from groups previously inexperienced in conflict and unacquainted with the constraints of union action (for example, women). The radicalisation of action has often compensated for the lack of radicalism in demands. Perhaps this merging of the instrumental and expressive aspects of conflict signifies that when a demand is not negotiable it is expressed as a provocation.

4. TOWARDS AN INTERPRETATION

It cannot be denied that in recent years there has been an appreciable rise in militancy, while at the same time new and more numerous forms of labour conflict have appeared. Does this mean that some sort of revival in workers' conflict is under way in Belgium?

Two points must be made before providing an answer to this question. Firstly, disputes have developed within very varied contexts over very diverse questions: disputes of a structural nature (those over plant shutdowns, rationalisation measures or overall social policy); those of a contingent nature (dealing with the effects of inflation and the rising cost of living); and those based on a particular situation(working conditions, matters concerning the wage hierarchy or inter-union relations). These contexts and these problems rarely exist in isolation, and the majority of disputes arises from the interaction of a wide number of basic contexts. Secondly, disputes are handled at different levels, and conflicts and subsequent negotiations reveal the complex and diverse nature of forms of bargaining activity and the lack of any relationship between them. In short, the trends in dispute activity which have been described here are by all appearances disorganised and disparate in character. They do not appear to tie in with any overall strategy, they arise from a wide variety of contexts, and those that are involved are very diverse in nature.

One thing must, however, be asked: what link or links, if any, are there between the disputes that have developed over the last few years? To reply to this question, three hypotheses must be put forward with a view to characterising these movements as a whole: these concern the limits of institutionalisation, the relationship between labour disputes and cultural changes, and the crisis in the system of economic management.

THE LIMITS OF INSTITUTIONALISATION

The most conventional hypothesis is to explain the development of disputes, and especially unofficial disputes, as marking the limits of institutionalisation; this does shed a certain amount of light on the effects of disputes, but it gives no indication of their causes. Trade union activity in Belgium has become considerably institutionalised, as a result of the particular features of Belgian society itself (a society devoted to the continual peaceful settlement of differences), the dynamics of the workers' movement (with its reformist ideology), and the features of union action itself (tending as it does towards professionalisation).

One of the most important effects of this situation is the extent to which union activity becomes increasingly technical in character with (a) a marked preference for a 'technical' approach to bargaining, whereby any initiative and responsibility are taken out of the hands of the work-force and passed on to the union machinery, and (b) the development of such practices as giving certain advantages to union members only, a positive and powerful encouragement to increased membership and part and parcel, both logically and from an historical viewpoint, of the established system of national level bargaining (Piret, 1971: p. 9). Within such bargaining procedures (both during the course of dispute activity and in defining national industry-wide agreements), union organisations tend to formulate demands within the guiding principles of concerted bargaining: negotiations take place over negotiable points, which more often than not comes down to saying that issues are literally bargained over in money terms. This has a dual effect. First, working conditions are placed in a straitjacket: demands that are wage-orientated are directly in the mainstream of neo-capitalism, with any increase in living standards being compensated by a rise in productivity (such as through increasing work speeds). The problem for the union here is to keep one step back from the context within which it puts forward claims, to raise demands both over working conditions *and* over the directions taken by the production situation itself. The second effect is that it inevitably leads to a reduction in the level of militancy among the rank and file.

Some light can thus possibly be shed on the increase in the number of disputes and their disorganised character. Dispute activity, especially in the case of unofficial disputes, is at one and the same time a reaction to institutionalisation and a form of pressure on institutional practices. From this viewpoint, such disputes are conflictual though indiscriminate forms of action. Strikes that have taken place either directly or indirectly against the results of national level bargaining have revealed the limits of any over-institutionalisation. Defining the threshold of tolerance comes down to providing an answer to the question of knowing why in certain circumstances institutionalisation is rejected while in others it is accepted. Disputes over *programmation sociale* have shown that institutionalisation is rejected when it is felt that it places obstacles in the way of trade union action or, more precisely, the smooth running of the machinery of redistribution. Put in more concrete terms, when the institutional machinery prevents the fruits of a favourable economic situation from being enjoyed, it is repudiated.

The current economic crisis will surely indicate the limits to which institutionalisation can go, and its inherent contradictions. Such institutionalisation, which is just one facet of the way in which society is run, will without doubt be used more than ever as a means of controlling disputes, while there is liable to be some move to neutralise its effects on the economy (by easing up on redistribution and the transfer of wealth, together with an attempt at incomes policy). The end result may well have the opposite effect to that originally expected, with further outbreaks of labour disputes.

LABOUR DISPUTES AND CULTURAL CHANGES

A further factor has appeared in disputes in recent years, which results from the increasing links between labour disputes and what may be called more 'everyday' problems. These links have two forms: certain labour conflicts may have repercussions on other areas of conflict, of a cultural or more strictly social nature, while labour relations may be affected by considerations that normally apply in other spheres.

Such repercussions on labour relations can be of two kinds. Firstly, in certain disputes, demands that originally arose in a context other than that of work may be grafted on to labour demands proper. For example, certain grievances which have a bearing on working conditions derived originally from new-found demands over health and welfare. There can be no question of a money trade-off (*via* 'dirty-job' bonuses) where health is in the balance. Placing a greater value on physical well being does not lie in the work situation itself, but has been introduced from outside. To take another example, for several years now district action committees have been developing as active agents of urban protest; and it often happens that labour demands, primarily over jobs and employment, come up in the context of urban protest, for example through opposition to land and property speculation, or urban or local redevelopment projects.

There is thus a connection between experience at work and experience elsewhere in several conflict situations and, beyond this, some kind of drift occurs from one area to another. This is very clear in the case of strikes involving women workers; the form which such disputes take, the numbers taking part, the degree of militancy, and the ideological tendencies cannot be explained without some reference to the feminist movement.

Finally, some disputes bring to light a dichotomy between experience at work (with its own particular conditions and the kinds of demands it makes) and experience outside work. The work situation as such (conditions at work, the hierarchical set-up and the constraints involved) has evolved only slowly, whereas outside work there has been a kind of pseudo-liberalisation, which has manifested itself in institutional crises (in the situation of the family, for example). This provokes a certain contradiction which finds expression in a wide variety of forms—for example, certain kinds of deviant behaviour ('marginality'), delinquency or industrial sabotage. In the same manner, clear signs of these tensions may be seen in several disputes and in particular in the way these disputes are carried out.

THE CRISIS IN THE SYSTEM OF RUNNING THE ECONOMY

One final element, though probably the most important one for interpreting the way in which conflict within society has developed, is most certainly the crisis that has arisen in the system of running the economy.

Roughly speaking, this crisis takes on two different forms. In Wallonia it is the crisis of traditional Belgian capitalism and the way in which it has been run. This situation is shown by a series of indicators, namely the obsolescence of the machinery of production (in the steel industry, mining and glass-making), the increasing dependence on technological innovation (Belgian capitalism has missed out on most of what technology has had to offer since 1945, as revealed by the register of industrial patents (CNPS, 1967)), the increase in investment from overseas sources (in sectors such as chemicals, the petroleum industry, mechanical and electrical engineering), the dismantling of Belgian combines since 1960 (Storms, 1972), and the transfer of investments to sectors such as tourism and housing.

Industrial development in Flanders, on the other hand, started more recently with the influence of firstly the new Flemish middle class (the political rivals of the traditional established bourgeoisie who had controlled the whole sector of small and medium-sized firms), and secondly the multinational concerns (in petroleum, chemicals, the motor industry, electronics and so on). The question here, then, is one of a form of economic colonisation.

In fact, traditional capitalism in Belgium has had an increasing part of its initiative taken from it. Control has increasingly moved abroad, while Belgian capitalist interests continue to look after certain overriding functions such as financial affairs. Like the traditional ruling class, the state is incapable of handling this kind of problem. The political machinery is very widely-based, but no political party or grouping represents any real alternative, while the greater part of any initiative is undermined by a latent conflict over the actual form that the state itself should take.

This is amply borne out in the whole debate over public initiative in industry. This particular bone of contention, aimed at making up for shortcomings in private investment, has been voiced over recent years within the labour movement. Initial experiences failed due to confusion between supervising the investment and applying the means of control, so that, in this respect, the state encountered exactly the same problems as private investors. Given this, recent disputes appear more defensive than offensive in outlook, and this is underlined by the number of disputes which have broken out in declining sectors and the ideological concepts (such as workers' control) that have arisen in areas that, technologically speaking, are doomed to die. Finally, the expanding sectors have seen the developments of a particular tendency based on defending differentials, as illustrated by strikes in the petroleum industry over wage questions rather than over working conditions.

It may be claimed that the last great offensive by the working class developed in 1957 and stopped after the strikes of 1960–1 and that since then, in spite of increasing militancy and the appearance of new forms of action, the majority of disputes is essentially of a defensive nature.

Having said this, will not the present crisis, affecting as it does all industrial societies, lead to the occurrence of disputes of a more offensive kind?

At the end of 1975, the employers and the unions in Belgium were negotiating the establishment of short-term guidelines for limiting the redistribution of economic resources. In other words, negotiations were taking place to cancel out the economic effects of concerted bargaining in the workers' favour, a measure which, in the eyes of the employers, appears today as the best safeguard of the system itself. If this were not enough, while freezing institutionalised conflict (concerted bargaining activity), workers' organisations are also being asked to oversee the situation themselves, in other words to maintain order. As has been seen, the labour movement has two possible ways of reacting to this situation. It may either insist on sticking to the rules of bargaining as they stand, in which case there is liable to be an increasing tendency to take a firm stand, which will deepen the crisis; or it may accept that concerted bargaining shall be placed in cold storage for a period, in which case there are substantial risks of a situation of repeated deadlock developing within the unions themselves.

Whatever the outcome, it is very probable that the present crisis will aggravate conflicts within both sides of industry. Tensions on the workers' side will be manifested in differences between regions, between strong and weak sectors and between different factions inside the working class. On the employers' side, relations are already strained between large-scale plants, the multinationals, and small or medium-sized firms, and also between industrialists and financial circles. All these divergent positions will, it is certain, affect the issues where the disputes occur, over what, and the directions taken by dispute activity.

NOTES

1. Throughout this analysis attention has been concentrated on the two main regions, Wallonia and Flanders, and not Brussels, which constitutes a separate, much smaller, region based primarily on service employment.
2. For further details on this point, see the analyses of V. R. Lorwin, 1968 and 1975.
3. The PSB (BSP – Belgische Socialistische Partij in Dutch) has retained a unified structure. The PSC is divided up into two separate organisations, the majority CVP (Christelijke Volks-Partij) and the minority PSC. The CVP and the PSC take part in governments in one bloc, and by and large share the same programme except as regards regional community matters. Of note is the fact that the PSC/CVP, an 'all-class' party, is prone to further internal divisions, between conservative and progressive factions, and the same is true, though to a lesser extent, of the PSB.
4. *The second agreement* (12.12.63) dealt with the third week of paid holidays and also included a 'social peace' provision up until the end of 1965. *The third agreement* (15.7.66) covered two points: a double holiday bonus, with no further demands to be made on issues concerning actual working hours. A 'social peace' provision went up to the end of 1968. *The fourth agreement* (7.2.69) was not signed by all the employers and was by and large superficial with regard to agreements at industry level. Source: CRISP, 18.5.73.
5. *Ibid*: p. 6. This hypothesis is illustrated by the following phrase taken from the draft agreement:

   '. . . [the] conclusions of the present negotiation will not give rise to any further or supplementary demands at industry or plant level.'

6. *The fifth agreement* (15.6.71) dealt with working hours, union training facilities, the payment of hours on union business and travel expenses. *The sixth agreement* (6.4.73) brought in a fourth week of paid holiday as from 1975, the full month's wage being guaranteed for the first month's holiday. *The seventh agreement* (10.2.75) included a declaration of principle on the harmonising aims of joint industrywide talks, and dealt with fixing a guaranteed minimum wage, modifying the ceiling adopted for travel expenses, and making recommendations on working conditions for young people and women workers. Source: CRISP, 18.5.73 and 18.1.74.
7. The CSC has more than 1000 full-time officers, and the FGTB more than 700 (Van Outrive, 1974: p. 9). As far as employers' associations are concerned, see Leemans *et al*, 1970; and Heyvaert and Molitor, 1974.
8. On the question of energy and the control of energy, see the Special Issue of *La Revue Nouvelle*: 'L'énergie – qui décide en Belgique', Vol. LXI (Feb 1975).
9. Church-run education represents more than 55 per cent of those of school age.
10. The level of wages is often higher in foreign firms than in Belgian companies (van den Bulcke *et al*, 1971: p. 269).

LIST OF WORKS CITED

Beckers, M., Frere, J. P., Saucier, R. and Torrisi G. (1973), *La Belgique Face aux Investissements Etrangers* (Louvain: Centre de Recherches Sociologiques).

Claeys, P. H. (1973), *Les Groupes de Pression en Belgique* (Brussels: ULB and CRISP).

CNPS (1967), *Recherche et Croissance Economique* (2) (Brussels)

de Bakker, B. (1970), *La Grève des Mines du Limbourg, janvier-fevrier 1970* (Brussels, CRISP, Ch. no. 499, 13 Nov.).

Debuyst F. (1967), *La fonction Parlementaire en Belgique* (Brussels: CRISP).

de Ronge, A. and Molitor, M. (1975), *Données Relatives aux Grèves en Belgique de 1947 à 1971* (Brussels, CRISP, Ch. No. 677–8, 28 Mar.).

de Vroey, M. and Carton de Wiart, A. (1971), *La Propriété et la Part de Marchè des Principales Entreprises Industrielles en Belgique (II)* (Brussels: CRISP, Ch. No. 509–10, 12 Feb.).

Heyvaert, H. and Molitor, M. (1974), *De l'Association Professionnelle à l'Organisation Patronale* (Louvain: CRECIS).

Laloire, M. (1971), 'Les mandats syndicaux', *La Revue Nouvelle*, LII, 11, 369–73.

Leemans *et al.* (1970), *De Patronale Beroepsorganisaties en het Overleg* (Leuven: Sociologische Onderzoek Instituut).

Lorwin, V. R. (1968), 'Belgium: class and language in national politics', in Dahl, R. A. (ed.), *Political Oppositions in Western Democracies* (New Haven: Yale University Press,) 29–70.

—— (1975), 'Labor unions and political parties in Belgium', *Industrial and Labor Relations Review*, 28, 2.

Molitor, M. (1971), 'Situation du syndicalisme belge', *Synopsis* (Jan. – Feb.).

—— (1973), 'Action syndicale et relations industrielles', *La Revue Nouvelle*, LVII, 3, 272–80.

Neuville, J. (1973), *Le Taux de Syndicalisation en Belgique en 1970* (Brussels: CRISP, Ch. No. 595, 9 Mar.).

—— (1974), Les Elections Syndicales de 1971, III (Brussels, CRISP, Ch. No. 631, 1 Feb.).

Piret, C. (1971), *Les Grèves de 1970: Descriptions et quelques Hypothèses* (Brussels: CSC).

Spitaels, G. (1969), *Le Mouvement Syndical en Belgique*, 2nd ed. (Brussels: Institut de Sociologie).

Storms, B. (1972), 'L'évolution du portefeuille de la Société Générale', *La Revue Nouvelle*, LVI, 11, 327–43,

van den Bulcke, D. *et al.* (1971), *Les Entreprises Etrangères dans l'Industrie Belge: Aspects Généraux, Régionaux et Economiques* (Université de Gand).

van de Kerckhove, J. (1973), 'Grèves spantanées, phénomènes et symptomes de crise'. *Recherches Sociologiques*, IV, 2, 335–56.

Vandewalle, J. F. (1975), *La Concertation Sociale Interprofessionnelle* (Louvain: working paper).

van Outrive, L. (1974), 'Les syndicats chrétiens et socialistes en Belgique, leur pouvoir dans une économie néo-capitaliste et concertée, leurs stratégies vers l'autogestion', *Recherches Sociologiques*, V, 1, 3–38.

Verly J. (1973), *Emploi et Structures de Production Régionales* (Louvain: IRES).

3 *The Contradictions of French Trade Unionism*

PIERRE DUBOIS, CLAUDE DURAND
and SABINE ERBÈS-SEGUIN

1 THE ECONOMIC CONTEXT OF INDUSTRIAL CONFLICT

Among Western European nations, France occupies a somewhat special position which, if we refer to those criteria normally used to describe industrial societies, can be defined as a mixture of the archaic and the modern. There is much within French society that is the result of contrasting and irreconcilable forces. The fabric of industry covers both high-growth activities and others (of which there are a considerable number) which have not yet progressed beyond the nineteenth century. Industrial expansion in France has proved vigorous, its pace not slackening off to any significant extent until the end of 1974. This in itself is something almost unique in Europe, though it is in contrast to the stagnation of pre-war years. The activity rate is such that alongside one of the longest working weeks to be found in industrial countries exist some of the longest annual paid holidays, giving rise as they do to an almost complete month-long shutdown of industry. Like all forms of relationship in French society, occupational relations operate through successive periods of deadlock, marking the extreme divergence that exists between the two sides of industry: employers who at times consider themselves to be so 'by divine right', are often strongly anti-union, and embody in highly personalised form the power that they hold; and the workers, a large proportion of whom, along with both the main unions (the CGT and the CFDT), reject the type of society in which they are living and criticise the way in which it is developing. To this must be added the existence of a very extensive publicly owned and nationalised sector, for the most part organised on monopoly lines. Here the rules governing employment and wage payment function in an entirely different way to those in the private sector.

Nevertheless, a widespread evolution is taking place, and this, above and beyond the more or less short-term economic fluctuations, affects the very structures of production. It accounts at least partly for the changes in behaviour that have occurred since 1968. While it is indeed possible to observe a reasonable stability in long-term strike statistics, the strikes themselves have evolved in a similar manner to those structural transformations that have taken place within French production. Here the years 1966 and 1967 represent an important turning point. What happened in 1968 was perhaps one of the prime consequences.

LONG-TERM ECONOMIC TRENDS IN FRANCE

An analysis of French economic growth reveals a certain number of phenomena whose role goes some way towards explaining present-day movements within society. While French production and the overall trends of evolution are basically the same as those of other Western European countries, there are differences between each country's economic history and economic 'periods'. Furthermore, developments in social behaviour are affected by disparities which occur over a period of time and by the ways in which structural changes take place.

Leaving aside the period of reconstruction in the immediate post-war years, it can be seen that the growth rate from the 1950s up to and including 1974 is without precedent in the history of France. The average rate however is no greater than that of neighbouring countries, averaging about 5 per cent per annum between 1949 and 1969, a rate slightly higher than those of the United Kingdom and the USA, and slightly lower than those of Italy and West Germany. However, this development follows a long period of economic stagnation, from 1920 to 1945, which affected all factors of production and investment, as well as the active population level. Growth is of itself therefore a new structural element; economic survival has been succeeded by continuous growth. In part this has been conditioned by an evolution in attitudes within industry—which, however, makes further changes in attitude necessary. Continuous growth also means that even now sectors with varying rates of development exist alongside each other. What is more, there is no uniform evolution in factors of production, either in time or extent. This leads to a whole series of disparities which, perhaps more than mere statements of principle, provide the basis of arguments put forward by the unions over forms of production.

(a) First of all, it can be noted that the level of *working hours* remained stable, though high, until 1966. In spite of an increase in paid holidays to three and subsequently four weeks (in 1954–6 and 1962–4 respectively), the annual average of working hours is still one of the highest among the industrialised countries, which means that the length of the working week has become greater. In fact it rose to forty-six hours in the sixties. Some tendency to reduce this figure has occurred only since 1963, when the active population started to increase.

Secondly, an important part is played by the labour market. It should in fact be pointed out that the active population had *decreased* during two of the preceding periods, 1929–1938 and 1946–1962. Increasing the length of the working week was therefore aimed in particular at remedying the deficiencies of a restricted labour market.

These two elements provide some explanation of behaviour in the employment field, and they will be analysed in greater detail in Section 2.

Society is extremely sensitive to any increase in unemployment, however slight. A certain number of unemployed does not have the same significance in an open labour market containing few obstacles to mobility as in a restricted, compartmentalised market. Disputes and demands over safeguarding jobs do not arise solely in periods of economic difficulty: witness the 1972 Joint Français dispute and the 1973 Lip dispute, which occurred during a period of expansion. Even though there is not an exceptionally large number of such disputes, they arouse considerable interest to the extent that evolution in a particular direction is called into question by such specific cases, such as the complete shutdown of entire industries (textiles, footwear, and mining from the 1960s), an absence of regional employment policy (Joint Français) or of company policy (Lip). As can be seen, these remarks are still true even at the present time, as the effect of a rise in the active population only aggravates particular problems of industrial reorganisation.

Also of note is the constantly high level of demands put forward over working hours, which evolve rapidly into a rejection of the economic system (Baumfelder, 1968).

Furthermore, even before any increase in the numbers of the active population had occurred, there was a noticeable continuing improvement in the 'quality' of the labour force – in other word in its level of training— and this had a growing influence on the relationship of the individual to his work. These include the difficulties experienced by often highly-trained young people in starting out on their working life; the crisis of the 'OS'[1] in the 1970s; and, especially, the increasing tendency to challenge hierarchy and decision-making practices within the plant. However, since the 1950s the increase in the general level of culture has also helped to raise the productivity of labour. At the same time the accelerating migration of manpower from low-productivity sectors to the more productive branches of the economy has led to improvements in its utilisation. It is for this reason that the attitude of the unions towards the subject of retraining is somewhat ambiguous. More than any other demand, occupational training cuts both ways[2]. It contributes towards the full integration of the worker into society, but also makes him aware of the reality behind the division of labour: and while it provides a means of individual advancement, it also leads to the worker being unsuited to the job he effectively occupies and is a factor which makes for changes in industrial structure.

(b) So, as working hours increased, there was a considerable rise in *labour productivity*. This was indeed a long-term trend which was common to all industrial countries, but it accelerated more rapidly in France from 1949 where it was also the sole element that had not experienced any stagnation in the pre-war period. Nevertheless, wide variations can be observed in the rises in productivity in different industries, which bear no relationship to overall developments in particular branches. Furthermore, until 1962 there was an *inverse* relationship between the rise in productivity and the degree of concentration. The least concentrated sectors were often those which experienced the greatest increases: for example textiles was particularly interesting in this respect.

This high, sustained increase in *labour productivity*, varying according to the industrial sector, is, in the view of more or less official observers of French economic growth (Carré *et al*, 1972; but see also Guilbert, 1975) largely attributable to a rise in labour effort, at least until the mid-1960s. Productive capital began to increase more rapidly only after 1963. At the same time, there has been a stagnation in employment in industry, with even a steady decline in some sectors. Put more simply, it may be said that, for the first fifteen years after the war, the labour factor assumed the largest share in growth; this is proved by the data on working hours and productivity. This weighs heavily on the economic conscience of the workers, and it is worth bearing these figures in mind when we consider the periodic appearance of demands concerning work-speeds and shortages at workforce level. These kinds of demand, often raised in post-war years, become less frequent in 1963–4, and then reappeared in a fairly clear and particularly spectacular manner after 1968. Whereas in the fifties and sixties these more often than not took the form of claims for financial compensation for the extra effort demanded, they now—and especially since 1970—constitute a direct challenge to the organisation of work.

(c) *Productive capital* has also experienced a considerable, though more belated, increase. There are two different reasons for this. On the one hand, while its rate of increase compares with that of other countries from the beginning of the 1950s, its take-off point was narrow, with a very low pre-war investment rate and no growth in the active population until 1963. Less effort was devoted to increasing productive capacity than to raising productivity. The relatively low efficiency of capital also resulted from the technological backwardness of the pre-war years. Moreover, the great majority of investments until 1955 was undertaken in those basic sectors under state control. The history of state planning in France is one of an unmistakable desire to achieve growth targets. The first two plans, which cover the ten post-war years (1946–56), are certainly no more than 'guidelines', just as subsequent ones were. However they had the dual effect of directing public spending and also of changing states of mind from being conditioned to stagnation and crisis to being orientated towards expansion. The role of subsequent plans became increasingly ill-defined until, with the (present) Seventh Plan, it is virtually non-existent. So when, after 1955, an improved balance in capitalisation was reached between the various different branches of industry, and private investment took over from the state, it cannot be said that this was due to any inherent dynamism on the part of private investors; they have been constantly jostled and jogged by the authorities.

Until around 1965, no substantial movement of change could be observed in *industrial structures*. There are, moreover, two distinct aspects to the problem. Firstly, technological concentration—the distribution of production units according to size—did not evolve to any extent until the 1962 census, and then, unlike the majority of other industrial countries, post-war growth occurred in undertakings that had not undergone any substantial modification in size since the beginning of the century. Concentration in this sense is still lower today in France than in the other countries of Europe. Between 1955 and 1965, the proportion of larger firms remained much the same, with the first ten industrial concerns representing about 6 per cent of the total turnover of industry. However, substantial reorganisations occurred among medium-sized firms, tending in particular towards improvements in productivity. The phenomenon of Gaullism is linked with this movement.

Nevertheless, since 1965 the trend has been completely reversed. At the same time that French industry opened out towards the export market, a wide concentration of industry was undertaken. This found its true political expression only with the arrival of Giscard d'Estaing as President.

It is tempting to see some correlation between the increase in exports and financial concentration, in that relaxing national boundaries signifies both a need to rationalise production according to capitalist criteria of cost-effectiveness, and the fact that the country has been opened up to external capital. However, a feature of the financial market in France is its extreme restrictiveness. Closed to multinational firms longer than other European countries, France opened up all the more easily after 1965 as its capital needs were strongly felt, and it was also during this period that the employers launched a vigorous offensive against state intervention in industrial investment.[3]

(d) Until recently, and even now to some extent, a large proportion of *productive investment* has been undertaken by the public sector. In the post-war years up to 1955 this took one-third of the total, while private savings were almost exclusively directed towards housing construction instead of towards financial shareholding. This led firms to resort to self-financing and to external markets. Until about 1960, self-financing together with fairly wide facilities for long-term borrowing were sufficient to supply their investment needs. Subsequently, however, there was a noticeable investment boom, though this was checked fairly sharply in the 1964 stabilisation plan. Firms then resorted increasingly to external capital, which explains the progressive takeover of the economy by multinational companies.

This brief insight into the long-term trends helps one to analyse the general directions of trade union policy. A long period of high continuous growth, achieved by the efforts of the working population (through productivity improvements and through state investment, has provided substantial increases in the purchasing power of the workers, but has not given rise to any increased participation in economic decision-making on their part. Quite the contrary: the major part of post-war social legislation dealing with worker representation in organs of decision-making, both within the firm ('*comité d'entreprise*') and at national level (national plans), has been emptied of all meaning, while that which has been acquired through nationalisation has been rapidly falling apart. In contrast, the efforts made by the workers and state investment have enabled firms to get back on an even keel and undertake substantial structural modifications. At the same time, since the mid-1960s they have turned to the international market, the actual effects of which are only just beginning to be felt. Some statistical details of the development of the French economy will be found in Appendix I.

THE TWO AREAS OF SOCIAL CONFRONTATION – PROBLEMS OF PERIOD DEFINITION

Given such an economic background, May 1968 can be seen as being less of an upheaval than may be thought. Within such a context, it resulted both from structural developments in the system and prevailing economic circumstances. The consequences for the workers of 'industrial reorganisation' went hand in hand with a sluggish economic situation in 1966–7; the end of 1967 marked the beginning of a revival in economic activity, and as such a particularly favourable period for putting in claims. This watershed made any change in relations between the two sides of industry all the more manifest, particularly as the foundations for such a change had already been set within the way economic affairs had evolved.

Alongside industrial structures that had undergone transformations, the system of industrial (and political) relations was archaic and inertia-ridden. If the desire for change is often expressed by workers in France in more openly revolutionary manner than in other countries, it is without doubt due to the enormous disparities that exist between the economic state of affairs and social practices. The whole period from 1960 to 1968 was a vacuum as far as negotiated agreements were concerned,[4] while widespread measures for restructuring industry were being carried out, along with very great increases in productivity. What 1968 did do was to give employers the chance of realising fully the dangers behind such a situation. Indeed it may be said that the crisis contributed to placing industrial relations in France more directly in line with the situation in industry.

However, these crises do not represent a breakdown in the development of social and economic relations. They are in part the result of these relations, and affect them in turn. The point of view of either side appears in a more radical and clearcut fashion, and though after 1968 the tendency to take part in negotiations was resumed, there was at the same time a noticeable hardening of attitudes, as much on the employers' side as in the unions. This phenomenon reappeared towards the end of 1974, as we again enter a period of crisis, though this time of directly economic origin.

It is therefore worth while analysing social relations in France since 1968 on two levels. In the first place, it is futile to give an outline of periods purely on the basis of socio-economic relationships, with the year 1968 firmly fixed as some sort of turning point. 1968 is an important date from the social point of view, but it has no particular significance in economic affairs. If viewed in narrowly economic terms, the social upheavals appear only as the result of previous transformations.

It is equally fallacious to base any analysis of social relations solely on contingent fluctuations in economic factors. Their only interest lies in providing a background to understanding variations in strike levels, in other words in illustrating the tactical capabilities of the unions, while they say nothing of the actual constitution of social relations.

Economic analysis enables the period since 1963 to be divided into the following three phases:-

1963: the features of the labour market are modified with the active population starting to rise; this is accompanied by productivity gains that are still largely based on manpower effort, in spite of an incipient transformation in the structure of industry.

1966–7: industrial concentration accelerates, and its effects on the level of employment begin to be felt. At the same time, technological changes are beginning to affect the system of production, the trend being to replace manpower by machinery, and hence increasingly to link productivity to the technological, financial and even human effort involved, while still reducing the number of jobs. However, the uncertain climate in which these movements take place mask what are in fact structural changes over a certain time. An initial pointer was to be the May 1968 crisis, and a second the world economic crisis which broke out towards the end of 1973.

End of 1973 – beginning of 1974: the economic crisis increasingly resembles a crisis of capitalism itself, with France lagging somewhat behind other Western countries. It is only from the autumn of 1974 that the term 'structural crisis' is heard from the employers' side.

So it is only since 1968 – and such is the importance of this date – that the conflict within society, as manifested in relations between workers and employers, has apparently originated simultaneously in two clearly differentiated fields, namely the structural field of fundamental conflict between models of society, and the contingent field of day-to-day tactical skirmishes—though the dominant class may try to maintain that there is no difference between the two. This bivalent nature of conflict is a permanent feature, although it only comes to the fore during those privileged periods (at least as regards analysis) which constitute moments of crisis. In fact, during 'cruising' periods—those in which no particular economic or social difficulties occur—the employers entirely dominate the structural field. They develop the mode of production, transform it from within, and take the strategic measures designed to maintain it; and pride of place among such measures goes to concealing the structural nature of changes in the employment situation. For example, until the end of 1974, both the Government and the authorities succeeded in passing off extreme modifications in the level of employment as being caused by a poor economic climate that would improve sooner or later while, in fact, they were the result of concentration in industry and increasing mechanisation of production: that is to say, structural changes within the system itself. The tendency in employer strategy as a whole is to change things like this so as to defend the basic principles of the economic and social order against encroachment on the part of the workers. It does so by making any solution as precarious as possible, by linking it to short-term contingent factors.

Hence, especially in periods of economic prosperity, as in 1971–2, employers in industry, and still more so the Government, have attempted to squeeze wages by playing on the fear of inflation and the notorious wage-price spiral. Along with this has appeared the notion of influencing wage levels by manipulating the labour market. Nevertheless, the world crisis that has been taking shape since 1971 shows how impossible it is to deal with relationships in the socio-economic field solely in terms of contingencies; neither the level of employment nor prices are linked to the prevailing short-term economic situation alone. So, since 1966 and 1967 in particular – those years in which massive changes began to occur in the economy in France—it is important to make as clear a distinction as possible between those disputes that are derived from day-to-day contingent bargaining and those that constitute a fundamental confrontation, challenging the very basis of established authority. The tendency has strengthened further since 1974 (Erbès-Seguin, 1976). Thus the inflation which took place in 1963 was without doubt more directly a contingent phenomenon than that which has developed since 1971, which resulted initially from the disruption of the international monetary system under the particular influence of multinational companies. And the employment problems which have started to appear in an acute form since the autumn of 1974 are due to the combined effects of a prevailing fall in world production levels and 'rationalisation' of the system of production, leading to cut-backs in the number of jobs available. Within the context of the economy, the effects of both aspects merge together in the short term, as far as both descriptions of economic developments and whatever awareness workers and unions have of them are concerned. It is for this reason that it appears difficult and somewhat inconclusive to attempt, as certain economists have done, to make a direct correlation between prevailing economic factors and, say, strike movements. A recent analysis of strikes in France in the long term (Scardigli, 1974; see also Erbès-Seguin, 1975) shows at the same time the absence of any long-term trend and

> a very high sensitivity of strike indicators to the economic and political climate. The workers appear to accommodate themselves to a fairly high rate of inflation, when it is accompanied by substantial rises in wage levels and a low rate of unemployment; however a high level of strike activity develops whenever economic expansion is disrupted, when there is a drop in spending power, and especially when strong monetary erosion is accompanied by a high level of unemployment and a reduced increase in saving.

Therefore both the tactical requirements of demands themselves and changes in the manner in which workers challenge the structures of the economy, and especially those arguments used to support what are apparently similar demands, must be taken into account. Any understanding of developments which take place in social conflicts must be derived from knowledge of the contents of demands—which, being of necessity detailed, is difficult to come by. From this viewpoint, May 1968 represents a point at which demands take on a radical turn that becomes more blurred in subsequent years of prosperity, only to appear once more in 1974.

Indeed, outside the crisis periods, the working class finds itself constrained to place its day-to-day struggle – though not the arguments it expresses – within the area of contingent situations: this covers the fundamental basis of areas around which negotiation takes place, but not the effective strike themes. However, when a crisis situation presents itself, one of its prime features is, if not to upset completely, at least to call into question, the existing power relationship. The confrontation then reveals its fundamentally structural character. Nevertheless, the implication behind any further pursuit of this tendency is that political action comes into play, and up to now it is this that has been lacking.

2 THE DEMANDS

THE 'NEW' DEMANDS

The primary element for analysing strikes is their demand content. For France, an important source of relevant statistics is the record of disputes collected by the French labour inspectorate (*inspecteurs du travail*). Recourse to this data is eminently worth while; indeed, one may well be astonished by the spurious interpretations often given to the development of disputes, founded on a limited number of spectacular cases that are changed about to a greater or lesser extent by a militant press which is ready to discover at every opportunity waves of new demands where a rigorous statistical analysis shows no more than perfectly stable trends.

What then is revealed by a statistical analysis of strikes? First of all, the overwhelming preponderance of wage demands (Durand and Harff, 1973). Whatever indices are used, wage demands come way out in front in the order of frequency of motives for strike action. They are five times more frequent than demands over trade union rights[5] and reduction in working hours, which come in second and third places, and ten times more than demands over job protection and working conditions, which come in fifth and sixth places.

While it is to be expected that what happened in May 1968 should have led to innovations in the content of disputes, as it certainly did with regard to the forms taken by disputes and the ideological directions of the unions, the statistical analysis of disputes reveals the social partners fully engrossed in permanent wage bargaining (*ibid*: p. 373), that the 'new' or 'qualitative'

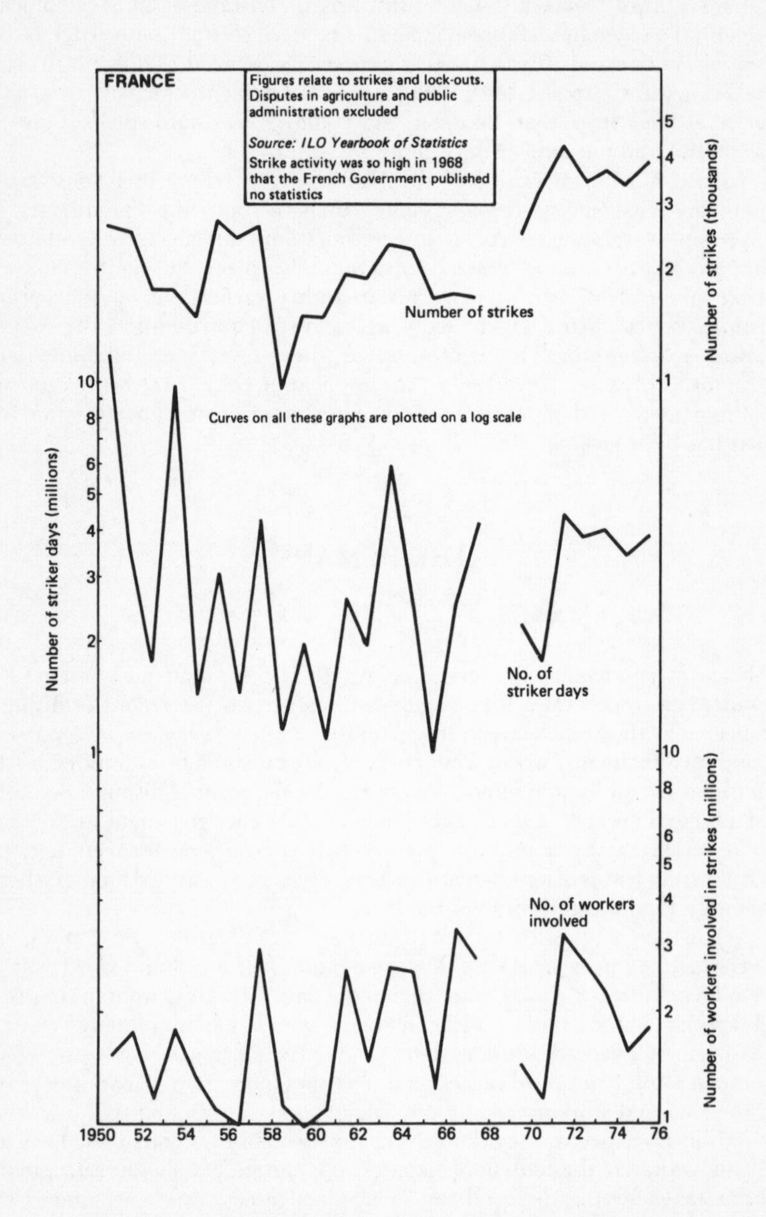

FIGURE 3.1: Industrial conflict in France, 1950–75 (log scales)

demands are limited to a small number of 'exemplary' disputes or remain within the realm of ideological controversy.

On this point, though, it is not our wish to treat the debate over so-called 'qualitative' demands too dismissively. Even if, from a methodological point of view, distinguishing between quantitative and qualitative, economic and non-economic demands may appear too perfunctory for the specialist, none the less this debate did exist after the May movement. It involved certain divergences in the interpretation of Marxist thought with, on the one side, a greater emphasis on the economic exploitation of the workers (economistic interpretation) and, on the other, a desire to go beyond considerations of exploitation to seek some challenge to forms of alienation within society that are not all linked to the economic system, such as social dependence, the industrial system or the quality of life (qualitative interpretation).

It is, however, possible that this debate, which incidentally encouraged reflection within the labour movement, especially on themes of self-management ('*autogestion*'), took place on an ideological plane distinct from actual demand-orientated movements, at least outside those periods of open crisis (May 1968 and the 1974 economic crisis). The effect of such crisis periods is to make fundamental debates come down into the arena of practical affairs, whereas in 'cruising' phases they remain the province of words and not actions.

THE EVOLUTION OF THE DEMAND CONTENT OF STRIKES

A comparison between post-May 1968 demands with those made before then (*ibid*: p. 368) shows that 'qualitative' demands even dropped back in importance: while working conditions fell from sixth to seventh place, working hours fell from second position in 1964 to fourth place in 1971. The explanation behind this is the prominence of the campaign in 1964 for a fourth week of paid holiday and, as far as plant-level disputes are concerned, this was more widespread ten years ago than present-day disputes over a return to the 40-hour week or a reduced retiring age. Militants tend to feel that these demands will be resolved by bargaining at the national level. An analysis of the contents of plant agreements (Bachy *et al*, 1974: p. 276) reveals moreover that under the general heading 'working hours', the provisions on paid holidays continue to be greater in number than those on the length of the working week and the lowering of the retiring age.

Retirement conditions had nevertheless been the theme of 24-hour protests ('*journées d'action*') on a national scale, and have an important place in central union policy. In fact, working hours and retirement conditions come top in the list of demand themes set out in the trade union press (Erbès-Seguin, 1973: p. 382): on the same level, for the CGT, as purchasing power (which comes only seventh in themes appearing in CFDT publications).

The disparity between the themes developed in the union press and actual dispute aims shows the wide autonomy of plant-level conflicts in relation to possible directives from the central organisations, and the extent to which the propaganda lines of the two largest unions actually diverge beyond those demands made in joint declarations over a united front.

Nevertheless, upholding union rights in the face of employer persecution of work-place representatives has been the aim of genuine united action by both unions in recent years, to the same extent as employment protection. This has had a real effect on the evolution of disputes, and defending union rights has risen from sixth to third place in plant-level strike aims. This affirmation of union strength at rank-and-file level may be one of the first concrete manifestations of the development of the demand content in strikes since May 1968. This is not without some significance, in that this demand may be interpreted as a claim for the recognition of some form of union influence at plant level.

Other indications of the evolution of strike demand content may be sought in a detailed analysis of the nature of wage demands. Post-May 1968 wage demands, for example, have a more egalitarian tendency than those made before May and they are directed more towards defending the spending power of underprivileged groups. Demands for flat-rate increases, fixed rises to offset rises in the cost of living, and for raising the wages of the lower categories occur proportionally more frequently than percentage demands (C. Durand and Dubois, 1975). More will be said later on the possible importance of this egalitarian trend.

The increase in demands for safeguarding the standard of living apparently results from the convergence of the main union organisations on a policy of defending living standards and the fortunes of under-privileged categories, and also from the overwhelming entry of these under-privileged groups (the 'OS', women workers and immigrants) into social conflicts; so much so that these groups appear to have largely overtaken skilled workers as the driving force in disputes.

On the other hand, the assumption that demand themes would progress towards direct demands over job control (Mallet, 1970) is apparently not supported by the statistical evidence, since the figures for wage demands linked to job control show a decline.[6] It would moreover be a mistake to assume that the labour movement is turning towards workers' control by lumping together such diverse manifestations as disputes over dismissals, demands over job classification, stoppages for improving working conditions and direct action with a view to a reduction in working hours.

Certain observers appear to think that there is something new in output control by workers or in deliberately slowing down production, and it is treated as some sort of *avantgarde* phenomenon. Yet it may be recalled that Simiand (1907) analysed go-slow tactics at the end of the last century, and that this has been the subject of repeated studies in industrial sociology.[7]

Output limitation takes on a different significance according to the technological environment and the nature of the work-group. It may be individual or collective; it may be union organised or unofficial; it may aim at controlling work organisation or simply act as a compensatory phenomenon or as an escape valve. All such manifestations cannot be given the same interpretation, and, *a fortiori*, neither can all cases of go-slow action be placed under the same heading as workers' action of a more elaborate form which testifies to increased consciousness; go-slows are often no more than a primitive form of economic bargaining.

Even though overtly political demands occur only rarely, we cannot ascribe a hidden political meaning to every economic demand. The discrepancy, admitted by the militants themselves, between the implicit significance of demands and the latent reasons behind disputes does pose a problem. It is not enough to say that such and such a conflict over wage levels and job classifications (like the one by production workers—'OS'—at the Renault Le Mans plant) in fact expresses dissatisfaction with working conditions for the wage dispute to become a strike over working conditions. The strike analysis that has already been quoted (Durand and Dubois, 1975) reveals that 62 per cent of demands for wage increases are admitted by union militants to be linked to frustrations over hierarchical relationships and alienation due to working conditions. The fact that workers may become accustomed to 'economic' negotiation behaviour, that worker action is confined within the bargaining system, and that the employers refuse to speak in any other language may also be an alibi for not changing anything in the system of negotiation. In 1968, for example, a period when the balance was tipped in the direction of the workers, did the content of the Grenelle negotiations reflect the meaning behind the May movement? If the workers' movement desires a socialist orientation, should it tie itself down with conventional rules of the game, or deal with problems at the level at which they are actually posed? A minority has expressed such a point of view: before his death, Fredo Krumnov (who was on the executive committee of the CFDT) refused to be shackled to the negotiation points put forward by the Government and instead waited to negotiate 'on the basis of our own objectives and not those of the establishment' (Krumnov, 1973). Hence, what is maintained is a form of demand strategy that differs from the habitual trade unionism of negotiation.

Industrial relations activity in France is still surrounded with ambiguity. When the economic climate is poor, when wage claims are unsuccessful, the union alters its line of demand by directing action towards non-negotiable points such as employment levels, job content, the plant structure, and the distribution of the national income (Erbès-Seguin, 1973). Is the class struggle waiting for the right moment, the one at which it has nothing to lose? This raises the question of the ideological significance behind demand activity, and the point has been highly debated between the trade union organisations in recent years during the controversy between the CGT and the CFDT over putting forward wage claims, and whether these claims should be linked to the existing wage hierarchy or not.

THE DEBATE ON THE WAGE HIERARCHY[8]

A survey carried out in 1971 showed that 77 per cent of CGT plant-level militants were in favour of wage increases which respected the wage hierarchy, while 84 per cent of CFDT militants were for non-hierarchical increases (i.e. wage rises that were not automatically applied across the scale of job classifications). The CGT's arguments are based on defending skill-levels and professional qualifications. For the CGT, qualifications are a fundamental element of life at work, they must be defended wherever they are threatened, and a watch has to be kept to see that they are correctly defined. The CGT defends the right to levels of training and culture against the tendency of capitalism to reduce the skill content of work and limit the workers' chances of receiving training strictly to its own requirements. Training and cultivation are conditions for the return to the concept of work as a creative activity overcoming alienation; they pave the way for the eventual takeover by the workers in the course of technological, economic, social and political evolution (Hostalier, 1973). Any desire to remove the wage hierarchy is seen as designating the executive and administrative grades (the *cadres*) as those guilty of the misdoings of the capitalist system and rejecting them from mass and class-orientated trade unionism (Desseigne, 1971). The desire to do away with the hierarchy system calls into question the alliances of qualified engineers and staff grades with the working class. The problem of the hierarchy is approached in terms of political strategy. It favours the capitalist aim of dividing the working class.

For the CFDT, 'to refuse to see that the wage hierarchy is an expression of the hierarchical form taken by established authority is to accept the organisation of society as it stands and play into the hands of the capitalist order.'[9] This union advocates a strategy of putting forward claims now which are incompatible with capitalism. The form taken by demands should prefigure the image of the world of tomorrow, a socialist and democratic world of self-management from which the power hierarchy is to be excluded.

Formulated in such a manner, these divergent views are apparently irreconcilable. Nevertheless, as far as both a common platform at the national level and plant-level demands are concerned, actual practice (while still not without its ups and downs) succeeds in achieving compromises which largely smooth over these ideological differences. At plant level, more often than not, the tendency is to compromise on wage questions: a demand for a percentage increase on top of a flat-rate payment. This compromise position is given theoretical form in the CFDT's notion of a 'binomial wage', made up of (a) a 'progress wage', which enables needs which are the same for all to be satisfied, and is identical at all levels in the hierarchy, and (b) a 'function wage', which is aimed at remunerating the level of responsibility, and remains a hierarchical phenomenon. The CGT for its part matches the demand for 'a single scale going from the labourer to the qualified engineer', each having his position within a clearly defined hierarchical set of functions, with a policy of re-evaluating low wages by raising the national minimum wage (SMIC) and giving differentiated rises to the advantage of under-privileged categories. This then also leads to the common strategy of 'reducing disparities'.

The result in practice is that there is very little difference in the aims put forward in demands, which is encouraged by the desire to present a united front in face of the employers. Furthermore, a detailed analysis of the relation between the demand practices and the ideological orientations of militants shows that, at grass-roots level, those demands which are not linked to the wage hierarchy do not explicitly have the same meanings of class struggle attached to them by the inter-union controversy. Anti-hierarchical attitudes reveal themselves to be linked in a more discriminating fashion to interests of self-defence rather than interests of class. Wage demands that are not based on the wage hierarchy appear to express the natural reactions of solidarity experienced by the mass of production-line workers, and occur more frequently with marginal and under-privileged groups, finding their expression more often among young workers and the unskilled.

Nevertheless, no correlation exists either between anti-hierarchical demands and radical forms of action or between these demands and giving disputes a political interpretation. At plant level, demands that are so expressed as to go against the wage hierarchy have an economic rather than a socio-political implication.

THE POLITICAL SIGNIFICANCE OF STRIKES IN FRANCE

There can, however, be no doubt that dispute action does take on a political significance above and beyond the industrial relations system of which it forms a part. The latent dissatisfaction with the constraints of dependency and alienation resulting from the situation at work means that strikes can be interpreted as the expression of revolt against the condition of the worker. This then takes on a fuller meaning, challenging the model of society established by the dominant classes, without necessarily obtaining expression at the level of political affairs. It may even be said that their own 'ethics' prevent the unions from intervening directly within the field of action covered by the political parties. Yet the very contents of their demands often question the overall options which exist within the economic situation or, in certain extreme cases such as May 1968, the political balance.

If it is true that plant militants recognise this latent political significance behind industrial conflict (Durand and Dubois, 1975: Ch. 1, part III) the extent to which it can be expressed at the level of political action in an immediate and direct fashion is bound to differ according to the context. In certain disputes (especially in the public sector, such as in broadcasting) strike action extends directly into the political sphere, while the strategy of undertaking widespread strike action, of 'generalising' disputes, as sometimes occurs at certain periods or in certain sectors of industry, creates a balance of power that can threaten the establishment.

Lastly, strike action expresses class struggle: militants stress the role of the strike in developing political awareness and in mobilising the working classes. By virtue of this, strike action can be said to 'point the way towards the coming socialist society'.

If we add together all these various meanings attributed to strike activity, the proportion of strikes with a political significance is considerable: something like one strike in two has, for those militants who led it, a direct political significance or provides a necessary hardening of attitudes towards the establishment, particularly for CFDT militants.

THE CONTEXT OF DEMANDS – CATEGORIES AND SECTORS

The latent political significance of conflicts does not, however, mean to say that a strike, as carried through and experienced, has its own logical pattern. There is no absolute correlation between demand content and forms of action. In actual practice they are very often poles apart. What happened in May 1968 is the most notorious example of a movement divided between revolutionary practice as regards forms of action (paralysis of the economy, occupation of plants, street demonstrations, the symbolic use of the red flag) and an extremely conventional demand content (for the 40-hour week and minimum wage guarantees). The ways in which worker militancy was aroused in the years 1967 and 1971 have not had any specific bearing on a particular category of dispute. Differences in militancy according to strike demand are minimal (*ibid*: p. 120–1).

Any propensity to undertake action which is not sanctioned by law during a strike (such as factory occupation, or the use of force) is greater in non-economic disputes; these are frequently strikes over obtaining rights and a protest against repression—in other words, conflicts in which forms of action and strike aims tend to become identified with one another. Strikes called over employment protection and working conditions have not, however, been statistically longer and tougher than those called for other reasons. Actions such as go-slows, absenteeism and aggressiveness towards supervisory grades remain more frequent manifestations of latent dissatisfaction over working conditions than open conflict.

The analysis of disputes within their context also shows that no one pattern of social conflict is limited to a particular social category. Undoubtedly there is a resurgence of militancy among the 'OS', women workers and immigrants, yet their actions have the same objectives as those of traditional categories of workers. Wage demands are no more frequent among under-privileged categories than among others, although their form changes. With unskilled grades, as is only natural, strikes over raising low wages predominate (accounting for 50 per cent of strikes involving the 'OS', as against 37 per cent among skilled workers, and 19 per cent among technical grades). Skilled and technical grades are more prone to put forward demands for percentage increases. The frequency of demands for standard of living increases is inversely proportional to position within the hierarchy.

Disputes over employment safeguards tend to occur more often with the more highly qualified categories, and demands bearing on work duration (working hours, paid holidays and retirement conditions) are more frequent in technical and craft trades than in production line work. 'Qualitative' demands—those which are put forward by more privileged categories of workers—only arise once essential needs have been satisfied (for example, once living conditions have been safeguarded). Demands directed towards further training and promotion are also the province of privileged levels – increased status and cultivation are pursued once the minimum vital necessities have been assured.

Strikes over working conditions are more frequent in mass-production work and in firms with a female labour force, and less in craft trades where the workers are not as exposed to the constraints of work-speeds and production-line work. In work requiring solely mental activity and in technical trades, the increases in demands concerning working conditions centre around shortages of numbers and deficiencies in work organisation, so that in a roundabout way technical grades and office-workers have the same preoccupations as production line workers.

As with occupational categories, interesting differences arise between the occupational sectors (i.e. public or private) as regards the nature of demands expressed during strike action (*ibid*: pp. 107–110). 'Economic' strikes are less frequent in the public sector, or they succeed less often than in private employment. Public-sector employment is the only area in which dissatisfaction on an economic level declines in importance as a latent cause of disputes. In order to avoid government measures to freeze wages in this sector, wage demands are recast in the form of claims based on job classifications, through which limited results may be obtained *via* drift in job grades. Giving demands that are based on job categories pride of place in public-sector employment is not however simply a strategic consideration: along with this type of demand comes reference to professional responsibility. Added to this are questions concerning work organisation or the statutes governing the firm (the defence of statutes of nationalised firms figures in 20 per cent of the disputes within the public sector and gave rise, for example, to the lengthy strike of broadcasting staff in protest against the reorganisation of French radio and television when the ORTF was disbanded at the end of 1974). Such demands denote the very particular direction in which action is taken in the public sector where questions of control predominate, the institutional setting being such that the unions already have a wider say in the control and organisation of undertakings.

3 THE INSTITUTIONAL STRUCTURE OF INDUSTRIAL RELATIONS

Before dealing with the question of the content and form of negotiation, it is important to show how the tendencies of French unions are placed with respect to the institutions of representation and to provide an overall assessment of their official negotiating capability, distinct from that of their opposite numbers in West Germany and Great Britain.

THE INSTITUTIONS OF REPRESENTATION

The main institutions of trade union representation at plant level are the plant steward[10] (*délégué du personnel*); the plant committee (*comité d'entreprise*), upon which depends the plant safety committee (*comité d'hygiène et de sécurité*); and the plant-level union branch (*section syndicale*), recognised as an established organ of representation since 1968, together with its in-plant union delegates (*délégués syndicaux*). The *comité d'entreprise* does not exist in the public area, but the same role is fulfilled by various different bipartite commissions (i.e. commissions on promotion, training and appointments) in which the unions have a much greater say than in the private sector (Dubois, 1974).

The creation of these established forms of representation marks an advance in the recognition of the status of trade unions in the plant. The plant stewards and delegates to the works committees are elected on lists presented by the unions, and the union branch delegates are designated by the unions themselves. Such an advance in official union negotiating capacity within the plant is not without its shortcomings. It is evidently more extensive in plants where union organisations are more firmly established. In other words, the institutions of representation operate more effectively in large undertakings than in small ones, and in the public sector rather than in private industry.

In small firms or in those that are only slightly unionised, there is often some confusion between the various forms, with the same person holding different offices, or even an insufficient number or complete lack of organs of representation (Dubois, 1971). Surveys conducted by the French Ministry of Labour reveal that several years after the creation of the *comité d'entreprise* numerous firms employing over fifty employees still did not possess one.

As regards the plant-level union branch, the vagueness of the legislation on this point means that its role varies from one plant to another. One recent survey (Bachy *et al*, 1974) indicates that the plant-level union branch may limit itself simply to stimulating the elected bodies, or that its role may be to override those of the plant stewards and works committee by taking over bargaining and leading dispute activity. Once again it is the amount of weight the union has within the plant which confers on the plant-level branch this pre-eminence over other organs of representation.

On the whole, the extent to which procedures involving these forms of representation are respected is not absolutely binding, and the efficacy of these institutions is very varied. They depend at one and the same time on the varying propensities of employers to negotiate or attach any status to the unions, and on the differing lines taken by the unions, which see themselves as either more or less participatory or oppositional bodies. Each side blames the other for the failure of the institutions of representation to function properly, with the unions accusing management of using them solely with a view to providing the outward signs of good occupational relations, and the employers accusing the unions of transforming them into an arena of confrontation and class struggle.

On the national level, the unions play a part in various national bodies, the Conseil Economique et Social, the Commissions du Plan, and the regional Comités de Développement and Conseils Economiques et Sociaux. These bodies are fraught with the same tribulations as relations within industry, though their activity is also affected by the political climate.

NEGOTIATING CAPACITY AND THE BALANCE OF POWER IN INDUSTRY

The repeated appeals of the established authorities since 1968 for a more participatory attitude in industrial relations have never really been effectively followed through, apart from the reformist line taken by the minority unions. The CFTC and Force Ouvrière challenge only the imperfections within the capitalist system and they seek to remedy these through negotiated and legislative means. Both these unions are in agreement with the viewpoint of the government and the more progressive employers over the need for reformist change, and they are therefore not in principle opposed to taking part in negotiations, to finalising agreements, and to regarding positively the content of statutory measures.

The situation is more delicate with respect to the CGT and the CFDT, since these unions question the very basis of the capitalist order and its present expression at the level of the state. There could be no question of their lending support to the present system or of accepting any accommodation with such a state of affairs. Nevertheless they remain favourable to negotiating some sort of compromise, which marks a step in the balance of power existing between what are antagonistic interests, and confers a minimum of guarantees on the workers. In this sense, an agreement may constitute an acquired gain in protecting the interests of wage-earners; it is not regarded as support for the prevailing state of affairs but as a temporary armistice, to be called into question at the first opportunity as changes occur in economic, political or social conditions. The CGT and the CFDT do sign agreements, but they immediately raise certain points for renegotiation; for these unions an agreement should never be considered as final. It is not part of the progressive creation of a different order of things, but an expression of the balance of power.

Yet behind such an offensive, based on ideological considerations, more often than not there lies a pragmatic strategy. The structures of bargaining are accepted as soon as they work more or less efficiently or if, in spite of deficiencies in operation, they are seen as constituting a victory for the workers. This may lead to some separation being made between the institutions of representation themselves (which at the very least enable information to be gathered) and 'economic' negotiation (where the unions refuse to be restricted within the confines of an incomes policy). The CGT and the CFDT will reject any agreement or any law which ties an improvement in the condition of the workers to the prosperity of the capitalist system, as this would have implications of class collaboration and the acceptance of the ultimate aims of capitalism (if we all work together, everyone will benefit from it); they will likewise condemn measures that either restrict workers' action or will only be accomplished over a period of years.

Since 1968, there has been a drop in the number of productivity agreements since, by fixing earnings increases to a rise in productivity, they were seen as a form of ideological manipulation. Both the CGT and the CFDT reject long-term agreements on wage questions and will have nothing to do with recipes for aligning increases in living standards with the prosperity of individual undertakings. Distrust of different forms of worker shareholding and plant productivity agreements[11] is a sign of apprehension about falling into a trap. Suspicious of having their hands tied by long-term agreements and of being manipulated, the unions prefer to go one step at a time and not restrict their possibilities of action. The reduced propensity of either side of industry to conduct negotiations outside actual dispute situations, at least at plant level, is linked to the absence of any consensus as to the ultimate aim of negotiations: for employers, as for unions, negotiations are a testing time.

The situation in France precludes a policy of occupational relations based on some sort of permanent mutual understanding. The low institutionalisation of dispute settlement arises from the same state of affairs. Research carried out by CRESST (*ibid*) shows that use of conciliation procedures, which reaches 35 per cent in engineering, drops to low levels in other branches of industry (2–6 per cent of disputes). Strike notice procedures are likewise rarely respected (4 per cent with proper notice in engineering) (Durand and Dubois, 1975). Furthermore, the prevailing political climate has always had an influence in France on the propensity to undertake strike action (Perrot, 1974; Tilly and Shorter, 1973), and this is the reason why it is arbitrary to wish to isolate occupational relations from the context of movements within society and considerations of power relationships.

CONTROL OF TRADE UNION ACTION

The low propensity of French unions to engage in official bargaining activity is also due to the nature of their relationship with the rank-and-file.

Inside the CGT and the CFDT, there is speculation about the effect on the attitudes of members of negotiating policy—whether or not to sign an agreement, whether or not to express satisfaction. Will signing an agreement lead to a reduction in militancy and sympathy towards the union? Could further action be undertaken over unsatisfied demands? What is the best way of attaining a level of consciousness sufficient to reveal the need for an advance towards socialism?

The fact that French unions are relatively weak in organisational terms means that they have to keep in close touch with feelings within the rank-and-file. However, the rules behind official negotiating practice mean that it is the 'professionals' who deal with the demands, and this places demand activity on shaky ground when it comes to relations with spontaneous action at rank-and-file level (Erbès-Seguin, 1971 (a) and (b)). In spite of the frequent occurrence of spontaneous strikes, unofficial strikes as such are nevertheless less common in France than in England or West Germany. This is due to the fact that spontaneous strikes are immediately taken over by the union organisation, even if the strike is considered to be inopportune or of no avail. Even illegal acts by the rank-and-file are covered by the representatives of the union, so that any tension that exists between the rank-and-file and the union does not fully see the light of day (Bosc, 1973). Such tension finds expression at certain instances during the dispute, most often at the beginning of strike action or at the end, when votes for a resumption of work are taken. These dissensions between the rank-and-file and official plant union or worker representatives are occasionally further aggravated by inter-union rivalry. Several surveys have brought to light the equivocal behaviour of competing organisations, which exploit dissatisfaction within the rank-and-file to outbid and outflank their opposite numbers. This kind of friction is more frequent when the strengths of the organisations are roughly the same (Kergoat, 1973).

The system of worker representation in the plant isolates the mass of workers from control over bargaining. However, since May 1968 any danger of the functions of representation becoming bureaucratised has largely been counteracted by the use of forms of self-determination in dispute action, with the practice—which has since become current—of holding mass meetings where worker representatives have to report in detail on the state at which negotiations stand, and also of having repeated ballots on continuing strike action or returning to work according to the results obtained. During these ballots, held both to decide whether to go on strike and on what forms of action to take, it is no longer rare to see the most predominant union voted down. In the 1971 Batignolles dispute, for example, the strategy of limited stoppages advocated by the CGT (representing two-thirds of the workforce) was rejected in favour of more aggressive action which led to a five-week strike.

The extent of spontaneity of action by the workers explains the relative independence of the content of plant-level disputes from central union programmes of action. This also tends to lead to differences in demand content according to the level at which bargaining takes place: grievances over working conditions are traditionally dealt with at plant steward level, plant-level disputes are overwhelmingly over wage questions, central union demands (retirement conditions, the 40-hour week, paid holidays, the level of employment and trade union rights) are dealt with at national level in the form of 24-hour protest stoppages and are usually resolved by legislative means or through national agreements between the unions and the employers' associations.

The legal recognition of the union branch in the work-place lends official support to any wider autonomy of action at plant level as far as dealing with grievances is concerned. Nevertheless, whether or not union officers from outside the plant intervene in a dispute varies, with the CGT maintaining a practice of greater direction from the centre than is the case with the CFDT.

4 NEGOTIATING PRACTICE

NEGOTIATION STRATEGIES AT NATIONAL LEVEL

The Official and Legal Framework

Given the existence of certain statutory measures in France in the area of occupational relations, is the legal intervention of the authorities aimed at defining the framework of negotiating relations between the CNPF (the employers) and the trade union organisations, or is it intended to encourage them to meet round the table? What the law[12] does do is define certain aspects of industry-wide negotiation at national level. It defines first of all its content: negotiations take place over 'a particular subject relating to working conditions, to guarantees on a social level, and in particular to conditions of employment; it may confer only advantages greater than those conferred by statutory means.' The law also defines the parties to negotiation, i.e. 'those recognised as being fitting parties to negotiation are the employers' organisations and those unions that are the most representative on a national level.' It defines the coverage of negotiation: this may be widened with the consent of, and provided no opposition is expressed by, a 'Higher Commission on Collective Agreements' (Commission Supérieure des Conventions Collectives). However, the law neither specifies the obligation to negotiate, nor the frequency or internal procedures of negotiations, nor the sanctions to be applied in case of infringement of its content.

The legal framework of the inter-industrial national agreement (La Convention Nationale Interprofessionnelle) is at once both more and less rigorous than that established for collective agreements in individual industries. It is more rigorous since it may happen that certain unions which are not representative on the national level (the CFT, the CGSI and other autonomous central union organisations) participate in industry-level negotiations, and also because to extend such agreements it is not necessary to have the unanimous compliance of the Commission Supérieure. On the other hand, the legal framework of national agreements is less rigorous since the content of individual industry agreements liable to be extended is binding, and furthermore, as far as industry agreements are concerned, the authorities may, by instituting a joint commission, impose an obligation on both sides to meet together and draw up such an agreement.

National-level bargaining is therefore somewhat ill-defined in law. However, the state has other legal means of exercising influence at this level of negotiations. It may extend the coverage of agreements by passing laws in a similar vein (e.g. the 1967 government orders on employment precede the 1969 national agreement on the same topic; the 1971 law on occupational training follows on from the agreement of 1970). The authorities may intervene on a financial level so as to help in finalising negotiations (for example, helping to set up occupational training facilities, providing unemployment benefit for workers over sixty, and releasing credits for improving working conditions). Finally, the law may remove obstacles of an institutional nature. The law of 27 December 1973 on improving working conditions no longer prohibits variations in working hours and part-time work, and it was only due to this that negotiations in this area could succeed.

The state, then, does intervene in the sphere of negotiations between the CNPF and the national trade union organisations – the legal framework is established and legislative measures may be applied to encourage or accompany negotiations. Recently, in May 1968 and in March 1969, industry-wide bargaining at national level resulted from the initiative of the authorities and with their participation. In the former case, the state, with a view to putting an end to the 1968 strikes, agreed to take the initiative in calling together the two sides that were involved in the confrontation; it also played an important part by, among other things, imposing on the employers various wage increases and a rise in the national minimum wage. In March 1969, the Tilsitt meeting, planned the previous year at Grenelle, was intended to 'examine the extent to which spending power had evolved during 1968 within the context of the overall evolution in economic and financial affairs.' Unlike in 1968, absolutely nothing was imposed by the state on the employers, and both the state and the employers have since continually rejected tripartite negotiations. It is now therefore apparent that direct intervention on the lines of the 1968 Grenelle talks is the exception: the state seems more anxious to organise the framework of national-level negotiations (i.e. the venue and the means towards negotiation), or to ensure that the maximum number of wage-earners benefit from an agreement (through extension procedures), while guaranteeing a minimum survival level (through the SMIC, and a series of laws aimed at the more under-privileged sectors), and it does this rather than intervene directly in actual negotiations. As will be seen later, 'encouragement' is more important than 'interference', to the extent even that the appeal and arbitration procedures provided for in law have for a number of years now fallen largely into disuse. This attitude appears highly compatible with the role developed upon the state by 'liberal' ideas such as those expressed in the CNPF policy statement of 1965, when the foundations were being laid for the profound changes in economic structures which were to appear in 1966–67 (see Section 1). From this viewpoint, not only is it the role of the state to allow for growth to be attained, while not actually creating it (by stepping back from industrial investment), but it must provide the necessary support and maintenance work behind negotiation, without going so far as to take it over entirely. This shift in the effective role of the state was already apparent in 1967, at the time the first government orders on employment also appeared during the period of industrial redevelopment. The aim then was to facilitate this process, as with the 1975 laws on unemployment compensation. The part played by the state in looking after 'those left behind by economic growth', the clearest evidence as to the division of labour between the state and the employers, is even greater during a period of economic difficulties.

State intervention is always undertaken in a fairly generalised form, so as to provide a framework for future negotiations between the CNPF and the central union organisations while not placing too many constraints on the actual content. Whether they cover worker shareholding, dismissals, continuous occupational training or trade union rights, the increasing number of laws passed since 1968 have in common the establishment of general guidelines, the effective application of which at plant level depends either on further official measures actually bringing the law into force (the *décrets d'application*), which very often take a long time to appear, or on the level of good will (or rather the balance of power) at the work-place where the intended measures are to be applied. The effective content of social legislation depends above all on the ability of the working class to make its acknowledged rights respected.

The law does very little then to modify the bargaining relationships which exist between the CNPF and the trade union confederations, and little more can be said as regards relations between the state and the unions. Meetings do take place, but they do not do so within any institutional framework. What is more, nothing obliges the authorities to deal solely with 'representative' unions: CFT and CGSI representatives have even been introduced into certain regional councils (1973). Finally, neither the law nor the constitution compels legislation to be passed in the social field. Negotiating relations between the state and the unions are not bound by the law; they arise from other factors, and more often than not depend on the situation prevailing at the time. All that is institutionalised is the existence of union representatives in a consultative capacity on the national Conseil Economique et Social (and its counterparts at regional level), the National Plan Commissions and the Commission Supérieure des Conventions Collectives.

For their part, neither the CNPF nor the unions have fixed any agreement as to their negotiating relations. No established national inter-industry agreement makes provision for the obligation to negotiate, or even to meet together at a particular date, although the agreements covering employment security and continuous occupational training provide for annual meetings to follow up the application of the measures. These meetings do not imply any modification in content and may be purely a formality.

Within such an institutional context, containing relatively few constraints, how do bargaining strategies come to develop on an industry-wide basis?

Bargaining Strategy: Typology and Evolution

Since 1967–8, a sharp increase in the output of regulations governing social affairs may be noted on three levels, with the development of state intervention (denoted by a steady increase in the number of 'social' laws and decrees), a growth in the number of inter-industry national agreements (signed by the employers and workers' organisations), and a rise in the number of plant-level agreements. This dual evolution (i.e. at both top and lower levels) should not hide the fact that the main body of collective agreements in France is still made up of industry-level agreements (those covering a single branch of economic activity). Most agreements are of unlimited duration, although several changes in recent years, have reduced their time-limit, with institutionalised wage revision at regular intervals and more or less permanent negotiation on all questions regarding occupational training and security of employment. The provisions of plant-level agreements only very rarely cover all possible areas, and more often than not deal with specific points (such as wage levels, wage payment—increasingly on a monthly basis—work-force financial participation measures, working hours and questions of levels of qualification).

THE STRATEGY OF THE STATE

Any bargaining strategy pursued by the authorities will depend upon the subject under discussion, together with other factors that will be analysed later on. Before looking into the way in which this strategy has evolved over recent years has been for procedures to be prolonged in order to hold one of protracted or speedy negotiations, of encouragement or interference, of promises or payoffs.

In order to produce a piece of legislation, matters can either proceed quickly or drag on. Except in the case of particular measures, the tendency in recent years has been for procedures to be prolonged in order to hold consultations with interested parties (*via* working parties, talks with either side, and possible interaction with negotiations already under way). However, this may be no more than a means of explaining away deliberate procrastination.

Giving promises is a strategy which extends that of long, drawn-out negotiations. Specific measures are announced, and then simply forgotten; application procedures may considerably restrict the full extent of innovation in a particular statute. The regulations themselves may be so ambiguous and so complex, and their enforcement so difficult to control, or the sanctions may have so little deterrent value, that it is impossible to put the law into effect. Developments in recent years have been marked by the frequent inclusion of promises as part of an overall programme, and by an increase in legislative measures, both in quantity (there has been an appreciable break since 1966) and quality (new areas such as working conditions are included). This much on the positive side should not let us forget those promises which have been made and then left on one side (especially as regards labour jurisdiction matters) and the noticeable non-application of controls and sanctions. When faced with union demands, the strategy undertaken by the authorities has been scarcely innovatory, with demands selected, priorities altered and satisfaction only partially obtained.

The strategy of encouragement and/or interference has, moreover, had its novel aspects in recent years. The authorities have jogged the CNPF into undertaking industry-wide bargaining on a national level by several devices: recommending negotiation (as, since 1967, over security of employment measures); recognising it legally (in 1971); setting a good example in public sector employment (from 1970 for worker shareholding); contributing financially (since 1963, agreements can be signed with a National Employment Fund (Fond National de l'Emploi); removing legal obstacles (variable working hours were permitted for the first time in 1973); and establishing permanent structures in which the CNPF and the union confederations meet together—in 1967, with the consultative committee to the national employment agency (Agence Nationale pour l'Emploi); in 1971, with the national body responsible for occupational training (Conseil National de la Formation Professionnelle, de la Promotion Sociale et de l'Emploi); and in 1973, with a special agency responsible for questions concerning the improvement working conditions; it was also considered having an agency for developing increased worker participation). One or other of these means was used when the question of working conditions was taken up in 1973. However, such measures do not impose an obligation to negotiate, and have no power to overcome clear resistance on the part of the employers. Encouragement then gives way to interference; nevertheless, in spite of government intentions, no breakthrough has been made in the field of worker participation in the management of undertakings.

THE STRATEGY OF THE CNPF

Despite state pressures, the CNPF has the final say as to whether or not it actually negotiates at the inter-industry level. In two areas (wages and questions concerning the distribution of power within the plant), and to one method (tripartite negotiation), it has refused consideration outright. Outside these limits, and on obtaining the go-ahead from its permanent assembly, the CNPF is prepared to enter negotiations. It defines the subject and voices its intentions to the union organisations, often receiving them one after the other; it fixes the date of the first round of talks, and how often the meetings are to take place; it makes the initial proposals, and the final ones as well; it then attempts to obtain the signature of the unions.

The strategy of the CNPF towards union demands is not much different to that adopted by the state, though it would prefer to reach policy agreements (the establishment of common guidelines which are subsequently to be negotiated more fully at lower levels). It would also like the unions to agree to abide by their signature.

Three changes characterise negotiating practice by the employers during the last few years. Firstly there has been a new level of acceptance of negotiation at the inter-industry level. This started at the end of 1967, the previous important agreement being back in 1961, and each year since 1968 has brought with it a fresh agreement or the revision of a previous one. Secondly, this national bargaining has extended into new areas; whereas agreements on retirement and security of employment are in line with past ones, those covering occupational training, wage-payment on a monthly basis and working conditions are original. Finally, negotiation has tended to become continual in the sense that since the beginning of 1973 we have entered a phase of revising and improving on existing agreements.

THE STRATEGY OF THE CGT AND THE CFDT

Here the prime aim is, of course, to select the overall line of demand, specify the precise objectives embraced within this, and give an indication of priorities. The second point is to prepare the ground for negotiations or for lobbying the authorities, by means of letters to the CNPF and the ministries concerned, press conferences, drawing up petitions, handing out leaflets, lobbying parliamentary deputies, and a campaign which may or may not involve national strike action. When negotiations are under way or when there is consultation with the authorities over projected legislation, tactics involve making counter-proposals, or raising the level of the debate by threatening to break off talks. The agreement is signed (after consultation with representative bodies within the union), though criticisms are still made of it; or the law is simply denounced as not going far enough.

In the last fifteen years, the strategy of the CGT and the CFDT has undergone marked changes, first of all in the area of unified action—though this has not been without its ups and downs. An initial joint declaration signed in January 1966 provided the inducement towards joint action up until the end of 1967, but further developments did not occur until the end of 1970. Since then, various series of joint demands have been pursued in a regular manner. A further change has been the launching of campaigns on unified themes. Whereas in the years 1966 and 1967 the aims of 24-hour protest demonstrations (*journées d'action*) were often ill-defined, if not widely disparate, those that occurred in 1971, 1972 and 1973 centred on themes which were given some priority, such as retirement, the SMIC, or spending power, and were backed at a local level by campaigns on union rights and the conditions of immigrant workers. The actual content of demands has also altered somewhat. Demands based on maintaining spending power, full employment and freedom of action for the unions occur throughout the whole period, while before 1968 reduction in working hours, the demand to negotiate over real wages (instead of simply the basic wage scales), and the repeal of the 1967 government orders reorganising the welfare system were occasionally placed on the same level. Pension rights, a high continuing rise in the rate of the SMIC and the improvement of immigrant workers' conditions only came to the forefront from the end of 1970, and improvements in working conditions in September 1971.

An interpretation is needed of such changes in strategy, and this will be attempted below. First, however, it is worth while comparing and contrasting negotiating practices at national level with what occurs at plant level during strike action. Limited though they may be, negotiations on the national level and social legislation have been carried out to an increasing extent in recent years. Given this fact, how can those strikes which reveal extreme uncompromising bargaining practices be explained?

In this respect, there is one area of particular contrast: negotiating practices at national level always remain within legal bounds, while at plant level strikes do not hesitate to break such bounds. The state, the CNPF and the union confederations accept the requirements of the law. The state extends agreements only after respecting all the procedures; the CNPF negotiates solely with representative organisations, it proposes improvements beyond a minimum set out by law, respects what it has signed at least in the letter (if not in the spirit), and invites all those unions that have accepted the agreement to take part in subsequent talks to prepare the application of the measures; the unions for their part respect formal procedures when rejecting agreements. The legal framework within which national level negotiations take place is not highly restrictive, but this is not always the case at plant level, which may explain in part any tendency towards undertaking action outside the law at this level.

NEGOTIATING STRATEGIES IN PLANT-LEVEL DISPUTES

The Statutory and Official Negotiating Framework

Negotiation with a view to the conclusion of a plant-level agreement, whether subsequent to strike action or not, is legally allowed but not required, though every industrial undertaking is of course bound to respect the provisions of labour law and also the relevant industry agreements, together with any agreement that it has negotiated with its employees. The law of 11 February 1950, revised in 1971, recognises the validity of the plant agreement, but allows complete freedom as to whether one is to be negotiated. Where no industry-level agreement exists, the various provisions normally contained within such an agreement may be set out in an agreement at plant level; while where there is an industry agreement, a plant agreement may improve on it, and also go on to cover the question of real wage levels. A plant agreement has to be reached with representative unions within the plant itself. Nothing further is imposed as a legal requirement. An employer is obliged by law to meet with representatives of the workforce during the course of the compulsory meetings with the plant stewards of the *comité d'entreprise*, but there is nothing which compels him to satisfy whatever demands are put forward.

But what are the requirements of the law when a labour conflict appears on the horizon? Before the strike is actually declared, usually nothing at all; provision is not made for prior conciliation, except where explicitly stated in the collective agreement. The work force, for its part, is not bound to give notice of strike action (except in the public sector and in certain branches of industry), and demands do not have to be stated before a strike actually starts. As for the employer, he is only bound to give a reply within six days to whatever demands are put forward by the plant stewards.

When the strike breaks out, the use of the law to encourage negotiation is that much greater, though it is far from having an over-riding influence. One thing alone is binding upon the strikers: demands must be expressed—a strike may not be undertaken without being backed by demands. The law furthermore provides for the automatic intervention of a third party *via* a compulsory conciliation procedure, and compulsory conciliation clauses must be included in the collective agreements. All other negotiating procedures which exist in law are in no way obligatory. If conciliation is not obtained, the parties may settle for recourse to mediation (the provision of mediation may also be imposed by the authorities). The mediator may summon both sides and a decision is reached, with reasons given. This decision becomes binding if not rejected by either party within eight days. Arbitration can also follow from a failure to obtain conciliation and, unlike mediation, it may not be imposed by the authorities. It needs the common accord of both sides, and the arbitrator, once designated, comes to an arbitration decision which must be supported by reasons and which has the force of law.

If an agreement is reached at the end of a strike, what legal scope does it have? A conciliation agreement, a mediation decision that has not been rejected within eight days, the arbitration decision and any other text signed by both parties are binding upon either side to the same extent as the provisions of the law or the collective agreement. If these are not put into effect, the usual means of appeal may be set in motion (*via* investigation by the labour inspectorate, with possible proceedings, judgement, etc), though certain of them may be rescinded and declared null and void.

There is never any obligation on an employer and strikers to sit round a table and negotiate. The conciliation procedures which bring them face to face involve a third party, and there is no obligation that an agreement must be reached. The other procedures for the 'peaceful regulation of labour disputes' are optional, though any constraint exercised during the course of negotiations is unlawful. Such then is the framework within which the various bargaining strategies oppose one another.

Analysis of Bargaining Strategies during Strike Action: Typology and Evolution

In the analysis of negotiation during strikes, there is one apparent contradiction, similar to what has been noted on a national level: when confronted with a strike situation, the majority of employers show some reticence about negotiation, yet the number of plant-level agreements is increasing. Several examples show that occasionally one and the same plant is involved in either case. Strike action gives rise here to a breakdown in the practices of negotiation.

NEGOTIATION DURING STRIKES AND THE EMPLOYERS' SIDE

The only legal obligations on employers are, in the case of conciliation, to present themselves to the conciliating body, to receive the work-place representatives (even if only for a couple of seconds in order to say no to their demands), and to abide by what they have signed. They are furthermore not allowed to include within a possible agreement any terms that are restrictive with regard to the law and industry agreements. In those strikes that have been analysed, these obligations have always been respected, and likewise there was never a case of any constraint being used in obtaining a signature to an agreement.

Those areas of negotiating activity that are covered by the law are respected. Beyond this, though, there opens up a vast area which is outside the law, namely that which provides the possibility of using different strategies: one which is directed towards real negotiation, or one which rejects it. The employers are free to choose what form negotiations take, when they are to take place, how intense they are to be, how often and who is to take part (whether to have talks with all the unions together or have them in one at a time, or whether to recognise spokesmen who have been elected during the course of the strike). They are free as to what strategies to apply during negotiation and in giving concessions; and they are free to alter this strategy at any moment. As regards the form that negotiations take, the majority trend is one of taking a hard line and not giving way.

Since the beginning of the Fifth Republic (1958), has there been any marked development in employer strategy over negotiation and concessions with regard to strike action? Due to the lack of studies which would enable any real comparison to be made, it is difficult to say one way or the other. There is some evidence of increased intransigence in strikes, but on the other hand negotiations at plant level are no longer the exception. A clear break has occurred, though any hypothesis to be drawn as to the evolution of the conduct of bargaining is by no means clearcut. With the habit of making negotiations may come increased flexibility as far as strikes are concerned; or, on the contrary, negotiation may be a means of preventing strikes altogether. If a strike arises, it is stopped without more ado.

It is illuminating to compare the strategy of the CNPF in national negotiations with that of individual employers when faced with a strike. The legal obligations are respected in both cases, though beyond this there are marked differences. Strike action may make the employers either more or less inclined to negotiate. An employer of a particular plant is not under an obligation to 'play the boss'; on the contrary, it is sometimes in his interest to sort things out as quickly as possible.

NEGOTIATION DURING STRIKES AND THE UNION SIDE

In almost all cases, the unions satisfy the obligations to appear before conciliation bodies and to put forward strike demands (some strikes do, however, break out in a climate of discontent with no exact demands, though they are always worked out subsequently). Since 1968, nevertheless, the five-day strike notice requirement in public service employment is no longer universally respected.

There is not a great number of legal restraints, but the law does proscribe and condemn certain negotiating practices such as direct action, sequestration, the theft of documents to be used in discussions, and the appropriation of manufactured articles for use as exchange currency. The unions may select opposing strategies—in other words, they may decide to have recourse to illegal action. Furthermore, while still remaining within the bounds of the law, they may either show good faith or exhibit intransigence in negotiation (the field of non-codified practices is very wide). On the whole, as regards choosing the moment and the material conditions of negotiation, and those who are to take part, they are seen to be more flexible than the employers, while some individual unions, though only a minority, do not hesitate to influence the way in which negotiations are going by using various illegal means which are not resorted to by the employers' side.

As regards the evolution of union bargaining practices, it is difficult to discern any particular trend. The most striking fact is the recent, though infrequent, appearance of a harder line being followed in negotiations. This is supported by a series of innovations: strike notice has been practically abolished in the public sector; recourse is had to a greater number of negotiators (including the workers themselves); and a face-to-face confrontation with the employer is sought, avoiding any resort to outside conciliation. It sometimes even happens that no demands are stated at the start of a strike movement, or sequestrations and direct action are undertaken, and documents or manufactured goods appropriated. Whereas in the past extra-legal activity was usually limited to the area outside actual working affairs (illegal action aimed at enforcing strike action), it has extended to the field of bargaining (illegal action directly influencing the course of negotiations).

NEGOTIATION DURING STRIKES AND THE STATE

The authorities do not intervene in labour disputes automatically; they have to take it upon themselves to do so. Beyond the conciliation, mediation, and arbitration procedures, they may reject intervention altogether, pleading the freedom of both sides to enter into binding agreements. However, the public sector has to be treated separately, since the authorities are directly involved through the intermediary of the administrators of the state-held companies. It will be seen below that their attitude in negotiations is founded upon intransigence (Dubois, 1974).

To summarise, it may be said that the authorities and the labour inspectorate intervene in an effective manner so as to encourage the fact of negotiation though not its outcome. Since the beginning of the Fifth Republic, the authorities seem to have accepted one thing: given the reticence of both sides of industry, they no longer press them to resort to formal procedures for the peaceful regulation of labour disputes. On the other hand, they intervene on a more informal level if and when the occasion arises. More than on the national level, they 'respect' negotiating freedom. When, in national-level negotiations, they wish to impose a certain development, legislative action may be taken or help provided through financial measures. At plant level, they make use of persuasion alone; there is nothing to indicate the existence of secret funds for the financial settlement of strikes or for supporting the assets of undertakings.

THE EFFECT ON BARGAINING STRATEGIES OF CHANGES IN LEGISLATION[13]

Legal measures underwrite a particular balance of power at a given moment in time, and are therefore often the result of the negotiating strategies themselves. Can the law in turn modify such strategies to a certain extent? Changes in the legal framework within which bargaining takes place have without any doubt influenced negotiating strategies on a national level, though they have had practically no influence on strike action. This may lead us to put forward the hypothesis that innovations in negotiating practices occur instead at plant level, and that these cannot be immediately acknowledged by the law, which is slow to underwrite changes in the balance of power.

Inter-industry national bargaining existed before the precise moment at which it was given official blessing in July 1971. It was not therefore the law which gave rise to the end result, and neither did it lead to any acceleration in its development; there were just as many instances of such negotiation from 1968 to 1971 as there were from 1971 to 1974. The fact that it is not possible for the authorities to extend these agreements would have rather the opposite effect of discouraging any enthusiasm amongst employers, and this could perhaps explain in part why the small and medium-sized firms withdrew from negotiations over working conditions. The new structures set up by the law have not stimulated bargaining as such on a national level, since this sometimes preceded the actual creation of the relevent institutions. On the other hand, a particular series of laws backed up by financial measures have indeed encouraged negotiations as much at a national level as at plant level (i.e. the laws on occupational training, and government orders on employment security and worker shareholding).

THE EFFECT ON BARGAINING STRATEGIES OF THE ECONOMIC AND POLITICAL CLIMATE

National Bargaining Strategies within the National Context

The negotiating strategy undertaken by the authorities and the employers is a means of facing up to and surmounting the crisis of capitalism in its various different aspects, while still retaining on an institutional level the basic foundations of the system, namely the private ownership of the means of production and the profits system, with the power of decision-making in the hands of a few together with the leap into growth, the economic policy which is used in an attempt to preserve capitalism.

When the frontiers of France were opened up on entry into the Common Market, the government and the employers were forced to embark on a particular economic policy. The emphasis has been on industrialisation (the top priority in the Sixth Plan) and on increasing the competitiveness of industry through the adoption of new techniques, increased concentration or company reorganisation. The aim is for industrialisation to secure the balance of trade, and any policy on employment or prices and incomes is dependent upon this.

The bargaining strategy of capital is therefore doubly relevant to such an economic policy. It is, first, of direct use to the policy itself, and it also to some extent avoids social troubles that are liable to upset the system altogether. Statutory measures and agreements have become more numerous in recent years than in the period before 1968, due in the main to the substantial number of provisions on occupational training and employment protection. It is not mere coincidence that the employers and the Government have had an overriding influence in dealings within both these areas. The competitiveness of individual plants within a context of rapid technological and economic change depends on the quality of the labour force at their disposal, its initial level of training and the versatility which further vocational training provides, labour mobility, its suitability to the work required of it, and how active in fact it is (through the elimination of elderly workers and those unable to or incapable of working).

As a result, retirement conditions have also been examined. The extreme reticence shown by the authorities and the employers in discussing this point may be explained by applying the same reasoning. A lower retirement age is not in line with a high level of industrial development since, in a situation of virtually full employment, it would lead to a reduction in the activity rate.

A third area is decision-making within the plant. The concept of worker participation is expressed in terms of worker shareholding (*'intéressement'*), a means aimed at encouraging undertakings to invest. Trade union rights do not come into negotiations, precisely because they call into question one of the basic pillars of the system: the undivided nature of authority.

A fourth area is working conditions. Increased industrialisation is only possible if the French labour force directs itself towards jobs in industry since, for various reasons, it is not possible to resort in an unlimited fashion to immigrant labour, while the headlong rise in the number of jobs in service industries means that emergency measures have to be taken (the change to monthly wage-payment was aimed at enhancing the condition of industrial workers).

However, the negotiating strategy of the state and the employers, made necessary by the choice of an economic policy which seeks to perserve the basis of the capitalist system, is somewhat muted and concealed by the prevailing situation. What are basically short- or medium-term factors within the economic, political and social field should not hide what lies in the background, though they do also influence the bargaining strategy undertaken by the unions. The impact of developments on the economic front has been dealt with above. In the political field, the prime need is to hold on to power, and it was with this in view that the workers were granted concessions in 1968. Approaching elections may also incite leaders to make more effort than usual. Measures favouring small shopkeepers and the independent trades (*viz* statutes of July 1972 and steering legislation voted in 1973), farmers and agricultural workers (September 1972 and early 1973) and under-privileged groups (social measures put forward by the Messmer Government in September 1972) were more often than not interpreted as being aimed at regaining the favour of those social groups which traditionally supported the regime before the 1973 elections. The same reasoning lay behind the CNPF proposal to negotiate over working conditions in the middle of the election campaign. The installation of a newly-elected legislative assembly or a cabinet reshuffle is also the ideal moment for announcing new measures; new leaders must be given credibility and made into popular figures.

For their part, the unions are just as sensitive to the political climate, especially before elections. The CGT and the CFDT have no desire to support the government which is in office; any satisfaction shown towards an agreement or a piece of legislation which is highlighted during an election campaign may look like confirmation of support for the regime.

Prospects in National Bargaining

Is it possible to forecast medium-term developments in national-level bargaining strategies? The movement of increased government regulation over recent years may simply be the result of contingent factors, and may have come about in order to make up for a period during which such intervention, aimed at instituting an 'official' body of rules, had been distinctly lacking in comparison in other countries of similar economic development during the same period. We feel however that this phase is more than just a passing phenomenon, and is in fact a trend which is destined to continue, even if we assume that there is no alteration in the present economic situation. In as much as this is so, it does not mean to say that this edifice of rules evolves of itself, and that each new rule is a contribution to building a more and more 'perfect' industrial relations system.

We believe that rule-making in this area will continue because, in rapidly changing economic circumstances, those rules which were drawn up at a given moment may become out-of-date (as regards either qualifications, work organisation or relative wage levels). Further rules are therefore created to replace those which are no longer suitable to the prevailing situation. The faster the changes, the quicker the rules become obsolescent, and the more necessary such a change becomes. Furthermore rapid changes within a society increase its instability and tend to emphasise social inequalities. In order to avoid shaking the doctrinal foundations of society, the employers and the Government take it upon themselves to replace those rules that are in force (even if they are not yet entirely unsuited for use) or to extend regulation to new fields (such as working conditions and continuous training) so as not to be overtaken by protest movements. Such new rules are, moreover, of use to the system.

This willingness to amend the rules that are in force and to institute new ones covering continually wider fields may also be explained by greater demands on the part of the workers and the articulation of additional needs (whether these result from an increased cultural level, union influence or a rise in the level of consciousness since 1968; or whether, on the other hand, they are ready-made needs encouraged by advertising and the media).

This raises two problems. Firstly, the risk that the Government may be tempted to reduce some of the growing legislative burden should not be ignored. It is in fact very likely, in our opinion, that the extent to which the state has stepped back from intervening directly in the economy (with an increase in the autonomy of public-owned and nationalised companies, and a reduction in its share of the money in circulation) will be accompanied by less intervention on a social level as far as the productive work force is concerned, though with greater intervention on behalf of those left behind by growth (those on the minimum wage, the elderly, the unemployed and handicapped people). This trend has already become apparent over recent years.

The second imponderable deals with the continuity of negotiations: 'the very frequency of talks may lead to a profound change in relationships between the negotiating parties' (Adam *et al*, 1972). Is there any chance of permanent bargaining coming about? The rapid obsolescence to which such rules as exist are prone ought to encourage recourse to negotiation, though in our estimation it will never cover all areas. The contemporary situation means that the employers negotiate in fields of use to the development of capitalism (i.e. wages, employment and occupational training); for this reason these particular themes could be the subject of negotiations on a permanent basis. On the other hand, negotiations covering questions that are not directly useful to the development of capitalism or which even go against it (union rights, improved retirement conditions and worker control over employment conditions) will remain tied to balance of power considerations. The employers will never agree to permanent negotiations on these points and, as has been the case at least until now, will not even negotiate *at all* on these questions, except to a relatively minor extent.

5 TRADE UNION DOCTRINES AND STRATEGIES

THE PATTERN OF UNIONISATION

The results of union elections suggest that the two main confederations, the CGT and the CFDT, have the support of about 80 per cent of the work force. The actual level of union membership, however, is only 20 per cent, a figure which includes wide variations between sectors. A rough outline of unionism in France is as follows (see Appendix 1, Table 8): the CGT numbers about two million members and is the leading union confederation, with membership covering wage-earners of all categories and occupations, with the exception of teaching. The CFDT has nearly one million members, and though previously it recruited more among non-manual occupations, it has tended in the last ten years to spread to other areas, like the CGT. Force Ouvrière has about 700,000 members, mainly in the public sector and in a few particular geographical regions such as the south-west. Its influence among the working class is relatively slight. The final union which aims at attracting members from all sectors is the CFTC, the original union which separated itself from what became the CFDT in 1964, retaining its Christian vocation in a period of 'deconfessionalisation'. Its impact on the whole is very slight; it covers in particular a few well-defined sectors such as banking and mining, though it is strong in some parts of northern France. There remain two other unions, which cover particular occupational categories: the FEN (Fédération de l'Education Nationale) for the various levels of teaching staff, and the CGC (Confédération Générale des Cadres) for executive and middle-management grades.

The distribution of union members according to industry is somewhat varied, with the most highly unionised sectors being engineering, chemicals and public employment. As a general rule, the law of December 1968, which formally allows the institution of union branches in undertakings with over fifty employees, has eased the task of the unions in those areas where they already had members, although it does not appear to have had any direct effect on introducing unionism where it did not exist beforehand. The level of overall trade union membership has risen only very slightly since 1950, and whole sectors of the economy, in particular in the service industries, remain untouched by the union movement, while it is often precisely these sectors which have an ever-increasing level of employment.

The occupational constitution of industry, and those changes which take place within it, also have an effect on union growth. Thus it may be said of the CGT that, as a widespread organisation with a mass basis, its membership is a reflection of the working class, especially the traditional working class. This does not simply mean that its most longstanding and certainly most solid nucleus is that of the working class 'élite', the skilled workers. At work-place level, at any rate, CGT militants and members are a fairly faithful image of the overall occupational composition within the plant. It is apparent, though, that this particular union, perhaps even because of its desire to represent the masses, has been less successful in obtaining much of a foothold among the so-called 'marginal' groups (the term itself is revealing), which include young workers, women and immigrants. As far as disputes are concerned, those that have been in the public eye since 1968, and particularly in 1971, often happen to involve just these categories of workers. Moreover it may be noted that where such disputes arise, the CGT often shows itself to some extent incapable, if not of grasping what is involved, at least of backing up the forms of action taken.

The CFDT had its origin in a federation of commercial employees, and was long conscious of the fact that its origins were not from within the working class. Recruitment at plant level was frequently greater among white-collar workers than among manual workers, while its militants had been formed via Christian youth organisations (such as the JOC—*Jeunesse Ouvrier Catholique*).[14] However, the basis of its membership widened during the sixties, and militants with more diverse backgrounds arrived on the scene. The emphasis that this union repeatedly placed on the condition of the more underprivileged groups(due to the influence of the social doctrine of the Catholic Church rather than the Marxist concept of the proletariat), made it more awake to the problems of those elements of the working population. A wider and more diversified membership, the increasing disappearance of its original precepts (with no other doctrine coming to replace them), and the fact that within the plant it often finds itself in a minority position *vis-à-vis* the CGT, have enabled it to be more in tune with rank-and-file feeling, particularly in 1968.

TWO WAYS OF DISPUTING SOCIETY

It has become somewhat conventional to differentiate between the CGT and the CFDT where their concepts of social change are concerned, while observing similarities in the strategies undertaken by them during disputes. Their distinctive characteristics were clear enough in the past, with a Marxist-orientated CGT and the CFDT of Christian reformist origin. However, since 1968, and in particular since 1970, the year in which the CFDT 'officially' entered the Socialist camp, the differences between the two are of increasing interest.

Among central union organisations, only the CGT and the CFDT contest the political and economic foundations of society and desire total change. The other unions are openly reformist in outlook, and it is for this reason that, quite apart the predominating influence which the CGT and the CFDT have, especially in industry, these two alone have been selected to analyse the position on the union side

The CGT is the only union confederation which is officially Marxist (since 1922). The analysis it makes of French capitalism is founded upon the class struggle, the basis of which is the ownership of the means of production and the exploitation of the labour force.

The meaning behind the term 'conflict' is thus perfectly clear for this particular confederation. It challenges the system of production as it stands, and considers that the relationships which exist within society are those of contending parties. It can therefore be said that its view of things is in complete contrast to that of the CNPF, which defends the principles of free enterprise and the profit motive (Vachet, 1970; Jacob-Ory, 1972). However, in accordance with Leninist principles, any change in the system should be obtained by political means. This is the role of the party, while the union exists to obtain the maximum advantages for the workers. The extent to which society is called into question is thus expressed only at an economic level, with regard to the distribution of the surplus value, although this also represents a fundamental opposition to present production relationships. Nevertheless, the union does not directly challenge the way in which industrial undertakings and society as a whole are organised, since change at this level can only come about following political change. Thus, to the question 'how can change come about in society?', the CGT reply that this is the affair of the political vanguard, organised within the Communist Party. This position determines a particular strategy, different from that of the CFDT.

It is worthwhile taking a look at the way in which the CFDT has developed towards taking up a radical stance with respect to society. Originally of Christian orientation, basing its doctrine on the social ideas of the Catholic Church, it did not have a particularly important role in social relations during the inter-war years. Subsequently, as its influence became wider, the increasing opposition it expressed towards the way in which society is organised long continued to draw its inspiration from a moralistic line which rejected an economic analysis and regarded 'people as people rather than as groups' (Schiffres, 1972). The transition from an analysis of industrial society on a moral level to one on a political level can be traced clearly back to the 1959 Congress, during which a report on 'Democratic Planning' was presented. As the author of this report pointed out (Declercq, 1971; see also Oppenheim, 1973), its aim was (a) to replace an economy based on profits with one based on actual needs, using public investment as the means behind this (including the nationalisation of the banking system) and (b) to alter the power distribution within society by, in particular, giving the workers a place in management activities.

Nevertheless, the CFTC (as it then was) remained for a long time (and still is) reticent as regards relations with the state, be it even a socialist one. This position was to contribute to its current endorsement of the self-management line, which guarantees the unions their autonomy and gives them due recognition of their areas of responsibility. A position such as this, in the tradition of Proudhon, is important in distinguishing the CFDT from the CGT, both as regards theory and strategy.

Hence a concept of conflict based on fundamental opposition had already been outlined within the CFTC in 1959, at the very moment at which it engaged upon on overall analysis of society. It should however be stated that at this time, and until 1968, the CFTC (later the CFDT) remained a very 'administrative' union in outlook, such unionism possibly being defined as one tending to 'treat occupational affairs and those of the plant itself as depending upon their general economic context . . . participation is upheld as providing access towards decision-making . . . Optimistic as to the possibilities of influencing decision-making, administrative unionism does not shy away from conceiving economic programmes in the long term' (C. Durand, 1971). Furthermore, the analysis which the CFTC/CFDT makes of areas of demand is not on the same level as that of the CGT. While the latter makes a distribution between demand action, which is the job of the unions, and all questions affecting political power, which are the province of party organisations, the CFTC/CFDT sees its role as a trade union organisation as relevant to the power structure in society as a whole (*via* control of investment) as well as in the plant.

As for the term 'class struggle', this appeared for the first time at the 1970 Congress, where the former Christian movement also for the first time struck up the 'Internationale'. However, this did no more than confirm what was already an accomplished fact. One of the hypotheses put forward below is that the extensive changes in production activity in France, which occurred around the years 1966–67 (see section 1 above), have led the CFDT to reach a level of awareness long attained by the CGT. What can at least be said is that the CFDT, like the CGT, bases its analysis of the situation in France, together with those actions that have to be undertaken, on a radical critique of the capitalist system, though the definition used by the former is only partly borrowed from Marxism. It is made up of three *mutually dependent* elements, since simply modifying the economic system is, in the view of the CFDT, not enough in itself to transform social relations. The attack must be made on three fronts[15]: (i) on the organisation of the economy, and the private ownership of the means of production; (ii) on those relationships in society which are based on hierarchical factors, with a minority in a position of power; and (iii) on the prevailing ideology and cultural system which alienate the workers and encourage delusions of personal success and private consumption to the detriment of collective interests.

In the CGT, it is the ownership of the means of production which *determines* the other areas, the superstructures. For the CFDT, socialism should be based on three pillars, *autogestion*, through which the workers become collectively their own employer, the social ownership of the means of production, and democratic planning.

STRATEGIES FOR SOCIAL TRANSFORMATION

The overall strategy of the unions may not be fully accounted for without reference to their role in the emancipation of the working class. The CGT thus places its demand activity within the general framework of the class struggle, though limiting the part it plays to one of putting forward demands. The path taken by the CFDT has been one of progressively widening its terms of reference to take in a concept of society which, after 1968, led it to become socialist, though based on the capacity of a union to undertake autonomous action, and closer in this respect to the 'Charte d'Amiens' than to Marxism. Indeed, according to whether it is believed that political consciousness can only be born *outside* the economic struggle, or that, on the contrary, it may be obtained from *inside* it, we find ourselves faced with a Leninist strategy of trade union autonomy limited to economic action (as practised by the CGT) or action aimed at self-management (as developed by the CFDT).

To the extent that Leninist strategy in changing society implies the supremacy of the party over the union movement, the specific nature of union activity should be founded upon concrete demands. This position is, however, difficult for the CGT to maintain, since any organised demand-orientated activity has both economic and political implications. Thus the union has no choice but either to confine itself to basic demand activity (making itself an organ of pure bargaining, which is contrary to its conception of class struggle) or, on the other hand, to carry out its strategy as part of an overall anti-capitalist strategy (which may result in it coming into competition with the party). The entire history of CGT attitudes towards economic planning in France illustrates this dichotomy. Following a phase during which the CGT adhered to the First French Plan, it virtually abandoned any programme of economic policy between the years 1950 and 1960. With the developing strategy of the Joint Left, its demands gradually fell into line with a certain political and economic viewpoint, especially after 1972 and the Programme Commun. It made a particular effort to reflect upon the specific role of trade unions; the construction of a socialist society is thus considered 'a common task in which the unions are actively involved. They are to be one of the main pillars of a society built for the workers' (Krasucki, 1972). Nevertheless, the way in which the work is divided between the party and the union is still clear, though there remains the problem of the unions having a long-term strategy of their own.

More recently, and especially since 1973, there has been an apparent loosening of the ties between the Communist Party and the CGT in the area of strategy.[16] Even though their common reference to Marxist doctrine determines their fundamental relationships, their fields of activity, and especially the means of undertaking this activity, have become more independent of each other. Recent (negative) evidence of this can be seen in the efforts made by the Communist Party in 1975 to recover some lost ground in influence at plant level. The official protest raised by the party against the obstacles raised against its in-plant activity somewhat belies its own failings in this area. On the other hand, union leaders gained an increasing hearing within political circles, and in November 1974 members of the Government accused union activity of becoming 'too political'. This ought not to be interpreted as one side trespassing on the area of the other, but rather as a more diversified and autonomous trend in union action which tends to loosen the tutelage of the Party. While the practice of day-to-day demand tactics raises hardly any problems in defining relations between union and party, there are liable to be three kinds of problem if any overall strategy is established: doctrinal ones, 'diplomatic' ones of relations between the CGT and the Party, and, even more likely, possible problems concerning relations with the non-militant rank-and-file. Indeed, most members and sympathisers support the union, whether it is the CGT, the CFDT, or any other, less for what it is than for what it does; less for its basic doctrine than for its actual activity within the plant. Hence the importance for the unions of securing tangible results in pursuing demands, which involves tactical questions developing out of the prevailing climate. Hence also the difficulty in defining strategies of action which go beyond the everyday sphere of activities, and imply 'going in for politics' (in the sense often understood by the uncommitted rank-and-file).

This also explains why such a strategy is easier to develop at levels further away from the work-place, and in particular at the national level, which has a more privileged position for the CGT than for the CFDT. As far as activities at plant level are concerned, any challenge to the organisation of the work process soon raises questions of control and the balance of power; since any change in the relationships within society has to be preceded by change on the political front, this problem has to be deferred until some period following the transition to socialism. Here again the CGT has no long-term strategy.

These two elements combined have various effects on the overall organisation of demand strategy within the CGT in the area of 'economic' bargaining. They enable some sort of *entente* to be reached with the employers, even if it is only provisional and founded upon 'agreement to disagree'. What the CGT proclaims is the need to negotiate the maximum number of advantages for the workers; moreover it prefers to negotiate at national or industry level. It thereby avoids raising concrete points about the organisation of work. At plant level, the efforts of the CGT are directed towards playing off grievances in money terms and bidding up the price of labour rather than challenging the way in which it is organised. Such, apparently, is the reason for distinguishing between 'quantitative' and 'qualitative' demands. Also, simply saying 'they can cough up' is a fairly straightforward way of challenging the profits system, and one that can easily grasped. It is, moreover, a demand that unifies everyone behind it, in line with the CGT's desire to be a union of the masses; and since the demand is seen from a Marxist standpoint, the CGT is, as it were, in advance of the employer's side. It has long now considered the true 'enemy' to be the national and international monopolies rather than individual employers. It inveighs against the *logic* of the system rather than against those individuals who incarnate it. This provides yet another reason for it to prefer negotiations at the highest level.

However, to the extent that the role of the union is to mobilise the mass of workers, it has to take charge of the interests of the greatest number. As has been seen, the CGT is inadequately represented among both marginal categories and certain high-growth sectors, and it is perhaps these areas which pose the real problems in society in the latter part of the twentieth century.

It can be said then that the CGT has taken up problems with the most appropriate party over a longer period and in a more effective manner than any other union, but whether the problems concerned have been the most appropriate ones is another matter.

Trade union action to bring the workers together has to base itself upon unifying political principles, on an overall vision of society. Unionism should be at one and the same time both a mass and a class phenomenon. However, it is not by accident that the area of action to be chosen by the CGT is that of relations with the state. This choice is linked with the primacy of political over economic strategy in attaining social change. When the time is thought to be ripe, it enables popular forces to be mobilised in support of action on a political level (the 'Union de la Gauche' and the 'Programme Commun' being the most recent manifestations of this), while still reserving actual trade union action for the area in which it has over-riding effectiveness, i.e. demands in the field of occupational relations. This effort towards unification means advocating nationalisation, a line which has been taken up and amplified by the CGT since the early part of the Gaullist period. The CGT has seen nationalisation as the prime means of putting an end to personal power within industry, enabling the unions to take part in company management. On this point at least there is some movement in CGT strategy towards long-term measures. This tendency has been increasing since 1971, and especially since the CGT adhered to the left-wing Programme Commun, giving rise to greater reflection on the role played by trade unions. Nevertheless, it seems that the demands raised by the CGT with regard to nationalisation are aimed at transferring ownership and setting up some form of state capitalism linked to radical political change, rather than at any change in the actual content of nationalisation. The question is similar to that of power and influence inside the individual firm: its actual constitution will not be examined until those political changes to which it is subordinated have taken place. Once more, the CGT can be said to deal with the appropriate institution, the state, which is both increasing its grip on the economy and making inroads into what had been acquired in the sphere of nationalisation back in 1945 (Dubois, 1974).

Unlike the CGT, the CFDT has no pattern of social organisation established from outside by a political party. It is even frequently reproached for not having a firm theoretical basis for its actions, and for having an exaggerated confidence in spontaneous activity as far as demands are concerned. We have already seen the historical reasons why this central union organisation evolved towards taking an overall analytical view of society, a process which the CGT had long since gone through. For a long time, until 1959, 'invoking the need for some sort of overall plan avoided making an analysis in terms of the system as such, and the CFTC contented itself with a reformist attitude based on the negation of the class struggle' (Oppenheim, 1973). It is interesting to note that around 1955, at a time when the CGT had an uncompromising attitude (rejecting even a temporary or highly limited form of compromise, refusing to elaborate any kind of strategy whatsoever in the economic field), the CFTC was using planning as an alibi to conceal both its failure to analyse the system and its class collaboration, both of which were linked together. It was at this time that the two unions were the furthest apart, their strategies subsequently drawing closer together due to political events (the coming to power of De Gaulle in 1958, and the end of the Algerian war in 1962, which enabled energies to be redirected to internal affairs) and also to economic events (structural changes within the system occurred at the beginning of the sixties, and in particular in 1966–7). If we examine the dates, we find the CFTC report on democratic planning in 1959, the first agreement between the CGT and the CFDT on joint action in January 1966, and the CFDT's entry into the socialist fold in May 1968, made official in 1970. All this is more than coincidence.

This turn of events has allowed the CFDT to evolve according to a dialectical process, with ambiguities showing themselves up progressively as the political and economic situation developed and as they were revealed by impetus from inside the organisation itself. The notion of planning had long enabled the most conservative and the most forward-looking elements to exist side by side, and was used by the latter to challenge the system of production directly for the first time in 1959. In 1964 came the elimination of the conservatives; yet, although modernist in outlook, the organisation remained very reformist deep down (C. Durand, 1971). Nevertheless, the agreement with the CGT was only possible because some form of evolution had taken place. The agreement was by and large a tactical one, and the rapprochement between the two unions has had it ups and downs, with relations most difficult in May 1968. Like all crisis situations, the May movement shed light on certain issues; the CFDT 'discovered' the class struggle and the socialist alternative through action at plant level. This was to play an important part in its future evolution. In 1970, the CFDT took on socialist colours, though with the anti-centralist, self-management inclination discussed above. As a result, the leap into the sphere of qualitative considerations has been made, helped along by the political situation, while the common understanding between the CGT and the CFDT went beyond the tactics to become an overall strategic position. The debate between them came out into the open, and from 1971 the union press started to publish searching articles aimed at examining more deeply those points at which their outlooks resembled or diverged from each other. And as far as similarities were concerned, the tactics of action counted more than points of doctrine. As has been shown, both unions have a somewhat different idea of socialism and the role played by the unions. However, it is not paradoxical to claim that, if for different reasons, neither union has any real strategy for change.

The position of the CGT is that the work is divided between the party and the union in such a way that at present autonomous action is only practically possible for the union at the level of demand tactics; a clear example of one of the habitual functions of ideology, namely facilitating day-to-day practice. The CFDT, for its part, does not yet have sufficiently elaborate theoretical foundations to provide the two-way process between doctrine and action which would allow it to formulate some strategy of change. Some efforts in this direction were made when the union still had a reformist basis, and it is therefore probable that some form of evolution will occur in the future. However, this tendency is opposed by the CFDT's anti-bureaucratic and anti-centralist attitudes, which are tied to a desire that the workers should take over control of their own destinies. Any theory of social change tends to be elaborated solely on the basis of activity at a low level, as a result of which the union refuses to take the easy course of resorting to an ideological stance.

If the CGT's dilemma hinges on the relationship between the economic and the political spheres (the union and the party), that of the CFDT lies in the dichotomy between the need to carry out a painful elaboration of theory, and its support for self-management at all levels, beginning at that of dispute activity. However, at present a sort of strategic vacuum exists within both unions; this reinforces convergent practices at the tactical level which, as far as they are concerned, are linked to prevailing factors and are therefore likely to continue to evolve on parallel lines. It may be said that strategy as such exists only to the extent that the unions have undertaken to carry out action on a joint basis—and the very fact of coming together is a strategy in itself.

There is, however, one important area in which the CFDT makes a particular effort as regards strategy, namely in making demands which challenge the way in which labour is organised (reducing work-speeds or rearranging hours rather than having a bonus increase as a compensation for more unfavorable conditions), and also in whittling away the wage hierarchy (with flat-rate rather than percentage increases). From this viewpoint, the considerable effort made to train members, which has always had a place within the union, is to some extent a form of overall strategy. However, it has been seen (in Section 2) that there is often some disparity between the demands put forward during a strike and those elaborated by the union.

The CFDTs policy of training the maximum number of militants is also linked to this union's traditional concept of individual responsibility, so that its internal structure and democracy differ somewhat from those of the CGT; according to the union, these differences influence their particular forms of action. Union democracy does not refer to the degree of freedom of political discussion or to a division into organised tendencies, which is rejected by all unions. It is a matter of understanding who actually takes which decisions. To start with, it is certain that the occupational constitution of an organisation has an effect on internal decision-making. However, it seems somewhat shallow to allow this factor a direct influence (as does Adam, 1970: p.34), since more often than not it is mediated by the form and degree of personal commitment, trade union doctrine and the autonomy accorded each individual union federation in determining fundamental options, as well as by the importance given to training within the organisation. Some ten years ago, there was a certain contrast between the two main unions in several respects (Erbès-Seguin, 1971 (b)). A higher CGT membership among skilled workers in the 'traditional' industries facilitated the appearance of militants who had a more highly-developed class consciousness—based on Marxist principles—than CFDT militants, who were more often of rural origin or from a non-working class background (white-collar workers and technicians, etc.). Two distinct forms of union democracy resulted (*ibid*). In the case of the CGT, the wide freedom enjoyed by the rank-and-file in determining immediate strike aims at work-place level contrasted with the way in which the union hierarchy fixed general objectives. This clear separation illustrates a form of internal democracy limited to immediate demand activity. In the same period, the CFDT had a form of democracy which was both more fully integrated and more 'technocratic'. Its militants had a broader overall training than those of the CGT, but whatever doctrine they may or may not have fundamentally believed in was much less assured in substance. They tried to produce decisions which succeeded more in integrating all levels of intervention into some sort of general objective, though possibly these objectives, when seen in plant-level terms, were less of a reflection of rank-and-file feeling.

This distinction has certainly not disappeared altogether. Nevertheless, several elements combine to make the internal democracies of the two main central union organisations comparable with one another. First of all, the evolution of the CFDT towards socialism has, among other things, largely done away with the trend towards technocratic decision-making: decisions on action and the content of demands are increasingly made at the lowest level. What is more, the lack of any solid doctrine which can be referred to means that overall objectives are affected more easily by demands originating from the work-place. Finally, the militants are of more diverse origin and, as is the case with the CGT, this increasingly reflects the constitution of the rank-

and-file. On the other hand, the apparently greater autonomy of the CGT from the Communist Party in the area of trade union action facilitates a similar sort of development. However, if this dual movement increases democratic decision-making in both unions, it also makes it increasingly difficult to work out ultimate strategic objectives.

On a tactical level, practice within the CFDT tends to take a more radical turn, and is more splintered than that of the CGT. Seeking as it does to open breaches within the system (a possible heritage of its reformist past), it tends to probe deep; a spearhead plays an active part in the more noteworthy, drawn-out disputes for which greater improvisation is required – a role in which CFDT militants have a better grounding. Its revolutionary attitude is reached through self-management in dispute activity. The CGT, on the other hand, has the weight and tradition behind it that makes it appear more like the leader of the working class. The training received by CGT militants is more concrete, based on strike organisation, on drawing up demands and on negotiating techniques. Its pre-occupation with attaining mass unified action gives it a weakness for demonstrations on a mass scale (the *journées d'action*, for example) and it is wary of plant-level operations which it may not be possible to control. It is less apprehensive about undertaking official bargaining activity than the CFDT, since it considers the risk of its being caught up in the system is not so great, both for historical reasons and because of the emphasis it places on economic demands (Erbès-Seguin, 1971 (a); CREDOC, 1972).

The attitude of both confederations over the question of strike funds apparently goes against this tendency. In fact, only the CFDT has a central fund, which has been compulsory since 1966. Benefit is paid to all members in proportion to subscriptions paid up, with payments being made from the first day of the strike except in the case of 'those general strikes of an inter-industry confederal nature'. By contrast, the CGT makes provision in its budget for only fairly small sums for its 'solidarity fund', though at federation (industry) level, the situation may be different. When a dispute arises, the CGT appeals to the solidarity of members and the public at large, considering that this has the advantage of attracting attention to the particular movement. Thus in the CFDT there is a 'bureaucratic' centralisation of strike payment, while in the CGT each federation has freedom of choice. In actual practice, though, the automatic payment of strike benefit to members means that they have greater freedom in calling for strike action, while a campaign to organise solidarity assumes the support of other federations, or even the confederation organisation itself.

RELATIONS WITH OTHER MOVEMENTS

On the whole, the labour movement in France does not have very close ties with movements within other social groups. Its disinclination to accept whole-heartedly the overtures of the students' movement in May 1968 gave rise in some instances to unfortunate misunderstandings. Following the enthusiasm created by the unified mass demonstration of 13 May, in which workers, students and teaching staff joined forces in a gigantic procession, subsequent student marches on the Renault plants (by which the torch of revolt was to be passed on to the workers) were confronted by closed factory gates, locked shut by the occupying work force. At the Flins plant, the students fought side by side with the workers, yet the workers only participated to a limited extent in the special worker/student action committees, with the CFDT alone half-entering into some sort of dialogue in the advanced technology sectors. However, the infiltration of extreme left-wing ideas into the worker movement has had more success, with a certain number of student militants taking jobs among the working population. Some emphasis should also be placed on the gradual penetration of ideas resulting from May 1968 into the labour movement (such as 'direct action' and *autogestion*).

The labour movement is, on the whole, just as impervious to movements among rural groups or from within the service sectors. Protest movements by vine-growers, small-shopkeepers and long-distance lorry-drivers have not benefited from any real solidarity on the part of the workers. Brittany was the only region in which some form of solidarity was manifested between industrial and rural workers in 1968, which is reaffirmed from time to time in a tough strike situation, and may be reinforced by a growing awareness of regional solidarity (Quere and Dulong, 1974).

The unreceptive attitude of the workers to the activities of ecological groups has meant that only very infrequent examples of co-ordination have occurred, though some forms of urban protest (over transport conditions) have occasionally given rise to common action on the part of the unions, citizens' defence groups and left-wing parties (Verdès-Leroux, 1974). Nevertheless, such co-ordination was highly ephemeral, the different groups having in fact very diverse aims.

The labour movement in France, a movement with a class basis, tends by its very nature not to venture beyond its own bounds.

NOTES

1. *Translator's note.* The current meaning of the 'OS' (*ouvrier spécialisé*) is the semi-skilled production-line worker.
2. This is moreover the reason why retraining is more frequently discussed and introduced by the employers rather than featuring as a trade union demand.
3. Cf. what has been called the Employers' Charter (Charte du Patronat Français), published in 1965 by the CNPF, the employers' confederation. It created a considerable stir both because of what it contained and because it was one of the first times that employer doctrine had been officially set down.
4. At least as far as overall nationwide agreements and social legislation are concerned. During this period there were in fact a few agreements in industry of some importance, in particular at Renault Motors (a state holding) and in chemicals.
5. *Translator's note.* '*le droit syndical*', i.e. not only the right to union membership but also the respect of certain legal measures in favour of trade union activity. Despite this, it is not quite 'union recognition' (bargaining agent) on the Anglo-Saxon model.
6. Among demands dealing with classifications and mode of payment, those linked to job control fell from 46 per cent in 1964 to 32 per cent in 1971 (Durand and Dubois: p. 51).

7. For reference, we may quote studies by Roethlisberger and Dickson or Roy and Lupton, and in France, C. Durand, C. Prestat, A. Willener, *Travail, salaire, production.*
8. *Translator's note*: since the War, basic wages in many industries have been calculated by using a fixed hierarchy of job co-efficients (the Parodi system).
9. 'Objectif CFDT – Remettre en cause la hiérarchie', *Syndicalisme*, 1307 (10 Sept. 1970) pp. 9–24.
10. *Translator's note.* This term has been preferred as being more in line with British practice, since the plant steward is elected as a worker representative on a plant-wide, basis. Cf. the in-plant union representative, who is 'delegated' by his union.
11. *Accords d'intéressement, actionnariat* and *contrats de progrès.*
12. Loi du 11 février 1950 sur les Conventions Collectives.
13. In interpreting bargaining strategies, the conclusions reached by certain surveys are taken into consideration. In our opinion, all of them seem to minimise the importance of the economic context, See: Sellier, 1961; Adam *et al*, 1972; Reynaud *et al*, 1971; Delamotte, 1971.
14. Until November 1964 what is now known as the CFDT was part of the CFTC (Confédération Française des Travailleurs Chrétiens).
15. *Syndicalisme hebdo.*, 4.11.71.
16. In this area, it is difficult to do more than guess at hypotheses. The signs take on such a high degree of subtlety as to make them not very easily accessible to the uninitiated.

LIST OF WORKS CITED

Adam, G. (1970), *L'Ouvrier Français en 1970* (Paris: Colin).

——, Reynaud, J. D. and Verdier, J.M. (1972), *La Négociation Collective en France* (Paris: Les Editions Ouvriers).

Bachy, J. P., Depuy, F. and Martin, D. (under the direction of Adam, G.) (1974), *Représentation et Négociation dans l'Entreprise* (Centre de Recherche des Sciences Sociales du Travail, Université de Paris Sud).

Baumfelder, E. (1968), in *Sociologie du Travail*, No. 2.

Bosc, S. (1973), 'Démocratie et consensus dans la grève', in *Sociologie du Travail* (Oct.–Dec.).

Carré, J. J., Dubois, P. and Malinvaud, E. (1972), *La Croissance Française* (Paris: Servil).

CREDOC (1972), *Syndicats et Patronat Face à la Politique Contractuelle* (Paris: CREDOC).

Declercq, G. (1971), *Syndicalistes en Liberté* (Paris: Servil).

Delamotte, Y. (1971), 'Les tendances récentes de la négociation collective en France', *Revue Internationale du Travail*, 103, 4.

Desseigne, G. (1971), 'Syndicat et hiérachie – faux débats et réalité', *Politique Aujourd'hui* (Feb.).

Dubois, P. (1971), *Recours Ouvrier, Evaluation Technique, Conjoncture Sociale* (Paris: Colin).

—— (1974), *Mort de l'Etat Patron* (Paris: les Editions Ouvriers).

Durand, C. (1971), *Conscience Ouvrière et Action Syndicale* (Paris: Mouton).

——and Dubois, P. (1975), *La Grève* (Paris: Fondation Nationale des Sciences Politiques, Colin).

Durand, M. and Harff, Y. (1973), 'Panorama statistique des grèves', *Sociologie du Travail*, No. 4.

Erbès-Seguin, S. (1971a), 'La fonction syndicale', in *idem* (ed), *Grèves Revendicatives ou Grèves Politiques? Acteurs, Pratiques, Sens du Mouvement de Mai* (Paris: Anthropos, 1971).

—— (1971b), *Démocratie dans les syndicats* (Paris: Mouton).
—— (1973), 'La presse syndicale en 1971, thèmes professionnels et économiques', *Sociologie du Travail*, No. 4.
—— (1975, 'Essai sur une approche sociologique des comportements ouvriers face à la conjoncture économique' (Paris: Groupe de Sociologie du Travail, mimeo).
—— (1976), 'Les deux champs de l'affrontement professionnel', *Sociologie du Travail*.
Guilbert, B. (1975), 'L'enjeu de la crise', *Temps Modernes* (Apr.).
Hostalier, F. (1973), in *Sociologie du Travail*, No. 2.
Jacob-Ory, A. (1972), 'Les syndicats patronaux dans le système économique' (Université de Paris, mimeo).
Kergoat, D. (1973), *Bulledor, ou l'Histoire d'une Mobilisation Ouvrière* (Paris: Servil).
Krasucki, H. (1972), in *La Vie Ouvrière* (organ of the CGT) (1 Mar.).
Krumnov, F. (1973), 'De la volonté de changement à l'action' *Le Monde* (29 Mar.).
Mallet, S. (1970), 'L'après-guerre 1968: grèves pour le controle ouvrier', *Sociologie du Travail*, No. 3.
Oppenheim, J.-P. (1973), *La CFDT et la Planification* (Paris: Paristema Action).
Perrot, M. (1974), *Les Ouvriers en Grève* (Paris: Mouton).
Quere, L. and Dulong, R. (1974), 'Mouvements Sociaux en Bretagne', *Sociologie du Travail* No. 3.
Reynaud, J.-D., Dassa, S., Dassa, J. and Macloug, P. (1974), 'Les évènements de mai-juin'68 et le système français des relations professionnelles', *Sociologie du Travail*, Nos. 1 and 2.
Scardigli, V. (1974), 'Les grèves dans l'économie française', (Paris: CREDOC).
Schiffres, M. (1972), *La CFDT des Militants* (Paris: Stock).
Sellier, F. (1961), *Stratégie de la Lutte Sociale* (Paris: Editions Ouvrières).
Simiand, F. (1907), *Le Salaire des Ouvriers des Mines de Charbon* (Paris: Cornely).
Tilly, C. and Shorter, E. (1973), 'Les vagues de grèves en France, 1890–1968', *Annales* (July-Aug.).
Vachet, A. (1970), *L'Idéologie Libérale* (Paris: Anthropos).
Verdès-Leroux, J. (1974), 'Les conditions de transport: objet de mobilisation', *Sociologie du Travail*, No. 3.

4 *Labour Conflicts and Industrial Relations in Italy**

IDA REGALIA, MARINO REGINI
and EMILIO REYNERI

1 THE ECONOMIC CONTEXT OF INDUSTRIAL CONFLICT

There exists a wide-ranging literature on the peculiarities and distortions of post-war Italian economic development, and the reader is referred to this for a detailed account of the process. In the present context it will suffice to describe those aspects of the Italian economic system which help explain the course of industrial conflict and the nature of trade union policy. We shall, therefore, limit ourselves to only a few points. Some basic statistical data will be found in Appendix I.

The years of post-war reconstruction, which determined the type of economic and labour market development which Italy was to experience, ended with the deflationary measures of the second half of 1947. Inflation, the central problem throughout the period of reconstruction, provoked sharp differences of view over economic policy, but the expulsion of the left-wing parties from government enabled the explicitly 'liberal' approach to prevail, and the problem was tackled resolutely through the control of credit and public expenditure.

Capitalist accumulation in the 1950s occurred against a background of tight money and controlled expenditure. Both measures were justified by the fear of inflation and the conviction that the problem of unemployment in Italy could not be resolved through Keynesian management, but rather through the accumulation of private capital. These convictions meant,

* The three authors have for a long time worked together on research into the theme of this essay, and have therefore had an opportunity of discussing the interpretations presented here. However, each has written separate sections and does not necessarily agree with all the theses set forth by the others. In particular, I. Regalia has written Section 6; M. Regini, Sections 2 and 5; E. Reyneri, Sections 3 and 4. Section 1 is the result of discussions between M. Regini, Michele Salvati (Università di Roma) and Alessandro Pizzorno, who has also supervised the whole work, and to whose suggestions the three authors are deeply indebted. Bianca Beccalli has made valuable criticisms of an earlier version of the text.

however, that the impulse given to capital accumulation through public expenditure remained relatively modest, and that a tight monetary and credit policy, together with the weakness of the unions, led large-scale manufacturing industries to strive hard for increased productivity, and to rid themselves of the pockets of inefficiency which had accumulated during the reconstruction period. As a result, the rise in permanent employment in manufacturing remained relatively modest until 1958–9, and recorded unemployment remained very high.[1] Such a situation weakened union action, and this weakness was accentuated by police repression. Management was able to dismiss any worker it wanted to, and demands and demonstrations of dissent were dealt with by government action. This still applied when, after the 1953 elections, the left-wing parties began to regain support. (Indeed, in many enterprises repression increased after 1954, partly because of American threats to withdraw orders from firms which still had Communist majorities on the *commissioni interne*.[2])

The post-Korean economic cycle ran from the trough of 1952 to that of 1958. As has been said, during this cycle unemployment persisted, and hence labour disputes and union action generally appear to have been little influenced by the level of economic activity. Hence, also, the rate of wage increases did not keep pace with the rate of increase in productivity. But in the subsequent cycle, that of 1958–64, there was a re-awakening of union activity. Both the level of industrial conflict and the rate of wage increases[3] rose much more rapidly, and were directly related to changes in the level of production – and, as far as industry was concerned, to changes in the level of employment as well. The same relationship between changes in production, employment, industrial conflict and wage increases appears in the next cycle, which ran from 1964 to 1971. The peak years for the four variables in the industrial sector were: in the first cycle, 1960 (industrial output), 1961 (industrial employment), 1962 (labour disputes) and 1963 (wage increases); for the second cycle, respectively, 1968, 1967, 1969 and 1970.

It can therefore be claimed that, from the 1958–64 cycle, the Italian unions escaped from their subordination to the political situation (which had resulted from both structural unemployment and the Cold War and its consequent political isolation of the PCI) and their position came to depend increasingly on purely economic variables, as in other advanced industrial societies.

There remained, however, certain features which distinguished the Italian situation from that elsewhere. A significant indication is provided by the timing of the two peaks of wage increases—1963 and 1970—which, according to Fuà (1973: 1197), did not correspond to those in any other country with the possible exception of West Germany after 1968. Another important phenomenon which began to manifest itself in the 1960s was the simultaneous decrease in both total employment and unemployment. The activity rate of the population as a whole dropped from 43.8 per cent to 37.4 per cent in the decade 1959–68. This indicated that there had been considerable concealed unemployment (or underemployment) in Italian agriculture in the 1950s, which came to light with migration and urbanisation, and which the increases in employment in the industrial and tertiary sectors were insufficient to absorb. In other words, the process of migration, which continued at very high rates between 1955 and 1970, involved a considerable loss of overall employment.

These various phenomena lead us to accept as highly plausible the hypothesis, put forward both in Italy and elsewhere, of a segmentation of the labour market into differentiated sub-markets, the passages between which are restricted by both economic and institutional factors. In some of these sub-markets, labour shortages may occur, leading to wages pressure and rapid pay increases, while at the same time the level of labour utilisation may remain low in other sub-markets. For structural reasons, the Italian working class finds itself in a position of relative strength in the modern sector of the economy, while in the more backward sectors there exist large segments of underemployment and part-time work, which make union activity difficult. During the 1970s the decentralisation of certain operations, or entire productive processes, to small or very small enterprises and to out-workers has reached significant proportions, even in the modern manufacturing sectors.[4]

These phenomena have been interpreted as the response of Italian capitalism to the growth of union power, which emerged in the 1960s and was consolidated in 1969, bringing with it an increase in labour costs and greater rigidity in the use of labour. In fact, the decentralisation of production made it possible to avoid bottlenecks resulting from labour shortages, and created a market of 'marginal' labour in which the supply of labour was much greater—and the workers in which were therefore in a position of structural weakness. In this way there is an increasingly accentuated dualism in the Italian productive system, and although it is difficult to identify it with precision, it certainly has the effect of increasing the area in which union action is difficult, if not impossible. The decentralisation of production and the resort to outwork, inserted into a productive structure already characterised by a myriad of small enterprises co-existing alongside a few large-scale ones, helps explain the policy of the Italian unions. They have been less willing than unions in other advanced capitalist countries to pursue a bargaining strategy which benefits only those workers in positions of strength: that is, those employed in the modern sector of the economy. This tendency has been accentuated since 1971 by the intensification of the economic crisis. As we shall see in Section 5, the prolonged recession (interrupted by only a very brief recovery) raises problems about the protection of employment,[5] especially for the weaker sections of the labour force. At the same time, the very high rates of inflation are forcing workers in stronger bargaining positions to advance demands to make up for the decline in the purchasing power of wages. The reaction of the unions to this change in the economic situation has been to place the protection of employment at the forefront of their strategy, and to try to defend the purchasing power of wages with such devices as the *contingenza* (see p.155, note 12), which benefit the entire labour force and not merely its strongest elements.

2 QUANTITATIVE TRENDS AND DIFFUSION OF CONFLICTUAL ACTION[6]

The period 1968–75 was characterised by a strong resurgence of conflict and by a renewal of trade union action. At first, these phenomena were concentrated in some very advanced sectors of the working class and of the unions, where they acquired radical aspects and made for a crisis in the existing system of industrial relations. Later on, they partially spread to other sectors, geographical areas, etc. Furthermore, the contents and forms of industrial action thoroughly changed at the same time, giving rise to a new system of industrial relations.

In this section we shall only outline the quantitative trends of labour conflicts and bargaining activity, and briefly describe their diffusion into the different areas of the national economic structure and different sectors of the labour force. This first analysis will be done mainly on the basis of statistical data. The most relevant characteristics of the conflicts, and the changes in union structure and in the system of industrial relations will be dealt with in the following sections.

From the quantitative point of view, labour conflicts underwent an unprecedented growth in this period. According to the three indicators provided by the national statistical sources (see Figure 4.1), they touched areas seldom or never reached in previous times. Conflictual action in the period 1968–75 was, as a whole, far more intensive than in the two periods into which we can conventionally divide union activity after the years of Reconstruction (i.e. 1950–8, 1959–67). Industry was the main arena of this intensification of conflict; but conflictual action also increased sharply in the service sector. On the other hand, the agricultural sector, which traditionally had a high level of conflict, shows quite a modest growth in recent years.

The traditional pattern of strike activity in Italy, whereby most of the time spent on strike results from the renewal of national contracts in the main industries,[7] has not basically changed even in this period. Such was the case during the fifties, when the general level of conflict was very low; and it remained so throughout the sixties, when it was much higher, even though the hours of work lost through plant-level conflict increased sharply. However, after 1968 plant conflicts became more and more important, and their impact on both public opinion and, in particular, on trade union policy was much greater than their quantitative weight. Conflict and bargaining at plant level first became important in those factories and industries in which trade unions were more militant, and then spread to other sectors of the economy. In manufacturing industry, where this phenomenon was particularly widespread, the numbers of plant conflicts in this period (except in 1973) were higher than in any of the previous years.

As we have seen, the big factories of the manufacturing industries, and in particular those in the metal-working sector, remain the most important areas

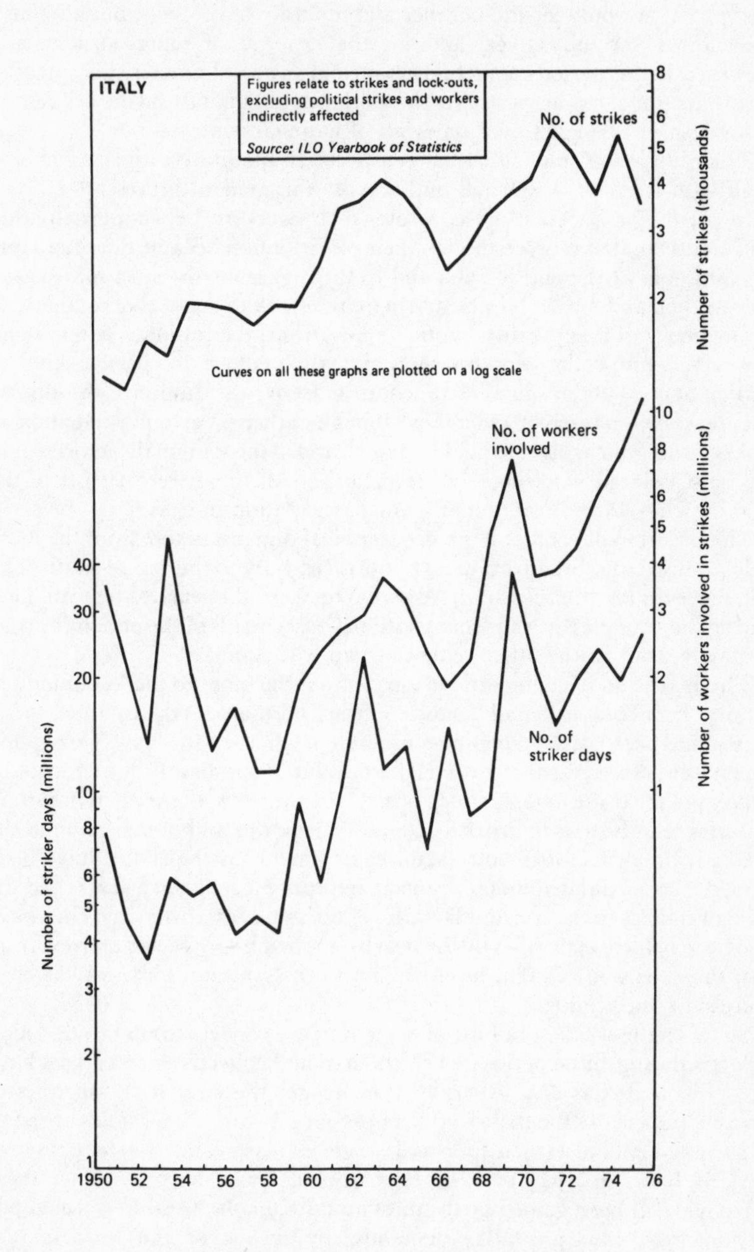

FIGURE 4.1: Industrial conflict in Italy, 1950–75 (log scales)

of trade union activity in this period as we shall see in the following sections, this is true, not only for the number and intensity of conflicts, but also for their forms and objectives, and for the renewal of union structures. However, in this period conflictual action and its new characteristics spread for the first time to other sectors of the working class, mainly on the occasion of some sharp struggles over renewals of national contracts.

This diffusion of conflict has many aspects. Its qualitative aspects will be dealt with later; here we shall outline only this general process.

In 1968, for the first time, white-collar workers began participating consistently in strikes, even though their participation became quantitatively relevant only at the end of 1969 and in the bigger factories. In some cases, during 1968 and 1969, this new participation took on aspects of sudden and unforeseen militancy, often autonomous from the unions. After 1970, however, white-collar workers showed a different, more passive kind of participation, under increased control from the unions. A similar phenomenon – namely an increased though rather passive participation in strikes – was typical also of female workers, and of those in small factories or in the most isolated workshops of big factories. All these were sectors of the working class with a traditionally low participation in strikes.

The diffusion of conflict has a geographical dimension too: from the more industrialised and urbanised areas of northern Italy to the centre-south. The differences in the intensity of strike action between these areas were still high during the struggles over the main national agreements of the period (in 1969 and 1973); but in the other years this gap was closing.

This extension of conflict in industry – from the more to the less unionised sectors, from big to small factories, from northern Italy to the centre-south – has been partly a spontaneous result of imitating the first big struggles, which were successful and very well known. But it has mainly been due to the strategy of the trade unions, which tried to use the strength they had in certain factories or industries in order to extend their power and organisation to the weakest. Small factories, and factories in general in the south, have been helped by co-ordinated union action at enterprise level, which also raised the level of conflict in the weakest factories of the same enterprise; and they have also been helped sometimes by the nearby, more militant factories. Nevertheless, the extension of plant-level conflict to the southern factories has been quite slow and limited.

So far as the weakest industrial categories are concerned, the trade union strategy during those periods when the national collective agreements have been renewed has also generally been to get the strongest categories of workers (especially the metal-workers) to put forward the most advanced or important demands (such as equal wage increases and the reduction of working hours in 1969, and the *Inquadramento Unico* in 1972). Once these objectives had been gained by the most militant unions, the others would put forward and obtain similar demands, by means of the 'principle of comparison'.

More complex is the relationship between conflict in industry, and conflict in agriculture and in the tertiary sector. Detailed statistics show that agriculture is the only sector in which, even after 1968, the volume of labour conflicts remained at the same level as – or lower than – in the early sixties. However, a more modern kind of conflictual action has been spreading in recent years, namely strikes more directly aimed at damaging production in the big agrarian enterprises—although in some situations, particularly in the south, traditional symbolic actions, such as interrupting traffic on important roads and occupying town halls, are becoming important again. In these cases we can see agricultural labourers and small peasants united together as they used to be in the past. But, on the whole, the trend is towards a homogenisation with industrial action, as is made clear by analysis of the demands put forward for the renewal of the national contract of the agricultural labourers in 1971.

The diffusion of conflict in the tertiary sector has taken place mainly in imitation of what has happened in industry. This process has not been led by the trade unions to the same degree as in those industries in which unions are weaker, in small enterprises, and in southern factories; but more often it has been a spontaneous attempt by the workers to keep up with what has been obtained in industry, often against the will of the central trade unions. This is especially true for the public service employees, whose higher propensity to strike accounts for most of the increased conflict recently shown in the whole of the tertiary sector. In most of the service sector, those demands which have actually been put forward have been traditional wage demands, accompanied by tough strike action. On the other hand, in the civil service and in other sectors which were state owned, the national trade unions, and sometimes left-wing groups outside the unions, have tried to put forward more general and political demands (such as the reform of the transport system, schools, hospital organisation and so on). But these more sophisticated demands, requiring long-term and difficult bargaining with the government, have often been set aside by the more direct action of employees for wage increases, resulting in some conflict between the trade unions and the rank-and-file, who are charged with being 'egoistic' and 'particularistic' (*corporativo*).

The development of union action in the private service sector has been somewhat different. Here again, in a very few situations there has been an explosion of militancy which has not been controlled by the unions, imitating the most advanced demands and forms of action of the industrial workers. This has mainly occurred in a few large department stores in the main cities. It has been followed by an increase in and diffusion of conflictual action under trade union control, not only in the large retail sector, but also in sectors characterised by small productive units and by precarious employment in which the unions have traditionally been weak (one recalls the mobilisation of hotel workers in 1971, which surprised the unions themselves). In the private service sector at least—unlike developments among public employees—important conflicts between rank-and-file action and union policy did not take place.

3 DYNAMICS AND PROTAGONISTS OF MOBILISATION[8]

The most intense, widespread and innovative period of conflict in post-war Italy began gradually. In 1968 the initial outbreak of workers' militancy was unexpected and quite unforeseen by the unions; but it was still far from being widely diffused, and both the forms of action and the demands were mainly traditional. To contrast the Italian situation with that in France, the term 'creeping May' (*mai rampant*) was therefore coined.

In the spring of 1968 conflict reached a high level in only about ten big factories of the northern regions, in very different geographical areas and industries, with varied occupational structures. However, they had some features in common: low union membership, low conflictual action in recent years and, as a result, strongly compressed demands. No militant union existed either in the metal-working firms which had grown up in the early sixties in non-industrialised areas with a deferential Catholic ideology, or in the old strongholds of textile paternalism based on communitarian links. In other factories, after the strong union tradition that went back to the days of the Resistance had been violently broken, the Socialist-Communist confederation CGIL had partially reconstructed itself in the early sixties, but had been able to resist the subsequent ebbing of strike activity and the new wave of repression. The intensity and the harshness of the conflict thus appear in an inverse relationship to the existence of a union organisation able both to satisfy the workers' demands and control their behaviour.

Another feature which characterised all these conflicts and reappeared afterwards in other cases when mobilisation began was the comparison mechanism. In some factories conflict broke out in order to obtain equal pay between old and new employees or with other factories of the same company; in others to restore the dynamics of differentials frozen for years; in yet others to defend the traditional privileges of some groups of workers. Lastly, both the old and the new paternalism were plunged into a crisis from which they could not recover when their workers came to compare their own conditions, which had been guaranteed to be the best possible by their 'good employers', with those of other workers in the same area or industry.

But the internal dynamics of conflict were different. All the conflicts occurring in factories without a record of industrial action began within the framework of a dispute initiated by the union; the workers' participation was mostly passive at first, needing external stimulus from the union or from students, and only exploded later. Conflict began violently and sometimes spontaneously in factories where there already existed groups of workers experienced in collective action, identified on an occupational or political basis.

The protagonists of the first phase of mobilisation were by no means all young semi-skilled workers. The few isolated militant strikes in 1967 and several conflicts in the spring of 1968 were led by workers employed on process production, older craftsmen or textile workers. Furthermore, two of the most important conflicts involving semi-skilled workers were not started by them:

the printing workers set off the 'avalanche' of wildcat shop strikes in the summer of 1968 at Pirelli, and in the spring of 1969 at Fiat the first shops to stop spontaneously were those composed largely of skilled workers from northern regions. However, these older skilled workers had taken action to maintain their own relative privileges, and their active role soon ended. After 1970 they not only participated passively in the strikes, but even hindered other workers in their conflicts and supported strikes out of self-interest only.

On the contrary, the young, mostly immigrant, semi-skilled workers, who had been almost excluded from the industrial relations system until 1968, did not begin to establish themselves as autonomous protagonists in important conflicts until the autumn of 1968 and the spring of 1969, finally dominating the scene in the 'hot autumn' of 1969. It was therefore necessary that conflictual action should have become established as well as achieve some important victories—and that in the political elections of May 1968 the left-wing parties should have succeeded in raising the expectations of the working class—for it to be possible to break the heavy subjection of semi-skilled workers to the factory system. But the stronger and the more lasting the bonds of those workers not accustomed to unions and to industrial work, the more violent and innovating their liberation.

This process often came about in two phases. In some factories, the first conflict in 1968 only cracked the deference, while a second one in 1969 broke it once and for all, employing new forms of mobilisation. The liberation of the young semi-skilled workers was much more rapid in the factories, which only began to struggle in 1969, when the contagious influence of other conflicts was already being felt. The firms involved were mostly either marginal in size or geographical position or, on the contrary, ones with good union control before 1968 but with a system which functioned largely for the older skilled workers and much less so for the others.

After 1969 conflictual action spread to sectors of the labour force which were not traditionally 'strike prone', particularly outside the industrial working class, as described in section 2. New protagonists emerged: white-collar workers, public service employees and civil servants. The office workers' behaviour was ambiguous from the beginning; from the winter of 1968 to the spring of 1969, they alone went on strike (for the first time in Italy) in the major northern factories. The conflicts always began after a plant agreement had been made for blue-collar workers only which excluded them from any benefits, and they were led by medium-status office workers, often graduates, who were harder hit by the rationalisation of work than those already performing unskilled jobs. Their demands confirmed that white-collar workers went on strike in order to recover salary and status privileges. On the other hand, the proposals of the students' movement for grass-root democracy had a profound influence on the young graduates. The great importance of meetings, referenda and autonomous groups in leading conflict indicates widespread hostility towards the unions, which were judged to be either bureaucratic or too political, but in any event 'external' organisations. The militancy of these 'technicians' soon disappeared: in some factories they even went on strike in protest against the manual workers' conflict at the end of 1970. By contrast, the lower-status office workers, who had broken their traditional deference towards the management more recently, continued to take an active part in union disputes.

In non-industrial sectors conflictual action spread in different ways, according to union traditions, the composition of the labour force and, above all, the degree of job security. In commerce and other services there was a well-established paternalism and low union membership because of the precarious nature of jobs and the fragmentation into numerous small units. Once again, it was something completely new when these workers, mainly women, went on strike in the big shops and in the big chains of hotels and restaurants. From 1969 to 1971 there was intense, widespread militancy which invariably declined when the economic crisis and job insecurity became worse. The same happened to the weak components of the industrial labour force, the workers in small firms. When industrial conflict was at its most widespread, the unions in some areas had even been able to organise and bring out on strike women out-workers, but their resistance was soon overcome as work orders were transferred to other areas.

In the public services the unions were already relatively strong even before 1969, and in some cases the traditions of conflict were very old. The return to militancy after the wave of workers' conflicts was therefore normal, even if it reached very intense levels. Furthermore, where the unions were strongest and attempted to control mobilisation, some ex-union leaders associated with left-wing groups formed autonomous rank-and-file committees which could call strikes for wage demands.

From 1969 to 1973 there was also virtually uninterrupted conflict in public administration: the postal service, schools, local and central government, customs, firemen, etc. A common attempt was made to achieve salary increases which would re-establish differentials over industrial workers or other sectors. Conflicts in the various sectors of public administration followed each other in continuous succession. Claims of this kind were familiar in the public service, but the usual patronage-type unions were unable to deal with this contemporary explosion of demands. Paradoxically, the CGIL, which had always opposed sectoral thrusts from a minority position, greatly increased its membership. This can be explained by the fact that the civil servants accused the major unions in the sector of not succeeding, as they had in the past, in satisfying their demands as the workers' unions had those of the industrial workers. They saw the CGIL as the workers' union *par excellence*, and the most effective means of satisfying their demands as well. The flow of young graduates with left-wing views was also important, particularly in the schools.

But traditional sectoralism never disappeared in public administration or the public services. Frequent and uncontrolled strikes for big salary increases blocked essential services for long periods in 1975; the patronage-type unions reappeared and there were serious tensions between national confederations and public administration unions, which were more in favour of taking up spontaneous rank-and-file demands. In particular, some groups of public servants tried to recover economic privileges partly lost as a result of the egalitarian wage policies of the confederal unions. For the first time, the strikes in public administration preceded rather than followed the actions which had been planned for the end of the year by workers in major industries; in fact they replaced the usual disputes in big factories, which were now being hit by frequent, massive suspensions of work and the fear of redundancy. This is obviously explained by a far greater job security, as well as by the fact that in public administration the mechanism for automatically adjusting wages to the increase in the cost of living was less efficient than in industry.

The mobilisation of workers in the mass media and scientific research was greatly influenced by the student movement, and followed directly from it. More traditional demands about wages and working conditions followed discussions about the possibility of lessening the gap between manual and intellectual work.

Lastly, while rural small-holders, whose political behaviour has always been moderate, began to demonstrate alongside workers from the big chemical plants in order to get the price of fertilisers reduced and to scoff at the leaders of their compliant organisation, other self-employed workers and those in a position of authority – judges, lawyers, doctors, etc.—moved openly against the working class.

All these centrifugal thrusts originating from the non-industrial sectors pose serious problems for the CGIL, which aims at a unitary strategy because of the electoral demands of the left-wing parties to which it is attached. This does not affect the Catholic CISL, which aims to defend the particular interests of its own members and takes little interest in the compatibility and consistency of the various demands.

4 THE NEW FORMS OF ACTION[9]

THE NEW FORMS OF ACTION INSIDE THE FACTORIES

In the wave of conflicts which began in 1968, the plant level assumed a much more important role than in the past. This is not only because the workers' mobilisation began at this level and because for the first time the plant disputes were so widespread; but also because the factory, the shop, even the individual place of work, became the physical location in which the workers carried out their struggle, using very radical tactics.

'Internal conflicts' ('spot strikes', 'rolling strikes', lightning strikes, go-slows, etc.) were certainly no novelty in the history of Italian trade unionism, but their precedents went back principally to the early fifties when the employers' repression succeeded in crushing union organisation and in preventing strike action at the plant level. For a long time, therefore, workers' conflicts were forced to assume the more traditional form of abstention from work outside the factory gates, even though, in the early sixties, some more strongly unionised firms experienced 'articulated' strikes (stoppages of one or two hours, or, very rarely, of half-an-hour) which did not require the worker to leave his post.

The 'absolute' novelties introduced in 1968 were the enormous diffusion of conflict, its partial juridical recognition, some specific tactics (particularly the go-slow) and, last but not least, the connection with demands about working conditions. Moreover, the social, occupational and union characteristics of the workers who carry out these strikes nowadays are very different from those of the strikers of 15–20 years ago. However, strike tactics did not change immediately at the start of the mobilisation in 1968. In both the spring and autumn of 1968, conflicts nearly always followed the usual tactics (strikes of one day or of some hours either at the beginning or end of shifts), though with a high level of participation and violence. In fact, when it was still feared that the strike might fail, and there were few union militants at the shop level, it was preferable to avoid the further problem of coming up against the plant hierarchy—which work-place stoppages necessitate—and instead to exploit the active intervention of the few militants and union officials through such pressures as picketing. In the first half of 1968, the success of the strikes was often due to mass picketing, in which considerable groups of students frequently participated.

Picketing was still very important in 1969 and later in those cases in which the workers had been in a weak position for some time; but it gradually disappeared as conflicts successfully took root in the factories. It was then replaced by strikers' marches through shops and offices to pursue blacklegs and sometimes to seize managers.

The Radical Tactics of Action

The tactics of internal conflict are considered 'radical' because they upset the balance between the cost of the strike to the firm and to the workers which practice had established and almost made legitimate. Due to the weakness of both the workers and the union, this balance had settled at a perfect 'equity' between lost production and lost wages. The new forms of action aim instead at increasing the damage to the firm without increasing that to the workers by disorganising the productive cycle, preventing production from beginning immediately after the end of the strikes, and reducing production though continuing to work and, therefore, earning a wage which is less than proportionately reduced.

Since 1969 the 'articulation' of strikes has reached an unprecedented intensity. Strikes are not only articulated over time ('spot strikes'), but across space as well. In 'rolling strikes' brief stoppages follow periods of work in sequences which differ from shop to shop, from line to line, even from worker to worker, in such a way that at the same time some people are working while others are striking all over the factory. The result obviously upsets the production flow; the more integrated and rigid this is, the greater the impact. In the chemical and steel factories this form of action has sometimes seriously damaged plants or prevented them from functioning for many days after the end of a strike.

The timetable of stoppages for each shop or work-group is generally made known at the beginning of the week or of the daily work shift. The shorter the notice, the greater the damage to the firm, so in many factories, and above all in the metal-working industry, 'rolling strikes' were carried out unexpectedly; in each shop or work-group the stoppages and returns to work were announced by the 'shop delegates' (*delegati*) according to a timetable known only to them. This form of action may not respect the unity of the shop or work-group: for example, stoppages by the labourers who carry the pieces may alternate with those of the production workers. It is even possible to make stoppages individual, in such a way that in each group every worker strikes according to a different timetable. To this aim the 'registration strike' and the 'confetti strike' have been invented, in which the timetable of stoppages varies according to the last figure of the registration number or the colour of the card taken out by each worker at the beginning of the shift.

'Spot' and 'rolling' strikes are by no means 'wildcat' strikes even though they are often proposed by radical or opposition rank-and-file union leaders. In order that these forms of action should seriously damage the firm on one hand, while reducing workers' earnings very little on the other, it is necessary for there to be both widespread approval and a capillary network which can rapidly transmit the orders of the plant union leaders. Spontaneous action might prolong the stoppages and therefore upset the mechanism of the 'rolling strike', but it cannot intensify it. These 'articulated' strikes, which have taken place with varying intensity since the autumn of 1969 in all plant and national disputes, are very different phenomena from the spontaneous shop strikes, which were frequent in 1968–9 and 1970. The former are conflict tactics which involve all the workers in a factory in a particular dispute, while in the latter the conflict is spread by contagion and no unifying logic exists. Only the damaging effects on the production process are the same.

In fact, between the autumn of 1968 and the spring of 1969 the unions decided to carry out this radical form of shop-by-shop strike in order to combat the spread of spontaneous shop strikes. To gain control over the autonomous mobilisation of young, semi-skilled immigrant workers, the unions accepted the new forms of action, but used them in a more general conflict such as the disputes over national agreements, which of course only their organisations could manage in an efficient way. The second wave of wildcat shop strikes in 1970 was, on the contrary, the result of a complete breakdown of the 'new workers' ' sense of deference, brought about through forms of internal conflict frequently used during national disputes of the 'hot autumn' of 1969.

Much of what has been said about 'articulated' strikes also applies to the go-slow. However, the existence of a wide consensus among workers and capillary organisation on the part of the union are necessary to ensure that a go-slow lasts a long time in the whole factory, since to achieve this it is necessary that working times are reduced equally everywhere, and that the salaried workers strike in such a way as to lose the same amount of money as the piece-workers. But the beginning may be much less organised. In fact, in the factories where this form of action started for the first time in 1968, the go-slow began in some shops under the influence of a few rank-and-file leaders, afterwards spreading more or less rapidly through the whole factory. This form of action has been frequently used for shop disputes too.

To 'go slow' on the assembly lines, the workers must every now and then let a piece pass without doing what is necessary to it. From 1970 to 1972, outstanding examples of this type of strike occurred in several big car, electrical appliances and tyre firms. These sometimes approached sabotage, when the 'missed out' job was hard to detect at the checkpoint or when, on the same assembly line, each worker let different pieces pass, so that at the end not one completely assembled piece came out. However no explicit cases of organised sabotage were ever recorded. The work-to-rule is very similar to the go-slow, but traditionally it has always been the skilled workers who have carried this out.

Particularly during the phase in which workers' mobilisation was growing, the go-slow was often something more than a radical form of action. When demands concern a reduction of work-rates or of incentives, to 'go slow' means attaining the aim of the strike during the conflict itself, without waiting for an agreement. This is confirmed by the fact that both in 1968–9 (when this form of strike was carried out for the first time) and in several metal-working plants in 1970–1, many shops spontaneously continued to go slow after an agreement had been concluded, thus showing that they did not want to give up the victory which had been gained during the conflict (see page 118).

The Controlled Escalation of the Conflict and Forms of Strike 'to the Finish'

Traditionally the unions, when they needed to intensify their action, increased the hours of strike. The intensification of the forms of 'internal conflict' achieve the same result without increasing the loss of wages and reducing workers' capacity to resist long disputes. From the autumn of 1968 to 1970, the unions often had to regain control of spontaneous workers' mobilisation and therefore made use of these new forms of action to intensify the conflicts to a considerable extent. Serious disagreements spread, especially among the rank-and- file leaders, when the unions, which no longer needed to 'ride the tiger', began to moderate the escalation of conflicts in 1971–2.

Since the 'hot autumn' of 1969, when strong and immediate pressure on firms was needed, workers have begun to block factory entrances by uninterrupted mass picketing, made possible by an equally uninterrupted shop-by-shop strike. Until 1973, this occurred for several days and even for some weeks in many big firms during the final phases of national and plant disputes. In chemical factories the calling of a general strike was threatened—but very rarely carried out—in which even those few workers who were necessary to maintain the efficiency of the plant would not be allowed to work.

Even occupation of the plant has been used to give the 'final blow': for example, when the metal-working national agreement was signed in 1973, the biggest Italian factory, the Fiat Mirafiori, was spontaneously occupied. However, plant occupation continues to be much more widespread as a reaction to disciplinary measures or lock-outs. During economic crises (1966–7, 1971–2, 1974–5) small or medium-sized factories were nearly always occupied when the owners decided to close them down or to dismiss workers. In two or three cases the workers decided to carry on production alone until the firm was bought by a semi-state company. Sometimes the final phase of conflict escapes the union strategy of controlled escalation, and tendencies to continue the strike 'to the finish' appear, but such cases are fairly rare. In recent years the strike 'to the finish' has also been carried out by some small shops composed mostly of old, little unionised workers, who have strong autonomous bargaining power.

Violence often occurs in the final stages of a conflict, but both its protagonists and its physical location have changed. Struggles between police and workers in public squares in the early sixties, and outside factory gates in 1968–9, have been replaced by confrontations with black-legs, foremen, clerks and managers on internal marches.

Conditions, Diffusion and Consequences of the New Forms of Action Inside the Plants

From the autumn of 1968 to the spring of 1969 three important plant conflicts occurred which were destined to provide examples, since their particular features immediately spread. An analysis of these strikes suggests two conditions for the renewal of various forms of strike action: the mobilisation of the young, semi-skilled, mostly migrant southern workers, and the presence of dissident union leaders.

When mobilisation began, it was through these rank-and-file leaders that the semi-skilled workers heard about new proposals for conflict which had been drawn up by left-wing union and non-union groups, and made use of the recent experience of the student movement. As a result, while some believe these new features of conflict to be the spontaneous result of the mobilisation of young, semi-skilled workers, others consider it to be an intellectual construction which is only accepted by the 'new workers' because they are unaccustomed both to industrial work and union activity. But in the early conflicts both interpretations were relevant; and it can be said that only some of the 'novelties' were discussed in restricted circles of the unions or left-wing groups, and that if they were supported by the non-skilled workers this meant that they satisfied their demands and needs for action.

It can also be asked whether this renewal is simply the result of the introduction into the industrial relations system of a section of the working class which still lacked an identity and representation, or whether it corresponds to the specific structural conditions of non-skilled workers. In the first case, the internal conflict and the strikes which 'put the aims into practice' would answer to the most important need of a new collective entity, that of defining its own autonomous identity, by searching for forms of physical aggregation if necessary. In the second case, the new forms of action would depend on the fact that semi-skilled workers work in very rigid production flows. But both hypotheses seem inadequate if the evolution of the cycle of conflict is considered. In fact, the new forms of action have not disappeared, but have become much more moderate and institutionalised. This means that the non-skilled workers have, once and for all, achieved a new form of conflictual behaviour, but that this behaviour initially manifested itself in a very different form to that in which it finally established itself once the new protagonists had become fully socialised in the union. From the autumn of 1969, radical forms of action also spread to factories and shops with an old and highly qualified labour force. However, in these situations a renewal of action has not always taken place; this has invariably been the case where there was a predominance of non-skilled workers.

The plants themselves have proved to be the most effective variable in explaining the varying degrees to which these forms of conflict have been diffused, the frequency of 'spot', 'sudden' or 'rolling' strikes and go-slows increasing with the size of the plant. Furthermore, these actions are more frequent in industries, such as cars, steel and rubber, whose labour force is mostly comprised of young, non-skilled workers. Lastly, as far as the consequences of strike action are concerned, 'internal action' allows an almost uninterrupted mobilisation of workers, avoiding the risks both of long truces and of the conflict 'to the finish'. Moreover, it requires the active participation of every worker; at first it provokes frequent liberating outbreaks, and afterwards makes a definitive change in the social relations of the factory. Above all, the new forms of action lead to a decentralisation of conflict, since they give more responsibility to the 'shop delegates' (see page 143).

Employers' Reaction and Unions' Response

In the phase when conflict was developing, firms were obliged to submit to the initiative of the workers and unions. However, when the economic recession of 1971–2 brought the first signs of a new decline in workers' militancy, those forms of action which were most costly to the firm, particularly spot strikes, rolling strikes and go-slows, were immediately subjected to harsh attack.

Sometimes these actions were taken to the courts as sabotage, but essentially management took steps to recover the old balance between the damage to the firm and that to the striking workers. Firms refused pay during the brief intervals between two stoppages, and during go-slows proportionally reduced the fixed wages guaranteed by the national agreements. When shop or work-group stoppages occurred in firms with a rigid production flow, workers in shops 'above' and 'below' those on strike were prevented from working and suspended. The aim was to provoke full strikes all over the factory rapidly to weaken workers' resistance without greatly increasing the damage to the firm; and to isolate the most militant shops by attempting to hold them responsible for the suspensions.

The Italian courts, especially the lower ones and those in the big northern cities, often pronounced verdicts which were favourable to the workers, and the 'Workers' Charter' (*Statuto dei Lavoratori*: see page 152) has sometimes even been interpreted in a way which the unions had not dared to hope for.

However, union strategy became more prudent after 1971–2. The unions feared that management repression would lead to discouragement or rebellious outbursts, and at any rate a reduction of union control. Besides, having once reached a favourable equilibrium in the industrial relations system, the unions aimed to make the new rules of the game definitive. Some plant or local unions and the left-wing union factions opposed this decision, but with little success. The 'responsible' behaviour of the unions was designed to ensure that the forms of conflict did not go beyond the level of intensity accepted by the management. This strengthened their power further, since only a union organisation can control a rolling strike or a go-slow in its fine details, while workers who overstep union instructions provoke reprisals which affect the whole factory.

THE NEW FUNCTIONS OF THE FORMS OF ACTION OUTSIDE THE FACTORIES

When strikes failed during the fifties and mid-sixties, the unions substituted other forms of action: tents and sit-ins in public squares, urban demonstrations etc. They had a double purpose: to give the impression that the conflict was still continuing, and to exert pressure on the political system so that it should intervene in favour of the weaker side, that of the workers.

After 1968 the centre of industrial conflict moved inside the factories; however, the various forms of external action did not disappear, but were added to the internal ones, assuming different functions in the course of 1968–75. At the beginning there were frequent and sometimes spontaneous demonstrations and marches, the student movement having a large, even direct, influence. The fundamental function was to strengthen the collective protagonist, in much the same way as the students had done: by marching through the town the workers, and especially 'new militants' such as young semi-skilled workers and office workers, provided themselves with tangible proof of their own strength. The enormous and rapid diffusion of the most strictly 'expressive' aspects of the conflict (slogans, posters, songs) had the same function. Nearly a year later, the great mass demonstration, both local and national, was one of the means used by the unions to show their power and to recover control over the rank-and-file.

Afterwards, when frequent demonstrations for social reforms were taking place, the unions intended to link plant conflicts to social ones, but with little success. As a result, in 1972–3 demonstrations tended once more to be a means of achieving solidarity—in this case for a working class which remained strong at plant level, but which could neither gather other social forces around itself nor have any profound influence on the political system. Another sign of the same phenomenon was the rapid spread of 'open' plant meetings, in which local administrators, politicians and so on participated. As the economic crisis worsened, it appeared more and more clearly that demonstrative actions were again tending, partially at least, to replace those which required a heavy mobilisation of workers.

CONFLICTS THAT 'PUT THE AIMS INTO PRACTICE' AND CIVIL DISOBEDIENCE

From the autumn of 1968, forms of action were carried out in many plant and shop disputes, which anticipated the satisfaction of the demands without waiting for the agreement. Such strikes are said to 'put the aims into practice' or 'forestall the goal'.

The go-slow is certainly the most important of these actions: the workers reduce the rhythms of work to the level they would like the management to recognise as normal. But there are others. In 1970 workers in many factories introduced their own reduction in working hours. It was not only a question of banning overtime; in order to get a firm to apply immediately a new timetable—which, according to the industry agreement, was to come into force a year or two later—the workers decided unilaterally to put it into practice. But during the 'hot autumn' of 1969 union officials participated in plant meetings, one of the demands made in national disputes.

In these cases, the distinction between conflict and demand tends to disappear, since the conflict loses its traditional characteristic as a means of pressure for obtaining satisfaction for the workers' demands, while the demand becomes identified with the way in which the conflict is conducted. The workers appear to want to control their own wage and working conditions by conflict, rather than by agreement; and, in contrast with collective bargaining, conflict does not necessarily lead to legitimating the employer. Furthermore, the union is seen simply as an organisation for arranging conflict and not as an institution for bargaining over workers' demands. For these reasons some people have talked of a return to 'direct action', which characterised the anarcho-syndicalist phase of the workers' movement. As a result, even when conflictual action was developing, the unions were never in favour of strikes of this kind, apart from some left-wing factions. When the industrial relations system began to be reorganised after 1971 the unions intervened decisively to rationalise strike action in relation to bargaining and confirm their own role in mediation. In particular, the go-slow was reduced to a simple form of conflict; any connection with demands was eliminated, and it was established that work rhythms could not be reduced beyond a certain point and only for short periods.

Blocked at plant level, direct action continued at the social level, even if it was only sustained by local or industry unions. During the 'hot autumn', some local industry unions proposed not paying rents and public transports fares in support of the conflict. For the first time, workers' action was not limited to pressing the government to reduce the cost of some services, but extended to direct action. The self-reduction (*autoriduzione*) of rents continued in some working-class districts, but it was only sustained by extreme left-wing groups. Instead, 1974 saw the introduction of another form of action which was destined to be more widely diffused and supported by the unions: self-reduction of the tariffs of public services such as transport, electricity, gas and telephones. Some Fiat commuter workers spontaneously refused to pay an increase in bus fares; their examples quickly spread and 'bus delegates' were elected, thanks to the support of the metal-working union. At almost the same time a self-reduction of electricity tariffs began, with equal success; in a few weeks, tens of thousands of self-reduced bills were paid to the national electricity company through local or plant unions. In 1975 some plant unions also began the self-reduction of telephone tariffs, but the opposition of the national confederations was greater and less success was achieved.

Actions which 'put aims into practice' at the social level tend towards civil disobedience, even though this term is never used—while other, more typical, actions of civil disobedience fail (such as the refusal to pay television licences to protest against biased programmes). Direct action is opposed to the strategy of the national unions, which seek to obtain social reforms from the government by continuous bargaining and with the sole support of general strikes, both national and local. It therefore presents the same problems for the role of the unions as direct action at plant level.

In contrast to the above, the device of the 'reverse strike' has recently been employed. This very different form of direct action was widespread in Italy just after World War II, ranging from the occupation of uncultivated land to prolonging working hours in industry beyond the timetable. In 1975 workers at two important motor car factories (Alfa Romeo and Leyland-Innocenti), who had been suspended as a result of excess production, occupied the plants for several days and, according to union instructions, began working without the management. However, no car was produced and the 'reverse strike' ended up as a simple occupation, without the assembly line workers developing any tendency towards self-management.

THE EVOLUTION OF THE LEVELS OF DECISION IN CONFLICT

The process of decentralisation in Italian industrial relations will be examined later (see Section 6). Here we shall consider only the degree to which the control of conflict is centralised or decentralised—in other words, how the subject that decides the times and the means of conflict can vary at the same bargaining level. From this point of view, the most important characteristic of conflicts since 1967 is the decentralisation of strike decisions; so that even in important disputes, such as national industry-wide ones, the lowest level union organisations decide how to strike, with a greater or lesser degree of autonomy.

In the national disputes of 1969, forms of action which had previously been seen only in plant disputes were used for the first time. This was made possible by the fact that, at national level, only the quantitative limits of the abstention from work were defined, but not the ways in which they were to be put into practice. It was therefore up to the plant unions to decide whether to use more or less radical forms of internal conflict. This not only answered the need to exploit strong rank-and-file militancy, but above all offered the union organisations at plant level a continuous form of participation in the running of the conflicts in order to restrain their spontaneous and centrifugal tendencies. Starting from the 1972–3 national disputes, the industry unions, while still retaining the operational decentralisation of strike decisions, strictly limited the autonomy of the plant unions, indicating the maximum degree of intensity which could be reached by internal conflict. In several firms this provoked the 'factory councils' (*consigli di fabbrica*) to go beyond the industry unions' instructions.

A similar pattern can be found at other levels as well. The national unions decided that any intentions to strike on the part of shops or work groups should be submitted to the preventive consent of the *consigli*, composed of all the *delegati*. Also, plant disputes often developed into company disputes, in which case control of the conflict passed into the hands of the national industry union. More recently, after a lapse of many years, national confederations once again tend to check the decisions and forms of conflict carried out by industry unions. For the time being, however, this return to the centralised regulation of the forms of action is only official in the civil service and public services.

THE NEW FORMS OF ACTION IN NON-INDUSTRIAL SECTORS

In non-industrial sectors the renewal of conflict presents very different problems from those in industry, because the productive function and the union tradition are often different.

In commerce and in other non-essential services (hotels, restaurants, insurance companies etc.) the productive situation is fairly similar to that in industry; until 1968, furthermore, there had been no experience of conflict nor any union presence. As a result, conflictual action was modelled on that of the manual workers from the outset; the unions did not object at all because the number of people suffering from the lack of services as a result of strike action was relatively small and hardly included workers, and the situation enabled the unions to establish themselves in these areas for the first time. On the other hand, militancy declined before the unions had been able to establish themselves to a sufficient extent to think about the problem of controlling mobilisation.

The attitude of the unions was very different in the public services and public administration, not only because of the different productive function, but also because patronage-type unions had often carried out forms of action which were very damaging to users, without worrying about the dangers of isolating public workers from public opinion or from other workers. This had been possible since in these sectors the balance between costs and damages of strikes had always been potentially more favourable to the workers than it had been in industry, as a result of the higher job security. For example, up to mid-1975 in some public administrations the wage deductions for striking were usually made in instalments or even not made at all, with the result of encouraging conflicts 'to the finish'.

With some exceptions at the beginning of mobilisation (particularly in sectors where it was a question of creating a union organisation), the policy of unions associated with the national confederations, and above all with the CGIL, was always to avoid strikes which greatly damaged users and to search for new forms of action which encouraged the support of public opinion. Therefore, besides absolutely rejecting strikes 'to the finish' and sudden strikes, the confederal unions tried to carry out actions which did not completely halt the services involved: for example, in urban transport, strikes which occurred on holidays or outside the rush hours, or were limited to the workers who sell and check tickets, etc. Furthermore, the unions insisted that the hours of strike themselves should be used to inform the public of the reasons for the conflict by means of demonstrations, distribution of leaflets and meetings with the users (with patients in hospitals, with students and parents in schools, etc.). Sometimes these actions were even proposed in place of striking.

As a result of these measures, when confronted with a serious crisis the confederal unions can play the very important card of calling on concrete support from the working class. Thus in 1973, for the first time in Italy, they called a general strike in support of a teachers' dispute which was degenerating into such exasperating forms as the blocking of examinations.

Although they continue to reject all legal regulation of strikes, the unions have recently proved to be in favour of self-regulation of forms of action in the public services and administration. As early as 1967, the railway union voluntarily promised the government that they would in future respect the rules regarding the forms of strike which had been carried out previously, and in particular that they would give at least a week's warning. The most resolute position is held by the CGIL, the organisation which has the largest working-class membership and which is therefore most interested in relating the employees' demands to the successful running and reform of the public services and administration. The CGIL often criticises or even openly disowns its sectoral unions when they agree to support forms of action which breach these considerations.

Traditional forms of conflict in the public services and administration, such as sudden strikes, strikes 'to the finish' and working to rule, continue to be preferred by the 'autonomous unions' or by the extreme left-wing groups when they succeed in upsetting the control of the confederal unions. Sudden strikes when traffic is heaviest have been called in urban transport services and on the railways; for several months in 1975 there were sudden strikes nearly every day among airline pilots (the so-called 'wild eagle' strikes). Strikes 'to the finish' declared by 'autonomous unions' achieved a high degree of participation among teachers, high-grade ministerial staff, street sweepers of some southern towns and other small sectors of the public administration. Customs officers, Post Office and Treasury employees worked to rule for long periods, completely blocking the services. During a hospital strike patients were not cared for, but the confederal unions immediately succeeded in preventing this very unpopular form of action. Sometimes public servants used strikes as blackmail, continuing them 'to the finish' just before an important date-line, with serious consequences for users.

The outbreak of conflict in the public services and administration from the beginning of 1975 was characterised by an important resumption of these uncontrolled forms of action. In the absence of any manual workers' mobilisation this provoked, on the one hand, the reopening of a heated debate on the limits of the right to strike, and on the other a severe reaction from the confederal unions which went so far as openly to justify the Government's decision to bring in troops on the railways as an anti-strike measure.

5 THE NEW DEMANDS

THE EMERGENCE OF NEW DEMANDS IN 1968–9

From the autumn of 1968, and throughout 1969, the intensive labour conflicts which first affected the large metal-working and chemical plants and then entire sectors involved in the renewal of national contracts, rapidly developed a new set of features. Even the objectives changed, often radically undermining traditional union approaches. It is not possible to speak of a comprehensive new bargaining strategy in the union movement at this time, but rather of the emergence of new demands, often spontaneous and not linked to any precise overall plan.

(a) Above all, changing a long-standing practice in the Italian union movement, wage increases and productivity incentives began to be sought as a fixed sum, equal for everyone, and not as a percentage of the minimum wage-rates for each grade. As far as is known (Pizzorno (ed), 1974, 1975), this was a movement which arose spontaneously and spread rapidly throughout many metal-working and chemical plants.
(b) In certain assembly-line plants, the unskilled and semi-skilled workers, for whom no career opportunities existed, sought *generalised* upgrading, rather than that based upon individual merit or upon particular circumstances. In the two largest Italian car factories, Fiat and Alfa Romeo, workers in the assembly sections quite spontaneously raised the bargaining cry of 'second grade for all' (Rieser, 1969).[10]
(c) Another fairly widespread demand in this period was for control of the piecework system. In itself this was not an innovation on trade-union policy, especially since the improvements obtained related almost solely to wages. But in some factories (well-known cases in autumn 1968 were Pirelli and Candy) the strikers employed the technique of a slowing-down in work rates. When negotiations were completed, the workers spontaneously decided to continue working at a permanently slower rate than that stipulated, using the increases in piecework rates obtained to work less rather than earn more (Regini, 1974). Implicit in this was the demand by the workers for control of work rates.

As we have observed, all these demands were, for the most part, spontaneous; they were not part of an overall strategy, and their incidence was still fairly limited. What types of workers were responsible for advancing the new demands, and what change occurred in their relationships with other parties involved, to bring about this substantial break with the past?

The main group involved was that of the semi-skilled workers, especially those working on assembly-lines, where there was little union organisation. The relationship between these workers and other groups in the labour force gradually changed during the sixties. The increase in their numbers and potential strength in the labour market was not matched by any relative improvement in their position. On the contrary, the range of qualifications and wage-differentials continued to grow, partly as a result of union encouragement.

Their relationship with the union organisations, moreover, was not strengthened. The Italian unions (especially the CGIL), based as they were on the skilled workers, and organised largely *outside* the work-place, showed a serious inability either to understand the needs of the unskilled workers, or to integrate them into trade-union activity.

The crisis in these relationships helps to explain the nature of the new demands which arose spontaneously in 1968–9. Once mass mobilisation had started, the semi-skilled workers joined in by attacking the very means by which the factory structure ensured their passive collaboration (incentives and promotion based upon individual merit), while relegating them to a position of sub-ordination to other workers (lower grades and smaller wage-rises). Furthermore, they put forward demands for real and visible change which arose from their most immediate needs and experiences, which were simple and whose implementation could be easily supervised. This was in marked contrast to traditional bargaining demands, which tied wage demands to the growth of productivity, and which were generally advanced through the trade unions.

THE CHANGE IN UNION POLICIES AND THE NEW TRENDS IN DEMANDS AFTER 1969

As we have seen, the new demands arose spontaneously from the needs of certain groups of workers; but it was the trade unions which subsequently translated them into an overall and long-term bargaining strategy, worked out, not without pain, during 1969, and finally consolidated after 1970. According to some, in the passage from sporadic rank-and-file demands to a policy for the entire union organisation the demands were both enriched and better elaborated; according to others, they were emptied of the revolutionary significance which initially characterised them.

We can, however, go beyond this simplistic debate. Firstly, it needs to be noted that, on the whole, the unions, especially at plant level and in the advanced industrial sectors, did not reject these radically new types of demands. Instead, they accepted that their traditional bargaining strategy was in crisis, and used the new spontaneous demands as the basis for developing a more advanced policy. The unions were forced into this not just by the contingent need to re-establish control over an increasingly widespread rank-and-file spontaneity, but also by the even more basic need to use working-class mobilisation in order to acquire greater power in the system of industrial relations. In order to establish an organisational presence at factory level and force recognition by employers, weak trade unions, like those in Italy before 1968, must first obtain the effective support of the great majority of the working class. They must, therefore, be capable of absorbing the demands of an expanding group – the semi-skilled workers.

On the other hand, however, such demands were not simply supplied by the union organisations; they were sifted and modified. And these modifications did not merely moderate the more radical demands of certain groups of workers by linking them with those of other groups in an overall package; they also, and more importantly, made them *negotiable* in such a way as to strengthen the power of unions. During 1969–70, in the same metal-working and chemical sectors in which the new demands had first emerged, there was therefore a process of adjustment. From the convergence of rank-and-file demands and the strategy of the unions, two main new tendencies in bargaining objectives emerged more clearly: the demands for greater equality and for greater control of work-organisation. These demands formed the basis of the policies which, from about 1970, were formally accepted by the whole union movement. But in addition we should observe that as well as the two types of industrial action undertaken at plant and sectoral levels, there was a third type, undertaken at national level, which was aimed at government as well as, or even instead of, the employers as such; this involved the pursuit of social and economic policy objectives.

If these were the new directions which the renewal of bargaining strategies took (and we shall analyse them in detail in the next three sections), there were, nevertheless, two further areas, by no means new, which remained of central importance.

The reduction in hours continued to be pursued in all industries at national level, while at plant level there was an increasing tendency to seek a more rigid application of negotiated reductions in working-hours than in the past. This was done to avoid a reduction in hours becoming an increase in overtime (and hence in wages), and to use it instead to force employers to increase employment.

Finally, demands relating to union rights and powers continued to appear, at both national and factory level.[11] In industrial sectors other than metalworking and chemicals, the renewal of objectives took place largely at national level by decision of the unions, and only later spread to the factory-level. In the private service sector, almost only in the department stores and supermarkets was there any strong rank-and-file pressure at local level for a revision of objectives. In the public service sector, on the other hand, the very few changes in policy did not even take place at the level of the national category unions (except partially in a few cases such as the railway union in 1931, the state employees' and the hospital workers' unions in 1972), but were developed by the confederations (especially the CGIL), often against their own category federations, and against a large part of the rank-and-file. In this sector, in fact, policy renewal meant, above all, rationalising the tangled mass of relative privileges enjoyed by public employees, and equalising earnings and working regulations. This was met by widespread hostility from many sectors of the rank-and-file.

But, in relation to the theme with which we are concerned, what is most important to stress is the role which the confederations maintained in the overall bargaining policies of the trade unions, which is illuminated by their activities in the sector of public employment. In the 'division of labour' between bargaining activities at plant and category (i.e. industry or sectoral) level on the one hand, and at general (i.e. involving the whole labour force) level on the other, the confederations made themselves the official protagonists of economic and social objectives, and of the unification of the trade union movement. The latter constituted the newest aspect (see page 147); the equalisation of economic treatment, however, continued a trend already typical of the sixties.

Let us now examine separately the elements of the three new bargaining policies which characterised trade union policy in this period.

EGALITARIAN DEMANDS

The Meaning of Egalitarian Demands

We have already seen how strong egalitarian tendencies, which had the effect of redefining wage and status relationships between workers in the same plant, emerged in 1968–9, and how the unions substantially accepted them. What motives underlay these demands? Various interpretations have been advanced about the meaning of equal (lump-sum) wage increases for all to those groups of workers who demanded them. The trade union elements which sought to play down the importance of these demands attribute it to a simple reaction against a management policy which had increased wage differentials too far – that is, beyond the objective differences in the value of the workers' abilities. A different, traditional, 'solidaristic' interpretation has also been advanced: workers struggle together for a common purpose, and hence they must all have the same privileges; they all have the same needs and it is therefore fair to give more to those who have less and *vice versa*. Yet again, others see these demands rather as a sign of rejection, by unskilled and semi-skilled workers, of a hierarchical system of qualifications based on criteria of skills which modern forms of productive organisation never permit them to attain. This latter interpretation is more satisfactory because it takes account of the simultaneous demands for a single grade (*qualifica unica*) or for upgrading *en masse* (and not on individual merit). The system of skills based on the old criterion of individual capacity was rejected because the technology developed for assembly-line workers gave rise to 'uniformly unskilled' jobs, and did not enable workers to acquire skills through a period of apprenticeship, except in the case of a limited nucleus of the working class. It is also possible that the discovery of their capacity to disrupt the flow of production through brief stoppages in a few work-places (see Section 4), made the assembly-line workers aware that they were as indispensable to an extremely integrated production process as highly skilled workers.

But what were the aims and motives of the trade unions in accepting egalitarian demands, and thus reversing their traditional policy lines? We have already noted the more general reasons in the preceding section. In particular, it was useful for the unions as a whole initially to favour the least represented groups of workers in order to gain recognition as the *general* representatives of the working class as a whole. In terms of the capacity to mobilise the workers it was also useful to eliminate the most arbitrary divisions between them (for example, the fourth and fifth grades). But this exhausts the common interests shared by all sectors of the unions. The CGIL could not in fact oppose the interests of its activists and more militant members – those with specialised skills – too strongly. As a result, it was initially opposed to equal (lump-sum) wage increases for all, and later sought to interpret them in the most limited way, as we have indicated. Moreover, it rejected automatic upgrading *en masse*, which conflicted with its traditional defence of the 'professional value' of the worker. However, its more advanced sectors sought to develop the concept of a 'new professionalism' among semi-skilled workers, identified by their 'adaptability' and by the basic education required by modern forms of productive organisation, or which could be created if the form of organisation were modified. On the other hand, FIM-CISL (the metal-workers' federation of the Catholic CISL confederation), which was much weaker and was seeking to build up—in competition with FIOM-CGIL—a following among the mass of unskilled and as yet non-unionised workers, made itself the spokesman for the new demands almost unconditionally.

During 1969–71 different attitudes towards this question were reflected in a variety of solutions at factory level. Traditional demands for the upgrading of certain groups of workers continued, but meanwhile there emerged demands of an egalitarian type, aiming at the straight abolition of the lower grades (generally the fourth and fifth) and at automatic up-grading based on length of service. On the other hand, it took longer at plant level to develop the policy of linking upgrading to the establishment of a 'new professionalism', evaluated with new criteria or acquired through job rotation or job enrichment.

The Choice of Inquadramento Unico as the Central Union Demand

From late 1970 onwards, however, there was a gradual convergence of these initially differing attitudes. A new union proposal received the support of all sections of the unions: this was the so-called *Inquadramento Unico* (IU) for both blue-and white-collar workers.[13] Why was it that this issue, even if in different ways, was accepted as the new battleground by all sections of the movement? The most obvious answer is that it was a compromise between the radical version of egalitarianism on the one side, and the defence of traditional skills or a 'new professionalism' on the other. In fact, the latter prevailed; but for the union left wing, the abandonment of radical egalitarianism was compensated by the hope of an attack on traditional methods of work organisation which would be implicit in the call for a 'new professionalism'. Furthermore, where unskilled workers and radical tendencies were strongest, greater emphasis could be placed on automatic upgrading rather than promotion based upon individual skills. But besides providing a compromise between different factions of the movement, IU presented other advantages for the unions as organisations during 1971–3. It enabled them:

(a) to counter the opposition to egalitarian demands shown by the skilled workers in various plants after 1970–1;
(b) to rationalise and control wage structures, reducing the area available for paternalistic manoeuvring towards white-collar workers by management;
(c) to co-ordinate plant-level bargaining by setting out future guidelines, which had to relate to the methods of application of IU (since at national level only general characteristics were laid down): this made future plant-level bargaining policy predictable and selective;
(d) to put a premium on the technical bargaining skills of union officials, since IU was a rather complex matter to negotiate.

Thus, once control over the rank-and-file was no longer in danger, the trade unions adopted a policy which, again through the demand for IU, involved rationalising industrial conflict and reasserting control over it.

The discussions, demands and results of the egalitarian movement are best exemplified by the metal-working sector, but to some degree at least, they involved the whole of the rest of the Italian working class. In most other industrial sectors the egalitarian policy was widespread. Equal pay increases for all became the rule at national level in 1970, with certain exceptions in the more privileged categories (for example among workers in the power plants). In some sectors (e.g. textiles) egalitarian tendencies were very marked, and drastically reduced the number of grades; in other sectors (e.g. chemicals, where 'job evaluation' was widespread) there were uncertainties and ambiguities.

Outside the traditional manufacturing sectors, the situation was rather more contradictory and difficult to evaluate, partly because of the lack of information available. By 1971–2 IU was demanded by such groups as the gas workers and hotel workers, and then spread further. In general it seems there was a strict correlation between egalitarian demands and organisational and technological structures. Where the latter factors had the effect of removing differences between various elements of the work-force – of 'homogenising' it – egalitarian demands tend to arise. In the mass distribution sector, for example, where the organisation of the work-force tends to create large groups of workers similar in many ways to assembly-line workers, egalitàrian demands appear, expressed as requests for 'a single skill-grading for all sales personnel', for a reduction in the number of grades, or for automatic upgrading (based on length of service). In agriculture, on the other hand, technological and organisational developments have moved in different directions – away from general labouring and towards a series of specialised jobs—with the result that there has been a tendency to move away from traditional 'solidaristic' objectives towards those which put a premium on the qualifications of the upper strata of *braccianti*. In 1971, the unions were still demanding pay increases in percentage terms.

Finally, in public employment, where the 'autonomous' unions developed, simple economic objectives which favoured the most privileged groups of workers traditionally predominated. A drive towards unified, and in some way egalitarian, demands came only (and not always) from the confederations, especially the CGIL, and some of their affiliates. Recently some of these have succeeded in reducing wage inequalities (for example, hospital workers and state employees, both in 1972).

THE BATTLE FOR CONTROL OF THE ORGANISATION OF PRODUCTION

Ideology and Rank-and-file Demands in the 'Battle Against the Capitalist Organisation of Production'

Moves towards greater wage equality arose from strong rank-and-file pressure and were subsequently worked out, and partly modified, by the unions themselves; on the other hand, the 'battle for control over the organisation of production' – a slogan which summed up many of the most innovatory demands arising from plant-level industrial action after 1968 – was decisively shaped by intellectual and overtly ideological influences. Without bearing this in mind, demands which concerned the organisation of production might seem to be simply the same objectives that had long since been achieved by unions in other countries, or that had been promoted by the employers themselves. However, in reality such demands contained much greater ambitions. In particular they strove to express an original, and clearly anti-capitalist, policy, albeit one conducted through union-based action, for 'class-oriented' rather than 'business-oriented' trade unionism. As a result of the limitations which we shall examine, the reality fell short of these ambitions; nevertheless, in this particular case it is extremely important to appreciate the *intentions* of those involved, if we are to understand their demands, the place of these in an overall bargaining strategy, and their consequences.

The ideological origins of the 'struggle against the capitalist organisation of production' were varied. For several years before 1968, certain Marxist groups, dissenting from the line taken by the bulk of the Italian labour movement, had identified the organisation of production at factory level not as a simple reflection of the state of technology, but as the expression of power relations between the working class and the employers. Put in Marxist terms, productive forces (including technology and work organisation) were not neutral, but were themselves determined by existing relationships of production. Hence the need for a battle against the organisation of production which, even if waged through 'trade union' (rather than political) means, could not be limited to the improvement of working conditions. It had to serve to show that technology was not neutral, and it had to turn industrial action at plant-level into a conflict over power, and thus give it a political connotation.

Other minority groups within the union movement, of Catholic inspiration, saw the Taylorian organisation of production as a factor of alienation. Even though they discounted the limitations imposed by working within the existing, capitalist, relations of production, they considered it as part of an advanced (and not purely 'business-oriented') union's role to attempt to change existing forms of work and productive organisation.

These attitudes were very much in a minority in a trade union movement which largely accepted as natural and neutral the existing forms of the organisation of production. However, during the conflicts of 1968–9, a rejection of certain aspects of the prevalent forms of production (incentives, extremely high work-rates, exhausting or dangerous working-conditions, hierarchical structures etc.) appeared at rank-and-file level. The various minority groups working both inside and outside the unions were initially able to make use of this mass rejection and give it some ideological justification.

However, it proved difficult to translate it into precise demands, and to give it effect over a broad front as part of a coherent strategy. Accepting (for reasons already examined) the important policy changes implicit in the new demands, the unions took this task upon themselves. During 1970 and early 1971 the metal-workers' unions in particular placed the struggle 'against' the organisation of production at the centre of their plant-level bargaining activities. Their principal demands concerned the following: (a) abolition of, or strict limitations on, incentives in the piece-work system; (b) a reduction in the work-rates and work-loads, and an increase in rest time allowed; (c) a refusal to accept risky or noxious tasks in return for danger money; (d) a reduction in working hours and the abolition of night shifts; (e) rigid observance of the 40-hour working week, with minimum recourse to overtime.

As a result the trade unions succeeded in transforming rank-and-file rejection of certain aspects of the organisation of production into precise and radical (though obviously still negotiable) bargaining demands, but without as yet putting them into any overall framework. In other words, in 1970–1, union demands were linked together only *negatively*, although they had a common tendency to emphasise the 'autonomy' of the needs and interests of the workers themselves from the exigencies of productivity. But the strategy of a struggle 'against' capitalist organisation of production remained abstract until an answer was provided to the problem of precisely *what* was being struggled *for*.

The Making of Union Policies on the Organisation of Production

In the debates both inside and outside the unions there were certain responses to this problem, which derived from ideological positions preceding the outbreak of industrial conflict. The main proposals were of two types – either aiming at an *alternative* organisation of production, or at *control over* it. In the latter case, there was a further division over whether such control was to be directly exercised by the workers themselves, or whether it was to strengthen the power of their union representatives.

But while there was broad agreement over the struggle 'against' the existing organisation of production, the question of ends and objectives provoked divisions within the union movement, and there was great difficulty and uncertainty in elaborating suitable demands. During the period 1971–3 the unions experimented with various solutions to these difficulties.

(a) *Direct rank-and-file control* over the organisation of production did not usually emerge as a formal demand. But, after 'hot autumn', the shift in the balance of power at shop level in favour of the working class which occurred in numerous large-scale enterprises was such that in practice this type of control was obtained. The fact that such matters as work-rates, work-loads, rest periods, etc. were not mentioned a great deal in plant-level agreements did not indicate an absence of union action in these areas, but suggested that those problems which arose were generally dealt with directly on the shop-floor, by rank-and-file pressure, and through the *delegati* (shop-delegates). Only in a few cases (such as Fiat and Olivetti in 1971) were such matters dealt with in detail in plant-level agreements.

(b) The explicit demands, on the other hand, were mainly aimed at extending the *control of the representatives* of the workers over the organisation of production. There were widespread calls for committees and working-parties to study questions related to piece-work, grading-systems and health hazards. Above all, the demands about the work-place environment were designed to fulfil this aim. Very few of these were in fact directed at obtaining immediate and concrete results, such as the modification of certain types of equipment, or measures to reduce health hazards; instead, the majority tended to strengthen the power of the unions to control the work-place environment. Such objectives were very rarely amenable to immediate control by the workers themselves; they required medical and technical expertise (for example, recording the health records, and the exposure to health hazards, of individual workers, and the collection of statistical data on the work-place environment). The objectives were often vague or elastic, as in the case of the right of investigation. Furthermore, they enhanced the role of union officials, rather than the workers themselves, as in the case of the establishment of committees to control the work-place environment. As a result, the demands were very advanced in terms of union power in the work-place (although they did not extend to any assumption of managerial responsibilities through participation schemes, which the unions flatly rejected), but they created a gap between the rank-and-file and the union organisation, since they were often highly technical in nature, and when written into formal agreements gave no impression that a substantial concession had been obtained.

(c) As well as attempting to control the productive process, the unions also began to work in the somewhat ambiguous direction of an *alternative, and new, type of productive organisation*. There was much discussion in Italy, especially during 1972 and 1973, of the need to 'overcome Taylorism' and to find 'a more human means of producing goods and services', 'a new method of making cars', etc. In such slogans the original themes of the trade union left were taken up by more conservative elements, and by the PCI. An 'alternative' system of productive organisation was seen largely as a technical and managerial question, and hence in terms of changes which could be introduced at shop-floor level, such as job rotation, enlargement and enrichment, work-groups and production 'islands'. Demands for a change from line production to production islands at Olivetti in 1971 and Fiat in 1973 were symbolic of this approach. Such experiments had already been carried out in other countries on the initiative of management, but in Italy they were sought by the unions, with the general aim of creating a 'new professionalism in the workers' (as we have already seen on page 126, in the case of the *Inquadramento Unico*). Such an approach on the part of the unions was criticised in two ways. Firstly, it was said to achieve only symbolic, and extremely limited, results, since the general rule in industry remained the parcelling of labour into jobs with only single, or very limited, functions attached to them. Secondly, it was said to give no genuinely 'alternative' type of productive organisation, but only marginal adjustments which served to re-integrate the potentially alienated worker into the work-place situation.

From the Attack on the Capitalist Organisation of Production to the Defence of Union Power.

From 1971 onwards, the economic crisis, and the various political reactions to it, changed the framework in which the battle against prevailing forms of productive organisation took place. New difficulties were thus added to those we have already seen.

In the first place, inflation made wages once again the central issue of concern to the rank-and-file, just as the economic crisis forced the union leadership to moderate its demands. As a result, the strategy of the union leaders, based on issues which were linked to control over the work-place on the one hand, and social reform on the other, suffered in terms of its credibility among the rank-and-file. In fact, in order to be acceptable such a strategy had to be accompanied by sustained success on the wages front.

In the second place, the threat to employment forced the labour movement from attack back on to the defensive. It became more difficult to demand costly modifications to the organisation of production, or even to obtain the implementation of existing agreements (such as the creation of a new career structure foreseen in the *Inquadramento Unico*). Productive processes were, in fact, altered unilaterally by management through restructuring. Union demands had thus to be diverted to such questions as the guarantee of earnings, control over restructuring, and defence of the 'rigidity' of the labour force, so that management was not free to deploy it as it wished.

Thirdly, the first signs began to appear of one of the main managerial responses to the increase in trade union power – the decentralisation of production outside the large-scale enterprises, through sub-contracts, work carried out in the home or in small-scale concerns. As a result, union control over the organisation of production could no longer be limited to individual enterprises; it had to extend over a whole area. Demands for the elimination of sub-contracting, and for control over various forms of 'precarious' employment, began to appear. Such demands became increasingly important, both at plant and national level, from 1971 to 1975.

In recent years, therefore, conflicts over the organisation of production have moved from the search for technical innovations towards preserving the power and position of the unions. Today, in a strike, it is the employers who make demands about the organisation of production; they seek greater utilisation of plant and equipment, with more use of overtime and shift-work, less absenteeism, and greater mobility of the labour force. In the face of this prolonged attack, the unions have on the whole succeeded in holding their own; they have obtained guarantees on earnings, maintained a *de facto* block on redundancies, opposed any non-negotiated mobility of labour, obtained some measure of control of marginal employment outside the factory, and thus acted as a barrier to the decentralisation of production. But this has required notable concessions to the employers, and particularly a slowing-down of new union initiatives and a return to centralisation within the union movement itself.

As we have seen, egalitarian tendencies have been extended, however falteringly, from key enterprises to the whole economy, including those areas in which unionisation was most limited. The same cannot be said about the battle for control over the organisation of production, at least in its more aggressive version, which has been limited to certain large-scale enterprises—especially those involving assembly-work, those in the textile sector (where it has been aimed at control over the piece-work system and work-loads) and those in the chemicals sector (where the principal aim was control over the work-place environment). In the public sector, only those categories where there are large numbers of blue-collar workers (e.g. railwaymen in 1971, and bus-drivers in 1973) have made significant demands of this type. The unions have also discussed changes in labour organisation in the public administration, but here they refer essentially to changes in the hierarchical structure of authority.

ACTION FOR SOCIAL REFORMS AND FOR A NEW ECONOMIC POLICY

In this section we shall examine those social and economic policy objectives which have played a central part in the overall strategy of the Italian union movement since 1969. They have had varying consequences, and only some of them actually represent new departures; nevertheless, we shall consider them together for the following reasons:

(a) To begin with, none of them is directly concerned with labour relations within the enterprise but with the position of the working class in the overall political, economic and social system.

(b) In the second place, these demands are all aimed more at the public authorities (especially the government) than at the employers, though the latter are also involved to a certain extent.
(c) Finally, and perhaps most importantly, these objectives arise more from the strategy of the union leadership than from direct rank-and-file pressure. It is important to realise that the union movement as a whole has an objective need to *aggregate* the varying interests of the different sectors of the working-class around certain unifying aims, in order to avoid imbalances and conflicts within the movement. At the same time the confederations have an interest in bringing control of bargaining activity back into their hands, and wresting the initiative away from shop-floor militants and the individual industrial unions. Both these organisational interests (the reaggregation of rank-and-file demands and the recentralisation of bargaining activities) were served by union campaigns linked to general objectives which were not limited to the work-place. Except in rare cases, such campaigns were in fact run by the confederations, which saw in them a means of overcoming particularistic pressures, and at the same time of counterbalancing the decentralisation of bargaining activities – a process which was characteristic of the period after 1968, and which changed power relations within the union organisation in favour of the 'category' or industry unions and the *delegati*.

Action for Social Reforms
In 1969 the so called 'struggle for reforms' began with a series of demands over housing policy, and with considerable rank-and-file participation. There was almost complete agreement (at least verbally) within the unions on the need to channel working-class mobilisation towards social objectives beyond the work-place. Various factors account for such a decision. Above all, the profound economic and social imbalances produced by rapid capitalist development left the Italian ruling class unable to respond with measures of rationalisation. And the Italian trade union movement itself, with its strong tradition of politicisation, had always paid greater attention to economic and social problems than to the specific conditions of employed workers. New variables were added to these long-term elements in 1968–9: the great increase in union power, at a time when the mobilising and innovating capacities of the parties were in severe doubt; the need to ensure that the living conditions of workers' families did not worsen, thus cancelling out the benefits won in factory-level bargaining; and the confederations' desire to react to centrifugal and divisive tendencies in the movement, to aggregate and co-ordinate various types of demands, and bring them together at national level.

All through 1970, and for part of 1971, the unions therefore pressed the Government for reforms in housing, the health services, education, transport and the taxation system. These demands were backed up by general strikes articulated on a regional basis, by meetings with the political parties, and, particularly, by frequent meetings with the government. But the results were very disappointing, amounting to only a general, and not particularly advanced, new law on housing, and certain promises about the health service.

Although it was never in fact officially abandoned, by the middle of 1971 the 'struggle for reforms' could no longer generate rank-and-file support, and ended in failure as far as the unions were concerned. The reasons for this failure – which was in marked contrast to the striking successes obtained during the same period in plant-level industrial disputes – were much discussed both inside and outside the union movement.

To put it at its simplest, there were two distinct types of approach. On the one hand, it was emphasised that the reform strategy had met with enormous resistance, much greater than could have been foreseen; it had, in effect, overestimated the willingness of the more progressive sectors of capitalism and the political class to implement reforms which would eliminate such social imbalances as had become harmful not only to the mass of workers but to the productive system itself. Given the nature of the Italian economy and political system, such sectors nevertheless also had an interest in defending the parasitic sectors which would be hardest hit by reform, while certainly benefitting from the rationalisation and stabilisation of the system which reforms would bring.

On the other hand, there was a tendency to emphasise the *weakness* of the reform movement. There were some, especially in the confederations and the parties of the Left,[14] who blamed the failures on the low level of mobilisation, which itself resulted from a lack of rank-and-file interest in wider social questions and the narrow, work-place-directed horizons of the individual unions. Others, however, argued that the confederations had led the struggle for reforms in a remote and elitist way, with the result that there had been little popular participation because the rank-and-file had had little opportunity to influence the direction of the struggle.

In effect, as we have already observed, the confederations had a clear interest in emphasising the strategy of reform, and in organising it in such a way as to maintain central control. This gave them several advantages. It allowed them to co-ordinate bargaining activities according to a scale of priorities, to regain a pre-eminent position in the trade union movement, and to obtain privileged status as a body which the government had to consult on important economic and social problems. Only by bearing in mind all those advantages which accrued to the confederations, independently of the amount of success achieved by the struggle for reforms, can one understand why the union movement was so slow to change its strategy, despite its obvious failures, the criticism (and self-criticism) it provoked, and the various demands for a change of direction.

Demands on Economic Policy

However, as in the case of enterprise-level disputes aimed at changing the organisation of production, a change in the economic situation was the factor which forced the confederations to alter course and make rather different demands from the government. As early as 1971, but much more so in 1974–5, the economic crisis and the high rates of inflation (which threatened employment and the real income of the workers – in other words, the very basis of trade union strength) gave questions of economic policy priority over issues of reform. In 1971, the three confederations launched a campaign to defend employment levels and to develop the South; at the same time they began to insist upon the need for what they called 'a new model of development'. The following year, facing large rises in the cost of living, they called on the government to hold down charges for major public services, and to control prices. But, given the worsening political situation, and the paralysing crisis of trade union unity, these demands – like those for reforms – met with no real success.

From late 1972 to early 1974, during the partial economic recovery, the major industrial unions (especially in the metal-working sector) regained the initiative. Firstly, they organised a national demonstration at Reggio Calabria – in the heartland of fascist reaction – calling for measures to develop the South. Next, they demanded that the investment plans for the South made by state and partially state-owned industries should be negotiated alongside the renewals of the national agreements. Finally, during 1973 and 1974, after the renewal of the major contracts, they started negotiations with the largest industrial groups with the aim of forcing them to contribute to an improvement in the social services, and especially to undertake more new investment in the South. The tactic of dealing with employers instead of the government, and thus jointly tackling the crisis in order to avoid further damage to the productive system, was one which found temporary favour with the confederations themselves. In autumn 1974 they launched an 'autumn offensive' in which they demanded support for low-income groups (pension increases etc.), guaranteed wages, and a reassessment of inflation adjustments at the highest level. This temporary change in the activities of the confederations, moving from the sphere of economic policy back towards wage-related issues, arose from 'the fear of a wave of unco-ordinated wage demands [at factory level], in response to the rapid increase in the cost of living (over 20 per cent in a year) and the lack of reforms'.[15] It was also part of an attempt to form an alliance between capital and labour against the state, which remained unwilling to make concessions yet bore the brunt of demands of this type.

The results of the confederations' efforts were important, given the seriousness of the economic crisis; they included a recovery in the purchasing power of workers' incomes which helped the lower paid in particular, and a guarantee of wages at 93 per cent of the original level in all circumstances (a greater concession than probably any other union movement in Europe was able to achieve).[16] During and after this dispute, the confederations called for reductions in the prices of certain public services (electricity and telephones), partly to combat the tendency towards *autoriduzione* which was being supported by certain local unions in some areas.

But in 1975 the basic problem of the government's economic policy returned to the centre of the stage, and the confederations once again came to play the major role. The union movement became the point of reference and the spokesman not just for the workers, but for all those who believed that during the crisis priority should be given to safeguarding employment and to restimulating the economy through investment in the South and a radical restructuring of industry. It has been claimed that on these questions the union movement has now become the legitimate representative not only of its own institutional base, but of 'the people' as a whole. In effect, it is consulted by the government on all important economic problems. But the results of its efforts continue to be fairly modest. Besides, the very nature and scope of the theme on which it has concentrated its activities – the creation of a 'new model' of economic development – has to a certain extent stimulated anew the action and initiative of the political parties, which naturally leaves the unions less room for manoeuvre.

Although the results of the unions' efforts are still ambiguous, it is possible to draw certain conclusions from the change of emphasis from the 'reform strategy' to that of the 'new economic policy'. The former was essentially an *offensive* strategy, aimed at using the strength acquired by the union movement at factory level to change society. However, the innovations it aimed at were realised on paper only. The latter approach developed out of the economic crisis, and consisted in the first place of an attempt to *defend*, at the macro-economic and at the political levels, employment and the purchasing power of wages. In the latter case, the recentralisation and co-ordination of bargaining activities in the hands of the confederations was not, as before, the result of a political choice, but of necessity. This made it much more difficult for the lower levels of the union movement to adopt a more radical bargaining strategy. Moreover, the seriousness of the crisis in fact made several of the movement's objectives mutually contradictory. For example, there was a demand that employment should be protected in those industries in the North which were in difficulties, at the same time as the movement was also pressing for more investment in the South. And both demands were in potential conflict with a third – the demand for a major restructuring of industry.

Some of the results of the unions' attempt to use their work-place strength to influence basic economic policy have been of a conventional type – such as the offer to bargain for certain managerial and governmental policies by offering concessions on labour mobility (within or between factories, on hours and shift issues). But it has also led to a shift from general demands for a radical and comprehensive change in economic policy to immediate bargaining demands.[17] This, and the direct (and not merely symbolic) action undertaken by the employed workers of the North to help the depressed areas of the *Mezzogiorno*, represent perhaps the most novel and innovatory aspects of the union movement's strategy during the economic crisis.

6 CHANGES IN THE INDUSTRIAL RELATIONS SYSTEM[18]

A profound transformation of the system of industrial relations at every level took place in Italy after 1968. As we shall see, the process of change took three different but inter-related directions. From limited areas of the productive system (large industrial plants, especially in the north) it gradually spread to the whole of the industrial sector and right through the labour force (including services, public employment and agriculture); within the union it began at rank-and-file level and spread upwards, involving first the lower levels of the individual industrial unions, and then the higher levels and the confederations as well. As far as the overall system of industrial relations were concerned, the unions were the first to face the traumatic challenge of change; they were followed by the employers' associations and the state itself. The change therefore involved in the first place the weakest points (individual plants) and the weakest participants (the unions, especially the 'category' or industrial federations) in the traditional system of industrial relations (see below). It did not occur in a linear fashion: a decisive break with the past, which corresponded, very broadly speaking, to the years 1968–72, was followed by a period of readjustment which probably even today (1976) is not yet complete.

The catalyst of the change was the exceptional increase in labour disputes. Such change had, however, been developing inside the union movement for almost a decade (although the way in which it eventually occurred, and the forms it took were, in part, rather different from the original conception). For this reason, explanations which see the growth of industrial conflict as the decisive or exclusive cause (a view popular among many extra-parliamentary groups) seem inadequate, as do those which insist on the substantial continuity between the post-1968 situation and the tendencies promoted by the unions in the early sixties. This latter explanation (which is common in trade union propaganda) sees the unions as the principal promotors of the change. The first type of explanation under-rates the importance of the unions' ability to take over the process of industrial action, even when it arises spontaneously, and to 'generalise' its impact; the second type fails to show why the process of change accelerated rapidly only after 1968.

THE TRADITIONAL SYSTEM OF INDUSTRIAL RELATIONS: LINES OF CHANGE.

The Weakness of Trade Unionism

After the brief period of union unity represented by the unified CGIL, which was formed after the fall of Fascism, the basic characteristic of the Italian system of industrial relations in the fifties and much of the sixties was the extreme weakness of the unions. The principal manifestations of this weakness were the division of the unions along ideological lines, the centralisation of both the organisational structure of the unions and the bargaining process, organisational absence at the work-place, and the low level of membership. Divisions in the union movement profoundly influenced the peculiarly political character of Italian unionism. In a sense the dependence of the unions upon the political parties was a result of this: it is possible that a single united union confederation would, of necessity, have had to develop a position which was to some extent independent of the parties, whereas the ideological pluralism of the unions tended to hinder the emergence of a strictly 'union-oriented' environment, and to encourage the idea of trade union action as an extension of more general political action.

A further characteristic contributed to the marked politicisation of Italian trade unionism. The unions (albeit in different ways for the CGIL, which is largely Communist and Socialist in orientation, the Christian Democratic CISL, and the Social Democratic/Republican UIL) were not principally associations which could provide particular benefits and advantages for their own members; in Italy there are no resistance or strike funds, and no closed shop. Agreements apply indiscriminately to union members and non-members. As we shall see, the forms of worker representation at factory level are independent of the type and extent of unionisation among the workers. Even the technical services (*patronati*) run by various unions on matters relating to social security are aimed at non-members as well as members. This separation of trade unionism from the immediate material concerns of the individual members is partly linked to the union's status as a free association (we shall return to this below), but above all to the idea of the union as the general representative of all workers (and hence not just of the members), which is typical of the Communist and Socialist tradition, but in practice came to be adopted by the minority confederations as well.

In terms of membership, the unions were undoubtedly very weak. At the end of the fifties total membership could not have been more than 3.5 million[19] (2.2 million less than in 1947). For the CGIL in particular, the membership curve until 1968 is extremely telling (see Table 8 in Appendix I). If the scant benefits resulting from membership, the prolonged offensive against union activists, the employers' tendency to recruit employees among the 'democratic' unions (CISL and UIL) or among the so-called 'yellow' (employer-organised) unions, are all taken into account, the decline in CGIL membership may even appear comparatively modest. Why was it not greater, or why at least did the other confederations not succeed in becoming stronger than they did? It might be answered that the traditional left-wing politicisation of the Italian working-class, particularly after the struggle against Fascism, prevented this from happening. But the CGIL also survived because an explicit alliance between the Italian employers and the other confederations, which might have strengthened the latter, was never realised, despite the alliance at the political level between the employers' association (*Confindustria*) and Christian Democracy. It is likely that such an alliance did not offer sufficient short-term advantages to the entrepreneurial class, since the CGIL still remained the major union among the industrial workers, while the CISL was particularly strong among white-collar workers and in the public sector. Nor did the employers, either in the fifties or the sixties, see the necessity for encouraging a strong trade union alternative to the CGIL (which could have controlled the rank-and-file in exchange for recognition by management and the political authority) since the overall combativity of the working-class was low.

From the organisational point of view,[20] the CGIL for a long time favoured a confederal structure, which permitted co-ordination between all productive sectors. Behind this lay a concern to protect the interests of all workers as a class, including the unemployed and agricultural workers (Foa and Trentin, 1972); but its result was to restrict the ability of the union to respond flexibly to different situations. Symptomatic of this was the critical organisational absence at factory level. In the work-place there was, in fact, only a general body representing the workers, the internal commission (*commissione interna*) elected by all workers in a given plant, from *political* lists of candidates supported by the unions. This body had many limitations: it had few representatives on it, compared to the total number of workers, it had few powers (formally speaking, it had no right to engage in bargaining), and it had no organic link with the external trade unions. What is most important, however, is the fact that the unions remained *outside* the work-place (Treu, 1971: Ch 2). In this context the attempts by CISL to organise its own branches at plant level are hardly relevant.

Even the structure of bargaining is highly centralised. For many years 'interconfederal' agreements were the rule: these were reached at national level between the union confederations and the employers' organisations, wage-levels being determined for the whole of industry (Giambarba, 1972).

To some extent, the unions were forced to bargain at a centralised level by the emergency situation in the country as a whole. But centralisation of the bargaining process also suited the unions, or at least the CGIL, because it seemed more appropriate for defending the interests of 'the whole class'. What the union failed to foresee was that this would weaken the union still further, since it was impossible to control wage increases conceded by the most dynamic enterprises (in the export goods industries). In the largest factories (Fiat is an obvious case) the union vacuum became ever more serious, and the CGIL was forced to review its own policy and undergo some measure of 'self-criticism'.

The Employers' Front

Thanks to the weakness of trade unionism, the entrepreneurial class and employers' organisations have not had to regard the unions as significant. Instead they established privileged relationships with the Government and the Government parties, through direct alliances or clientele type exchanges (Pizzorno, 1970). However, the only attempt by Italian employers to assume direct political responsibilites by presenting their own candidates at local and general elections in the mid-fifties was a failure. The lack of success of Confintesa – the alliance between Confindustria, Confcommercio and Confagricoltura (the peak organisations of industry, commerce and agriculture) – in fact marked the beginning of a progressive differentiation of the Italian ruling class.

The first formal break in the solidity of the employers' front came with the establishment in 1956 of the association of state or partially state-controlled industries (Intersind), but this did not have any appreciable consequences until the beginning of the sixties. More immediately obvious were the differences between oligopolistic enterprises geared to exports and generally small firms selling to the domestic market. From the second half of the fifties the former introduced a policy of conceding wage increases which set them apart from the remainder of the employers' front. Confindustria increasingly became the bulwark of small and middle-sized industries (without high margins of expenditure), and these ran the organisation until the end of the sixties.

The Role of the State

The state's role in the system is formally neutral: there is no institutional provision for its intervening in industrial relations through reconciliation, arbitration etc., and this is so out of respect for the 'autonomy' of the parties directly involved. A consequence of this policy of institutional 'non-interference' was the informality of Italian industrial relations. The two articles of the Republican Constitution which concern the rights of union association and of strike action have never been activated. Even today trade unions and employers' associations are free private associations enjoying no special recognition, and the relationships between them are regulated by ordinary civil law. Thus there are no regulations governing the forms of strike beyond the laws protecting private property. Nor is there any fixed obligatory procedure for the resolution of labour disputes. (Public employment is an exception, since here labour relations are fixed by legislation, and the right to strike is limited in some respects – even if with little real effect).

The Crisis of the System in the Sixties.

The system of industrial relations which emerged in the fifties therefore directly reflected the different strengths of its principal participants. This meant, however, that a change in the power of one of the participants could have very extensive effects on the whole system. This occurred in the early sixties, when the strengthening of the workers in the large industrial plants in the North resulted in a great increase in labour conflicts. The individual unions immediately called for a policy of 'articulated bargaining', to regain control of wage drift, and the setting up of union branches within factories.

On the employers' front Intersind, recently formed and in search of an identity, was the first to respond openly to the unions; in 1962 it signed an agreement giving them the right to negotiate certain matters at plant level. On the other hand, the opposition of Confindustria held firm. As a result, some large enterprises (Fiat, Olivetti) effectively abandoned the Confindustria policy, and, taking a more flexible line, supported the policies of change and social reform which were linked to the entry of the Socialist Party into the centre-left coalition.

The second trade union objective—penetration of the work-place through the establishment of union branches—was, however, a failure. The extremely low level of unionisation explained the workers' lack of interest in an innovation which concerned union members. The unions themselves (especially those in the CISL) hesitated to give these bodies other than organisational functions. Nor, finally, did management have any interest in supporting bodies which did not really represent the workers, and were, in the last analysis, given only lukewarm support by the unions themselves.

However, the recession of 1964–6 gave the employers' front new strength, and returned the conflict to the national level, while at factory level the union climate appeared to be moving back to that of the fifties. Nor, at the political level, was it possible to reach any agreements which would bring about even those reforms which were admitted to be urgent.

THE RUPTURE OF THE TRADITIONAL SYSTEM AND THE STRENGTHENING OF THE TRADE UNIONS: 1968–72

Unlike those of 1960–3, the conflicts which began in 1968 with the upturn in the economy had extensive and long-term, although erratic, effects upon the system of industrial relations. Initially, the unions moved very cautiously, bearing in mind the memory of both recent and past defeats. Subsequently, however, they succeeded in using the mobilisation of the workers as a means for obtaining a more important and permanent role in the industrial relations system.

A new variable in the situation was a widespread though confused demand from the workers for participation in, and control of, their trade unions. Thus one principal result of the changes induced by the upheavals of this period, namely, the emergence of a new form of worker representation and trade union presence in the work-place, did not arise through the ability of the unions to extend their organisational structure inside the factory, but from their awareness of, and response to, demands emanating from the rank and file. At the same time the crisis within Confindustria deepened, and the 'co-operative' approach of Intersind came under severe strain. The state also came to play an increasing role in the resolution of industrial conflicts; the introduction of the 'workers' charter' (Statuto dei Lavoratori) in 1970 was, as we shall see, the most discussed, but not the only, example of this.

The Strengthening of the Trade Unions

THE EMERGENCE OF TRADE UNION REPRESENTATION AT FACTORY LEVEL

The development of new plant-level structures took place in stages, at each of which certain features of the previous situation were modified; the process may be seen as the elimination of alternatives.

(a) *The period from 1968 to the first half of 1969*: During – or sometimes after – many plant-level disputes, new and different forms of worker organisation and representation arose. These bodies were developed to make up for shortcomings in the organisation of the conflict, and to analyse and find alternatives to what were seen as unsatisfactory approaches. The need for better organisation was greatest where the unions were weak, or almost absent, in the work-place, and where mobilisation of the workers was most difficult. In such circumstances, work-group representatives were elected on an informal basis during the disputes to keep contact with the union leadership outside the plant, and with the *commissione interna*. Where, on the other hand, the unions or the *commissioni interne* were stronger, discussion and criticism were more developed, and the forms of organisation which resulted (action committees, unified rank-and-file committees (CUB)) had a distinctly political connotation.

In neither case, however, would it be possible to argue that the movement was 'spontaneous' in the sense of having originated among workers who had no previous political experience, either in the unions or parties, or in other political groupings. In the first case, where the greatest need was for basic organisation, individual industrial unions outside the factory promoted, albeit indirectly through their activists inside the plant, these new departures as a means of penetrating the factory. In the second case, where the basic concern was to challenge the political direction of industrial action, the initiative came from union and party activists in the PSIUP (the extreme left-wing Socialist Party) and even the PCI, or from the followers of the extreme left-wing groups, which in 1968–9 were strengthened by the growth of student militancy.

These organisms all developed, however, as effectively united bodies, superseding both inter-union rivalry and the distinction between union members and non-members within the working class. In fact their emergence marked the end of ideological warfare between the confederations, and also focussed attention on the question of trade union democracy, a matter which hitherto had been little discussed in Italy. There were rank-and-file demands that open meetings should have decision-making powers, instead of being used by the leadership as forums for the diffusion of information; other demands involved the right to participate in negotiations and in decisions about the forms and objectives of industrial action, and the right to approve prospective agreements.

Trade union responses to these challenges varied according to the organisational strength of the unions. Where they were strong, they were less willing to change the attitudes towards factory-level organisation which they had developed in the sixties. But where trade unionism was less well-entrenched, there was a greater receptiveness to the new demands. In these circumstances, plant-level agreements were concluded which granted the right of assembly at the work-place, with trade union participation, and established the so-called *delegati di cottimo, o di linea* (shop delegates dealing with issues concerning piece-work or the assembly-line). These *delegati* were not, however, at all the same as those who emerged during the most intense period of industrial conflict; they had the strictly technical task of supervising central aspects of working conditions (incentives, work-rates etc). For the unions this type of control, which the workers had never previously enjoyed, was in itself a substantial concession to obtain from management. But for those workers who were demanding participation and *direct* control over the work-place situation, it seemed an inadequate advance. In many cases, the disappointment engendered was very considerable—for example, at the Fiat works in the spring of 1969.[21]

(b) *The second half of 1969: the 'hot autumn'*. During the tense atmosphere which developed in mid-1969, plant-level conflicts spread rapidly. These often involved new groups of non-skilled workers with little previous experience of union activity. New and infectiously anti-authoritarian calls for direct control by the workers were made. In this atmosphere it was very difficult to identify with certainty the attitudes of the militant workers who led the mobilisation, and who often took on the label *delegati*. Were they the 'first nucleus of shop-floor power, or merely an element of democratisation and strengthening of the trade unions?' (Augusti, 1970: 245) This perhaps somewhat abstract question was hotly debated by the New Left. Some groups, such as Lotta Continua, saw the extension of shop delegates as inevitably strengthening the unions (and hence, in their eyes, as something to be fought against); others cherished the idea that it heralded the birth of workers' control, with the formation of a 'shop-stewards' movement' independent of the trade unions (Castellina, 1972).

This last suggestion may not have been historically impossible; it did not occur, however, because the individual unions most involved in the rank-and-file agitation (in particular the metal-workers' federations), managed to come up with proposals which allowed them to regain the initiative during the general mobilisation for the renewal of national agreements. The two main proposals, which were forwarded jointly by the unions, were extremely successful; they entailed firstly, consultation with the shop-floor workers over how some of the bargaining demands should be defined – an entirely new departure in the Italian system – and secondly, the promotion within the factory of committees of activists from individual shops to direct industrial action alongside the internal commissions.

The advantages which accrued to the unions as a result of their initiative were considerable. On the one hand, in those areas where their credibility appeared to have been compromised in plant-level disputes, the unions regained the confidence of the workers, and won the support of new activists. On the other hand, they were able to make widespread and direct contact with the rank-and-file in many plants which hitherto had not been touched by industrial action. The reassertion and extension of the trade union presence was also facilitated by the massive use of meetings *inside* the work-place – a practice which had not been used since the immediate post-war period. The unions included the right of assembly among their bargaining demands, and sought to end the management veto against allowing union officials inside the factory (officials were often carried through the factory gates by enthusiastic and militant strikers).

(c) *The period of experimentation (1970–1)*. With the conclusion of the national agreements, the main industrial unions obtained both the right of assembly and the recognition of a given number of union representatives within the work-place (rights which were soon extended to all productive sectors by the Statuto dei Lavoratori of May 1970). The unions thereby realised their longstanding ambition—dating back to 1960—of securing a presence within the factories.

However, the problem then arose of what role the *delegati* were to play. It immediately became clear that the union representatives—activists from the various unions, who were nominated by the unions themselves—were not the same thing as the *delegati*. This was not only because the number of union representatives stipulated in the agreements was much lower than the number of *delegati* who were elected during the 'hot autumn', but also because each represented different groups: whereas the *delegati* represented above all the work-group by which they were elected, the union representatives represented the union in its relations with management. Yet it proved impossible to simply eliminate the *delegati*, and to declare the *delegati* experiment closed might jeopardise a great deal of the rank-and-file support which the unions had built up, and risk an escalation of wild-cat strikes.

The unions were nevertheless concerned over the implications of continuing the experiment. The smaller unions (especially the UIL) were afraid of being under-represented, since in the informal elections of the *delegati* the CGIL emerged with increased strength. The CGIL itself was worried about the fluidity of a system which had little solid organisation, and which might yield to corporatist and sectional temptations and pursue the specific interests of restricted groups of workers, rather than the general interests of the class. On the other hand, the theoreticians of the trade union left were in favour of maintaining the *delegati*, as were branches of the unions themselves in those areas in which they were aiming at an immediate and complete reorganisation (the Labour Chamber in Turin, for example, or the CISL metalworkers' union, FIM). These groups saw the *delegati* as the means of constructing a new, united trade union system, built with the support of rank-and-file workers. The definition of the role of the *delegati* which found greatest favour was in fact that of a PCI left-wing theoretician, Garavani; they were to be 'the expression of the compact work-group; that is to say that they correspond to management organisation turned on its head' (Garavani, 1971: p. 21).

During 1970 and 1971 the strongest industrial unions finally decided to continue the experiment, and began to tackle the many immediate problems which arose from it.

Why did the unions decide to continue the *delegati* experiment? They did so partly because they were forced to by its popularity among the rank-and-file; partly because it helped to unify the trade union movement (see below); and partly because the increase in union membership in 1970 persuaded them that although in theory the existence of *delegati* who did not belong to the union was a threat, in practice it posed little problem. It also seems likely that the more dynamic industrial unions realised that, at a time when they were expanding their organisation, the only solution to the existence of activists among the rank-and-file was to bring them up inside the union, accepting them unconditionally as the grass roots structure of the 'new' trade unionism, and thus broadening the basis of support for union representatives in the work-place. In this way the possible development of an independent workers' control or shop-steward movement was conclusively prevented.

(d) *The establishment of the 'delegati' and the 'consigli': (1971–2).* In December 1970, the CGIL became the first of the three confederations to declare itself in favour of the new grass roots structure for the unions, based on the *delegati* and the *consigli* (factory councils, composed of all the *delegati* in a given plant). In 1971 the CISL unofficially followed suit. In March 1971 the three metal-workers' federations decided to eliminate the old structures, such as the internal commissions and the union branches, and to establish methods of election and functions for the new ones—the first of the individual industrial unions to do so. After 1971, this practice spread to other sectors, although it met with resistance in the field of public employment. In the agreement establishing the new CGIL-CISL-UIL federation in 1972 (see below), the adoption of these new structures was officially sanctioned.

Having adopted the *delegati* and the *consigli*, the unions then had to impose them on management. In most cases management had been forced to negotiate with the councils during the most intense periods of industrial unrest, and to acknowledge the obsolescence of the internal commissions. However, the employers were generally reluctant to accept a new bargaining organ inside their factories without first discussing its nature and its rights. This reluctance led some of the industrial unions (for example, those in the chemical sector in 1972) to demand that the councils should be formally recognised as the representative organs of the union in the work-place when new national agreements were to be negotiated. Other industrial unions, such as the metal workers, pursued a different line, preferring *de facto* to formal recognition, and thereby following the advice of the three confederations to be cautious in defining the powers of the new structures. This difference may be seen as reflecting the different bargaining powers and levels of unity enjoyed by the various industrial unions. Organisationally weaker and more divided, the chemical unions may have had more to gain from a formally negotiated agreement with the employers, than from a fluid situation in which a great deal depended upon the continuing ability of the union to make its weight felt. Even today, at a national level, work-place representation has still not been formally defined; recently, however, management has appeared more willing to accept the presence of the new structures, as they gradually become more stable and subject to union control, and are extended and consolidated within the work-place.

But who, or what, exactly are the *delegati* today? They originally developed during industrial conflicts as activists and representatives of their own individual and limited work-groups; they were then accepted by the unions as their representatives inside the work-place. As a result, they have not entirely lost a basic ambiguity arising from these dual sources of legitimacy. Since 1971, the unions have made great efforts to get representatives elected to the councils who are as sympathetic as possible to the interests of their organisation, and who are then willing to pursue its policies even when they do not entirely coincide with the immediate interests of their work mates in the shop or the more restricted work-group. Officially, the general methods of electing the *delegati* have not changed: they are elected by the work-group, without prior nomination; their mandate may be revoked by the group; and they have no obligation to join the union.[22] In fact, however, clarifications and modifications have gradually been added which have facilitated the election of activists more acceptable to the unions. It has also become permissible to co-opt on to the councils activists who have not been elected as *delegati*. Nevertheless, this development has not prevented the continued election of a certain number of delegati who are either linked to political groups outside the union, or who still owe their election not to union support, but to their concern for specific issues of importance to their immediate work-groups. Indeed, their presence can have serious consequences when they promote strikes in their particular shops against the will of the official union. However, the union authority over rank-and-file structures was reasserted through the collective organ which co-ordinated union activity in the plant – the council—rather than at the level of individual *delegati*. From 1971/2 onwards, once the period of most intense mobilisation had passed, organisational needs again came to the fore, and the necessity of a division of labour in the representative process arose. Since the number of council members in the large enterprises was quite high—on average there was one *delegato* for every 50–70 workers—the secretariats and the council executives were strengthened. The competence of older activists who were specialists in complex aspects of labour relations was again of value. Trade union power within the factory came to be exercised at many different levels, in sharp contrast with the stereotyped image, widespread in 1969, of direct representation based on the mandate of the work-group, with no intermediaries or specialists. Thanks to this process of organisational rationalisation, it also became possible to control those *delegati* who were not linked to the unions. In practice, the executive directed union policy in the factory and was empowered to conduct negotiations with management. Meanwhile the *delegati* themselves were restricted to two roles: as two-way channels of information between unions and workers, and as decentralised means of supervising problems in the work-place.

How much had really changed for the unions, when compared to the previous system based on the internal commissions? Taking over a system of generalised representation of the *whole* labour force in a given plant, and not just that of their own members, the unions acquired both the right to be present inside the factory and a means of contact with the rank-and-file which they had never previously enjoyed. The fact that this system of representation was based on individual shops (and, in the case of white-collar workers, offices) made it possible for the union to gain and disseminate information, and gave flexibility to its actions. It is true that certain questions remain concerning the degree of union control over the new structures, but in practice they appear today to have achieved considerable autonomy.

THE PROCESS OF UNION UNIFICATION

Efforts to reunite the trade union movement began in the early sixties, and the industrial conflict which broke out in 1968 gave them new life. The two organisational dimensions of the movement – on one side the industrial unions,[23] and on the other, the three peak organisations, or confederations, which link the various industrial unions together – were impelled towards reunification in rather different ways. The industrial unions were moved by the situation which developed at rank-and-file level, while the confederations were motivated by the general political situation.

(a) During 1968 and 1969 pressure for reunification arose from the workers. The emergence of a new generation of grassroots leaders who had not lived through the divisions of the early post-war era, and the real unity of action within the movement resulting from increased industrial conflict, helped to generate this pressure.

Initially, the running was made by the joint initiatives of certain industrial unions. These consisted of consultation of the work-force on bargaining demands, the organisation of joint mass demonstrations, and the joint election of worker representatives to organise industrial action during the renewal of national agreements. Some unions even proposed that agreements should extend beyond joint action into the sphere of organisational unity.

The confederations, however, were much more cautious, and were critical of some of the initiatives taken by individual industrial unions. Their main fear was that the links between industrial union and confederation might be weakened to the detriment of the latter.

(b) The confederations began to play a more active role in 1970. The first joint meetings of the executive councils of the three confederations took place in the second half of 1970 and the beginning of 1971. Joint documents dealing with the aims and features of the reformed trade union movement were drawn up, and a timetable was planned for the so-called 'organic unity' of the movement – the merger of the three existing confederations into a single united organisation. This acceleration of the unification of the confederations was probably linked with two aims: regaining the initiative over individual industrial unions, and presenting a united front in their negotiations with the Government over social reforms.

The change was, however, rather too sudden to be entirely credible. Indeed, it can be seen as a bid to nip dissent in the bud; in actual fact, inside the CISL and UIL, the groups most closely linked to the Christian Democratic, Social Democratic and Republican parties remained an obstacle to unity, calling for 'democratic' guarantees from the Communists.

(c) By 1971 it was already evident that reunification in the short term was out of the question. The centre parties had come out openly against it, and even on the left there was concern at the possibility that unification of the movement might take place at any cost, even that of 'de-politicisation'. To this was added a general deterioration of the economy and the political situation, and at the same time, the period of industrial unrest had passed its peak. As a result, the gap between the policies of the confederations and those of the individual unions, which in 1970 had seemed to be closing, was reopened.

At confederal level the stalemate was overcome by an agreement to create a Federation of CGIL-CISL-UIL, and this was realised in July 1972. The federal solution allowed the confederations to undertake common action in some areas – pressurising the government for social reforms, or for new economic policy – while guaranteeing that each confederation would maintain its existing organisational structure. This avoided problems of sharing out power in an integrated organisation, and effectively allowed each confederation to pursue an independent strategy, behind a facade of unity.

At the level of individual unions, progress towards unification varied enormously. It was greatest in industry – particularly among the metalworkers who were the first to establish a united federation comprising the three former unions. It was slowest in those areas where the unions were most closely aligned to the political parties, such as the public employment sector, where clientelism was still rife.

Unlike union penetration of the work-place, the reunification of the unions appears to have come to a halt – because greater resistance to the change was encountered at the political level.

THE REDEFINITION OF THE BARGAINING SYSTEM

As we have seen, the Italian structure of collective bargaining was relatively highly centralised, and efforts after 1962–3 to establish a system of plant-level bargaining met with great difficulty. As a result, the action of the workers after 1968, focussed as it was at the level of the individual plant if not at that of the even more restricted shop, represented a sudden and unforeseen change of direction. The bargaining process became decentralised, particularistic and fragmented. The centrifugal forces which were set in train in 1968–9, and again in 1970, were supported by local union organisations in an attempt to regain ground within the work-place which they had slowly lost over the previous twenty years. In the heady atmosphere of mass mobilisation, plant-level bargaining, which had formerly been considered as complementary to national bargaining, tended to be advanced as an alternative to it.

These developments had significant repercussions on collective bargaining in each industry at the central (i.e. national) level. During the 'hot autumn', negotiations at this level were used as a means of consolidating and generalising for the whole industry lessons which had been learnt in individual plant-level disputes. In a sense, therefore, the traditional process (by which bargaining objectives were set by the industrial unions) was reversed; plant level bargaining established the objectives, while the role of the external unions was changed to one of aggregating, selecting and generalising these rank-and-file demands for their activities at plant-level.

The weakness of the new system lay in the difficulty of controlling rank-and-file action. The discovery of bargaining strength can generate in the advanced industrial sectors powerful centrifugal forces capable of spreading rapidly. Once the unions have consolidated and strengthened their position inside the work-place and in the overall system of industrial relations, they no longer have any interest in fostering these tendencies among the rank-and-file. In addition, as plant-level bargaining comes to play the key role in the process, the importance of united action in support of demands advanced in national negotiations is considerably diminished. This did not occur in 1969, but it did in 1973, when there was a certain amount of disappointment among workers in the larger enterprises over the results of national bargaining, for they had already obtained in their plant negotiation conditions which were, on certain issues, a great deal better.

With the increase of direct union activity in the work-place, the role of the confederations in the bargaining process also changed. Between 1969 and 1971 their main efforts were transferred to negotiations with the Government on the introduction of those social reforms which centre-left governments had until then failed to introduce. This strategy of negotiating reforms directly with government can be seen as an effort by the confederations, faced with an increase in the importance and power of their component industrial unions, to find a new and independent sphere of activity (see page 133). What was new, and indeed something of an anomaly in the Italian tradition, was not that the confederations were adopting a *political* role, but that they were presenting their activities as a substitute, at least in part, for the traditional functions of the parties.

THE OVERALL INCREASE IN UNION STRENGTH

As a result of all the changes we have reviewed, the movement's organisation was strengthened to an unprecedented extent. This could be seen in three areas: the rise in membership; the extension of its organisational presence to smaller and medium-sized enterprises, and to geographical areas in which the unions had previously been weak; and the growth of unions linked to the three confederations, in sectors in which the so-called 'autonomous' unions were strongest. Between 1968 and 1974, union membership grew by over 50 per cent (50.2 per cent for the CGIL and 54.5 per cent for the CISL) (see Appendix I). And since, as we have seen, union membership in Italy does not bring any special privileges, this rise would indicate a high degree of satisfaction with union policy on the part of the workers.

Recent studies have, moreover, shown how the increase in membership has been accompanied by a decline in the importance of the ideological outlook of the union, since the increase has affected all the unions together (Reyneri, 1973). They have also shown that there is a tendency towards equalisation of the level of unionisation of the work-force. The unions are therefore gaining ground in areas where previously they were weakest – the non-industrialised regions and the smaller enterprises (Amoretti, 1974).

This is also borne out by the available evidence on the spread of union organisation at grass-roots level, which shows the development of an unprecedented network.[24] Such a growth emerges particularly clearly from the data relating to the metal-working sector, which had the strongest trade unions and which experienced an enormous spread of unionisation. At their peak in 1965, the internal commissions in this sector numbered some 1,023 and represented 552,148 workers. Before 1968 the maximum number of representatives on the commissions and of union activists had been about 12,220. In 1972, 4,291 factory councils were elected, and these contained some 42,886 *delegati*, representing in all 1,055,592 workers.[25] The number of enterprises in which some form of plant-level organisation of the work-force existed therefore appears to have increased almost four times, as does the number of activists upon whose support the unions could rely.

A final and very important indicator of increasing union strength was the expansion of those unions belonging to one of the confederations in the sector of public employment (Razzano and Cini, 1974: 90). In this sector CGIL membership rose by 15 per cent over the period 1968–73, that of the CISL by 8 per cent, and of the UIL by 18 per cent. At the same time the 'autonomous' unions in this sector lost ground. The most notable example of this was among the school-teachers; the CGIL increased its following here from 4,000 members in 1968 to 90,000 at the beginning of 1975.

Changes in the Employers' Organisations

The outbreak of industrial conflict in 1968/9 undoubtably found both the management of the enterprises concerned, and the employers' organisations in general, unprepared. In fact, this partly explained its success. All subsequent behaviour of the employers can be seen as an attempt to regain the initiative over an increasingly aggressive trade union movement.

In March 1970 the leadership of *Confindustria* changed hands. The new president sought to participate in the negotiations between the union confederations and the government on the question of social reforms, but he received a severe rebuff. Aware of their own new-found strength, the unions were in no mood to allow any interference which would alter the balance in their direct confrontation with the government. During 1970 and 1971, while the trade union offensive was at its peak, the employers were thrown on to the defensive. Meanwhile the employers' associations went through a profound crisis which involved not merely *Confindustria*, but also the employers' organisations in each industry and Intersind – the latter having, as we have seen, attempted to build a cautious understanding with the unions during the sixties.

As a result there was a hardening of employer attitudes which resulted in a campaign against the power of the unions, in which they were joined by certain elements of the government. It concentrated upon the alleged anarchy in the factories, upon the problem of absenteeism and on the low level of utilisation of capital equipment. In 1972 the president of Confindustria even accused the unions of 'subverting democratic institutions'. Within their enterprises the employers resorted to tough measures – lock-outs, sackings, attempted prosecutions, and even sometimes connivance at the incursions of Fascist mobs – measures which often had the effect of increasing the militancy of the workers. However, their most effective action was what has been called a slow-down in investment. A significant indication of the difficult situation in which the employers found themselves was their tendency, widespread in 1970–1, to negotiate directly inside their enterprises rather than through the employers' association. Management seems in fact to have been caught in the cross-fire between the union-organised mass mobilisation on one side, and the intransigence of employers' associations on the other.

The only new element was the so-called 'Pirelli Report', of February 1970. This influential document called for a reorganisation of Confindustria and a rationalisation of the services it offered to its members. It suggested a policy which would take account of the new-found power of the unions, while at the same time giving individual employers a greater say in the shaping of that policy.

It was, however, the recession of the second half of 1971 – helped by the decline in investment and precipitated by the dollar crisis – which, by raising the level of unemployment, gave the employers a chance to regain the upper hand. Between October 1971 and January 1972, a series of official meetings took place between the three union confederations and Confindustria. The unions, especially the CGIL, hastened to emphasise that these talks were simply to exchange views on the question of employment. But Confindustria had greater ambitions, and floated the idea of an agreement with the unions for a joint approach to the government on the twin problems of economic growth and social reforms. In exchange for assurances about the level of employment the unions would accept a framework agreement to regulate collective bargaining, a greater formalisation of the structures of worker representation in the factories, and a system of 'wage co-ordination'. Despite some wavering on the part of CISL and UIL, the unions rejected the offer. The CGIL evoked the corporate state in defining the proposal as a 'corporative co-administration' which would effectively sanction employer-control over the process of economic development. However, the Confindustria proposal was not entirely abandoned. It has consistently reappeared in the political debates of recent years as a suggestion for a 'social compact' (*patto sociale*) between labour and capital to defeat what are seen, in Ricardian terms, as the groups which live off parasitic rent extracted from the productive sector.

The formation in 1972 of the Federmeccanica, a federation of the employers' associations operating in the metal-working sector (in which national agreements were about to come up for renewal), marked the end of the defensive period for the employers. This new organisation, created inside Confindustria, was to deal with the unions at national level, and therefore had greatly increased powers compared with the existing sectoral employers' associations, whose functions were limited to technical tasks. Its creation was an implicit criticism of the policy of Confindustria towards the unions, and perhaps at the same time a recognition of the need to offset the increase in union power with a re-organisation and a more rational co-ordination of employer policies. What was most striking, was the much more aggressive way in which Federmeccanica entered the negotiations for the new agreement; for the first time an employers' association reacted to union demands with its own agreed set of proposals.

Changes in the Role of the State and the Statuto dei Lavoratori

In recent years the role of the state has changed from one of passive 'neutrality' to an ever greater involvement both through legislation and through its ability to act as an agent of mediation and conciliation.

Passed in 1970, the Act best known as the 'Workers' Charter' can be interpreted in two ways: either as a temporary deviation from the norm of an informal and unstructured system of industrial relations, or as the beginning of a new pattern. The latter seems more probable, especially if we consider that less than four years later the Charter was followed by a new framework for labour law, the precursor of a more general reform of the legal system. The idea of a workers' Bill of Rights goes back to the demands of the CGIL in the fifties for an act to protect the constitutional rights of the workers at the workplace (Cazzola, 1972). The Charter itself, however, was the direct result of the upheavals of 1968–9; the political climate of the period was decisive in ensuring its parliamentary approval, and in the final draft the Charter included many of those demands (such as the right of assembly in the workplace) which had been thrown up by mass mobilisation.

As a recent study has observed, opinions vary as to the significance of the Charter (Rossiti and Treu, 1974):

> On the one hand there is a view (held by large sections of the employers, the government and legal bodies) that the Charter, and 'abuses' in its application, may be subversive elements in both the political system and the economy. On the other hand there was harsh criticism from parts of the left, who, especially at the beginning, opposed the Charter on the grounds that it was aimed against the workers and at the limitation of industrial conflict, or in a hardly less subtle way argued that it would be most useful to the trade union bureaucracies to nip any potentially radical tendencies in the bud and bring disputes to a close as quickly as possible.

Nevertheless, although the Charter establishes principles for the regulation of both industrial disputes and trade union organisation (favouring in particular the confederations), it also does a great deal to protect and help the workers and the activists themselves, including those not belonging to a union. According to the study just quoted, the Charter could therefore have a dual effect: it could regulate conflict, while at the same time making it more radical.

The Charter has therefore been interpreted in various ways: but how has it been used in practice? It has, certainly, rapidly increased the number of *individual* workers who are prepared to resort to the law to obtain redress for their grievances. On the other hand, the unions themselves, particularly where a high level of unionisation of the work-force gives them a powerful position, have made little use of the Charter. In general this results from their traditional reluctance to resort to the law in labour disputes, which is seen as a tacit admission of weakness. In particular, the unions are often afraid to risk a negative outcome, which might prejudice any previously strong position held by them.

In recent years the state has also played an increasingly important part in labour disputes through direct intervention. Such mediation and conciliation as it engages in is still, however, carried out on a largely voluntary and unregulated basis. At the central level it is done through the Minister of Labour, while at local level it is done through the latter's field offices, the prefects, and, more recently, increasingly through the competent offices of the regional administration. A recent study (Veneziani, 1972) has highlighted the importance of the role of the specialised field offices of the Ministry of Labour, in comparison with that traditionally played by the prefecture. For the more important negotiations (national agreements etc.), the Minister of Labour himself is coming to play an increasingly important part. The same study also suggests that public intervention is today tending away from a purely 'neutral' position, towards a more positive role of putting forward proposed solutions, based on the constraints of economic planning. It might therefore be argued that public intervention has been aimed at finding a way of implementing planning in an indirect way, given the difficulties of obtaining the explicit consent of all the parties involved.

THE READJUSTMENT OF THE SYSTEM UNDER THE PRESSURE OF THE ECONOMIC CRISIS: 1973–5

During the upheavals of 1968–72 there was a substantial decentralisation of power in the union movement, but since 1972 there has been some reversal of this trend. On the one hand, the economic crisis created a need to co-ordinate union activity in order to maintain employment levels and to contain inflationary wage pressure. On the other hand, the unions themselves, having strengthened their position among the workers, would win considerable political credit if they could demonstrate an ability to restrain wage-demands in those sectors where the workers were contractually strong; and they would also gain support from workers in contractually weaker situations if they could channel the overall increase in union strength towards support for these lower-paid groups. Faced with calls from various quarters to regulate the industrial relations system by law, the unions responded with a policy of 'self-discipline' in collective bargaining and 'self-regulation' of strikes. In return for this restraint in the strategically powerful sectors, they demanded a change in economic policy and measures to support the weaker sections of the economy. In this way, exploiting their power and support within large-scale industry, the unions sought to bargain, with a certain amount of success, for help for agriculture, for the backward areas of the South, for certain sectors of public employment (education, for example), for the pensioners and so on.

Unlike the situation in the fifties, however, the centralisation of union policy today does not mean that action at plant level has been abandoned. This would be impossible in any case. New representative structures at this level, and a generally great awareness by the workers of their own power, have made shop-floor power and independence of action a permanent feature of the system of industrial relations. Union activity at factory level had therefore to continue, but in negotiations with the large-scale enterprises in particular, it dealt with a whole range of issues going well beyond the work-place: demands for investment in the South, demands that firms should make contributions to local government to improve social services, etc. (see page 134). Clearly, therefore, such a policy has transferred the impact of plant-level action, and of the demands which arise from it, into the more co-ordinated national bargaining system which is developing. Today, for example, meetings with the large monopolistic employers are held at national level, with the industrial unions being joined by the union *confederations*, as well as the factory councils of the various enterprises whose role has in fact been drastically reduced.

All in all, then, the unions today tend to see their role as that of promoting *planned* growth, which will permit a more equitable distribution of income and the elimination of areas of privilege. The great difficulty for the unions is that this role is an open-ended one, growing in size and complexity. It demands a virtually continuous bargaining process with government and employers (Confindustria has somewhat softened its former tough approach recently, especially after the change of leadership in the association in 1974). The unions have to find ways to ensure that demands which have been met concerning issues outside the work-place are subsequently implemented. How, for example, are they to make sure that a programme of planned investment is implemented? How can they ensure that funds appropriated from industry under union pressure actually find their way into the social services for which they were intended?

There is, finally, a problem of ensuring continued rank-and-file support for policies which do not necessarily bring immediately visible benefits. It was certainly no coincidence that in 1974, for the first time for many years, leaders of the union confederations were jeered at major public meetings. Moreover, the slowness with which the new *consigli di zona* (area committees) have taken root, is at least partly due to the difficulty of mobilising support for a policy which is centred on issues not immediately relevant to the work-place. (These committees were to have served as a means of co-ordinating at local level all union action outside the immediate work-place.)

Once more the unions are appealing to the 'political' consciousness of the workers. Yet the politicisation of the Italian trade union movement today does not seem to express an ideology so much as a more generic group solidarity.

NOTES

1. According to the calculations of Salvati, 1976, permanent employment (those who, in the week of recording the data, worked more than 32 hours) in manufacturing rose in the 1952–8 cycle by only 8 per cent, while in the subsequent cycle (1958–64) the increase was around 20 per cent. According to ISTAT, the 1959 figure for 'recorded' unemployment was still 1,135,000, against a total employed labour force of about 20 million.
2. The *commissioni interne* are discussed in detail on page 139.
3. In the metal-working sector, taking 1954 as the base 100, negotiated wages rose only to 110.7 in 1958 but to 192.4 in 1964 (Salvati, 1970a).
4. It has been calculated that outwork, which escapes being recorded in official statistics, amounts to one million workers in industry alone (Garavini, 1974); another estimate puts it at 1,720,000 (*Rinascita*, 1976, No. 9).
5. According to EEC statistics, recorded unemployment in Italy grew from 609,000 to 1,090,000 between 1971 and 1975.
6. This section has drawn on: Beccalli, 1971; Carabelli, 1972; Guidi *et al*, 1974; Halevi, 1972; Regini and Benetti, 1974; *Quaderni di Rassegna Sindacale*, 1972 and 1974.
7. The years in which national contracts for the metal-workers (the largest and most militant category of workers) were renewed by and large coincide with the peaks in the curve of strike hours for the whole of the economy.
8. This section has drawn on: Accornero, 1971; Accornero and Cardulli, 1974; Bolzani, 1974; Lelli, 1973; Regini and Reyneri, 1971; Marchese, 1974; Reyneri, 1974 and 1976; Turone, 1973.
9. This section has drawn on: Accornero and Cardulli, 1974; Bianchi, 1974; Orazi, 1975; Dina, 1970; Foa, 1975.
10. The jump from third to second grade was the critical one, since the third was traditionally the last of the semi-skilled grades, and the second the lower of the skilled grades.
11. It should be noted that demands involving union rights do not seem to have been concentrated in any particular phase of the period 1968–75. On the one hand, important new rights were obtained from the very beginning of the period. For weak trade unions enjoying limited recognition, as in Italy, demands relating to rights preceded and accompanied, as we have seen, demands relating to working conditions. On the other hand, when the employers' resistance hardened (especially after 1971) or when the economic crisis worsened (from 1974), there was a slow change of emphasis towards demands relating to social and economic policies, rather than to union rights. But the question of union prerogatives still retained great importance in this later period as a defence of positions already obtained, such as a refusal by the unions (at least formally) to limit the extension of plant-level bargaining, the independence of the factory councils, the right of public employees to take strike action, and the power to control the use and deployment of the labour force.
12. Particularly in pensions, and the so-called *unificazione del punto di contingenza*, i.e. the unification – for all workers – of the basic salary upon which cost of living increases are calculated and compensated for.
13. This involved a single grading scale, within which white-collar grades were interwoven with blue-collar ones. It was to be possible to work right up the scale; but while at the lowest levels it was possible to be upgraded on the basis of length of service, at all other levels it was based solely on skill level. Since, however, ordinary workers in highly mechanised plants possess no skills of the traditional type, firms were requested to create a 'new professionalism' through 'training programmes, job rotation, job enlargement and job enrichment' (as set down in 1972 in the demands for renegotiation of the metal-working national agreement). The proposal was thus linked to the new demands discussed on page 122, and involved the reduction of wage differentials.
14. The PCI, initially favourable, came to attack sharply (in 1971 through Berlinguer himself) the union movement's attempt to engage in a direct struggle for reforms; instead they put

forward their own organic 'reform policy', which was, they argued, the task of the political parties.

15. *Quaderni di Rassegna Sindacale* No. 51, Nov.–Dec., 1974, p. 220.
16. 93 per cent of net salary was guaranteed to all workers who were put on the so-called 'Cassa Integrazione Guadagni' (to all those who were made either partially or totally redundant – i.e. on a less than 40-hour week). The Cassa was renewable on a three-monthly basis.
17. In fact, there are practically no union bargaining platforms – even in enterprises with special problems – that have not been built around demands for certain types of investment and of social services. Moreover, during the renewal of labour contracts in the major industrial sectors in 1975, the unions demanded the right to participate in decisions concerning employment, investment and restructuring of industry.
18. In addition to works cited in the text, this section has drawn on the following: Accornero, 1973; Aglieta and Bianchi, 1970; Albanese, 1973; Bianchi and Frigo, 1971; Censi, De Pamphilis *et al.* 1973; Centro Studi CISL (ed), 1975; CGIL, 1971; Confindustria, 1973; De Masi and Garavini, 1972; FIM-CISL, 1971; Foa and Trentin 1962; Forbice and Chiaberge, 1975; Romagnoli, 1975; Salvarani and Bonifazi, 1973; Treu, 1971.
19. See Turone (1973: 262). It is to be noted that, as a result of intense rivalry between the unions, membership figures until the sixties were always inflated and hence unreliable.
20. In organisational terms, Italian unions (including the CISL and UIL, which conformed to the CGIL model) consist of two structures: 'vertical' structures of 'category' federations (organised on a national, provincial and zonal basis) which organise white- and blue-collar workers in a given productive sector (e.g. metal-working, chemicals, building) and to which is entrusted the task of protecting the specific interests of those categories, above all through the national contracts; and, on the other hand, the 'horizontal' structure of confederations which, at various levels, co-ordinate the action of the category unions and are responsible for activities which involve all workers, irrespective of category.
21. In June 1969 a leaflet distributed at Fiat criticised the plant agreement instituting assembly-line shop delegates: 'The shop delegate is the most aware member of the group in which he works, and he enjoys the confidence of his work-mates. He is neither proposed nor nominated by any organisation outside the factory . . . he is responsible only to the workers, and to no-one else. He must be capable of dealing with the factory authorities. . . . His job is not to transmit problems to the internal commission, but to deal with them himself, until they are resolved. Moreover, his role must not be limited to dealing with a given aspect of working conditions: shop delegates must be able to negotiate with the employer on all matters of consequence to the body of workers.' Quoted in *Classe*, No. 2 (Feb. 1970) p. 247.
22. There are, however, rumours of a possible decision by the three confederations to demand union membership as an essential prerequisite for election as a *delegato*, although such a decision would still appear to be unpopular if taken. In any case, the problem is more theoretical than real, since the great majority are already union members, and dissent from union policy does not necessarily correspond to non-membership.
23. *Translator's note*: The reader will recall (see above, note 20) that political divisions between the three main confederations also divided their constituent unions. Thus in each industry there were three industrial unions, linked respectively to the CGIL, CISL and UIL. Where, in this section, reference is made to *joint* action by the industrial unions, this refers to action jointly undertaken by the three unions operating in a given industry (e.g. FIOM, FIM and UILM in the metal-working sector) and not to action undertaken jointly between unions in *different* industries.
24. See *Quaderno di Rassegna Sindacale*, no. 51, Nov.–Dec. 1974, p. 192.
25. See *Esperienze e Orientamenti* (June 1973) p. 78.

LIST OF WORKS CITED

Accornero, A. (1971), 'Le lotte operaie degli anni '60', *Quaderni di Rassegna Sindacale*, Nos. 31, 32.

—— (1973), *Gili Anni '50 in Fabbrica* (Bari: De Donato).
—— and Cardulli (1974), 'Le lotte in Italia 1970–1975', *Quaderni di Rassegna Sindacale*, No. 5.
Aglieta, R., Bianchi, G. *et al.* (1970), *I Delegati Operai* (Rome: Coires).
Agosti, A. (1970), 'Documenti per una discussione sui delegati operai' *Classe*, No. 2.
Albanese L. *et al.* (1973), *I Consigli di Fabbrica* (Rome: Editori Riuniti).
Amoretti A. (1974), 'Risultati e problemi del tesseramento e del finanziamento al sindacato' *Quaderni di Rassegna Sindacale* No. 50.
Beccalli, B. (1971), 'Scioperi e organizzazione sindacale, Milano 1950–1970', *Rassegna Italiana di Sociologia*, No. 1.
Bianchi, G., Frigo, F. *et al.* (1971), *I Cub: Comitati Unitari di Base* (Rome: Coires).
Bianchi, S. (1974), 'Lo Sciopero a scacchiera', *Prima Communicazione* (Apr.–May).
Bolzani, P. (1974), 'La Massificazione del lavoro non manuale', *Classe*, No. 8, (Feb.).
Carabelli, G. (1972), 'Analisi del assenteisno e della conflittualità nella media e grande industria' (Milan, mimeo).
Castellina, L. (1970), 'Tesi sui delegati', *Il manifesto*, No. 1.
Cazzola, G. (1972), 'La CGIL e il diritto sindacale', *Quaderni di Rassegna Sindacale*, No. 46.
Censi, G., De Pamphilis *et al.* (1973), *Delegati e Consigli di Fabbrica in Italia* (Milan: F. Angeli).
Centro Studi CISL (ed.) (1975), *Sindacato e Sistema Democratico* (Bologna: CISL).
CGIL (1971), *Strutture Unitarie sui Luaghi di Lavoro* (Rome: CGIL).
Confindustria (1973), *Le Rappresentanze dei Lavoratori in Fabbrica* (Rome: Confindustria).
D'Agostini, F. (1974), *La Condizione Operaia e i Consigli di Fabbrica* (Rome).
D'Antonio, M. (1973), *Sviluppo e Crisi del Capitalismo Italiano, 1951–1972* (Bari: De Donato).
De Masi, G., Garavini, S. *et al.* (1972), *I Consigli Operai* (Rome: Samonà e Savelli).
Dina A. (1970), 'Un esperienza di movimento politico di massa: le lotte interne alla Fiat', *Classe*, No. 2 (Feb.).
FIM-CISL (1971), 'Sull organizzazione', *Quaderni FIM-CISL*, No. 3.
Foa, V. (1975), *Sindacati e Lotte Operaie, 1943–1973* (Turin: Loescher).
Foa, V. and Trentin, B. (1962), 'La CGIL di fronte alle transformazioni tecnologiche dell'industria italiana', in Momigliano, F. (ed.), *Lavoratori e Sindacati di Fronte alle Trasformazioni del Processo Produttivo* (Milan: Feltrinelli).
Forbice, A. and Chiaberge, R. (1975), *Il Sindacato dei Consigli* (Verona: Bertari).
Frey, L. (ed.) (1975), *Lavoro a Domicilio e Decentramento dell'Attività Produttiva* (Milan: F. Angeli).
Fuà, G. (ed.) (1974), *Lo Sviluppo Economico in Italia*, Vol. II (Milan: F. Angeli).
—— (1973), 'Cicli e tendenze di fondo dell' economia italiana nell' ultimo ventennio', *Rassegna Economica*, No. 5.
Garavini, A. *et al* (1969), *Lo Sviluppo di un'Economia Aperta* (Naples: Edizioni Scientifiche Italiane).
—— (ed.) (1972), *L'Economia Italiana, 1945–1970* (Bologna: Il Mulino).
Garavini, S. (1969), 'Strutture dell' Autonomia Operai sul Luogo di Lavoro' *Quaderni di Rassegna Sindacale*, No. 24.
—— (1974), *crisi Economica e Ristrutturazione Industriale* (Rome: Editori Riunti).
Giambarba, E. (1972), 'La contrattazione del dapoguerra a oggi: il livello interconfederale', *Quaderni di Rassegna Sindacale*, No. 35.

Guidi, E. *et al.* (1974), *Movimento Sindacale e Contrattazione Collettiva 1945–1973* (Milan: F. Angeli).

Halevi, J. (1972), 'Evoluzione ed effetti degli scioperi negli ultimi vent anni' *Quaderni di Rassegna Sindacale*, No. 38.

Lelli, M. (1973), *Ternici Lotta di Classe* (Bari: De Donato).

Leon, P. and Marocchi, M. (eds) (1973), *Sviluppo Economico Italiano e Forza Lavoro* (Padua: Marsilio).

Marchese, C. (1974), 'Le strategie rivendicative nel pubblico impiego', *Quaderni di Rassegna Sindacale*, Nos. 47 and 48.

Orazi, A. M. (1975), 'Le lotte per l'Autoriduzion', *Fabbrica e Stato* (June-July).

Paci, M. (1973), *Mercato de Lavoro e Classi Sociali in Italia* (Bologna: le Mulino).

Pizzorno A. (1970), 'I sindacati nel sistema politico italiano': *Rivista Trimestrale di Diritto Pubblico*.

—— (ed.) (1974–7), *Lotte Operaie e Sindacato in Italia, 1968–1972*, six volumes (Bologna: Il Mulino).

'Rapporto Pirelli' (1970), in *Mondo Economico*, No. 8.

Razzano, R. and Cini, D. (1974), 'L'organizzazione sindacale nel pubblico impiego', *Quaderni di Rassegna Sindacale*, Nos. 47–8.

Regini, M. (1974), *La Candy*, Vol. II in Pizzorno (ed.), *supra*.

—— and Benetti (1974), I vincalo posti dalla forza lavoro occupata alla sua utilizzazione nell'azionda. (Ancona: mimeo).

—— and Reyneri, E. (1971), *Lotte Operaie e Organizzazione del Lavoro* (Padua: Marsilio).

Reyneri, E. (1973), 'I livelli di sindacalizzazione della for a lavoro in Italia', *Rassegna Italiana di Sociologia*, No. 3.

—— (1974), 'Origini del nuovo ciclo di lotte', in Accornero, A. (ed.), 1974: *Problemi del movimento sindacale in Italia, 1943–1973* (Milan: Annali della Fondazione Feltrinelli, Vol. XVI).

—— (1976), 'L'inizio della mobilitazione operaia: protagonisti, aspetti nouvi e ruolo del sindacato', in AA. VV., *Lotte Operaie e Sindacato: il Ciclo 1968–1972 in Italia* (Bologna: Il Mulino).

Rieser, V. (1969), 'Alcune note su caratterie e propettive delle lotte operaie alla Fiat' *Vento dell 'Est*, Nos. 15–16 (Dec.).

Romagnoli, G. *et al.* (1975), *La Democrazia nel Sindacato* (Milan: Mazzotta).

Rossiti, F. and Treu, T. (1974), 'L'applicazione dello Statuto dei Lavoratori', *Sociologia del Diritto*, No. 2.

Salvarani, G. and Bonifazi, A. (1973), *Le Nuove Strutture del Sindacato* (Milan: F. Angeli).

Salvati, M. (1970a), 'Slittamento salariale e sindacato, con particolare riferimento all industria metalmeccanica, 1954–69', *Rassegna Economica*, No. 6.

—— (1970b), *Sviluppo Economico, Domanda di Lavoro e Struttura dell'Occupazione* (Bologna: Il Mulino).

—— (1974), *Lotta di Classe e Organizzazione Operaie* (Milan: Mazzotta).

—— (1975), *Il Sistema Economico Italiano: Analisi di Una Crisi.* (Bologna: Il Mulino).

Treu, T. (1971), *Sindacato e Rappresentanze Aziendali* (Bologna: Il Mulino).

Turone, S. (1973), *Storia del Sindacato in Italia: 1943–1969* (Bari: Laterza).

Veneziani, B. (1972), *La Mediazione del Pubblici Potei nei Conflitti Collettivi di Lavoro* (Bologna: Il Mulino).

5 *From Corporatism to Polarisation: Elements of the Development of Dutch Industrial Relations*

TINIE AKKERMANS
and PETER GROOTINGS

I INTRODUCTION

One of the most important functional requirements of capitalist industrial relations is the incorporation of the main working-class organisations – the trade unions – in order to prevent the outbreak of wide conflicts which would threaten stability. This process has developed very successfully in the Netherlands. Post-war union leaders have seen themselves as sharing responsibility for the effective functioning of the system, though this should not be seen as an automatic and one-directional process. A number of conditions needs to be fulfilled if incorporation is to take place:

(a) incorporation of the work-force: in the early post-war years there was fear of unemployment and poverty but thereafter the growth of the welfare state provided a new legitimacy;
(b) ideological integration of the union movement: the 'economism' of trade unionism, which separated it from the wider labour movement, was indicated by the cultural *embourgeoisement* of the unions and by their separation from politics;
(c) control over the membership: this was secured by centralisation and bureaucratisation within individual unions and the federations;
(d) control over workers in general: this was secured by the monopolisation of representation by the so-called 'responsible' unions.

A final functional condition in the Netherlands is the organisational and ideological division of the union movement.

The incorporation of Dutch unions has probably distinguished itself from similar developments abroad by its rigidity, characterised by the corporatist pattern of industrial relations (tr. Hoeven, 1972: p. 17): the institutionalised and more or less voluntary co-operation of the major class organisations, with the state wielding important, and eventually decisive, influence as a third party. It is supported by a common ideology which assumes a basic mutuality of interests—in other words, a rejection of class struggle, and even of a struggle over wages (Kleerekoper, 1971: p. 156).

However, this period has now ended, and changes have taken place in both the ideology and the policy of the recognised unions. Co-operation has been more or less replaced by negotiations involving conflict with both employers and the state, while the latter has changed its role from that of a mediator to being a party to negotiations. Maybe its influence has not diminished, but it has acquired a different quality.

Before discussing this process we clarify the methods we have used. We have not provided a politico-economic analysis of relations between labour, capital and the state, but rather a sociological analysis of the ways in which relations between categories and collectivities have developed, though our broadest frame of references is the Dutch class structure. In Section 4 our study of labour conflicts is largely restricted to the actions of the workers; strictly speaking one should consider conflict as a relationship rather than as the actions of one party, and we have tried to place these actions in their wider context. It is important to point out that, although we speak of 'workers' actions', in fact the workers rarely actively pursue an autonomous strategy and ideology, but react to the actions of employers and the state.

Our approach is justified by the available studies and sources. There is no tradition of sociological research on the problems of the Dutch labour movement (Teulings, 1973 (b): p. 3), and there are few analyses which cover long periods of time and relate events to socio-economic and political developments (the exceptions are Albeda, 1971; and Teulings and Leijnse, 1974). Strike statistics published by the CBS cannot be regarded as adequate, nor is their classification scheme very useful for analysis (Cornelissen, 1970). We have had to resort to press reports for much of our material, with the attendant problems of the arbitrary nature of the coverage and biased reporting (Teulings and Leijnse, 1970; Smolders, 1973; Pauli, 1970).

2 THE DEVELOPMENT OF THE INDUSTRIAL RELATIONS SYSTEM IN ITS SOCIO-ECONOMIC CONTEXT

CORPORATISM

The basis for extensive co-operation in industrial relations had been laid before World War II (Teulings, 1973 (a): p. 242; Kleerekoper, 1971: p. 69; Windmuller, 1969: pp. 83–6), and the final forms were worked out during the war by elites of employers, unions and the state (Windmuller, 1969: pp. 103–8). Associated with this was the transformation of the social-democratic SDAP into the progressive-democratic PvdA in 1946, and of the social-democratic NVV into a general union federation. In the early years the structure created by these developments existed alongside another labour movement, based on workers' class unity and led in part by the Communists: the EVC. The development of the corporatist structure involved the defeat of this movement.

The structural pivot of the system became the centralisation of consultation in the Stichting van de Arbeid (a bipartite consultative body representing employers organisations and the three union federations, which was established in 1945), and in the Sociaal Economische Raad (the SER, an advisory council for the government in which independent 'crown members' sit alongside union and employer representatives, which was established in 1950). The SER was the central organ of the PBO (Industrial Organisation under Public Law), which provided for the creation of both industrial (horizontal) and product (vertical) organisations (*schappen*) in which 'all those who are working in a certain industry or group of firms, which are in one way or another related to each other, are organised and co-operate' (*Wat is PBO?* p.5). Several aspects of bargaining were subject to legal regulation by the Buitengewoon Besluit Arbeidsverhoudingen (Extraordinary Decree on Labour Relations, BBA) of October 1945, which gave the authority to approve, modify or reject all collective agreements to the College van Rijksbemiddelaars (College of National Mediators). This body also had the power to grant and to refuse extension of the provisions made with the recognised unions to other groups. Recognised unions were accepted by the state and employers as representing all Dutch workers, and were therefore given seats in all organs of co-operation, in exchange for which they gave up all claims to organise at plant level. The employee representation councils (*kernen*) which had existed before the war and which, in a number of cases, seemed to develop into effective and autonomous plant organisations of workers (especially in the building and metal industries), had to disappear. They were replaced by legally established works councils (Works Council Act, 1950) of which the employer was chairman and which served a purely consultative purpose based on an ideology of co-operation.

This institutionalised structure of relations developed in the period of the post-war boom and the Cold War. After the first five years there was no organised opposition to it from within the labour movement.

THE TRADE UNION MOVEMENT

Four organisational blocks are usually distinguished within the post-war union movement:

(a) the Nederlands Verbond van Vakverenigingen (NVV), founded in 1906 as a socialist, centrally organised counter to syndicalist and anarchist organisations. Since the Second World War it has ceased to be distinctively socialist.

(b) the Christelijk Nationaal Vakverbond (CNV), founded in 1909 as a Protestant reaction to socialist and other organisations. It still rejects concepts

of class antagonism and favours consultations between the 'social partners'.
(c) the Nederlandse Katholieke Vakverbond (NKV) was founded as the Katholieke Arbeidersbeweging (KAB) and changed its name in 1964. Its starting point was Catholic social doctrine and the Papal encyclicals *Rerum Novarum* and *Quadragesimo Anno*.
(d) These three federations with their affiliated unions form the 'recognised union movement'. The fourth block is a residual category mainly comprising those unions which have not affiliated to the three federations. Most of these are white-collar groups (the category unions), but they also include radical groups and semi-permanent action committees.

The degree of unionisation rose from 30 per cent in 1947 to 40 per cent in the 1960s, and now stands at 38 per cent. The NVV has around 40 per cent of all organised workers, its membership having increased considerably of late. The NKV has 24 per cent and the CNV 14 per cent, and both are declining. The independent groups have about 22 per cent and are increasing, partly because of the growth of the organisations themselves but also because some unions have left the main federations. Over the years the unions have failed to keep pace with the growth of employment in the tertiary sector, while the main federations have also failed to attract the growing numbers of white-collar workers, who are more likely to join category unions.

Salaried union leaders are not elected by the members but appointed by the union staff and executive (Windmuller, 1969: pp. 210–7). This has certain consequences: the existing group of officials can set the style of leadership; the leadership develops a collective outlook; union officials tend to exchange places with managers of other institutions (parliament, government, broadcasting, scientific institutions); and leaders' policies can be implemented with little difficulty.

The Dutch union movement has been highly centralised since the beginning of this century, a tendency which has been strengthened by the increasing complexity of industrial relations, which has enabled union leaders to emphasise their own responsibility within it. As a result, the leadership and union members are estranged from one another to a considerable extent; it is hardly possible to speak of a 'rank-and-file', since union members are more like the clients of an organisation which is offering a service. Combined with the weakness of the unions at plant level this leads to a high level of membership turnover (*ibid*: p. 200). The unions have tried to tackle this by such devices as compulsory union membership (limited to the printing industry only), repayment of union subscriptions by employers to the members (in the cigar industry) (*ibid*: pp. 194–200), or payment by the employers of a premium per member to the unions to finance their general work. In 1969 and 1970 there were a few strikes in the metal industry to secure this last demand. In the pre-war years unions could attract members through unemployment benefit, but this is now dealt with by the state, and the unions have therefore developed a range of services to members, such as claiming back pay, legal advice, provision of health care and other welfare facilities. These have been an important element in membership recruitment in recent years (*ibid*: p. 206; van de Vall, 1967). Finally, the recognised unions have held to their monopoly of legal and national recognition in order to maintain their position among the workers.

THE EMPLOYERS

Employers are also organised into Catholic, Protestant and general (i.e. 'liberal')groupings (Terpstra, 1973). They operate in the various sectors of industry and on the national level are joined in organisations for industry, agriculture and trade. The collective central employers organisations co-operate on matters of social policy, and in 1969 the Protestant and Catholic national federations amalgamated to form the Nederlandse Christelijke Werkgeversverbond (NCW). Much larger than this is the non-confessional Verbond van Nederlandse Ondernemingen (VNO).

The paternalistic effect on employer/worker relations of there being no union presence in the plant, to which reference has already been made, was reinforced by the structure of Dutch industry up until the late 1960s. In 1963 88 per cent of all firms employed fewer than ten persons, while only two per cent employed more than fifty. On the other hand, 55 per cent of the total labour force was employed by this two per cent. In 1971 70 per cent of firms still employed less than ten persons and only 8.8 per cent employed more than fifty. Given that many companies, especially in manufacturing, were still family concerns, it is easy to understand Windmuller's description of the mentality of the main employers as being 'the business world's counterpart of the "regents' mentality", which still accounts for the notion prevalent among some high government officials, that authority carries its own legitimacy within it' (Windmuller, 1969: p. 239).

On the other hand, the Netherlands has been the headquarters of a number of very large multi-national firms like Unilever, Philips or Shell. These were able to develop an autonomous personnel policy which for a long time was able to compete with the unions.

THE STATE

Wages Policy 1945–68

For over twenty years after the Second World War there was a highly centralised wages policy. All collective agreements[1] were tested against national norms fixed by the authorities after consultation with the Stichting van de Arbeid. The policy was initially introduced as an instrument of post-war reconstruction, but was maintained afterwards. It was supported by the unions because of their anxiety over the level of employment (Terpstra, 1973: p. 2).

Over the years increasing flexibility had to be introduced into the initially very tight controls because severe labour shortages developed, giving rise to a form of wage drift known as 'black wages'. In 1964 there was a deliberate loosening of controls to make possible the 'whitewashing of black wages'

(Windmuller, 1969: p. 368), but this went further, resulting in a major wage explosion. Thus it was a combination of deliberate policy by employers and the nature of the labour market, rather than actions by the recognised unions, which challenged central attempts at wage control.

By the end of 1966 increasing unemployment enabled the central authorities to regain control. Because of growing tensions between the centre and the associated organisations, control of the policy was removed from the Stichting van de Arbeid and replaced, for the last time, with the College van Rijksbemiddelaars.

Strike Legislation[2]

Since the introduction of the Extraordinary Decree on Labour Relations, strikes have increasingly been judged illegal by the courts, leading to the virtual loss of the right to strike. Encouraged by both the employers and the recognised unions, the government has worked on a Bill since 1958 which would regularise the position, recognising the legality of strikes but imposing a range of conditions, such as the need not to break the law, violate c.a.o. agreements or existing norms of relations between employers and unions and the norm of 'carefulness', or to breach the principle of proportion between goals and means. Moreover, the right to strike is limited to those unions which are admitted to central bargaining and to strikes over the negotiation of c.a.o.s. Since 1972 unions and employers have become less sympathetic to the Bill, and it has been put on ice, though it is still in effect legally. In 1974, when the Government and the Stichting van de Arbeid discussed strike legislation again, the unions said they wanted total withdrawal of the Bill.

STRIKES IN POST-WAR YEARS

Strike Activity in the 1950s and 1960s

Strikes have been of little importance in the Netherlands—a conclusion which can clearly be drawn from figure 5.1. Since 1950 the number of strike days exceeded 100,000 in 1955, 1956 and 1960 only. The strike pattern of the first twenty years after the war differs in three ways from that of the pre-war years. Firstly, the absolute number of conflicts was much reduced (van de Vall, 1967: pp. 116–18); secondly, most of the strikes which occurred were unofficial, the number of these being in fact higher than in the pre-war period; and thirdly, each strike was concentrated in a small number of firms (Lammers, 1965). Although the indicator used (the number of strikes divided by the number of enterprises involved) is crude, the trend away from broad strikes within branches of industry towards strikes in single firms seems clear. As can be readily concluded from preceding sections, the recognised unions rarely organised strikes, sometimes appeared as strike breakers, and were indeed often the object of the strike.

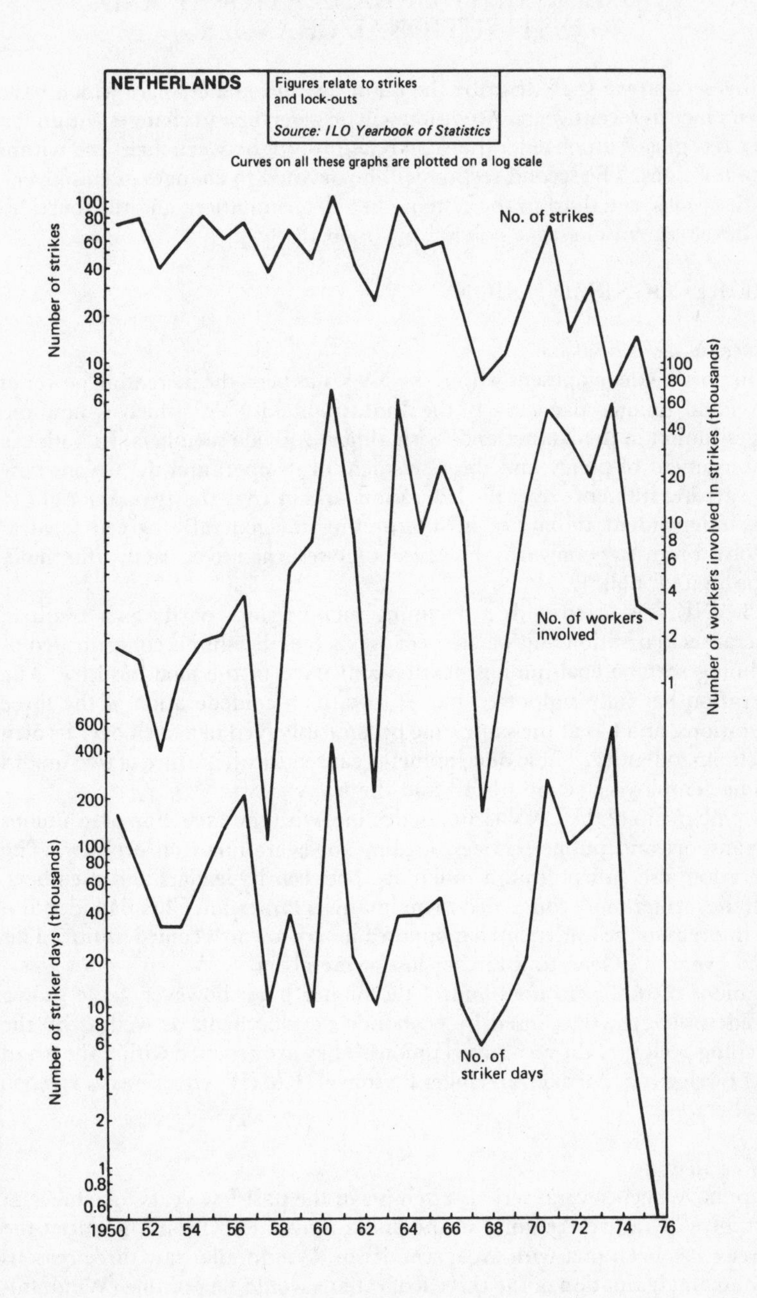

FIGURE 5.1: Industrial conflict in the Netherlands, 1950–75 (log scales)

3 SOME RECENT ORGANISATIONAL AND INSTITUTIONAL CHANGES

In this section we shall describe the main institutional changes which have taken place in recent years. Attention will be given first to changes within the three recognised union federations, in relationships between them and within certain unions. The second section will be devoted to changes in employers' organisations; the third to the system of co-determination; and the fourth to the development of wages policy from 1968 to 1974.

THE RECOGNISED UNIONS

Changes in the Federations

An important development within the NVV has been the increasing power of individual unions, particularly the Industriebond-NVV which is now the biggest union in the Netherlands with almost 200,000 members. In both the establishment of policy and the assessment of its operation the unions now have greater influence over the federation, and in 1972 they won the right to take independent initiatives in interpreting the federally agreed Central Accord. From 1973 onwards, however, they returned to a strictly 'internally co-ordinated' policy.

The NKV is faced with a declining membership, partly as a result of general secularisation and partly because its membership is concentrated in declining sectors: coal-mining, textiles and parts of the food industry. The federation has fully supported moves towards a confederation of the three federations, and has at the same time become involved in a crisis over its own continuing identity. These developments caused the departure of two unions of office employees (Unie BLHP and the BVA).

Membership of the CNV is also in decline, with the exception of its unions in transport and public services, leading to severe financial problems.The federation also suffers from a difference between its leaders and members, with the former more concerned to maintain its Protestant Christian identity. For this reason the leadership has opposed moves towards confederation. This could eventually lead to a further loss of members.

Unions of staff personnel and of the higher paid, however, have shown considerable growth, caused by economic developments as well as by the 'levelling policy' of the recognised unions. They are grouped within the Raad van Overleg voor Mediaal en Hoger Personeel (RMHP) covering ca. 130,000 members.

Confederation

There have been several serious attempts in the past few years to achieve at least formally a greater unity in the union movement. From the outset the exercise has been met with great scepticism. Windmuller saw three reasons why no amalgamation of the three federations would be possible (Windmuller, 1969: pp. 136–7): pluralism constitutes such an integral part of Dutch society; formal doctrinal differences are unbridgeable, especially for the CNV; while at the same time pluralism never really caused any difficulties in day-to-day inter-federation relations (for example, co-operation continued informally after the mandate of the Catholic bishops in 1954 forbidding association with socialist organisations).

Why then has there been such a move for greater unity in recent years? At least three explanations can be put forward: firstly, maintenance of the divisions was becoming financially unwise; secondly, the tendency to reject formal groupings on religious or other lines has developed strongly, especially among Catholics; thirdly, there is pressure from the membership for greater unity.

Some forms of institutional co-operation between the three federations have existed for a large part of the post-war period. In 1958 the Raad van Overleg (Consultation Board) was founded by them to co-ordinate some aspects of policy. From 1963 onwards, the NVV and KAB started to publish collective programmes of action, and in 1967 the CNV joined this for the first time. Since 1968 the NKV has taken repeated initiatives to encourage closer co-operation, and in early 1976 the NKV and NVV finally formed a confederation: the Federatie Nederlande Vakbeweging (FNV). At the same time, a number of developments have taken place which have led to greater co-operation among individual unions across the two federations.

It seems that, instead of a greater unity within an ideologically standardised union movement (one of the original aims), the development of the confederation has ultimately shown exactly the opposite: greater organisational and ideological disunity. We now have two large blocks, FNV on the one side and CNV and RMHP seeking closer relations to each other on the other side.

Plant Work

The most important development of recent years within the recognised union movement has been what is generally known as 'plant work'. It was started in 1962 by the then ANBM (NVV metal-workers' union), one of the forerunners of the present Industriebond-NVV, mainly to create an organisational structure at plant level. Research by this union into the problem of membership turnover had demonstrated the gulf which had opened up between members, leaders and the apparatus itself (Buiter *et al*, 1962 and 1963). This was caused, *inter alia*, by the extremely centralist policy, which was itself failing as indicated by the growth of unofficial strikes and organisations. The union reaction was to add a plant-level union structure to the local organisational body. The members within a plant formed a 'plant (member) group', the chairman of which (initially appointed by union leaders, but later chosen by the members) was the 'plant steward', who had the task of maintaining direct contact with the union. A new paid function was also created, that of the plant group trainer, who had the job of advising plant groups on their development and functioning. Further, the scope of the union's policy was extended to the personnel policy of the enterprise.

The plant work started in four firms in 1964. By 1970, before the Rotterdam dock strikes, it had spread to 125 firms in the metal industry (covering 10–15 per cent of workers in the industry). Since then it has grown steadily. By 1971 it covered 207 plants (50 per cent of all workers in the industry); and by 1973 there were 500 plant-member groups, mainly still in metals but by now also in chemicals and textiles as well (Poppe, 1971). The metal unions of the NKV and CNV had started plant work in 1966.

Since the early 1970s this new structure, which had at first been an instrument for communication and the more effective promotion of interests, has undergone ideological change. It is increasingly presented as 'a democratisation movement of enterprise and union' (van Beekfeld, 1974), and it has been given more importance in the general strategy of the industrial unions of NVV and NKV: firstly in the c.a.o. strikes, which presupposed a membership that was to be mobilised quickly (Leijnse, 1973), and then as part of the movement away from existing labour-management relations at enterprise level which has developed in these unions. In this connection it might be expected that problems would arise over the relationship between plant-work and works councils (see below). The former potentially breaks through the framework of participation and aims at a form of workers' control; those advocating it have in mind developments in workers' self-management elsewhere, especially in Yugoslavia. Meanwhile other unions have begun to take up plant work – for example in construction and the civil service – and its eventual development remains unclear and highly ambiguous.

CO-DETERMINATION IN THE ENTERPRISE: FORMAL CHANGES AT FACTORY LEVEL

Although participation by employees in company management was discussed before the Second World War, its realisation is a post-war development. A series of complex legislation has been introduced, forming part of the legalistic and centralised overall industrial relations system, and dealing with participation at the level of sectors of industry and at the national level (the PBO) as well as that of the enterprise; but in this section we deal with the latter only.

Works Council

Works councils are legally established consultative bodies in which employee representatives sit under the chairmanship of the employer; the unions are not involved.

In 1971 a new Works Council Act was introduced. Although it was claimed that it met objections that existing works councils did not provide for genuine participation, the unions were not satisfied because they feared competition from the works councils. In general a company's works council can make known all its views about the firm and make proposals (article 23). Unless 'weighty interests' oppose this, the council has an opportunity to advise on central general policy decisions (article 25). It is consulted on certain decisions in the 'social' field (that is, in connection with incentive rates and other kinds of payments), unless these issues are regulated by the c.a.o. Finally, the employer needs its approval on certain matters (working rules, firm saving schemes etc), and it is involved in some areas of co-management (welfare institutions, job consultation, supervision of compliance with measures on working conditions and safety). The works council is still chaired by the employer.

In October 1973 the Minister of Social Affairs again consulted the SER on works councils – the usual first step in the preparation of legislation. In recent years there have been controversies over their operation.[3] Some stress their value as co-operative bodies, while others regard them as an instrument in the hands of management and would like to see them replaced by personnel councils on which workers alone would be represented and which would have the task of promoting employee interests. The first view is held by the CNV, the second more and more by NVVand NKV. Traditionally the unions have had little influence at plant level and employee representation has been carried on by the works councils (Windmuller, 1969: pp. 399–400). Since under the Act of 1971 the elected members of the council will be able to meet without the employer chairman during working hours, it has been claimed that the function of authentic representation of employee interests which was carried out by the earlier *kernen* has returned (Bos, 1972); but this is an exaggeration in our opinion.

WAGES POLICY, 1968–75

Since 1968 the system of wage determination has been relatively free from control, although new attempts have been made to return to central controls. The first attempt (the Roolvink Wage Act of 1969–70) failed, while the second (the Enabling Act of 1973) succeeded for a year.

In November 1967 the Stichting van de Arbeid advised that wage vetting should be abandoned; wages should be fixed through free collective bargaining, though the government could continue to intervene afterwards in the interests of the economy as a whole. This advice was accepted. Terpstra has suggested the following causes of this liberalisation after over twenty years of control: increasing economic differentiation; increasing difficulty in securing consensus over what constituted the general interest; the unwillingness of the unions to accept that wages alone, and not prices, should be used as an instrument of economic policy; the need to bring wage structure and determination into line with the rest of Europe. He also argues that this liberalisation increases the scope for conflict (Terpstra, 1973: p. 3).

However, the degree of centralisation remains high. Only in 1968 did the SER not give precise indications of the degree of allowable wage increases in its bi-annual reports. As early as 1969 the acceleration of inflation (caused partly by the introduction of Value Added Tax) and increasing public expenditure caused a renewal of centralisation. The SER imposed a maximum of 5 per cent for wage increases, though later it also formulated political conditions for the establishment of a national wage agreement: the Government should co-operate by, for example, not increasing VAT any further (de Jong, 1974).

On the other hand, there was a distinct evolution between 1967 and 1969 in that direct intervention by the Government in individual negotiations had become unacceptable to the unions. The Government could act through general measures alone. In 1969 it introduced the *Loonwet* (Act on Wage Formation), which would enable it *inter alia* to annul those parts of a c.a.o. which, in the opinion of the Minister of Social Affairs, were contrary to the national interest (Clause 8). The Bill was passed by Parliament only when the Government threatened to resign otherwise, and the NVV and NKV withdrew from the SER and the Stichting van de Arbeid, announcing that they would not return until Clause 8 had been set aside. In October the SER reached agreement on a number of conditions to be put to the Government for the future of wages policy; ministers then declared that they would no longer make use of Clause 8, and the NVV and NKV returned to the organs of consultation and co-operation. Some centralisation continued, in that the Stichting directly consulted the Government over acceptable wage increases in the 'Conversation of Leidschendam'. The recognised unions were still prepared to follow a policy of moderation, provided it was on a voluntary basis. However, these talks did not end in agreement, and the Government announced a new wages measure, to which the NVV and NKV responded with a one-hour strike. Nevertheless, all three federations declared their continued willingness to moderate demands, if not to fight inflation, then to make possible certain increases in social spending; in other words, moderation was now combined with political demands.

Further shifts took place after autumn 1970. Firstly, the federations included representatives from the bigger individual unions in their bargaining delegations, in the hope that this would then have a moderating effect on the unions' strategy in c.a.o. negotiations. In the central bargaining of autumn 1971 the federations declared themselves willing to limit the increase in real wages to 3 per cent in order to fight inflation, provided that their demands for income levelling, profits controls and increased house-building were met. However, the SER Board of Economic Experts considered the unions' commitment to moderation insufficient and supported the employers' demands that there be no increase at all in real wages. The central negotiations therefore failed, one of the reasons for which was that the employers preferred at this time to negotiate at sectoral level; unemployment was rising in some sectors, notably house-building and the docks. The industrial unions were therefore left to pursue their own negotiations, which led to a major conflict in the metal industry in 1972 (discussed in Section 4).

Discussions continued over wage and price restraint and possible direct Government intervention. The latter was rejected by unions and employers alike. The unions would not agree a wage measure with the Christian-Liberal Biesheuvel Government because it did not give enough priority to reducing unemployment and was cutting public spending. The VNO feared that state intervention would simply lead to conflict, as it had in 1970. This explains why one of the coalition parties, DS 70 (a conservative breakaway from the PvdA) found no hearing for its insistence on wage and price controls. As a result, the party withdrew from the coalition in July 1972, and in 1973 the PvdA joined the Government, thereby making possible a closer co-operation between Government and union movement.

The unions sought a social contract with the Government and employers. In exchange for wage restraint they demanded from the government an expansion in housing; educational reforms; improvements in the minimum wage; a long-term policy on investment, budget and incomes; maintenance of the trend policy for civil servants; moderation in all incomes, not just wages; only a small increase in VAT; and no deterioration in welfare facilities. From the employers they demanded willingness to reach agreements at central level, and provision of union facilities within the enterprise. The most important demands concerned wages, but so long as there was some real improvement in wage levels the unions were prepared to exercise restraint. The employers and such institutions as the Central Bank urged the priority of the fight against inflation, and blamed wage increases for the economic difficulties. In a statement in May 1972 the VNO and NCW had called for limitations on the growth of public spending, guarantees of compliance with agreements, and limitations on wage and price increases, amounting to a nil increase in real wages. They rejected statutory enforcement of such a policy.

The loose accord which resulted from these different positions was roughly as follows: there was some provision for a threshold arrangement; the government which was about to assume power would be confronted with the remaining union demands; there was 'narrow scope' for wage increases, which the unions interpreted in terms of egalitarian demands. The scope for real wage improvements was fixed at 3½ per cent, but this was left to be negotiated in sectoral c.a.o.s.

The ways in which the unions tried to realise their egalitarian demands will be described on page 176. After the conclusion of the strikes which these had involved, the wave of c.a.o. strikes of the early 1970s also came to an end, partly because of the decreased enthusiasm for action among workers and unions, and partly because of the new situation created by the 'oil crisis' of late 1973 and further economic deterioration. Before the full implications of the latter had made themselves felt, the unions made their demands for a central accord for 1974. Although these indicated some reversal of the egalitarian trends in the industrial unions, at the same time these were generalised into other sectors: they claimed a 2½ per cent increase in c.a.o. wages, half as a percentage and half on a flat-rate basis; and improvements in the threshold arrangements. In November 1973 the Government announced that it was preparing an Enabling Bill which would make possible the statutory imposition of conditions of employment. This was said to be a temporary emergency measure, covering prices as well as wages, which would be brought into force only if the consequences of the oil crisis made it necessary. Otherwise, the government's views on the coming central accord were close to those of the unions, though given the redistributive elements in the policy there was some political controversy, with the right-wing parties opposing the 'imposition from above' of redistribution.

In December the Government introduced the Enabling Act in the light of the oil boycott. Apart from the extreme left-wing groups, there was little opposition to this. Discussions between the Government and the unions were limited to fixing the size of the wage increases and the duration of the Act. A flat-rate basis of pay rises was agreed, and in the light of disagreement between the unions and the employers over the duration of the Act the Government made no statement on this issue.

Before the Enabling Act was put into operation there was another conflict between the union federations and the employers, this time over the nature of the wage increase; the employers regarded it as advanced money for the price-increase compensation, while the unions wanted a separate wage increase. The unions left the Stichting once more. Ultimately the Government favoured the unions with its measures. It also limited dividend payments and announced a strict price policy and fixation of several fares.

As soon as the situation seemed to clear, the union federations demanded free collective bargaining starting on 1 April. They declared they were prepared for a Central Accord on the base of the original 1973 demands, if Government would introduce fiscal measures to sustain employment and help the lower paid. Employers advocated measures in favour of investments.

The Government promised *f*2.5 milliard, equally divided over investments, wages and public spending. Talks between the three parties in March, involving also independent organisations of employers and employees (the so-called 'small Stichting'), ended without result. Government thereupon decided on new measures based on the Enabling Act, once more meeting the union demands to a large degree.

In June the three federations published an Emergency Programme containing political demands. The degree to which Government would meet these demands would be decisive for further c.a.o.s. For the first time the NVV and NKV on the one hand and CNV on the other showed a division of opinion on a number of issues.

In August the federations were prepared once more to work for a Central Accord, in which this time some sectoral differentiation should be possible. In case of a break-down on the central level, negotiations would be continued on the level of the branches. Demands concerned wage increases, extension of the scope of c.a.o.s to higher income groups, and full publicity of incomes. For the first time certain statutory measures for 'creaming off excess profits' and provisions for education leave were demanded.

The FME also advocated c.a.o. arrangements differentiated according to productivity differences.

Discussions between the Government and the 'small' and 'large' Stichting were deadlocked on wage issues; the non-material issues were not even discussed. After the Government announced a spending of *f*3.5 milliard which was judged insufficient by both sides, consultation in the Stichting was broken off.

After the Government had declared that it would not interfere in c.a.o. bargaining this time, the unions decided to raise the same demands. Tough and protracted negotiations on the level of the branches, *not* sustained by any strike action, resulted in rather meagre c.a.o.s in which no agreement was reached on the non-material issues.

4 LABOUR CONFLICTS, 1969–75

A SHORT CHRONOLOGY OF STRIKE WAVES, 1969–75

In order to give some impression of events in the past few years, we shall give a brief outline of the most important strikes that took place. By 'strike waves' we mean simple empirical point of conflicts which occurred at around the same time.

Towards the end of 1969 unofficial strikes took place all over the country for a cost-of-living allowance to keep pace with suddenly rising prices. Starting in a straw-board factory in Oude Pekela in September, they spread quickly throughout the Groningen region, not only in straw-board but also in potato flour, metal, chemicals, cigars, building and among taxi drivers. The official unions refused to support the strikers, among whom were several unpaid union officers, because they felt they had to respect the existing c.a.o.s. Representatives from the various plants formed a 'joint committee of action' which met frequently, organised meetings and campaigns and remained in existence after the dispute was ended.

In the following years there were strikes in several sectors, usually over wage issues. In 1970 the Stichting van de Arbeid tried to stop a large wild cat strike in the Rotterdam docks by paying a flat sum of *f*400. This decision caused a '400-guilders-wave' over the whole country, accompanied by several strikes. In some cases workers remained on strike after their unions had reached agreements with the employers. Three major disputes took place over the negotiation of c.a.o.s (in 1971 in building and in 1972 in metal manufacturing, and in 1973 in several industries). The last of these differed from the previous two in that, instead of there being a large degree of initiative with local union representatives, the unions maintained a tight central control. The strike lasted over six weeks, and an average of 57,700 strikers was involved at 140 plants. It ended abruptly when the unions instructed their members to return to work because negotiations were to be resumed; at some plants strikes continued unofficially for several days, but from then on no major wage disputes occurred.

From 1973 onwards the labour conflicts were to a large degree over loss of employment. Sometimes they took the form of occupations. The first organised occupation in the Netherlands took place in 1972 at ENKA in Breda (Noord-Brabant). Following a decision to close several factories by the top management of the holding company (AKZO), the workers formed a committee which organised an occupation, based on the example of the Upper Clyde Shipbuilders in Scotland. At first the unions rejected the idea, but when the employers continued with the plan after it had been criticised by two expert boards, a very well prepared occupation was launched, during which production was stopped. It lasted five days and was successful in that the firm had to drop its plans for the time being. Shortly afterwards a successful occupation was organised in the Noord-Brabant screw factory of Van Thiel United at Beek en Donk. The management had proposed closure of the factory, and the workers continued production during the occupation. The Industriebond-NKV and Industriebond-NVV gave assistance. The occupation ended after six days when another firm agreed to take over the factory and conserve employment. In the years following a number of minor occupations took place, mainly in the southern provinces.

SOME GENERAL QUANTITATIVE ASPECTS

The strike statistics (see figure 5.1) show that although the absolute number of disputes was not at all high, the other two indices (average numbers of workers involved and striker days) give some reason to believe that the importance of industrial conflict has increased, at least as compared with the previous twenty years. Since 1970 the ratio of striker days per 100,000 worker days has remained above ten, something which had not occurred once during the 1960s. The peak years were 1970 and 1973, but 1971 and 1972 were also high, while 1974 showed a considerable decline. This continued in 1975, making the strike totals again among the lowest in the world.

According to the CBS, the majority of recorded strikes are unofficial, though in 1971 and 1973 most strikers were involved in official actions, which also accounted for most strike-days. Moreover, the CBS data gives a somewhat distorted picture for 1972 by classifying the metal industry strikes as unofficial protest strikes. The absolute number of strikes carried on by trade unions during this period was higher than before, while the years 1969, 1970 and 1972 were characterised by a number of large unofficial strikes. In 1969 these were concentrated in the northern Netherlands, in 1970 in Rotterdam and surroundings, and in 1972 throughout the country though mainly in the west.

Strikes were most frequent in traditional sectors: metal, transport equipment (including shipbuilding) and transport. Hardly any strikes occurred in the newer sectors, such as chemicals, or in the tertiary sector. Developments in the building industry have been notable; in the past it has been a strike-prone industry, but in this period there was a remarkable decrease in strike activity.

It is not possible to conclude directly from this evidence of an increased level of conflict that Dutch workers and their organisations have become more militant; a more precise insight into the qualitative character of the growth in conflict would be necessary in order to do so. For this reason, in the following sections an analvsis will be made of the development of the *content of demands*, the *forms of action* and the *groups in action*.

THE CONTENT OF DEMANDS

In categorising and analysing the contents of demands, at least three difficulties arise. The first is to find any acceptable scheme for doing so.[4] We shall use one which differentiates between the three main groups of workers' interests: demands concerning the price of labour; those which concern the conditions and use of the labour force; and a residual category which has no direct relationship to the production process.

The second difficulty concerns what is being categorised if stated demands are accepted. Do these demands refer to the real problems, or are they merely substitutions of problems to which no solution can be found? Would it not be better to try to analyse the 'consciousness' underlying the demands, rather than the official terms in which they are stated? Although we recognise its disadvantages, we have to admit that we can only analyse demands as they are stated, the only form in which they appear publicly. More systematic research into individual disputes would be necessary before further propositions could be made.

The third allied difficulty is how to distinguish after a strike between the different kinds of demands which were made during the course of it. It is commonly known that during a dispute several different demands may be raised, but that only a few of them are retained throughout the strike.

Demands Concerning Wages

During the period under review wage demands centred mainly around two issues: protecting the real standard of living; and abolishing or reducing wage differentials, and preventing further discrepancies from arising. There were also some other issues which were specific to particular sectors.

The presentation of demands designed to protect the real standard of living depended on what the workers involved felt to be the immediate causes of the deterioration. In the first place there were, of course, demands for a straight increase to offset a rise in the cost of living. As we have seen, prices suddenly rose in 1969, and this was closely related to the initial outbursts of conflict. Since then the unions have succeeded in incorporating threshold agreements into the c.a.o.s, sometimes after strike action. A second issue was resistance by workers in certain enterprises to the withdrawal of bonuses, allowances, profit shares and so forth which had been paid above the agreed wage rate. These have usually been paid by the employer in times of prosperity to attract and retain labour, but he may reduce them if he thinks the firm's economic position makes it necessary to do so. On the other hand, these allowances become a fixed part of a worker's income, especially when they have been paid for a long period, and their withdrawal means a considerable loss of income. Demands for their retention, which were made at several firms in the first half of the period, are very defensive by their very nature, being directed merely at maintaining levels already reached by the workers. We know of only one dispute, a two-week strike at the Nieuwe Noord Nederlandse Scheepswerven (ship-building) in Groningen in 1971, where workers justified their demands for an extra week's wages by referring to the favourable results of the enterprise.

Strikes for the abolition of wage differentials can also be divided into several groups. Firstly, some developed from regional wage differences, which had resulted partly from the structural situation of regional labour markets but also from institutionalisation resulting from the introduction of municipal classes (different grades of local-authority area) after the war. Another immediate cause has been the process of concentration and centralisation which has been going on since the 1960s, leading to firms from different regions being amalgamated. Regional differences then coincide with wage differentials within one company. The same happens when firms from different branches of industry, with different levels of productivity, merge. Several strikes have been called for the abolition of such wage differentials within one company. Strikes against regional wage differentials were also conducted within individual sectors. In addition, there were strikes to end local differentials; against differences between workers doing the same work; by women for equal pay; and, since 1969, by organisations of young workers for the abolition of special 'youth rates' and for the introduction of minimum youth wages.

The wages policy of the unions in these years called for more attention to be paid to the low paid, 'who suffer most from inflation'. One feature which is remarkable in this context has been the growing resistance of union members to percentage increases. Demands for flat-rate increases were a particular feature of the large unofficial strikes of 1969 and 1970. Only in 1973 did the big industrial unions follow with demands which demanded, rhetorically at least, that the incomes of wage and salary earners should be levelled up. Employees in higher income groups resisted these demands, while the employers argued that income distribution was a question for the Government, not them. It should be noted that conflicts did not arise over the total amount of wage increase, but over the distribution within an accepted norm (the growth of productivity).

Finally, in considering issues specific to individual branches, of considerable importance was the demand for higher guaranteed wages, especially in the transport industry (taxis and goods traffic), where earnings comprise relatively low basic wages and high bonuses. Demands about the grading of jobs have always been made by individual groups within an enterprise.

Demands Concerning the Organisation of Production

The demands which can be grouped under this heading refer to the direct work situation. In view of their character and the almost complete absence of the unions from the plant (at least at the beginning of the period), it is hardly surprising that the majority of strikes in which these demands have been important have been unofficial, though some of these were later taken over by the unions – itself a novel development.

The most important issues have been: resistance to the introduction of continuous working; resistance to redundancies resulting from closures and reorganisations; and discontent over the growing intensification of work. Towards the end of the period several unions formulated demands in the central agreements aimed at acquiring more union influence at plant level.

Although one might assume that problems about the organisation of work are very specific to the individual plant, issues such as continuous working led to workers being mobilised throughout several different companies.

The most important issue in recent years has been the threat of redundancy following closures or rationalisations. Workers have taken a more radical position than their unions, firstly in protesting at all against redundancies, and then in demanding the conservation of employment. Only in 1968 did the unions develop a strategy at all, and then it was limited to securing favourable redundancy payments and easing the social consequences. After the ENKA case they began for the first time to question managerial decisions, demanding that plans for closures should be vetted by expert committees and the substitute employment provided, and finally resisting the closures themselves. However, pressure by the workers themselves remains the decisive factor (SWOV; Benschop and Kee, 1975: pp. 87–104).

Forced by the necessity of coping with these relatively new problems at plant level and their consequences for relations between unions and workers, and of building up a membership which could be mobilised for action, several unions have begun to include demands that the union presence in the workplace should be strengthened in their programmes for central agreements. These demands have developed particularly since 1970, and although in the first instance they may represent a reaction to the unions' former absence at plant level, they are increasingly combined with decentralising and democratising tendencies in the organisational structure of the unions (van Beekfeld, 1974; Leijnse, 1973).

A final group of fairly common demands concerns the consequences of strike action for the workers. Before returning to work workers usually demand compensation for wages lost during the strike and an end to any repression against the strikers by the employer.

Demands with no Direct Relation to the Productive Process

We shall discuss here political and sympathy strikes, though it should be emphasised that neither has been of great importance.

The only explicit political strike by the unions was on 15 December 1970, when the NVV and NKV called a one-hour strike against the Wages Bill which has already been discussed (page 170). There were also unofficial strikes against the Strikes Bill in 1972. Sympathy strikes have been largely confined to dock workers participating in international action, for example the boycott of ships carrying Chilean copper in 1972.

Also relevant under this heading, however, is a remarkable development in the c.a.o. policy of the unions. Since 1971 they have insisted that, in exchange for co-operation in the government's anti-inflation policy, certain conditions must be met. For example, groups outside the collective agreements (mainly in the higher-income groups) must also moderate their pay increases, and the savings resulting from general moderation should be used by the state to finance certain social services such as housing and education (Smolders, 1972: p.159). Furthermore, to try to ensure that general moderation would not favour strong firms and weaken the position of the unions, they formulated demands aiming at statutory settlement for excess profits in favour of the workers.

Typical, finally, of Dutch industrial relations is the continuous plea by the union movement (and most left-wing political parties) for an incomes policy covering all sorts of income, which has to be seen against the background of the traditional Dutch *wage* policy.

THE FORMS OF ACTION

During each dispute, the workers concerned use a number of different forms of action: negotiations, delays in collective consultation, strikes, calls for solidarity, etc. The scope for a particular action is, of course, determined by the nature of the demand and the particular situation of the workers involved, and also by their economic and legal position, their place in the productive process and their former strike experience. Finally, managerial strategies are important, though we cannot discuss these here; in any case, they are usually surrounded by secrecy.

Traditional Individual and Collective Forms of Action

All Dutch workers have lacked the basic right to strike since World War II. Strikes by public employees were illegal from 1903 to 1974; they have to restrict themselves to forms of action short of a strike, such as working to rule or protest demonstrations. But despite this prohibition, the bus and tram drivers of Amsterdam have struck several times without action being taken against them. Other groups of quasi-governmental personnel (hospital, welfare and education employees) used large national protest demonstrations, as have groups of young or female workers whose specific interests (education, minimum youth wages and equal pay) were not amenable to action at plant level and needed parliamentary attention. Bans on overtime have been used only rarely as the sole means of action, as have periodic strikes (stopping work for a couple of hours one day in each week). This technique was, however, used by the straw-board workers in 1969, because of the financial position of the workers themselves and the economic position of their industry. In the second large straw-board conflict (1973)—protesting against the introduction of continuous working and demanding a free Saturday—the workers paid less attention to claims by the employers and unions that the firms could not bear the loss; they simply stayed at home on Saturdays until agreement had been reached.

Strikes by the Unions: Selective Strikes
Although strikes are still regarded by the unions as a last resort, the resurgence of official industrial action is one of the most important developments of this period. Working-to-rule, protest demonstrations, overtime bans and delays in consultation have all formed part of union strategies in their c.a.o. strikes. The strikes are used by the unions to pursue specific objectives, and this gives them a very instrumental character.

The major strikes have been selective, for example those in the building industry in 1971 (de Jong, 1972; Ramondt, 1971b; Vroemen, 1971); the metal industry in 1972 (Smolders, 1972; Akkermans and Krijnen, 1972; Teulings and Leijnse, 1974; Groenevelt, 1972; Industriebond-NVV, 1972; KEN, 1972); and in industry generally in 1973 (Teulings and Leijnse, 1974; Nieuwstadt and Snels, 1973; Brej, 1973). Sometimes pressure was put on those firms which were thought most likely to concede; on other occasions the unions tried to cripple a whole industry by striking at certain strategic points—for example, during the building strike they tried to use strikes at cement factories for this purpose (Ramondt, 1971(b)). In all these instances only a few plants were allowed to strike for the duration of the whole action. These strategies were used for largely organisational reasons: protracted overall strikes would be expensive in terms of strike pay. However, they lead to difficulties if they do not take into account the expectations and experiences of the workers on strike. This became very clear during the two official strikes of 1971 and 1973, when the strategy was not fully accepted by the workers in those plants which were selected for action (*ibid*; de Jong, 1972: p. 40; Teulings and Leijnse, 1974: pp. 165–8). Similarly, the sudden ending of the strike by union authority caused some dispute.

Factory Occupations
Though still rare, factory occupations need to be mentioned as an important form of action in the recent conflicts. They represent an entirely new phenomenon in Dutch industrial relations, though to a certain extent it is difficult to distinguish them from spontaneous strikes in which the workers simply remain in the factories. At first purely unofficial, these devices began to attract union support. In some occupations workers continued with production throughout.

THE ROLE AND POSITION OF DIFFERENT GROUPS IN INDUSTRIAL CONFLICTS

The Workers
The big unofficial strike movements of 1969 and 1970 were, to a large extent, carried out by workers from the traditionally militant and strike-prone parts of the Netherlands, Groningen and the older industrial areas in the west. The national strikes by the recognised unions in the following years were also centred on the west, but began to involve both large and small firms in other

areas too. Districts and plants where there had been no strikes since the war, or indeed ever, participated for the first time; and the most protracted strikes were in the east and south. Campaigns against redundancies and factory closures were most radical in areas with high unemployment. Factory occupations have occurred almost exclusively in the southern provinces of Noord-Brabant and Limburg.

There have been only a few disputes in which women took part predominantly or exclusively, but the overall proportion of women in the work force is low (about 25 per cent), and they are mainly employed in declining industries or in the tertiary sector.

Despite the insecurity of their position, most immigrant workers supported strikes in the firms in which they were employed. Only a small number of short, mostly unofficial strikes of immigrants alone took place; these were mainly caused by the specific situation of these workers: bad working and housing conditions, differential wages, poor food. In 1974 and 1975, however, a number of large demonstrations by foreign workers took place to protest against Government plans to limit their numbers and to expel workers without residence permits. Unions and other groups also launched firm protests. Again, the number of immigrant workers is small: although it has increased since the 1960s it is still less than three per cent (Heemskerk, 1971).

Since 1969 several national demonstrations have been organised by the bodies of young workers: NVV Jongerenkontakt, KWJ and CNV Werkende Jeugd. These campaigns are primarily aimed at government and at parliament, seeking to lower the minimum-wage age from 23 to 18, improved education and better housing facilities. They have achieved some success in these areas. The Catholic group (KWJ) has also been active in various local disputes, especially in the south. This has led to some friction with the unions, especially those of the NKV.

The solidarity of white-collar and staff employees has certainly not been great during wage conflicts. During the big disputes of 1972 and 1973 it was usually only the production workers who went on strike, and the same usually applies to smaller disputes. As a result, relations between the main unions and the organisations representing these employees have been poor.

There have been some exceptions to this pattern, especially in campaigns against factory closures which affect manual and non-manual workers alike. For example, staff members at ENKA played an important role in securing the expert investigation which criticised top management in the ENKA dispute (Teulings, 1973). It could, however, be argued that the fragile bond which existed after this was broken by the industrial unions when they launched the strikes of 1973, of which the staff organisations did not approve. Apart from resisting the reduction of differentials, higher personnel have very rarely been involved in strikes of their own. The main exception was a strike by flight-control staff at Schiphol airport in June 1970 (de Jong, 1970).

Office staff outside industry (in trade, banks, etc) have not been involved in any of the actions of recent years. Their organisations are highly conservative.

There is a very varied pattern among public employees. Since 1959 their pay has been determined by the 'trend policy', whereby the level of salaries is based on changes in the average national wage (de Hen, 1973). The government does not want to be a trend-setter in improving wages and working conditions. So far the unions have complained about the restrictions on bargaining which this involves, and in 1974 the ABVA successfully demanded the right to strike for public employees.

The Unions

Unions can react in different ways to spontaneous and/or unofficial workers' actions: they can dissociate themselves; they can try to mediate between employers and workers; or they can support the action and take over the demands themselves. For Dutch unions there are both legal and ideological barriers to taking the last course. Until recently there was a legal obligation on unions to hold to what had been agreed in a c.a.o.; and there is still considerable concern for the 'national interest' within the unions. Nevertheless there have been important developments in recent years, in that the recognised unions are increasingly willing to support unofficial actions. This does not mean that every unofficial strike can count on financial and organisational support: actions for wage increases are unlikely to, but strikes against dismissals and so forth may well do so.

The unions at least in part dissociated themselves from the strikes of 1969 and 1970, as a result of which these actions became, to some extent, strikes against the unions. The important role played in the strikes by many unpaid union officials probably protected the unions from further negative consequences. For the unions to take over an unofficial action does not mean that they completely accept the workers' position; they have sometimes intervened to give support which inhibits the extension and radicalisation of the workers' demands (Teulings and Leijnse, 1974; pp. 99–123). Furthermore, if the union gives support it then takes over the leadership of the strike. Of importance here is the employers' tactic of refusing to negotiate directly with strikers and talking to union officials only; and there is also a tendency for negotiations to be transferred to higher levels in the central organisations if the unions and management cannot reach agreement. As a result, little remains of the workers' original demands.

During the early years of this period, the unions took the view that an agreement reached by them with management should be accepted by the workers concerned. If this did not happen, they refused to give further support. But during the tug-boat strike of 1971, they began for the first time to pay attention to the opinions of the workers themselves (Ramondt, 1971(a)). Moreover, in a number of unions the unpaid officials in the plants have increasing autonomy in promoting workers' interests: for example, the attempts (mainly by the industrial unions) to include unpaid officials from the plants in their bargaining delegations, and the involvement of groups at plant level in the organisation and preparation of the c.a.o. strikes.

The Employers

The policy of employers and their organisations towards industrial conflicts will usually contain the following elements: the integration of employees to prevent conflict; the ending of disputes as quickly as possible, using whatever means are made available by the power relationships of the moment, including repression; and prevention of the extension of a dispute to other plants or sectors, and in particular avoiding setting precedents.

The employers' organisations and 'progressive' employers lay increasing emphasis on making the existing consultation and communication structures function as well as possible, and on introducing new ones in order to prevent manifest conflicts. In Sections 1 and 2 we described forms of codetermination which exist within the enterprise, and the formal changes at the factory level. In this framework the plant work on the part of the unions is seen as mainly disintegrative.[5] Employers' reactions to plant work had not been unsympathetic at first, but this changed during the 1960s as they came to fear the development of a shop-steward system. Only in plants in which the unions are weak can management take the liberty of refusing minimal facilities to union officials. Where plant work cannot be prevented, attempts will be made to institutionalise it through rigid rules. There have also been some moves for the legal institutionalisation of plant work.

If the integrative policy fails, employers try to terminate conflict as quickly and for as low a cost as possible. Their behaviour shows a number of characteristic features which have not changed over the years. In the first place, there is a tradition of going to court over every strike that takes place, which nearly always results in their securing a postponement of the strike. In the 1960s, less use tended to be made of this where unofficial strikes were concerned. Instead the employers refused to deal with the employees directly, using the unions as intermediaries. This use of the unions is another employer tactic to which the unions have begun to show some resistance in recent years.

Other forms of repressive action have not normally been supported by the courts, such as dismissal of strike leaders or refusal to pay wages to 'those who want to work' but are prohibited by the strike. In 1971 the employers threatened the use of lock-outs, but in practice they did not do so on any scale.

After previous discord, the employers succeeded in 1973 in forming a strong united front against the union campaign for income levelling. After the failure of the central negotiations the unions tried to force a national c.a.o. through strikes in individual plants. The employers had considerable success in co-ordinating resistance to this. The main condition for (and at the same time the result of) this was that the employers' organisations, especially the federations, exercised a great influence on member firms. A special Office of Industrial Employers was set up in the VNO headquarters. The organisations have always exercised some influence over their members both through the availability of anti-strike funds and the possibility of expulsion, and this was greatly strengthened in 1970 by the introduction of an Onderlinge Werkgevers Garantieregeling (OWG: Regulation of Mutual Guarantee) by the VNO and NCW (SER; Teulings and Leijnse, 1974: p. 85). Employers in whose plants strikes had occurred could count on compensation provided that their policy was approved by the central federations.

The employers' organisations have taken a harder and more professional line during the past few years. They seem to want to make it clear to the unions that polarisation does not pay. This development could be described as a tendency to make greater use of repression; they have not departed from their integrative goals, but are supplementing these with strong action, helped now by economic conditions. In general the employers' organisations have developed into adequate opponents for both government and unions. They try to react against policy developments to which they are opposed (for example, the vetting of investments according to social criteria); and they do this with an extensive apparatus of scientific experts and through publicity campaigns.

5 THE PRESENT STATE OF THE INDUSTRIAL RELATIONS SYSTEM

INTERPRETATION OF CHANGES IN THE CONDITIONS FOR INCORPORATION OF THE UNIONS

Some changes have taken place in all the factors which we listed on page 159 as functional conditions for incorporation:

(a) *Incorporation of the work-force*: Workers' levels of aspiration increased during the 1950s and 1960s (ter Hoeven, 1972). Combined with increasing job uncertainty since the late 1960s, this helps to explain their increased militancy upto 1973.

(b) *Ideological integration of the union movement*: The unions give lower priority to the 'national interest', or at least they are concerned to extract concessions from the state in exchange for their taking a moderate line, though the movement is still very divided on this. This results from the union leaders being forced to pay more attention to the interests of their members. In so far as the situation is affected by the ideological division of the union movement, while pressure from members and financial problems favour a confederation, this is opposed by continuing ideological differences and existing organisational structures. The NKV seems to have the most difficulties, while the CNV will probably become a social movement, losing its more utilitarian members to the more effective NVV (Akkermans, 1974). The most relevant development in fact has been the discussions within the union movement on the nature of the enterprise. According to Albeda (1974), there are two main views on participation: acceptance of integration within the structures of consultation, and subordination of the representation of members' interests to concern for the enterprise as a whole; and a more conflictual model in which representation of the workers is seen as involving opposition to management. The former is more compatible with the existing system of works councils, while the latter has been involved in the development of plant work. However, plans for reformed works councils which exclude the employer are compatible with the latter, though the unions would still want to ensure that the councils were not rivals to them.

(c) *Union control over membership*: The union federations have lost something of their standing over wage policy to the big individual unions. This has been accompanied by conflicts within the federations, especially the NVV. At the same time, the unions' grip on their members has also decreased. In the 1950s there was considerable membership turnover, while in the 1960s there have been unofficial strikes, new organisations and some opposition to the unions. They have tried to reinforce their control through several means, the most prominent of which has been plant work. Although this can be seen as a kind of functional decentralisation, it may turn out to be a means of internal democratisation, with all the attendant consequences.

(d) *Control over workers in general*: The monopoly of representation by the three big federations still exists, but the independent unions have grown considerably in the past ten years. The recognised organisations make continuous efforts to maintain their monopoly, but continued exclusion of the 'responsible' independent organisations is irrational in terms of the functioning of the system. Their acceptance is therefore to be expected, though the enlarged union movement which results will show increased internal contradictions. There has been a certain revival of radical unionism, which has had the effect of alerting the recognised unions, and has also resulted in a few new independent organisations.

This discussion may suggest that some recognised unions have become somewhat less reliable as controlling elements in the economic system. It is true that the 'radicalisation' of the unions has resulted more from pressures than from conscious choice, but this is not to deny its reality. Without using the term 'business unionism', it can be said that certain unions are representing their members' immediate interests more pragmatically and efficiently. However, little research has been done into this question, or on the wider issue of the challenge it represents to the existing social order.

The 'power' of the union movement has also been discussed in a merely political way; employers' complaints that the unions have become 'too powerful' provide evidence that industrial relations are becoming tougher rather than indications of a real increase in union power. We have already seen that union power within the enterprise is still very restricted, especially within large plants. Moreover, within industrial relations as a whole the position of the unions seems to have weakened. Peper sees 1973 as the turning point here,[6] and gives three reasons for this: a reduced tendency to strike since 1973, because of unemployment increasing; the ideological differences between different branches of the movement coming increasingly to light; and the development of different organisations for officials and higher staff intensifying the organisational divisions.

There have also been complaints that it is impossible to govern without the agreement of the unions. Although this is true—the fall of the Christian–Liberal Biesheuvel cabinet in 1973 probably had much to do with its growing rejection by the trade unions—it is not a completely new situation. What is new is a phenomenon which we have already discussed, namely the increasing inability of the unions to reach central agreements, in the beginning mainly as a result of rank-and-file pressures, but later more and more as a result of resistance by employers. Peper suggested that this would prevent any return to the earlier centralism. In reality it caused continuous interference by the Government.

Finally, the Dutch union movement still retains very legalistic features which might ultimately prove decisive. In both the form and content of their policy aims the unions have a strong tendency to make regulations, either as legislation in the strict sense or in the form of contracts.

THE DEVELOPMENT OF THE INDUSTRIAL RELATIONS SYSTEM

We believe that the Dutch industrial relations system has changed from a corporatist to a neo-capitalist type. It has lost its high level of stability, and peaceful co-operation has been replaced by more or less conflictual negotiations. The state seemed to acquire a less decisive role. At the same time, however, the essential willingness of the unions to co-operate with the state, while varying with the 'colour' of the Government, has not disappeared.

Peper (1973: pp. 126, 7) has described this tendency as the replacement of the integration model by the coalition model. The formal contracts which are so central to Dutch industrial relations 'typically fit in a structure which will assume the features of the coalition model', in which development is especially promoted by the Government. Under this model the parties (employers and unions) stand up for their particular interests, while the Government develops a responsibility for socio-economic policy (*ibid*: p. 26). He considers this model best reflects the dynamic and greater level of conflict of the emerging pattern of industrial relations.

Windmuller (1969: ch. 11) has claimed that the most important development of recent years has been the decentralisation of the system, but he still doubts whether the various participants will create the conditions necessary for an easy transition to a greater autonomy for collective consultation at the level of the individual concern, or of the industry, according to the situation (*ibid.*). The following factors are among those which need to be considered. On the one hand there is the drive of 'employers and employees, but employees in particular, for greater freedom of action within the scheme of a labour market in a situation of full employment'; and on the other is 'the resoluteness of the government in wanting to be able to check the growth of wages, with a view to the expected inflationary stress' (*ibid*: pp. 18–19). Since Windmuller wrote this in 1969 this last factor still applies, but the labour market has changed considerably and the workers' striving for greater freedom has been deprived of much of its base.

A further complicating factor mentioned by Windmuller is the process of concentration in the organisations of both employers and employees. It is clear that this cannot promote decentralisation. De Jong (1974: p. 41) directly challenges Windmuller's whole decentralisation thesis. He argues that 'one can see a constant negotiation – also about wages – between the central organisations. The most important reasons for this development are . . . the development of the rate of inflation . . . and the political demands of the unions which have not basically changed in the course of the period described.' Economic developments, he claims, have worked in both directions. The Common Market, for example, represents a growth in centralisation, while full employment and the growth of the tertiary sector (with its tendency towards independent union organisation) are instances of decentralising trends (*ibid*: pp. 89–91). Given that full employment has become a phenomenon of the past, we conclude that the Dutch industrial relations system will remain highly centralised.

There was, however, a remarkable tendency towards decentralisation or 'liberalisation' until 1973 in terms of the role and influence of the state, especially in incomes policy, as described in Section 3. A crucial issue in eventually determining the degree of centralisation will be the role of the unions in the plant, including the future of works councils and plant work. These ambiguous issues have been discussed at several points above.

THE STATE OF THE SYSTEM

We have described the Dutch system as essentially corporatist, yet the component organs envisaged during post-war reconstruction were never introduced in their entirity; the regulating bodies which were to be established according to the law have only been implemented to a limited extent. In agriculture and mining the PBO developed quite strongly, but in more modern branches of industry like chemicals and electrical engineering it completely failed to take root (Windmuller, 1969: pp. 290–2). As such, the system is now clearly in a crisis. As Teulings writes (1973: p. 242):

> The history of the Dutch trade union movement since the end of World War II can be described within the frame of the development of the quickly growing 'corporative' structure of this country. In none of the world's industrialised countries since the war has 'corporatism' realised itself as a social form of organisation so completely and extremely as in the Netherlands. This peaceful socio-economic co-operation between trade unions of various political opinions, and their links with their social partners and the state, have only become less close in the early seventies under the pressure of new forms of struggle among workers and trade unions. Most of the institutions of 'industrial co-operation' which have existed for more than twenty years, have lost their functions and have given notice.

Indeed, the crisis goes further than the structures of co-operation and concerns the whole ideology. The different aspects of this crisis can be summarised as follows: a loosening of co-operation, plus a move from co-operation to negotiation; tougher negotiations; a greater level of conflict; no overall decentralisation perhaps, but certainly a temporarily less decisive role for the state in wage policy, and a shift in union activity to the level of the enterprise; ideological disintegration; and a hardening of attitudes on the part of the political parties; and, despite these tendencies, overall willingness on the part of the unions to co-operate with the state.

Perhaps it is best to describe the present stage of development as one of *polarisation*, a hardening of relations (de Jong, 1974: pp. 4, 40–41). Windmuller suggests it is a process of *modernisation* in the sense that the Dutch system may be seen as moving towards the pattern which is more familiar in many other Western countries (1969; see also ter Hoeven, 1972: pp.17–19; Peper, 1973). But that cannot be accepted without considering developments in those countries, and there are some indications that some of these are shifting in a more corporative direction.

NOTES

1. Collective agreements (hereafter called c.a.o.s) contain agreements on wages and working conditions. In 1940 fifteen per cent of the occupied population were covered by c.a.o.s; by 1962 it was 70 per cent. Those remaining outside are in the higher income groups. Until 1968 c.a.o.s specified maximum as well as minimum norms.
2. This section draws heavily on P. Baudoin and J. Jacops, 1973; H. van de Berg and P. Fortuyn, 1973; H. Drenth, 1966.
3. There have been several disputes in which workers and unions have had to enforce recognition by employers of the councils' limited rights: for example, in the Rotterdam docks (A. Teulings and F. Leijnse, 1974: p. 24); and in many cases of reorganisations, mergers and takeovers (E. Piehl, 1974)
4. The CBS distinguishes between the following 'points of issue': demands for wage increases; other wage demands; other demands concerning working conditions; protest strikes; those where no classification is possible. According to these official statistics the most prominent point of issue in 1969 and 1970 was wage increases; in 1971 there were four conflicts within the category 'other demands concerning working conditions', and the number of strike days in these was more than 90 per cent of all strike days that year. In 1972, 70 per cent of workers involved in strikes were engaged in twenty-one 'protest strikes'. The most common demand in 1973 was 'other wage demands', where official strikes were concerned, and 'other demands concerning working conditions' for unofficial strikes. The latter also constituted the point at issue in six of the fourteen strikes occurring in 1974. Most workers were, however, involved in 'other wage demands' (50 per cent, while the biggest single categories of strike days were over wage increases (40 per cent) and protest strikes (30 per cent).
5. F. van der Ven speaks of 'the problem of the non-integrative activities of the union within the enterprise, as this has become actual at this moment by the propagandisation of the "plant work"' (van der Ven, 1972: p. 9).
6. In *NRC-Handelsblad*, 23 November 1974.

LIST OF WORKS CITED

Akkermans, T. (1974), 'Het CNV en de eenheid van de nederlandse vakbeweging', *Eltheto*, no. 46 (July).

Akkermans, T. and Krijnen, G. (1972), *Het Metaalkonflikt* (Nijmegen: I T S).

Albeda, W. (1971), 'Les Pays-Bas: Les relations de travail', in Guy Spitaels (ed.), *Les Conflicts Sociaux en Europe* (Bruges: Marabout).

Albeda, W. (1974), 'De Nederlandse arbeidsverhoudingen op een keerpunt', *Economisch-Statistische Berichten* (12 June).

Baudoin, Piet and Jacops, J. (1973), 'De ontwikkeling van het stakingsrecht in Nederland' (unpublished paper, Nijmegen, Jan.).

Beekveld, C. van (1974), 'De vankbeweging en demokratie. Researchreport' (Nijmegen: Sociologisch Instituut).

Benschop, A. and Kee, T. (1975), *De Bedrijfsbezetting van de ENKA Breda* (Nijmegen; SUN).

Berg, H. v. d. and Fortuyn, P. (1973), 'Het Stakingsrecht in Nederland, een overzicht van de gebeurtenissen na de 2e wereldoorlog', *The Elfder Ure*, No. 12.

Bos, W. (1972), *Werkgeversorganisatie/Ondernemingsorganisatie* (Retterdam: Universitaire Pers).

Brej, B. (1973), *Een Kwestie van Principe* (Baarn: Meulenhoff).

Buiter, J., Poppe, C. and Wallenburg, H. (1962), 'Lager vakbondskader als communicatieschakel'; 'Modewerkers in de vakbeweging'; 'Interne leiding en organisatie van een vakbeweging', *Socialisme en Democratie*.

—— (1963), 'Herorientering in de vakbeweging', *Socialisme en Democratie*.

Cornelissen, I. (1970), in *Vrij Nederland*, 24 Oct.

Drenth, H. (1966), *Stakingsrecht* (Nijmegen: SUN).

Groenevelt, A. (1972), 'Achtergronden van de metaalstaking', *Te Elfder Ure*, No. 11.

Heemskerk, C. (1971), 'De (gast) arbeid', *Nesbic-bulletin*, Vol.6, Nos. 10/11 (Oct./Nov.).

Hen, P. de (1973), 'De ABVA, een vakbond die sneller groeit den het overheidsapparaat', *Vrij Nederland* (2 Jan.).

Hoeven, P. ter (1969), *Arbeiders tussen Welvaart en Onvrede* (Alphen a/d Rijn: Samson).

Hoeven, P. ter (ed.) (1972), *Breukvlakken in het Arbeidsbestel* (Alphen a/d Rijn: Samson)

Industriebond-NVV (1972), *Metaalakties februari 1972* (Amsterdam).

Jong, J. de (1970), 'De aktie van de verkeersleiders', *Social Maandblad Arbeid*.

—— (1972), *De Bouwstaking van 1971* (Deventer: Kluwoi).

—— (1974), *Het Nederlandse Systeem van Arbeidsverhoudingen* (Rotterdam: Universitaire Pers).

KEN (1972), *Metaalstaking 1972. Massaal Antwoord op Verscherpte Uitbuiting en Politieke Onderdrukking. Verslag en Analyse* (Rotterdam: KEN).

Kleerekoper, S. (1971), *Inkomensverdeling en Inkomensbeleid* (Alphen a/d Rajin: Samson).

Lammers, C. *et al.* (1965), *Medezeggenschap en Overleg in het Bedrijf* (Utrecht: Het Spectrum).

Leijnse, F. (1973), 'Demokratisering van de vakbeweging', in Teulings (ed.), *Onderneming en Vakbeweging*, q.v.

Nieuwstadt, M. v. and Snels, G. (1973), 'Progressiviteit en arbeidersstrijd: over de stakingen in Nederland', *Internationale Korrespondentie*, Nos. 32/33.

NRC – Handelsblad (23 Nov. 1974).

Pauli, H. (1970) 'De pers en de havenstaking', *De Groene Amsterdammer* (11 Nov).

Peper, B. (ed.) (1973), *De Nederlandse Arbeidsverhoudingen; Continuiteit en Verandering* (Rotterdam: Universitaire Press).

Piehl, E. (1974), *Multinationale Konzerne und Internationale Gewerkschaftsbewegung* Frankfurt a/M: Europäische Verlagsanstalt).

Poppe, C. (1971), 'De ontwikkeling van het bedrijvenwerk', *Sociaal Maandblad Arbeid* (Sep.).

Ramondt, J. (1971a), 'Sleepbootstaking in Rotterdam. De bonden volgen de arbeiders als de arbeiders dreigen weg te lopen', *De Groene Amsterdammer* (13 Feb.).

Ramondt, J. (1971b), 'De bouwstaking en de boedelscheiding van het kabinet De Jong', *De Groene Amsterdammer* (19 June).

S.E.R. *Informatie en Documentatiebulletin*, No. 32 (10 Sep. 1970) and No. 47 (22 Dec. 1971).

Sleepers in Staking (een onderzoek naar achtergronden, en verloop van het konflikt in de Rotterdamse stadssleepdienst verricht door de onderzoeksgroep krisissituaties) (no place, no date).

Smolders, Y. (1972), 'Chronologies overzicht van de belangrijkste gebeurtenissen voor en tijdens de metaalstaking', *Te Elfder Ure*, Vol. 19, No.3/4.

Smolders, Y. (1973), 'De metaalstaking van 1972 en de pers', *Te Elfder Ure*, Vol. 20 No.2.

SWOV *Afvloeingsregelingen in Nederland* (Utrecht, no date).

Terpstra, G. H. (1973), 'De verhoudingen tussen werkgevers en werknemers in Nederland', *Europese Dokumentatie*, No. 2.

Teulings, A. (1973a), 'Gewerkschaften und Arbeitskämpfe in den Niederlanden', in O. Jacobi *et al.* (eds): *Gewerkschaften und Klassenkampf: Kritisches Jahrbuch '73* (Frankfurt a/M: Fischer).

Teulings, A. (ed.) (1973b) *Onderneming en Vakbeweging: Ontwikkelingstendenties in de Arbeidsverhoudingen* (Rotterdam: Universitaire Pers).

Teulings, A. and Leijnse, F. (1970), *f 75,–ja, f 25,–nee* (Rotterdam; Universitaire Pers).

Teulings, A. and Leijnse, F. (1974), *Nieuwe Vormen van Industriele Aktie* (Nijmegen: SUN).

Vall, M. v. d. (1967), *De Vakbeweging in de Welvaartsstaat* (Meppel: Boom).

Ven, F. v. d. (1972), *De Crisis in het Rechtssysteem de Collectieve Arbeidsovereenkomst* (Alphen a/d Rijn: Samson).

Vroemen, J. (1971), 'De stakingsoverwinning in de bouw en hoe verder', *De Nieuwe Linie* (3 June).

Wat is P.B.O? (publication of the Ministerie van Economische Zaken, 1955).

Windmuller, J. (1969) *Labor Relations in the Netherlands* (Ithaca: Cornell U.P.).

6 *The Intensification of Industrial Conflict in the United Kingdom*

COLIN CROUCH

I ECONOMIC AND POLITICAL CONTEXT

THE ECONOMIC CONTEXT

Economic Problems and Policies

During the period under review in this study the long-term decline of the British economy became acute, and it is in the context of a considerably worsening economic situation on several dimensions that the disintegration of Britain's characteristic post-war industrial relations system should be seen. Although several new factors had appeared by the end of the 1960s to intensify the economic problem, the underlying weaknesses had been present throughout the post-war period; but for several years they had been largely denied major political significance by the fact that mass prosperity was advancing at an unprecedented rate. Certainly prosperity rather than relative decline was the relevant experience for the working population of the 1950s, whose immediate past included a world war, high unemployment and an international economic depression. Although they appear in retrospect as a period of low growth and a deterioration in Britain's position as a dominant trading nation, the 1950s seemed at the time to be an era of increasing wealth and full employment.

However, intermittent crises had demonstrated from early on the underlying instability. The early stages of movements towards economic expansion involved a deterioration in the balance of payments, which in turn led to a loss of confidence in sterling and a foreign exchange crisis. The official response to this would then be to use monetary and fiscal weapons to halt the expansion. In the course of this process governments revealed a reasonably consistent pattern of preferences between the major goals of post-war economic policy: full employment, a stable foreign exchange rate for pound sterling, stable prices and economic growth. Priority was given to the first two; economic growth was restrained whenever a balance of payments crisis occurred, and a low but persistent level of inflation (the inevitable result of a low growth rate coupled with full employment) was tolerated until it became implicated in balance of payments crises. Orthodox monetary and fiscal policies were used to maintain a shifting balance between these available policies. By the early 1960s the decline in Britain's economic position resulting from a persistently low rate of growth had become a major issue; but at the same time the implications of expansion for the balance of payments were becoming increasingly severe. In a search for more flexible instruments of policy the Conservative Government tentatively adopted a strategy of economic planning (thereby setting up tensions within the Conservative Party which became major controversies by the 1970s). The planning would take two forms: indicative planning for industrial development based on the French model but with far less direction than in France, the principal instruments of planning being tripartite discussions on a purely voluntarist basis; and income restraint, again to be secured through tripartite and voluntary machinery.

Among the limitations on this policy was the unwillingness of the Trade Union Congress to co-operate in wage restraint given existing government policies (Dorfman, 1973; Allen, 1960). By 1963 a general election was imminent and the Government threw caution to the wind, pursuing a 'dash for growth' policy without heeding the growing balance of payments deficit. In addition to short-term electoral gain, it was hoped that a policy of growth would help create a climate in which planning and incomes restraint might become acceptable to the unions. Although the Conservatives lost the election, the incoming Labour Government adopted a broadly similar strategy, claiming greater chances of success because they would pursue growth as a higher priority, because a socialist party was the natural party of planning, and because Labour's connections with the unions would make an incomes policy more attainable (Panitch, 1976: Ch. 3). Under the slogan of 'a planned growth of incomes', Labour set about establishing a more elaborate network of institutions and preparing a National Plan.

The detailed policy record, where it directly concerns industrial relations, is discussed in Section 4. But it is necessary to spell out here some of the wider related economic developments. The familiar pattern, with a pivotal role for balance of payments crises and consequent foreign exchange crises, continued as before. By the summer of 1966 the Government, rejecting the possibility of devaluing the pound, virtually abandoned its planning strategy and returned to the crisis measures of previous Conservative administrations. But in November 1967, in a further crisis, the pound sterling was finally devalued.

Devaluation provides the immediate introduction to the period under review. It marked the end of the Government's initial strategy. From then until it fell in 1970, the prime goal of Labour's economic policy was the pursuit of a satisfactory balance of payments. This had several implications relevant to industrial relations. Prices rose in the wake of devaluation. Fiscal and monetary policy were employed with considerable severity to reduce demand, resulting in gradually rising unemployment and high taxes. Increasing emphasis was placed on incomes policy as a further instrument for reducing the pressure of demand. By 1969, when incomes policy appeared to be having insufficient success, the Government temporarily and unsuccessfully switched its attention to policies of legally restraining trade union activity as an alternative means of reducing pay increases.

Although none of these policies achieved clear success, and may in some respects have been self-defeating (see page 251), by 1970 the target of a balance of payments surplus, for which so many other policy goals had been sacrificed, was achieved, while the underlying rate of productivity improvement in British industry was rising. But alongside these developments was a considerable increase in the rate of inflation. This was partly the consequence of devaluation and the rise in wage claims after the relaxation of incomes policy as workers sought to restore ground lost through price and tax increases. But the first signs of the rise in international commodity prices, which were to dominate the first half of the 1970s, were also making their impact. Rising prices replaced the balance of payments as the major economic issue of political relevance.

Britain's economic situation in 1970 differed in several ways from that which had been characteristic of the latter 1950s. The level of government intervention in both industry and industrial relations was considerably higher; full employment no longer enjoyed its former priority; the pound had been devalued; productivity was improving, but inflation was at considerably higher levels; and the level of industrial conflict was much higher. These changes were complex, and in some ways puzzling, especially the co-existence of (relatively) high rates of pay increases and unemployment.

The Conservative Government elected in June 1970 reversed some key aspects of economic policy, believing in a return to the free market and an abolition of controls. Incomes policy was ended; public spending was cut; government aid to industry was reduced and there was an attempt to redistribute income towards wealthier groups. Crucial components of this policy were the use of a higher level of unemployment and a strategy of resisting public-sector wage claims as alternatives to incomes policy in combating inflation. But neither was effective. The expected relationship between the level of unemployment and the rate of inflation failed to develop. In the state of 'stagflation' experienced by several Western countries, wages and prices rose alongside unemployment. At the same time the policy of resisting public-sector pay claims resulted in several major confrontations between the Government and determined unions and workers, in most of which large pay rises were successfully achieved after prolonged strikes.

The underlying improvement in productivity which had begun in the late 1960s continued, and given stable prices might have been sufficient to absorb the pressure of wages, but external price increases rose further. By 1972, in the light of continuing pressure for higher incomes, price rises, high unemployment and the fact that several major industries were in difficulties, the Government changed the entire direction of its policies. Moves were made to renew the tripartite discourse on economic planning and co-operation over price and wage restraint; Government aid to private industry expanded massively; and there was a return to statutory price and wage controls, starting with a freeze modelled on that of 1966. These developments were accompanied by a return to the 'dash for growth' economic policy of the pre-1964 Conservative Government. Interest rates were relaxed and taxation reduced, though one consequence of the former was a massive rise in house prices which increased the problems of many families. The defence of the pound sterling was finally abandoned as a policy goal and it was allowed to float in the foreign exchanges, declining in value for many months. The balance of payments worsened severely.

The statutory incomes restraint achieved some early success. Unions and employers abided by it, with few exceptions. Unemployment declined and certain underlying improvements in industrial capacity continued. However, there was little improvement in the relations between Government and unions, the incomes policy being resented as much as the Conservatives' previous strategies. Inflation stemming from commodity price rises continued. Whatever success the Government might have eventually had in securing growth alongside stable prices and full employment (in the new policy context of a floating currency and a not unsuccessful prices and incomes policy) was constantly undermined from this source. And to the extent that price controls were more effective than wage controls, the rate of profit in industry was continuing to decline faster than in previous years; the prospects for future investment were not encouraging. But the final blow to the policy came in autumn 1973 with the massive rise in oil prices, which both increased the rate of inflation considerably and had important implications for industrial relations.

At the end of 1973 there were major disputes involving the application of the incomes policy in three public-sector industries which were central to the rapidly changing energy situation: the mines, electricity generation and the railways. Two years previously, the miners had gained a significant victory over the policy of public-sector wage restraint. This time, despite the changed energy situation, the Government was determined not to allow the incomes policy to be breached. The National Union of Mineworkers banned overtime, and several weeks later called a national strike. The Government introduced drastic energy-conservation measures which damaged British industry throughout 1974. A three-day working week was imposed on all industry and commerce, and major cuts in public lighting and heating were introduced.

The crisis was resolved only after a change of government at the end of February 1974 (see page 199). As in 1964, a Labour Government took office against an economic crisis and balance of payments deficit, though of a much higher order than that of a decade earlier. Inflation was expected to reach 20 per cent during the year; it had become the single over-riding preoccupation of economic policy. A central goal was to prevent external price increases from being translated into *pro rata* wage increases. Thus incomes policy was still at the centre of economic policy. However, no formal policy of incomes restraint was followed, let alone of statutory control. Instead, the Government sought voluntary measures by the unions in exchange for egalitarian and interventionist social and economic policies. This strategy, known as the social contract, is further discussed on pages 200 and 243. By the summer of 1975, however, the pressures for income restraint became stronger and the unions were formed to commit themselves to a stricter policy.

Changes in Industrial and Occupational Structure

Despite the various attempts at incomes control discussed above, for most of the period under study the real—let alone the money—incomes of wage and salary earners continued to rise faster than the rate of price increases and productivity combined. The rise continued to be lower than that achieved in other western European countries, but this was mainly a reflection of the continuing relatively slow growth of productivity in Britain. To the extent that pay increases could be neither passed on in price rises nor absorbed by improvements in efficiency, they were gained at the expense of investment. This was particularly true from late 1971 onwards, when a series of voluntary and statutory pressures operated more severely on prices than on incomes. This intensified an already existing tendency for British industry to invest at a lower rate than several other European countries. Alongside this, wages pressure worked with other tendencies within the economy to enforce an increasing concentration of industry from the late 1960s onwards.

This process began under the 1964–70 Labour Government, which established an Industrial Reorganisation Corporation to facilitate and provide public finance for major mergers within the private sector. It was part of that Government's strategy for increasing the level of investment and for improving efficiency, using public institutions and money but not challenging private ownership. The rationalisations which accompanied the mergers, which were taking place elsewhere in the economy without state intervention, also resulted in considerable redundancies, contributing to the increase in unemployment which occurred from the late 1960s onwards.

Under the Conservative Government of 1970 similar processes continued, though initially under different means. Until 1972 the state withdrew from direct involvement in industrial reorganisation, but fiscal and other incentives to profit-making encouraged takeovers, asset stripping and redundancies. In 1972 the Government returned to measures of giving state support to industry, and launched a programme rivalling Labour's in size. By the end of the period state assistance was needed, not just to engineer industrial concentration, but to rescue companies threatened by bankruptcy following the rapid rise in inflation.

Heavy state aid, and increasingly state rescue operations, continued under the Labour Government of 1974, but with a major change in emphasis. Increasingly the purpose of intervention was to preserve jobs and prevent redundancy, a policy started under the Conservatives and contrasting considerably with the earlier pattern of mergers. Also, following the shift to the left in Labour's policy during the years of opposition, the state sought increasing degrees of control, ranging from participation in the equity to outright state ownership.

The changes in industrial structure resulting from the above and other factors resulted in several shifts in the pattern of industrial output and employment during the period under review. Despite the decline in the overall level of employment, the gross domestic product continued to rise until the crisis at the end of 1973. The resulting rise in *per capita* GDP was however somewhat reduced by a large movement of labour from productive industry to service employment. Between 1965 and 1975 employment in coal mining dropped from 600,000 to 350,000 and in manufacturing industry from 9,133,000 to 7,994,000. There were also declines in the public utilities, in transport and communication and in distribution. The major increases were in financial services (from 664,000 to 1,168,000) and professional and scientific employment (from 2,753,000 to 3,250,000). There were also increases in catering and hotels and in both national and local government service (see Table 1 in Appendix I).

Something of the unusual nature of this period is seen in the fact that, during a period of decreasing levels of employment and a decline in the labour-intensiveness of industry, wages and salaries rose steeply per unit of output in manufacturing industry. In part this is a result of the increasing numbers employed in non-productive industry, but it also partly reflects labour-market pressures. Taking 1970 as equal to 100, the index of wages and salaries per unit of output in manufacturing industry rose from 75.1 in 1965 to just 83.3 in 1968. By the following year it had risen to 88.5, and by 1973 it stood at 124.5.

THE POLITICAL CONTEXT

The foregoing discussion of economic changes has already given some indication of the main political developments of the period, but these will now be considered directly.

From October 1964 Britain was governed by a Labour government, elected with a tiny overall majority (five, soon falling to three) on a programme of economic modernisation and social reform. After eighteen months in office Labour went to the country in April 1966 and was returned with a majority of 100. Within three months a national seamen's strike and a major sterling crisis had led the Government to impose a statutory pay freeze and other deflationary measures, which resulted in both internal party splits and public unpopularity which persisted until the end of the Government's life. The details of these specific events are discussed in Section 4. The Government's deepening national unpopularity can probably be very simply related to the increasing severity of its fiscal policies and, later, the price rises which followed devaluation. The situation within the party was more complex. The Government did in fact introduce most of the social policy reforms which it had promised, and not until after devaluation did the social services begin to suffer from the surrounding economic crisis. But as targets for economic growth were abandoned, the great planning enterprise lost the appeal it had enjoyed in 1964. Most importantly, at least where the present study is concerned, the only aspect of planning which retained any teeth was incomes policy, which became increasingly severe between 1965 and 1969. The party's left wing became progressively disillusioned as the planning strategy which they had seen as a step towards socialism became a device for subjecting trade unions to legal control. The divisions in the party became particularly manifest as the Government introduced a series of Acts to impose a statutory incomes policy. On the occasion of the first of these, after the 1966 crisis, Mr Frank Cousins resigned from the Cabinet.[1] Mr Cousins, a left-wing general secretary of the Transport and General Workers Union, had temporarily left his union post to become Minister of Technology in 1964—a major gesture of the Government's close relations with the trade union movement and their mutual expectations from the planning process.

By 1968 the Government was in considerable difficulties. The devaluation crisis had meant a major change of policy and some ministerial resignations. The gulf between the Government and its supporters on the one hand and the Left in Parliament, the extra-Parliamentary party and the unions on the other was growing wider. Public unpopularity also deepened. In the local elections of that year Labour lost control of all but its most strongly held areas, and did very poorly in Parliamentary by-elections. However, this situation did not result in street demonstrations or an escalation of general conflict on the pattern seen in France. Although there were student revolts in that year in Britain as elsewhere in Europe (though on a much reduced scale), there was little evidence of any significant general political amalgamation between them and industrial unrest.

In 1969 the Government began to move away from incomes policy towards its attempt at introducing new legal controls over unions' activities (see page 244). This resulted in massive conflict with the unions and within the Parliamentary party. Left-wing MPs joined with those sponsored by trade unions and declared that they would vote against the Bill to introduce the controls. It was in the shadow of that Parliamentary revolt that the Prime Minister reached agreement with the TUC (Panitch, 1976: Ch. 7; Ellis and Johnson, 1974; Jenkins, 1969). From then on (June 1969) the position began to change, both internally and externally. The Government no longer attempted major statutory intervention in incomes policy or industrial relations, and began the process of repairing relations with the unions which was to become so central to Labour by 1974. As a result the internal party disputes quietened. At the same time, economic circumstances began to improve slightly with the recovery of the balance of payments. Early in 1970 the Government introduced a mildly reflationary budget, and by the time of the election campaign of June of that year it was universally expected that Labour would be returned to office.

But the Conservative Party made the price rises, which were becoming an important public concern, into a major election issue. They promised cuts in taxation and legal curbs on industrial militancy as solutions to the problem. Attacks on trade unions, always avoided in previous British general elections by the Tory party, were among the prominent themes of this campaign. The

Conservatives secured a majority of 32 and formed the next government.

The Conservative Party in opposition had shifted its policies considerably from those of the early 1960s, which had drifted towards economic planning and incomes policy. In the wake of the 1964 and 1966 defeats the *laissez-faire* wing of the party had secured a greater influence. The new Government set about implementing the new policies, some of which were described on pages 193–4. The industrial relations policies will be considered in detail on page 245. Other measures affected the welfare state and taxation policy, and further intensified the estrangement between the Government and the unions. Although the Conservatives had warned in opposition of the dangers of controversial state intervention in industrial relations, and had argued the case against incomes policy partly on those grounds, their own Industrial Relations Bill resulted in more controversy than any of the previous measures. Within Parliament, the Bill was very strongly contested by the Labour Opposition, while the unions simply refused to have anything to do with it (Panitch, 1976: Ch 6; TUC, 1970; Heffer, 1971). They would not accept consultation with Government over its mere details; the TUC took up a position of non-cooperation with the Bill after it became law; and there were various one-day strikes by increasingly large groups of workers during its passage through Parliament. Industrial and political conflict were becoming merged in an unprecedented way. The implementation of the Act was marked with further conflict as important unions, principally the TGWU and the Amalgamated Union of Engineering Workers, refused even to attend hearings in the new National Industrial Relations Court which had been established under the Act.

By 1972 the Heath Government had embarked on its major *volte face* in nearly every area of policy, some indications of which were given above. Part of the new policy involved a return to the pattern of tripartite national talks to secure agreement on incomes restraint and economic objectives, and overtures were made to the unions. However, this did not involve a lessening in the new level of political tension over industrial relations questions. The series of major public-sector strikes continued; the Industrial Relations Act was just beginning to have an effect; and the new policy involved a statutory incomes policy of greater legal severity than that of the previous Labour Government. The final stage of the Heath Government's relations with the unions, and the culmination of the increasing politicisation of industrial conflict, came at the end of 1973 with the mining dispute. The prospects for 1974 were of continuing price rises and industrial conflict, with probable increasing unpopularity for the governing party, which would have to go to the country by June 1975 at the latest. The Prime Minister decided to go to the country immediately, in February 1974, calling the election specifically on the one issue of 'Who governs Britain?' – the government or the trade unions. The party which had entered the 1970 election pledged to end incomes policy was now calling an election in 1974 on the one issue of the maintenance of a statutory incomes policy. The Conservatives' central election slogan was 'Firm Action for a Fair Britain', the latter phrase being a reference to the elaborate procedures for fixing the relative pay of different groups of workers under the incomes policy; again, the party which in 1970 had called for a return for market principles and an end to state intervention in incomes was now adopting the opposite policy. Meanwhile, Labour, the party which had championed an incomes policy from 1964 to 1970, stood as the party of free collective bargaining and opposition to state interference in incomes determination.

The February election was the first in Britain to be called on a specific issue for over sixty years; and it was the only occasion on which a major party had broken one of the basic assumptions of British politics: that the boundary between industrial and political conflict must be maintained at all costs.

A Conservative victory was widely predicted, but the result was in fact very different. The Conservatives slipped back badly, and Labour made enough gains in seats to overtake them as the biggest single party, but did by no means well enough to secure an overall majority, and in fact secured fewer overall votes than the Conservatives. The Liberal party made gains (the increase in their vote was extremely large, but under the British electoral system small parties have difficulty in gaining seats to match their votes). In Scotland and, to a lesser extent, in Wales, Nationalist parties which in the past had enjoyed only token representation, made important advances. The most dramatic single change was in Northern Ireland, where the Unionist Party allies of the British Conservatives lost their previous near-total grip and retained no seats at all. The issue here was nothing at all to do with industrial relations or the miners' strike, but concerned the continuing conflict between Catholics and Protestants in the Province which had involved open street violence since 1969.

Although the February election was called on the issue of industrial conflict, its outcome can hardly be interpreted as a public 'verdict' on that question, as the complexity of the results indicates, though it can perhaps be claimed that the large drop in public support for the Conservatives indicated a general unwillingness to pursue the politics of industrial confrontation. For a few days Mr Heath tried to produce an anti-socialist coalition with the Liberals to prevent Labour taking office, but this failed, and the minority Labour government came to office, immediately negotiating a compromise conclusion of the miners' strike.

As the Conservatives in opposition during 1964–70 had disengaged themselves from the troublesome new areas of planning and intervention to return to *laissez-faire* principles, so Labour between 1970 and 1974 had shifted its policies considerably leftwards, towards increased state intervention in industrial ownership and management, and towards non-intervention in collective bargaining and trade union affairs. The unions had increased their role within the party and made considerable policy demands, in an attempt to ensure no repetition of the 1966–9 estrangement. For the first time in many years the party and the TUC produced joint policy statements, on a strategy for tackling inflation.[2] The measures were mainly for improving the legal rights of trade unions, increasing state intervention in industry, and redistributing income and wealth. In exchange for this it was hoped that the TUC would eventually agree to try to persuade its member unions to show a degree of restraint in pressing pay claims under a Labour government. The general strategy of working towards an agreement of that kind was called the 'social contract' by party leaders. In the context of the February election the aspiration suddenly had to be translated into existing reality, and Labour leaders put forward the social contract as their alternative to the Conservatives' 'policy of confrontation'.

After the election the minority Labour government set about implementing the contract. The Industrial Relations Act and the incomes policy machinery (but not price controls) were abolished; food subsidies were introduced and various redistributive measures were implemented; and plans were made for major state interventions in the ownership and control of industry. In the coming months the level of pay increases continued to rise. It was clear that the Government would seek a majority at the earliest possible opportunity. By the early autumn Ministers began to elevate the social contract to an even more central place in Labour's publicly presented policy, and sought major commitments of support for the wage restraint provisions of the contract from the unions. Most importantly, at its Congress in September, the TUC accepted the idea of wage restraint in exchange for its new power over social and economic policy (TUC, 1975). A general election was called in October, the Government's campaign being rested entirely on the social contract (which had by now been expanded to include virtually every aspect of domestic policy) (Labour Party, 1974). The Conservative Opposition, which had not yet had time to reassess its policies after the February defeat, adopted a low profile; it concentrated its campaign on warnings against trade union domination of politics and advocacy of an all-party Government of National Unity under Conservative leadership to steer Britain through the inflation crisis (CCO, 1974). Labour secured its overall majority, but by only a tiny margin of three seats, though given the fragmented nature of the Opposition this proved workable. The Conservatives had dropped back further, and though the Liberals made no further advances the Scottish Nationalists secured several new seats.

The politics of the Government continued for a while to follow the left-wing course already established. Plans were being made for major state interventions in private industry; redistributive taxation was promised; and legislation highly favourable to the powers of trade unions and workers was introduced. However, these strategies together with continuing very high inflation resulted in a major decline in business confidence and a collapse of sterling on the foreign exchanges. In June 1975 the Government held its planned referendum on Britain's membership of the European Economic Community. This resulted in a decisive vote in favour of entry, while the Labour Left and most unions had campaigned for withdrawal. Not long after this, and amid continued pressure on sterling, the Government began to shift its policies. A form of incomes policy was reintroduced (see Section 4), and the Government sealed down its plans for intervention in industry. Plans for industrial recovery therefore began to rely increasingly on the private sector and its profitability, and Government policies came increasingly to correspond to the demands of industry and commerce.

INDUSTRIAL CONFLICT: QUANTITATIVE TRENDS

In reviewing overall quantitative trends in strikes it is important to bear in mind the problems of using available statistical data, as discussed in another paper in this study.[3] However, it is possible to consider broad tendencies indicated by the existing figures. Only bare outlines are considered here, since detailed discussions will be pursued in Section 3.[4]

The most significant feature has been an intensification of conflict indicated by all three major indices – the number of strikes, the number of workers involved, and the working days lost (see figure 6.1). The number of strikes rose from a low point in 1966 (a year containing a six-month statutory incomes freeze) to reach its highest level ever in 1970. After a sharp fall it continued to rise again from 1972 until the big decline in 1975. The figures for worker involvement show a similar tendency, but with the peak coming slightly earlier, in 1968. Thereafter worker involvement remained until 1975 on a plateau considerably higher than that of the previous period. The shift in the statistics on working days lost is even more dramatic. Again, climbing at increasing speed from a low point in the mid 1960s, it exceeded the figure for 1926 (the year of the General Strike) in 1971, and reached entirely unprecedented levels in 1972 and 1974.

A useful indicator of the contours of different periods has been given by Shalev (1973), and more recently in Table 1.6 of his paper in the present volume (page 17). His data show the continuous increase in the rate of stoppages outside coal-mining since 1950, with a sharp rise in the rate of increase in the most recent period (1968–73); the decline in a number of indicators (size, duration, involvement) during the 1964–7 period, again if mining is excluded; and the sharp increase in duration and size of strikes in the most recent period. This last point is related to a further important change in the early 1970s. As Shalev indicates in his present paper (page 9), in 1971 and 1972 the ratio of official to unofficial strikes outside mining declined considerably, though a more typical pattern had been re-established by 1973 and 1974. Behind these figures lay a shift in British strike patterns. Whereas the growth of small, short, unofficial strikes which had been so characteristic of the early 1960s continued (though becoming slightly larger and longer), the most impressive development in the early 1970s was of long, large official disputes; particularly important among these was a series of set-piece confrontations between the state and unions in the public sectors. These strikes are considered in more detail on page 228. It is notable that during 1968 and 1969 unofficial strikes alone rose substantially, the rise in official activity following from 1970. This lends *prime facie* support to the argument that the resurgence of official union militancy was a response to that of shop-

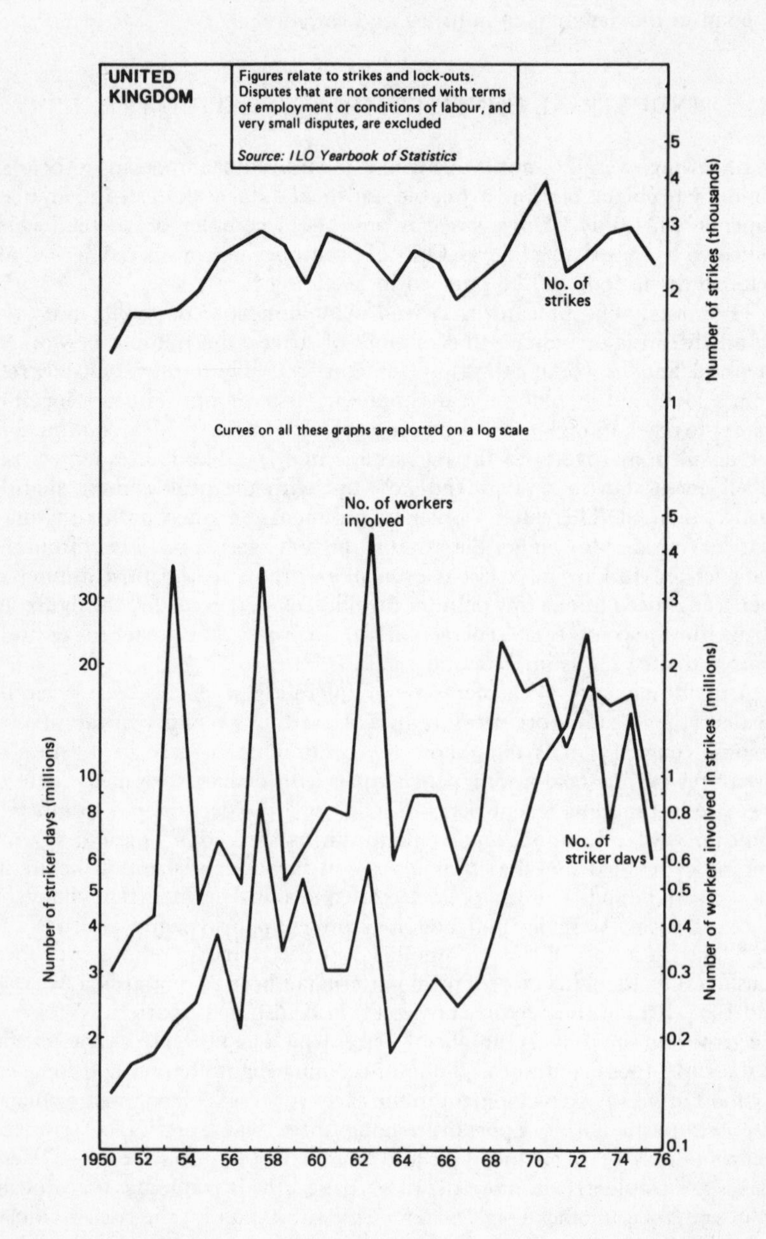

FIGURE 6.1: Industrial conflict in the United Kingdom, 1950–75 (log scales)

floor workers, though as the later discussion will show other factors were also involved.

As has been already indicated in some of the data discussed above, it is common in discussions of strike trends in Britain to separate coal-mining for some purposes of analysis. This is because of the distinctive history of strikes in this industry. Throughout most of the 1950s the number of mining strikes rose, constituting over 70 per cent of the total (Shalev, 1974: Table UK/1). By 1960 they had begun to decline, eventually constituting 7 per cent of the total in the period 1968–72. Finally, in 1972 and 1974 two major official strikes in the industry weighed particularly heavily in the overall statistics for those years. Meanwhile, throughout the 1960s strikes outside mining increased five-fold. In his paper in this volume, Shalev discusses the general issue of the exclusion of mining strikes, and elsewhere in the present paper the interpretation of the changes in mining disputes is considered; at present it is simply necessary to set them aside so that shifting patterns in other industries can be considered.

Only ship-building (like mining, a declining industry throughout the period) had not doubled its strike frequency between 1963 and 1970 (Shalev, 1973). Figures on relative involvement (the number of involvements per 10,000 employees) show: (i) the massive importance of transport equipment, but also of mining, transport, metals and machinery in the most recent period; (ii) the increasing importance of strikes in other industries as well (Shalev, 1974: Table UK/2). Even industries in which strike involvements are relatively low (such as textiles, public utilities, public services) saw major increases from 1968 onwards. Although relative strike proneness has not changed greatly, disputes are becoming important in industries which used to be immune.

Before leaving statistical data, a peculiarity of the British situation needs to be noted: 'political' strikes are not officially counted as strikes. In the past this has not been very important. However, one development in the resurgence of conflict has been the occasional appearance of political strikes. For example, Shalev (1973) estimates that the one-day stoppages (some official, some unofficial) against the Industrial Relations Bill in 1971 involved twice as many workers as the entire year's industrial disputes.

3 NEW CHARACTERISTICS OF THE PERIOD

Accounts of the historical context of Britain's industrial relations, like accounts of its class structure, frequently stress ambiguity and compromise. The trade union movement is old and deeply entrenched among society's institutions, and has close links with a political party which indeed it helped to found. For over a century the movement has maintained a high level of national cohesion with relatively little disturbance from conflicts between Communists and Socialists, Catholics and Protestants, manual and non-manual labour, or regional cultural differences. But alongside, and perhaps contributing to, these strengths, British labour has maintained a firm distinction between industrial and political actions, has rarely sought to use its national cohesion for any concerted purpose, and has been content with practices and institutions which have held the structure of income differences virtually static for nearly one hundred years. Conflict has been heavily institutionalised, unions have accepted whatever level of national integration successive governments have offered them, and the level of strikes has been lower than that in many western industrial societies.

But in recent years there have been distinct changes in these patterns, and in the activities of workers, unions, employers and the state. Although the pace of change in very recent years has been rapid, its origins can be traced back to developments which occurred in the late 1950s. Unlike some other countries, Britain did not experience a sudden resurgence of conflict in 1968, though it is true that by that time several significant developments had occurred. By the early 1970s the political context of industrial relations, and the level of overt conflict, had rendered much of the traditional account redundant. However, as subsequent sections will show, the historical mould of compromise has continued to shape the resurgence of conflict and the attempts of various groups to cope with it. Despite the changes, the ambiguities of compromise remain.

Evidence of the resurgence of conflict is found in the following phenomena:

(a) The rise in unofficial shop-floor militancy, indicated by: an increasing number and proportion of 'unofficial' or 'unconstitutional' strikes; an increase in the extent to which wages are settled at plant level (associated with the wider phenomenon of wage-drift); and a rise in the importance of shop stewards as opposed to full-time union officials. Although much has been made of the novelty of these developments, it is important to bear in mind that they mark a return to much earlier patterns of industrial relations; the pattern of trade or industry level bargaining through union hierarchies and employers' associations which has become known as the traditional pattern dates back only to the later 1930s. It should also be noted that the rise in unofficial disputes began in the 1950s, and was not a sudden phenomenon starting in the late 1960s.
(b) The exercise of unilateral controls by workers over the conduct of their work, and the willingness of workers to use unilateral pressure to seek the resolution of conflicts outside formal disputes procedure. This too is no sudden recent development.
(c) Resort to strike action on an important scale by formerly quiescent groups of workers. This is a much more recent development of the late 1960s and early 1970s.
(d) The extension of unionisation to increasing numbers of white-collar workers; here too the late 1960s mark a significant turning point.
(e) The extension of the scope of collective bargaining to wider issues than claims for increased pay or reduced hours of work which traditionally characterised union activity.
(f) In the 1970s, the return of long, large-scale official strikes, primarily in the public sector.

(g) An escalation in the level of both wage claims and settlements, including an increase in the frequency of claims; this became dramatically noticeable in 1969 in the course of what was then known as the 'wage explosion'.
(h) Again since about 1970, an intensification of the forms of industrial action taken by certain groups of workers, including the development of 'mass' picketing and 'flying' pickets, and occasional resort to the occupation of factories under at least temporary workers' control to resist closure and redundancies.
(i) At national level, political confrontations between trade unions and the Government, including a major extension of the Government's active participation in industrial relations.
(j) Associated with (i), an increasing tendency for unions at national level to raise wider political demands than their traditional preoccupation with 'industrial' issues.

These different aspects of the question will be taken up at various points in the following discussion.

THE NEW DEMANDS

The Initial Context

The traditionally modest and unremarkable nature of the achievements of British collective bargaining has been frequently discussed (Hyman and Brough, 1975; Phelps Brown with Browne, 1968; Routh, 1965). Of course, in part this results from the fact that unions are bargaining in a context of class domination. But even taking this into account the unions' own objectives have been modest and narrow. They have restricted much of their activity to the pursuit of wage increases which have not threatened the overall distribution of wealth or challenged the capability of the economy, and to the representation of their members in disputes over established and recognised rights within an accepted employer/employee relationship. Two important characteristics of the labour movement have helped to limit its objectives. First, unions have been deeply reluctant to become implicated in management in the sense of becoming management's tool, sharing its responsibility but not its power. They have therefore been content to maintain a separation between employer and employee, manager and managed, which has in turn meant full acceptance of subordinate roles for workers. Secondly, unions have been committed to the distinctively British conception of socialism in which the state is held to have the primary responsibility for providing such welfare benefits as pensions and health services. Therefore unions have not pressed employers to provide benefits of this kind, but have focussed their attention on wages and on reductions in hours; and in recent years the latter has tended to be equivalent to the former since reductions in working hours have been accompanied by equivalent increases in overtime working.

The modesty of traditional union aspirations is further indicated by the typical pattern of wage demands. Pay demands are usually for 'a substantial increase', supported by evidence of changes in the cost of living, the profitability of the firm or industry concerned, or pay increases recently secured by other workers. This last point is probably the most important of all. Known as the principle of comparability it appears at many levels of bargaining in Britain (Brown, 1973; Lerner *et al*, 1969; Parker *et al*, 1974). At shop-floor level, a claim will often be based on the fact that another group of workers in the factory, or in another local factory, has secured an increase. At the level of formal union claims the principle will again be used: a union may seek an increase because workers traditionally paid less than its members have had one, or because workers traditionally more highly paid have increased their differential. Within the public sector, especially the civil service and local government, comparability is often the principal basis of negotiations, with elaborate rules governing the comparisons which may be made. Finally, when governments appoint committees of inquiry into wage disputes the committees are often guided in their decisions by ideas of comparability (McCarthy and Clifford, 1966). It is not surprising that collective bargaining has rarely had other than a temporary effect on the overall distribution of income when many demands are couched in terms of the restoration or maintenance of existing differentials, and when comparisons with other groups of workers have been the most readily accepted formulae for agreements on both sides of industry. The failure of organised sections of labour to show anything other than temporary gains over unorganised labour may also partly be explained by the unilateral use of comparisons by employers. In some cases employers may deliberately set their wages according to those achieved in unionised sectors in order to deter their employees from bothering with union membership; elsewhere they simply use comparisons for non-unionised employees in order to maintain the stability of internal pay structures, or to maintain a position in a crudely conceived labour market.

But the very conservative and unadventurous aspects of British trade union demands may have radical implications (Hyman and Brough, 1975). Unions have used their insistence on general, non-specific criteria to counter Government and employer attempts to impose a rigorous market or managerial rationality on pay structures. In contrast, for example, with German unions, they have rejected Government pay ceilings or the strict linking of increases to productivity improvements. Union – and unofficial – claims have reflected workers' aspirations for a stable or improving standard of life, and perhaps also for a stable relationship between their incomes and those of workers considered close to them in the occupational hierarchy. During periods of expanding national wealth this demand can fairly easily be satisfied by modern capitalism. But during times of economic difficulty, when employers are trying to reduce labour costs and relate incomes more closely to output, those same aspirations can result in major conflicts.

The rate of real increases in workers' standard of living was for many years determined largely by the rate of productivity improvement, rather than by any redistribution of income (Phelp Brown with Browne, 1968). To the extent that money increases were secured which exceeded that level, they were absorbed by inflation. Inflation has thus had the same effect as a spurious increase in productivity by making it unnecessary for increases in wages and salaries to have any major distributional implications. Compromise and conciliation continued to provide workers with greater increases than employers would have liked for just so long as inflation and productivity together insulated the overall distribution of resources from the implications of these increases, and for so long as workers were victims of 'money illusion'.

Therefore, in the post-war period of potential labour strength, the continuing existence of Britain's peaceable and liberal industrial relations system was dependent on labour's own demands being modest, and their *effects* being further contained by rises in productivity or the rise in inflation.

The Emergence of New Demands

The increase in militancy in Britain has only partially taken the form of distinctively new demands. This results from the characteristics of traditional bargaining described above: if the traditional system has been *ad hoc* and unsystematic, with unions always retaining a measure of independence, a new level of militancy may emerge from that system gradually and without producing qualitatively distinct demands. The underlying development of a new level of militancy is no less real than in countries where its manifestations were more dramatic, but the break with the past is not so clear cut.

Since the early 1960s, there has been some broadening of demands (Roberts and Rothwell, 1974). Union claims have extended beyond simple pay demands to include improved holidays, occupational pension schemes, safeguards against redundancy and so forth. Unions and unofficial groups have become alert to problems of redundancy and have insisted on negotiating the terms of any lay-offs which occurred; more recently they have resisted the very fact of redundancy. Most productivity agreements in the latter 1960s had to include pledges by the employers that no workers would be made redundant by the implementation of the plan, or alternatively that redundancy would be by natural wastage or by voluntary response to generous offers of redundancy payment. In most cases it had been accepted by the employers from the outset that they would not have been able to secure agreement to the productivity improvements without such a pledge.

However, more significant developments in the nature of demands will be discovered if one considers the following dimensions: (i) the rising level of pay demands and settlements; (ii) demands for protection of the low paid; (iii) the growing importance in many industries of workers' unilateral job controls, and the response of management to these; and (iv) a new concern for wider political demands by the official union movement.

THE RISING LEVEL OF PAY DEMANDS:

There was a distinct rise in the level of both pay demands and settlements towards the end of 1969, and the characteristics of that rise will be considered shortly. But it is first necessary to set it in the context of the preceding years of post-war full employment and its consequences. Throughout the 1950s the pressure of pay increases was occasionally involved in general economic crises affecting the balance of payments and pressure on the pound sterling, as discussed on page 192. Much of this pressure for increased pay stemmed from local increases in excess of nationally negotiated rates. But the process of wage drift, as this was identified, cannot be simply equated with a rise in the demands of organised labour. To a certain extent the incidence of wage drift is a statistical by-product of the means employed for calculating orthodox pay increases (Wilkinson and Turner, 1972). Furthermore, collective action by workers is not necessarily involved in several of the processes which create 'drift'. In a fully employed economy with various sectoral labour shortages, many employers have unilaterally pushed up rates of pay beyond those negotiated nationally with unions, or in the absence of unions, as is often the case in white-collar employment. In contrast, it is in some of the most heavily unionised areas that pay has been most rigidly controlled, that is, in the public sector (Clegg, 1972: Ch. 9). The association between shop-floor militancy and drift *is* seen in those sectors where workers have been able to take conscious advantage of their strong market situation in order to turn certain payment systems to their own advantage. The most striking cases of this occur with piecework systems (Brown, 1973; Lerner *et al*, 1969; NBPI, 1965). When piecework was first introduced in British industry it was regarded with hostility by workers, because it was seen as a system for increasing managerial control over workers' output of effort and pace of work. But as workers gained confidence in using the power of the work group to withhold labour, so they became able to bargain over the terms of a piecework rate. Several characteristics of contemporary piecework bargaining demonstrate this improved power of the workers' situation: for example, the ratchet effect of the principle that a change in work arrangements may lead to a fortuitous increase in earnings but not to a fortuitous decrease.

A recent study of piecework bargaining demonstrates some of its significant characteristics (Brown, 1973). Its scope depends heavily on workers' awareness of the bargaining situation and their willingness to manipulate it; many of the potentialities of a piecework system will be realised only if workers are alert to opportunities for challenging managerial decisions or for advancing their own tactical position. Since the development of this awareness is likely to be a cumulative process, it is reasonable to assume that this kind of bargaining will spread to increasing numbers of enterprises over time. It is not likely that once bargaining has become established within a work-place it will be relinquished.

Although piecework is a form of wage payment highly suited to worker control, it is by no means only within piecework systems that work groups have expressed increasing demands. Workers on time rates and other forms of payment have been able to advance their position by claiming 'parity' with other groups of workers who are considered 'comparable' (Lerner *et al*, 1969). The comparable group may be pieceworkers within the same factory, workers at other firms in the same area, in other plants of the same company, or in other firms within the industry. An increase in the militancy of this kind of pay claim may take the form of extending the range of comparisons (Hyman, 1974). This has been important in very recent years as several firms have sought to replace piecework systems with such devices as measured day work. The purpose of such changes is to regain control over wage levels for management, and this has frequently been the result. However, in some cases workers (and unions) have sought to recapture the scope for bargaining by making increasingly ambitious claims for 'parity', using wider bases of comparison. Conflict over wage claims of this kind are likely to involve much larger groups than fragmented piecework bargaining. The implications of developments of this kind are discussed on page 233. It is important to recognise the *ad hoc*, unco-ordinated and modest nature of these gradually rising demands. In no sense has it been a concerted movement or a sudden development, and it has by no means affected all workers. Although the increase in unofficial shop-floor pay settlements is the predominant characteristic of the period, even that generalisation must be qualified. There have been several important incidents involving official unions, from 1956 onwards (Clegg and Adams, 1957).

As will be discussed in Section 4, by the mid-1960s governments were committed to an incomes policy to counter the continuing imbalance between pay and productivity. The policy was by no means totally successful, and few unions gave it unreserved support. Nevertheless, by 1968 the rising pressure of unofficial action indicated the resentment of workers at restraints on their ability to increase their incomes. In 1969 the legal constraints of the policy were finally relaxed. There was a sudden rise in the level of claims and settlements, which became known as the 'wage explosion'.

The interpretation of this explosion needs to take into account several factors. Firstly, to the extent that incomes policy had been effective, it had 'damned up' claims from several groups, particularly in the public sector (see pages 213,222), who had fallen behind those able to evade incomes policy controls. Secondly, the period had been one of sharply rising prices, first as a consequence of the devaluation of November 1967 and then from early steps in the increases in world commodity prices which were to dominate the early 1970s. Although increases in money wages rose faster than those in prices, these gross figures do not accurately represent the situation facing workers and their families (Layton, 1973). Not only is the price index only a rough approximation to the actual structure of prices rises faced by a particular family, but there is a major difference between wage and price rises. The latter rise at frequent intervals and particular prices rise at different times, whereas wages are only increased at fixed intervals of about a year. Therefore even if, taking grouped annual statistics, wages rise faster than prices, the experience of workers' families during most of a particular year has been of uncontrollably rising prices and a fixed income. Furthermore, the insecurity induced by high levels of inflation means that people are as concerned with what they fear will happen in the coming months as they are with the actual experience of previous months. It is notable that by 1973 government incomes policy sought to meet this element of fear of future inflation by the encouragement of threshold agreements. This marked a considerable reversal of the policy followed between 1965 and 1970, when incomes policy discouraged older agreements for cost-of-living bonuses on the grounds that they contributed to an inflationary spiral. By 1973 the fear of insecurity had become sufficiently important itself as a contributor to the spiral to warrant the temporary nation-wide introduction of cost-of-living arrangements (the 'threshold agreements').

Finally, it should be noted that data on price changes do not take account of changes in the impact of direct taxation. The 1964–70 period was one of considerably increased taxation, partly because of the heavy public-spending programme of the Labour Government, and partly because of the severely deflationary budgets which were part of the Government's strategy to restore the balance of payments. A particularly important aspect of this was the fact that rising money incomes were bringing into taxation brackets large numbers of manual workers who had previously not been affected by income tax. The significance of these taxation effects for an explanation of the sudden increase in pay demands has been studied in detail by Turner and Wilkinson (1972), who consider the increase in both pay increases and strikes during what was also a period of rising unemployment. They are primarily concerned with the implications of increases in taxation, and point out that (pp. 100–1):

> . . . the first general increase in the British strike liability coincided approximately with the introduction of the *average* wage-earner to the income-tax system's grasp, and that the more recent sharp increase in industrial conflict again approximately coincides with the date at which he became liable for the full rate of tax.

They also demonstrate (p. 72):

> . . . that the effect of increasing the individual's gross money income merely to keep in line with the rise in prices between 1960 and 1970 was to produce a rise in the proportionate burden of taxation for all single men earning more than £350 in the earlier year, and for family men who earned above £600 in 1960, so that *net* real income would have substantially declined. For the employee who earned £1000 in 1960, for instance, the effect of the shift to a higher tax curve involved in maintaining the same level of *gross* real income was to take an additional 5 per cent of the latter in tax, and to reduce his *net* real income proportionately more.

And, on a point relevant to the importance of the low paid in the resurgence of militancy, they show that, while pay settlements between 1968 and 1971 tended to favour the low paid (p. 39):

. . . this discrimination was almost entirely cancelled by the marginal effect of taxation. Indeed , workers at the highest level of earnings retained, on the whole, a larger increase in real terms than most other groups, and the smallest retained real advance was for the married man at a middling level of wages. The unmarried low-paid worker also did rather badly, and the lowest-paid family man was only permitted to retain his increase in gross real wages intact by the passing effect of the 1971 Budget's tax concessions, which removed him temporarily from the tax range.

It is therefore possible to interpret the wage explosion and subsequent high plateau of pay settlements in terms of an attempt by workers to protect their existing standard in life, and perhaps to secure continuous but minor advances in it. It may well be that, throughout the period, workers' expectations of the standard of living which they should be able to achieve were rising, but in the context of price increases, devaluations, freezes and increasing taxation described here, expectations of a constantly improving real standard of life would not themselves need to have increased in order to generate the dramatic increase in demands for money wages which occurred.

The growing scale of Britain's economic difficulties gave workers' demands an increasingly critical effect, while Government measures to retrieve the situation, such as tax increases and incomes policy only intensified these demands. Wage demands continued high under the Conservative Government until the reintroduction of a tough incomes policy in late 1972.

But the miners' dispute at the end of 1973 ended any prospect that the rate of claims and settlements would in fact stabilise, and 1974 saw a major revival, though the main source of the unprecedented increases in pay during that year was the threshold arrangement, which did not expire until November. The Labour Government abandoned incomes controls, and the level of pay rises in 1974–75 considerably outstripped the increase in the cost of living (though again, if changing levels of income tax are taken into account the relationship is not so striking).

It is clear that by the mid-1970s pay demands had come to have far more severe implications for the management of the economy than they had, say fifteen years earlier. Glyn and Sutcliffe (1972) have traced in detail the implications which this has had for British capitalism. They argue that employers have been unable to accommodate rising wages by simply increasing prices because of competitive pressures in export markets. It may be that they exaggerate the importance of this, but the presence of the phenomenon has not been seriously challenged. Its main consequence was a fall in the rate of profit, leading to a decline in investment, thus exacerbating the major structural problem of the British economy: low and inefficient capital investment.

This long-term tendency was intensified when the already high inflation of the early 1970s was supplemented by the consequences of the increases in oil and other commodity prices. Workers strove to protect their standard of living despite the sudden decline in national income, and governments imposed price controls. Although incomes policy contained workers' attempts for a period, the pressure on industry was still strong, and became intense during the initial period of Labour Government when price controls remained but incomes policy was relaxed. For a brief period from 1974 to mid-1975 it appeared that workers' militancy might force a major crisis of capitalist profitability, which the Government would meet with socialist policies. Caught between price controls and foreign competition on one hand, and pressure from workers for pay increases on the other, many firms, including some major ones, were threatened with bankruptcy and turned to the state for assistance. The Department of Industry under its then Secretary of State, Mr Tony Benn, seemed to be meeting these appeals with demands either for state ownership or at least state control, while encouraging workers who occupied firms threatened with closure to set up co-operatives. Government policy also appeared to favour a shift towards reliance on the state rather than the private sector as the source of new investment. These developments all contributed to the mood of panic among British industrialists and overseas holders of sterling. However, after the resumption of incomes policy and the transfer of Mr Benn to another department in July 1975, the pressures from pay claims abated and the Government again began to rely on private capital for industrial recovery, soft-pedalling its plans for intervention. Incomes policy became once more a means for protecting capital.

Whether Glyn and Sutcliffe are accurate in regarding industrial militancy as a direct challenge to capital is another matter. It is unlikely that there has been much conscious challenge to profits, and it is not even clear whether workers have come to have higher expectations than before. It is surprising that, despite the preoccupation of British sociology with the study of workers' perceptions and attitudes, very little work has been done on this particular question (Goldthorpe *et al*, 1968, 1969; Hyman, 1972a; Child, 1973). We know little of the aspirations of workers in terms of the criteria they use when making a pay demand, nor of their expectations for a certain standard of living. It is often claimed in the literature on the subject that their circles of comparison have been enlarged (Cliff, 1970; Hyman, 1972b), but there is no systematic evidence on whether this is so and, if so, in what ways.

However, whatever the workers' aspirations may be, the intensifications of conflict can be accounted for even without such knowledge. Given full employment, the stability of Britain's relatively unregulated industrial relations system depended on workers' being able to achieve a gently increasing standard of life through a moderate level of economic growth. By the late 1960s several factors had combined to render this balance difficult to achieve. A continuing low rate of growth and balance of payments difficulties (i) made inflation less tolerable to governments, (ii) led to devaluations and consequent price rises, and (iii) brought about harsh fiscal policies. Higher money incomes were increasingly needed to fulfil even modest objectives. But the increased pressure needed to secure these stimulated government counter-action; and, as will be seen in subsequent sections, this itself in turn stimulated further militancy and the politicisation of union demands. By the end of 1973 the new wave of commodity price rises, especially that of oil, intensified these pressures still further. The inflationary spiral reached unprecedented proportions. Until the mid 1960s inflation could be seen as a 'safety valve' through which conflicts between labour and capital could find a release, but this situation had changed dramatically by the 1970s. Price increases at levels which wiped out any gains from increased efficiency generated pay increases which themselves produced further price increases and cuts in investment which reduced further the possibility of economic growth rising to meet some of the pressure.

THE CAMPAIGN FOR THE LOW PAID

One aspect of the general rise in wage militancy may be considered separately as a qualitatively distinct development: the emergence of a concern for, and the increased militancy of, low-paid workers. Some elements of the possible causes of this have already been mentioned in connection with the work of Turner and Wilkinson on the effects of taxation changes. The first union to take up the issue of the low paid as a major question was the TGWU, which called the strategy 'social justice bargaining'. It formulated a target of £16 10s a week as a minimum wage in 1969 and this was later taken up by the TUC, the figure being increased from time to time as the cost of living rose. During the latter 1960s several unions negotiated pay settlements which made special provision for low-paid workers by awarding either flat-rate increases or increases which concentrated on the lowest paid and then 'tapered' as they moved up the scale (Layton, 1973).

A further aspect of the low-pay campaign, the new militancy of previously quiescent groups, is discussed on page 222. In part the new priority for low-paid workers can be traced to unions' re-engagement with the shop-floor and their realisation that in several industries the achievements of national level bargaining had not been great. But it may also be related in several ways to the incomes policy of the 1964–70 Labour Government. As will be shown, the groups most easily hit by incomes policy were low-paid public-sector workers who had begun to take action by 1969. At the same time, much of the official rhetoric around incomes policy concerned the low paid, ministers claiming that incomes policy could help them where collective bargaining had failed. Also, low pay was one of the criteria under the policy by which increases in excess of the norm could be achieved, though in practice it was not a helpful criterion (Hughes, 1972; Crouch, 1975). Unions responded to this situation in two ways. Firstly, there is some evidence that low-pay campaigns were a direct counter to government claims that incomes policy could do more for the low paid than bargaining; hence the significance of the TGWU's concept of 'social justice bargaining'. (A similar reaction can be seen in the campaign of the TGWU for increased old-age pensions, which was partly a response to the charge by politicians that pensioners on fixed incomes suffered from the 'inflationary' consequences of collective bargaining.) Secondly, and more important, since low pay was one of the criteria under which exceptional increases could be secured, several unions sought to adjust to this potential loophole by making their claims in these terms. This led to increased investigation of the position of low-paid workers by unions. Low pay emerged as a prominent issue in the late 1960s, but it has remained important in union demands, political rhetoric and the criteria of incomes policy.

The issue of equal pay for women became implicated in the low-pay campaign, partly because a large proportion of the lowest wages in Britain represent the differential rates paid to women workers, and partly because the general campaign for women's rights was beginning at that time. Women are generally less well organised in unions than men, and rarely involved in strikes. One aspect of the campaigns of the past few years has been an increase in the involvement of women in union activity and in conflict. Several unions have negotiated pay agreements which give larger increases to women, often as part of a longer-term strategy of moving towards equal pay. At the same time, general pressure for women's rights led to a succession of legislation for equal pay and employment opportunities in the 1970s by both Labour and Conservative governments.

The negotiation of pay increases biased towards the low paid creates problems for some unions which base their claims on the need to maintain differentials, especially the craft unions and some white-collar unions. This factor has certainly inhibited the extent to which the TUC could pursue a general policy for flat-rate increases. However, this has not emerged as a major division within the trade union movement. Many unions have both members who would benefit from assistance to the low paid and those who benefit from differentials, so sharp inter-union conflicts have been avoided. The general vagueness of unions' bargaining strategies has also prevented the issue from being raised sharply. Nearly all unions are willing to advocate help for the low paid, while at the same time stressing the need for differentials. The issue was posed more sharply when in 1975 the unions agreed a temporary flat-rate incomes policy; this caused considerable tensions among higher-paid employees.

DEMANDS FOR CONTROL

It is important not to put too much weight on the distinction between demands for job control and those for increased pay. Some observers have drawn attention to statistics which suggest that disputes over managerial control are assuming an increasing relative significance (Allen, 1966). Not only are these statistics of dubious value, but a dispute over work control may frequently be a disguised pay conflict (for example, a dispute over management's right to use certain forms of work measurement) (Hyman, 1972a). The evidence in sociological studies of the pecuniary attachment to work of most manual workers also indicates the central importance of pay issues (Goldthorpe *et al*, 1968a; Cotgrove *et al*, 1971), as does the tendency in recent years for agreements on the reduction of working hours to lead to a concomitant increase in overtime working.

However, it is possible to identify several different kinds of demands which might indicate a concern for workers' control over the organisation of work or an erosion of managerial prerogatives. The most important and entrenched worker controls are still those of skilled craftsmen, but if anything these have seen a decline in recent years as management has sought to bargain an end to them under productivity agreements. Increasingly important have been controls over piecework systems, overtime working and other strategies exercised by general workers (Brown, 1972), though these workers do not have the craftsmen's concept of preserving an occupational tradition, and their activity is more directly instrumental (D. Wedderburn and Crompton, 1972). Like craft controls, these actions represent very limited and narrow means of advancing workers' interests; the 'power' involved in being able, for example, to insist on working ten hours a week overtime in order to make up a living wage is not great.

An important development in the issue of control took place in the late 1960s, when employers developed the tactic of 'productivity bargaining'. An important purpose of this was to erode existing controls exercised by workers over their jobs, in exchange for which management offered, besides large pay increases, a degree of involvement in the affairs of the company. Against this, some unions tried to use productivity bargaining to extend the scope of workers' influence. The policy first became prominent when Allan Flanders (1964) published an account of the negotiation of an elaborate productivity agreement at the Esso Oil Refinery, Fawley. It received a major impetus when the 1965 incomes policy established increased productivity as a criterion for justifying pay increases outside the general norm, and the NBPI became a strong champion of the technique (see Section 4) (Crouch, 1974).

In its most advanced form, productivity bargaining involved a departure from usual 'across the table' bargaining. Instead of simply responding to workers' pay demands, employers offered large pay increases if workers would surrender job controls and accept major work reorganisations (often involving redundancies), new systems of payment (such as measured day work) and new criteria for assessing jobs (job evaluation). With MDW management was trying to reduce the incidence of bargaining, while job evaluation was used to replace bargaining by the 'rational' determination of pay differences. Although the objective was thus to establish a new set of working methods over which workers would have less unilateral control, during the process of the productivity bargain itself workers and union representatives were invited to share at a certain level in the process of decision-making; management usually hoping that this would encourage workers to identify more strongly with the firm and its interests (Crouch, 1977; McKersie and Hunter, 1973; Fox, 1974).

In a few cases unions took advantage of these latter possibilities to use productivity bargaining to extend the scope of negotiations to issues of managerial policy from which they were normally excluded. However, this was rare and in most cases where unions seized the initiative in productivity bargaining they used it to pursue the typical British union strategy of straight pay increases, especially when this provided a useful device for avoiding incomes policy controls (McKersie and Hunter, 1973).

Demands for workers' control as such has never been prominent in Britain, where unions have been jealous of their autonomy from management. However, in the past few years there have been striking developments here. In 1967 the TUC, without much prior discussion within the union movement, formally committed itself to the advocacy of workers' directors on company boards (TUC, 1967), and since the publication in 1972 of the EEC's proposals for participation in European companies it has elaborated a detailed policy and made it an important demand (TUC, 1973, 1974). The TUC has accepted the EEC concept of a co-determinative supervisory board overseeing the work of a purely managerial board, which would run the day-to-day affairs of a company, on the condition that (a) workers' representatives constitute 50 per cent of the membership of the supervisory board and (b) all elections of workers' representatives are conducted through trade union channels, with voting restricted to union members. A central concern here is the avoidance of the erosion of union strength through the establishment of alternative forms of worker representation, as has happened in some Continental countries; the TUC has also firmly rejected the European notion of non-union works councils. In 1974 the Labour Party committed itself to introducing measures of industrial democracy, and at the time of writing the Government is still considering the introduction of legislation on the lines of the TUC policy. Meanwhile, debate continues on the issue; several major unions, particularly the AUEW, fear that workers' participation, even on the terms proposed, would compromise unions' ability to represent their members' interests in conflicts with management.

The demand for participation has emerged from union leaderships without any great excitement at rank-and-file level. However, other developments which have taken place on the shop floor are also relevant to the issue of workers' control and may have stimulated the elaboration of the TUC's policies. During the early 1970s there were several cases of workers occupying factories threatened with closure or major redundancies.[5] This action is in itself a major departure as a form of workers' action, and is discussed as such on page 231. In most cases these occupations have ended with either defeat or the re-establishment of the company under orthodox management (as was the case, for example, after the lengthy, radical and much publicised sit-in by workers at Upper Clyde Shipbuilders in 1971). But in a small number of recent cases workers have tried to take over fallen firms and operate them as workers' co-operatives, doing so with some official support and encouragement during the first year of the present Labour Government. There are only a few examples, many difficulties have been placed in their way by the previous owners, and it is difficult as yet to make a full evaluation of them.

This evidence about the nature of demands for control is not unlike that on pay demands in its implications. Much of the activity described is well entrenched and not of particularly recent origin. In some cases (for example, unilateral job controls by non-craft workers) there has certainly been an increase in activity, but this has been gradual rather than a sudden escalation. Furthermore, much of it takes place at a relatively low level of bargaining. However, at the same time there are certain striking and very recent features (such as the occupations) which cannot be easily accommodated into the traditional pattern. And, as in the case of pay demands, workers' relatively unambitious control demands have important implications in the context of the current crisis, creating difficulties for management despite the low-level nature of the action itself. Whether it is true that increased managerial control would improve efficiency, it certainly represents the belief of management and government. Since the late 1950s an attack on 'restrictive practices' has been seen as one of the solutions to Britain's low productivity. Initially this was seen as a task for persuasion; productivity bargaining elevated it to a central managerial strategy, and also introduced the possibility of permitting a certain degree of participation in order to achieve it. The Industrial Relations Act (see Section 4) tried to take a more coercive approach. Unless and until measures of that kind are attempted again, the most likely measures in the near future will be more ambitious schemes for participation. The traditional British compromise over the control of work has been for workers to be allowed to control low-level aspects while management is left alone to run the company. This strategy of separation is beginning to break down from both directions, with the conflicting alternative implications which have been discussed.

GENERAL POLITICAL DEMANDS

There has recently been an intensification of union involvement in wider political issues. This needs to be seen in the context of a growth in direct state intervention in industrial relations. So long as the state was willing to leave voluntary collective bargaining alone, the unions were happy to play a relatively non-political role. But once the state began to interfere with this process, and through incomes policy express views about acceptable criteria for income increases and appropriate relative pay levels for different occupations, the unions were perforce thrown into a wider arena.

Traditionally, a firm division has been drawn between the concerns of the 'political' and the 'industrial' wings of the labour movement. Of course, at the level of formal union activity there is considerable inter-relationship between the two. Locally, trade union branches are frequently affiliated to the Labour Party. Unions' national conferences usually discuss wide political issues as well as their more immediate concerns, and much of the TUC's day-to-day activity is in this wide policy area. Unions also make their contribution to debates on all issues at the Labour Party's conference, where their votes predominate over all other sections of the party, and union representatives dominate the Party's National Executive Committee.

So far as policies are concerned, the unions have unequivocally supported extensions of the welfare state and redistributive taxation. On public ownership their position has been more divided, and orthodoxy has varied over time. Sometimes the unions in a particular industry have been in the vanguard of moves for its nationalisation, though this has varied from ardent to purely formal support (Banks, 1970). During the first two decades of the post-war period most of the union leaders were associated with the right wing of the party and lent their energies to helping it ward off moves for more extensive public ownership. In the early 1960s the unions were heavily involved in the divisions of the Labour Party over unilateral nuclear disarmament; by that time the right-wing domination of the union leaderships had begun to decline, and unions were ranged on both sides of that issue. But, important though union attitudes on these issues may have been, politics has been a rather minor concern for them, and the only occasions on which they have made major interventions have been in order to protect the continued freedom of bargaining (Richter, 1973). Furthermore, in considering the details of wider political activities mentioned above it is important to note that involvement in them was very much limited to a few figures within the unions, and changes in personalities in leading positions, which might indeed be accidental, could lead to dramatic changes in a union's policy position.

By 1970 a change had taken place. To some extent this can still be explained in terms of a change of leading personalities. By the end of the 1960s the two largest unions in Britain, the TGWU and the AUEW—which had both grown considerably through amalgamations—were led by men who strongly identified with the political Left. But their unions were not the only ones which reflected the same current of opinion, and further causes can be identified (Panitch, 1976: 148). Disillusioned with the Labour Government's policies of incomes restraint and its attempts to impose new legal restrictions on organised labour, the unions sought to reassert their role within the Labour Party, primarily by influencing its policies so that such steps would not be taken by a future Labour Government. They also wanted to ensure that the party would be committed to repealing the Industrial Relations Act which was being introduced by the new Conservative Government and to taking instead several measures to strengthen collective bargaining. Behind these developments, of course, the increased industrial militancy of the members was also a potent factor.

It should be noted that the issues on which the recent repoliticisation has concentrated are still compatible with the claim that the unions are active politically only when collective bargaining is threatened. For example, almost without exception, the evidence given by unions to the Royal Commission on Trade Unions and Employers Associations, 1965–8, was concerned with the defence of free collective bargaining. Disagreement with the 1964–70 Labour Government over incomes policy was not concerned so much with the fact of restraint or the application of certain kinds of criteria as with the statutory nature of the policy; and the major confrontation with that government, involving an unprecedented use of political strength by the unions, concerned an Industrial Relations Bill which sought certain limitations on their legal freedom of industrial action. Although during the subsequent Conservative Government the unions opposed a renewed statutory incomes policy, the miners were the only group to turn formal opposition into outright defiance; but the Industrial Relations Act introduced by that Government, which went considerably further than Labour's abortive Bill, met with almost complete non-co-operation by the unions. Finally, it is noteworthy that the major confrontation over the mines, which precipitated the general election of February 1974, essentially concerned the *means* by which the wage claim should be settled; the Government tried to insist on the use of its new administrative machinery for fixing pay, while the union wanted to return to the traditional method of collective bargaining backed by the sanction of industrial action. Even this major increase in the involvement of unions in political conflict was therefore consistent with the traditional stance of British unions.

However, alongside these actions, which are compatible with the old interpretation, new political demands were undeniably emerging. For many years the TUC had urged various general economic policies on the government of the day, especially at Budget time. But this activity was strictly separate from unions' bargaining activity; there was no attempt at using industrial action or bargaining power to demand the adoption of the policies proposed. When governments in the 1950s called for wage restraint the TUC would respond by saying that voluntary restraint by unions could be secured only if the government pursued policies of economic growth, stable prices and social justice, but this argument remained at the verbal level. It acquired slightly more substance in 1964 when the unions agreed to support the Labour Government's incomes policy on the grounds that that Government was committed to such objectives. But no precise policy demands were made, and not much wage restraint was offered. The episode cannot really be called bargaining or the raising of demands.

By 1967 it became clear to the TUC that the Government was increasingly seeking to use it as an agent in maintaining an incomes policy, while the Government itself had abandoned several aspects of the original policy, in particular the commitment to economic growth. It was difficult for the TUC to respond to this situation by disregarding incomes policy entirely, because it feared stronger measures of state intervention if it did so; but at the same time it refused to act as a state agency. Its response was therefore to formulate an economic policy of its own, published in its annual economic reviews. These set out growth targets and measures designed to reach them, and outlined policies on such issues as mergers and the welfare state. The policies were urged on the Government (with mixed success), and the general growth strategy was used as the context within which the TUC would determine its own voluntary incomes policy. In addition to the increased specificity of the proposals, this practice marked an important shift in TUC policy. Since its advocated economic policies were now influencing its own incomes policy, the clear division which had formerly existed between collective bargaining and political lobbying was being eroded. But the policy still did not involve making demands on the Government which were directly supported by threatened sanctions, and it was of limited significance since the TUC's incomes policy had little practical effect.

A further step in the politicisation of TUC economic policy occurred in 1971 when unemployment was rising, the Conservative Government was taking little interest in TUC policy, and the TUC itself considered that reflation was needed. In its *Economic Review* for that year it declared that pay claims must continue at a high level, because this was the only way that government measures to reduce demand in the economy could be countered and full employment regained.

As will be discussed in Section 4, in 1972 the Conservatives gave the unions a more direct opportunity to make political demands when, in a desperate attempt to achieve consensus on wage restraint, they offered to open a wide range of policy areas to negotiation between the Government, the TUC and the CBI. At the same time in discussions with the Labour Opposition the unions were engaged in a more explicit exchange of policy commitments between the unions and a future Labour government than had been the case in 1964. In the agreement known as the social contract the TUC sought understandings on Labour policy in the following areas: price and rent controls, food subsidies, redistribution of wealth and income through taxation, the public ownership of building land and certain industries, economic planning, transport and membership of the EEC. The terms of both these demands and the restraint which was offered in exchange remained vague in several key respects, but it does represent the strongest example yet of the unions engaging in a form of bargaining over political issues, and as such is an important departure in the raising of demands.

In common with the other forms of demand discussed here, these recent developments in the political role of unions mark a major shift in the traditional British situation. As discussed on page 239, in the straitening economic circumstances of the late 1960s, and even more strongly in the 1970s, the state took up the task of regulating and controlling industrial relations. This fundamentally threatened the old distinction between political and industrial action, with the ironic consequence that state attempts to control the situation led to the development of new demands in politically sensitive areas. The old system is by no means completely transcended, as the tentative nature of the various developments shows; it is likely that both politicians and union leaders would gladly return to their former habits, and they constantly seek to resurrect elements of these in their new machinery. But those developments which have taken place have produced a considerable and possibly irreversible weakening of the old model of compromise. Whether they should be interpreted as further steps in the incorporation of the union movement or whether they constitute a major advance in labour's political power it is still too early to determine.

THE EXPANSION OF CONFLICT AND NEW FORMS OF ACTION

The Militant Groups

Conflictual action, whether measured by the incidence of strikes, etc., or by the incidence of work-place bargaining, has not been distributed evenly across the economy. Certain groups with established traditions of militancy have continued to be significant, while new militancy has been observable in other sectors. These will be discussed in turn.

THE AREAS OF ESTABLISHED MILITANCY

At the time of the Donovan Commission four industries were considered to be particularly 'strike prone' especially in terms of unofficial strikes: motor cars, coal mining, docks and ship-building (Clegg, 1972: Ch. 8). In the search for 'common factors' in these industries, various authors have suggested a series of characteristics revolving round the issue of 'insecurity': piecework payment systems, high risks of redundancy, fluctuating demand and variable earnings. There has also been a tendency to identify the engineering industry in general (of which the car industry is a part) as that in which unofficial strikes are concentrated, relating that fact to certain institutional features of that sector, such as the prevalence of piecework and a cumbersome disputes procedure (Marsh, 1965; McCarthy and Marsh, 1966). In subsequent years there have been some changes in these patterns.

As noted in Section 2, there has been a gradual expansion of industrial conflict in a wide range of industries; if anything, it has increased at a faster rate in the less strike-prone industries than in those typically associated with strikes. In fact, the only two industries in which statistics showed a relative reduction in conflict were two of the four 'strike-prone' industries: mining and ship-building. The latter is an industry in considerable decline, in which new processes have gradually made redundant many of the old skilled crafts which were formerly such a dominant feature of the industry; the protection of their identity was a frequent issue in disputes (Cameron and Eldridge, 1968). The situation in mining is different, although during the period when there was a high level of unofficial activity in the 1950s the mines shared some characteristics with ship-building: instability (stemming here from piecework systems) and a declining industry. The reduction in unofficial strikes, to be replaced in the 1970s by an even more dramatic rise in national-level (official and unofficial) action, has been noted in Section 2, and is considered again on page 227, where it is related to changes in payment systems. In general, the shift in the pattern of mining strikes parallels that in the overall national pattern, despite the unusual history of conflict in that industry—a pattern of small, short unofficial strikes being replaced in the 1970s by one of large, long and often official ones.

The docks have continued to be an area of high conflict, and here too one can perhaps detect a tendency towards a wider scale of action related to changes in the organisation of the industry which were designed to tackle those very characteristics which led to its 'instability'. Two major changes have affected the docks since the early 1960s: decasualisation (designed to reduce the pattern of highly irregular work and earnings) and containerisation. The former led to the numbers of dockers being considerably reduced (through various voluntary redundancy schemes), while the earnings of those who remained rose massively. But implementation of decasualisation was marked by several wide-scale disputes over the terms on which it occurred. Containerisation concerns the major change in freight packaging and transportation which has taken place, leading to a movement away from the established port areas. Within these areas dock work is limited to union members and covered by union rules. Freight firms have taken the opportunity presented by containerisation of moving warehouses inland, outside the registered areas and hence outside union control. This has led to a series of major conflicts, both official and unofficial, between the employers and the registered dock workers. In 1976 the Government met the situation by extending the area covered by the registered dock labour scheme.

The car industry is a further instance where payment systems (primarily piecework) associated in the past with instability and disputes have been replaced. As yet it is too early to establish the results of this process. There is some evidence that it leads to a decline in the number and frequency of unofficial strikes, but there are also some indications that, as in the docks and (more dramatically) the mines, it may lead to a widening of the base of conflict, since the new payment methods involve negotiation at a higher level (Turner *et al*, 1967; Hyman, 1974). There has also been an increase in conflict and in the *scale* of strikes as workers in the less well paid firms have demanded parity with those in the highly paid Midlands factories.

NEW MILITANCY: LOW-PAID PUBLIC-SECTOR WORKERS

Government incomes policies have borne most heavily upon public-sector workers, particularly those without traditions of militancy. It is within the areas under their own control that governments have the greatest ability, and feel the greatest responsibility, to exercise income controls. Where the workers concerned are strongly organised and strategically placed (such as railwaymen or doctors) compromises may be reached; this leaves low-paid, poorly organised public-sector workers as the most vulnerable groups during incomes policy. Further, public-sector pay is less subject to drift and shop-floor bargaining, and hence less able to evade incomes policy. Finally, as shown on page 211, low-paid groups were hit particularly severely by taxation changes in the late 1960s; on page 213 the implications of this in new demands for increases to the low-paid were discussed. There are heavy concentrations of low pay among manual workers in both central and local government service, and though there are also low-paid groups in the private sector these are less thoroughly unionised.

One of the features of the resurgence of unrest in Britain has been the reaction of some of these workers. In each case, these were workers with established traditions of union *membership*, but with little history of official or unofficial militancy. They now found themselves engaged in protracted strikes against the Government (acting both as employer and as the state). In most cases unofficial militancy played an important part in providing the initiative, though the action took official form (Hyman, 1974).

One of the first examples was the major strike of local authority manual workers in 1969, when an unofficial demand for a £5 a week increase won mass support while the union leadership were negotiating a much smaller rise. The unions hastened to support the rising tide of membership reaction, and a prolonged and ultimately successful official strike was called. In the following year the unions adopted a militant posture from the outset, and again major concessions were won after a strike. Early in 1971 postal workers began their first full strike following government resistance to their pay claim. However, the union did not keep large reserves of strike pay, and after a prolonged stoppage lack of money forced a collapse of the strike in March. In January 1973 hospital ancillary staffs, gas workers and teachers were among groups taking industrial action of some kind to try and break the controls of the incomes policy which had recently been imposed. These attempts were not very successful. Health ancillaries were also important in May 1974 when they were joined by nurses (taking their first-ever strike action, and for their occupation a very radical step) in a strike to secure a major improvement in pay. The strikes were followed quickly by an official report which awarded major increases.

NEW MILITANCY: WHITE-COLLAR WORKERS

Trade union membership among white-collar workers in Britain has always been much lower than that among manual workers, with certain important exceptions. Because it has for many years been government policy to support trade union membership by public employees, such groups as civil servants, local government workers and administrative staffs in the nationalised industries have been heavily unionised; unions have also been significant among teachers at various levels. Among white-collar employees in private industry, however, the level of membership has been extremely low. Many employers have been prepared to accept unions among their manual workers, but have considered that their administrative staffs are part of management and owe special loyalties which would be incompatible with union membership. There is considerable evidence that the strength of white-collar unions has been dependent, not so much on the militancy of the workers concerned as on the support for union membership afforded by the government of the day and by employers (Bain, 1970). Throughout the 1960s the membership of white-collar unions grew, but more slowly than the rate of growth of the white-collar labour force. But in 1968 this pattern changed. From then the rate of increase has risen sharply, not only within the public-sector employments where unions were already established, but also in private industry (Bain and Price, 1976) (see Table 8 in Appendix I).

In addition to the increase in the degree of unionisation, there has been a rise in the militancy of those already organised. Some of these groups, in particular the draughtsmen and managerial and supervisory staffs, have been militant for several years, but there have been new developments, in particular affecting public-sector staffs held back by incomes policy. In 1968 and 1969 there were strikes among airline pilots. There had been sporadic unofficial strikes among teachers in the late 1960s, but in early 1970 the

National Union of Teachers called its first official strike, a selective action involving a range of schools throughout the country. Significantly the strike followed the union's rejection of arbitration on its pay claim because of lack of confidence in its impartiality, given the treatment of public sector workers under incomes policy. The following April doctors in the National Health Service took various forms of action following delays in the publication by the Government of a review of their pay. They refused to sign sick notices, while junior hospital doctors threatened strike action. Eventually the Government decided to pay the full recommended award to the junior doctors, but only a proportion to the highly paid members of the profession, referring the rest of the issue to the NBPI. The Conservative Party took up the doctors' cause, and following their victory in the general election a few weeks later rescinded the NBPI reference and paid the award in full. Finally, in February 1973 civil servants took their first-ever industrial action, holding a one-day strike and a demonstration in Trafalgar Square against the restraint of their pay claim under the Conservative Government's incomes policy. Outside the public sector a noteworthy dispute was the first strike by bank clerks in 1968. There was little support for a strike among the membership, so the executive of the NUBE struck alone, in their various branches throughout the country, being joined by just a small number of their members.

The rise in white-collar militancy has not only been reflected in the rise and activity of orthodox unions. There have also been interesting developments in the role of staff associations. These are bodies established by employers to provide a channel for employees' grievances and to forestall the emergence of autonomous unions. The associations are heavily controlled by the employers and rarely have any independent voice; they can certainly not call strikes. In some industries, principally banking, there have been long conflicts between the associations and unions seeking recognition. However, in recent years several of these associations have become more like autonomous unions, insisting on bargaining rights and control of their own affairs (Blackburn, 1970). In some cases this has resulted in the officers of staff associations taking the initiative in approaching orthodox trade unions for representation of their members; in others it has led to the associations themselves becoming quasi-unions.

A final important aspect of white-collar trade unionism is that the TUC is representative of both manual and non-manual unions. There have never been significant federations of white-collar unions alone, though until the past decade several such unions stood alone, outside the TUC. The two most important of these were the local government officers (who affiliated in 1964) and the teachers (1969). There have been attempts at setting up exclusive white-collar bodies, the most recent of which followed the 1971 Industrial Relations Act, when a few white-collar unions were among those suspended from the TUC for registering under the Act. Some of these groups tried to set up an independent body which could have relations with the Government, but very little came of it.

There is less unity between manual and white-collar unions over affiliation to the Labour Party. Few white-collar unions are affiliated, which partly reflects the preponderance of civil service, local government and educational unions in this group; these unions are either legally prohibited from having, or feel it would be unsuitable to have, a political affiliation.

As with other aspects of industrial militancy in Britain, interpretation of this evidence concerning white-collar unions needs to be very careful. Given the importance of government and employer recognition in encouraging union membership among these workers, it is difficult to see the growth of membership in straightforward terms as a move towards work-group collectivism. The strength of white-collar union opposition to incomes policy in the mid-1960s may partly reflect the preponderance of public employment in that category and the fact that incomes policy tends to hit public employees most easily; and partly the fact that these unions had fewer links enjoining on them co-operation with a Labour government. It would also be erroneous to identify a class-wide loyalty in such phenomena as left-wing white-collar unions or the existence of a single TUC. On the first point, some of the most militant actions of these unions have resulted from their insistence on differentials over manual workers. On the second, an important reason for the dominance of the TUC is the fact that it has effectively monopolised communication between the Government, organised employers and the unions. If a union wants its special interests to be considered during the framing of legislation, it will stand a better chance of so doing if its voice is represented in the TUC.

The Levels of Action

Traditionally, collective bargaining in Britain has been heavily surrounded by ritual and procedure, conciliation has been a major aim of representatives of all sides involved, and official strikes have been rare and soon resolved. One of the major indications that conflict has reached new levels of intensity during recent years has been a divergence from this pattern at several important points. These concern both the gradual rise of unofficial strikes and the sudden, more recent, resurgence of large official strikes. Other changes, concerning variations in the forms of action, will be considered on pp. 229–33, while changes in the institutional context of bargaining and conciliation will be discussed in Section 4.

THE RISE OF UNOFFICIAL ACTION

Alongside the emergence of work-place bargaining, with which it is closely related, the increasing importance of unofficial strikes has been a major obsession of commentators on industrial relations in Britain. Until the early 1970s about 95 per cent of strikes were recorded as unofficial, and the proportion had been reached after a gradual expansion since the early post-war period.

The distinction between official and unofficial disputes has been a particularly important one for employers and governments seeking order in industrial relations. Order can be secured when conflict is limited to a few highly predictable, institutionalised channels. It is sometimes claimed that employers most dislike unconstitutional, rather than unofficial, strikes. Whereas an unofficial strike is one called without the express sanction of the union concerned, an unconstitutional strike takes place contrary to established disputes procedure. This may lay down how much advance notice should be given for strike action, and a series of steps which should be exhausted before there is recourse to strike action. It is therefore in unconstitutional strikes that unpredictability is most important. But since in practice official unions rarely strike outside established disputes procedures, and since unofficial strikes rarely have any regard for official procedures, unofficial and unconstitutional strikes are for most purposes the same.

While for employers and government the distinction between official and unofficial strikes is important, it is doubtful whether it has a great deal of relevance to the workers concerned (Hyman, 1972a: Chs. 1, 2). There are of course important apparent differences. Unofficial strikes tend to be spontaneous and to arise more immediately from the situation and experience of the work-group. In this respect an unofficial strike may frequently be a sudden response to a managerial action, the exercise of an on-going countervailing power which may be an attempt to parallel the on-going sanctions enjoyed by management, whereas the official strike is a more formal and much more rarely used sanction. Unofficial strikes are likely to be brief, narrow in scope and restricted to more or less small groups of workers, while official strikes, when they occur, tend to be long and to involve larger numbers of workers. An official strike may be supported by strike pay given by the union; unofficial strikers rarely receive any form of financial support.

But beyond these differences the distinction should not be over-drawn, and in some cases indeed those already spelt out may not apply; for example, some unofficial strikes have been well planned in advance or have been of long duration. As discussed in the previous section, industrial action taken without the formal involvement of a union is not necessarily taken in defiance of the union; some evidence of workers' perceptions suggests that they conceive of their 'union' in terms of the local shop-floor organisation anyway (Goldthorpe *et al*, 1968a). Until very recent years the proportion of strikes which have been unofficial has been so great that it is unlikely that workers made many distinctions between whether they were striking officially or unofficially.

Other research has suggested that the simple distinction between official and unofficial does not reflect the complex reality of different forms of strike organisation. Research on the motor industry has distinguished between 'official unofficial' and 'unofficial unofficial' strikes (Turner *et al*, 1967; Clack, 1967). In the former case the works shop stewards (who may well be seen as constituting the 'union' by many workers) call a strike; in the latter there is a spontaneous walk-out by the work-force, with the shop stewards being either irrelevant or actually opposing the action. It was evidence of this kind which led some observers to revise an earlier view that it was shop stewards who were the main instigators of unofficial industrial conflict (Parker, 1968; Brown, 1973). They began to be depicted as potential sources of stability in industry, restraining unidentified 'militants' in the work force. Such an analysis can be interpreted in several conflicting ways. It has been used to argue that, were sufficient procedural and institutional changes made, stewards could become a new force for industrial order, just as the official union organisations had before them; the changes advocated range from structural reform of disputes procedures or union organisation to the imposition of legal responsibilities for 'leadership'. Alternatively, the same evidence could be interpreted as showing that conflict is inherent in the work situation, and that among an alert work-force the sole result of compromising the stewards would be the emergence of new leaders of shop-floor militancy.

A further point which limits the relevance of the official/unofficial distinction concerns the different policies pursued by different unions. In some unions a strike may be declared official only after a lengthy and highly centralised procedure, or after a ballot of all the members. In others, union officials may be empowered to declare strikes official with considerable flexibility, or the union may be prepared retrospectively to deem a strike official which had been started unofficially. Some unions are prepared to label as official most strikes which occur among their members. Several extraneous factors may influence these decisions, such as the liability to pay strike pay which some but not all unions incur if they make a strike official, and the particular strike procedures entrenched in union constitutions. For many years until 1972 the National Union of Mineworkers, which requires a national ballot of members before it can declare a strike official, called no strikes; but mining had the highest number of unofficial strikes in British industry. In contrast, the draughtsmen's union was able to claim in its evidence to the Donovan Commission that unofficial strikes rarely took place among its members, largely because of the union's flexible policy of declaring strikes official. A further point which will affect the significance of unofficial strike action in different industries is the great variation in disputes procedures. The tendency for workers to have recourse to the strike will be greater in industries where procedures are lengthy and believed to be biased in favour of the employers than where decisions can be reached quickly through methods which are considered to be 'fair' (McCarthy and Parker, 1966).

Final variables relate to different technical and circumstantial features of work. For example, it does seem that piecework systems are particularly vulnerable to fragmented group action which can be carried on unofficially while unions concentrate on fixing national rates, the two levels of action having little mutual contact (Brown, 1973; Donovan Report, 1968). It is for this reason that managements in several industries have sought to abolish piecework. However, this may eventually lead to an expansion of conflict on a broader base. The most striking instance of this is the mining industry, where from 1958 the gradual elimination of piecework correlated highly with a decline in unofficial strikes (Shalev, 1973). But when piecework was finally abolished in 1966 and all pay aspirations were focussed on the national negotiations, the unofficial movement began to take unofficial strike action in connection with national pay claims. Unofficial action at that level could not be ignored by the union, which stepped up its own militancy; the unofficial strikes of 1971 were followed by national official stoppages in 1972 and 1974. The National Coal Board has responded by trying to reintroduce piecework, and this has been strongly resisted by the union. Similar developments may follow the elimination of piecework in the motor industry, and this may explain the major strike in 1971 at the Ford Motor Company, a firm which operated without piecework. Some of the special problems of public-sector workers may be related to a similar source: there is virtually no local bargaining, and therefore the upsurge of militancy in the early 1970s had to be concerned with national negotiations. Unofficial militancy led rapidly to official action.

Unfortunately there is little systematic literature on these sources of variation in the bases of official or unofficial action, in the role that shop stewards will perform, and so forth. There is considerable evidence on the implications of technology for workers' attitudes (Wedderburn and Crompton, 1972), and a counter-literature which stresses extra-plant factors (Goldthorpe *et al* 1968, 1969), but little of this is related directly to the detailed study of militancy. Most of the research concerns the engineering industry, particularly motor cars.[6] Crucial though this is to the pattern of militancy in Britain, it is not the full story and significant variations may exist in other sectors. Some of these issues will be taken up again on page 233.

THE RE-EMERGENCE OF THE OFFICIAL STRIKE:
After 1970 there was a marked change in the British strike pattern. There was no notable decline in unofficial disputes, but a distinct increase in prolonged official strikes. It is difficult to determine to what extent this is a reflection of the process described above of unions accommodating themselves to the new militancy of their members, or a response to the switch in government policy away from conciliation. It is notable that most of the big strikes have taken place in the public sector, where governments have been able to impose policies of wage restraint more easily. This process began under the 1964–70 Labour Government, but its biggest development came with the Conservative Government of 1970, which openly adopted a policy of accepting prolonged strikes, especially in the public sector, in order to reduce the rate of wage increases. This strategy reflected that Government's view that it was the public sector which generated 'inflationary' wage claims ('competition' acting as an effective brake in the private sector); and that past government unwillingness to withstand prolonged strikes had been the main reason why these increases were possible in the public sector.

There have been some major strikes and other actions in the private sector (the building industry and the docks in 1972, and the Ford Motor Company in 1971) but most of the action was concentrated among nationalised industries and local authorities (e.g. local government manual workers in 1969 and 1970, health service employees in 1973, electricity workers in 1971, postal workers in 1971, miners in 1972 and 1973). In several cases (electricity in 1971, mines in 1972, docks in 1972, mines, railways and electricity in 1973) these strikes led to the declaration of a State of Emergency by the Government – previously a rare event in Britain. Several of these strikes were notable for the Government's attempt to move public opinion to condemn the workers concerned, adding a new resource to its means of beating a strike. In the case of the postal and electricity workers this had some effect on morale, but the miners were untouched. The culmination of this particular tactic was the calling of a general election in the middle of the 1973–4 mining dispute. With the exception of the postal workers, most of the groups involved in these conflicts before the Government's return to statutory incomes policy are either considered to have gained much greater increases than the Government had hoped to concede, or alternatively the dispute was handed over to conciliation machinery which ignored the incomes policy. The most celebrated example was the Wilberforce inquiry into the power workers' claim which explicitly rejected the Government's injunction to take account of the 'national interest' in proposing a settlement (Wilberforce, 1971).

These official disputes formed the most intense industrial conflicts of the early 1970s, apart from action over the Industrial Relations Act. Therefore, if one is speaking of a sudden escalation in industrial conflict in Britain, one is referring, not to a sudden rash of unofficial strikes (their increase has been a gradual post-war development which began to attract political attention from the mid-1960s onwards), but to a series of long official strikes which were in part a response to government action. In the past lengthy official strikes have been associated with desperate defensive actions by workers in periods of high unemployment and falling wages, such as the inter-war years. The development of long strikes ending in massive wage increases is a novel aspect of the recent situation.

Developments in Conflict Tactics

It is partly in this context of increasing resistance by government and employers that certain developments in strike tactics are to be interpreted. Once the Government had ceased to consider the ending of industrial conflict by compromise as its main priority in industrial relations, strikes were likely to last longer; therefore for the first time in many years in Britain unions had to pay attention to the tactics of industrial action. How might their resources be most effectively deployed to secure an advantageous agreement (Hyman, 1974)?

VARIATIONS ON THE STRIKE

One tactic which had already been developed was that of the token one-day stoppage. This occurs when a union wishes to give some intimation of its ability to call on action by its members and of the dislocation which a strike will cause, but does not yet want to pursue a protracted struggle. The effectiveness of this kind of action is largely limited to those workers who can produce a major effect by such a token, such as the railwaymen or the dockers, or to a dispute involving large numbers of workers throughout an important sector of the economy.

More important are such actions as bans on overtime, working to rule and go-slows. Although these activities enable some work to proceed and are therefore not as total as strike action, they have some advantages over strike action and are particularly disliked by management.[7] Since the workers remain at their jobs their earnings are not reduced so dramatically as during a strike, though they lose overtime pay and perhaps performance bonuses. Such action can therefore be carried on for a long time, and the implications of its disruption are sometimes cumulative. Management frequently has to make the difficult choice between putting up with the limited working or taking disciplinary action against workers who are withholding co-operation, thereby risking an escalation of the dispute to full-scale strike action.

Bans on overtime are of considerable importance in the many sections of British industry which are heavily dependent on overtime working, particularly when maintenance and repair work are normally carried on outside standard working hours. Working to rule as such is largely limited to occupations where management has set down elaborate rules for the conduct of work which are normally ignored by both management and workers in the interests of efficiency. The rules usually relate to safety, and this form of action is therefore limited to such occupations as the railways and electricity where the job has important hazards. When men are working to rule they abide by the details of the rule book with extreme rigour. But working to rule is really simply an extreme form of a more general weapon available to workers, withdrawal of the co-operation and give-and-take which normally characterise their relationship with management. Workers lacking the advantage of a rule book may achieve this by working slowly, or 'without enthusiasm'. The potentialities of this form of action, particularly for skilled and non-manual workers, were demonstrated by DATA during the late 1960s when it launched an aggressive policy of seeking pay increases. Draughtsmen worked 'without imagination', which meant that they would not use initiative in their tasks.

The realisation in the mid-1960s by several unions that the division between the national and local level of industrial militancy was rendering their typical activities out-moded, and the difficulties imposed on bargaining by incomes policy, led to some developments in conflict techniques. Some unions, in particular DATA and the TGWU, and later the AUEW, developed a strategy of carefully chosen selective strikes. Irrespective of any existing national agreements, a pay claim and possibly a strike would be launched against a small number of firms in an industry which was considered the most likely readily to concede an increase. This could then be used as a precedent for securing increases in other firms. Selective strikes were also used to enable a union to conserve its resources of strike pay during a lengthy dispute. The municipal employees did this successfully in 1970, while the failure of the post office strike in 1971 is generally attributed to the union's not taking such action. Other unions (prominently the NUM) solved this problem by not paying strike pay at all, but relying on strikers' wives claiming social security benefit.

A further development was the intensification of militancy during the course of strike action, particularly in picketing. In a typical British strike this is a relatively peaceful process in which a few pickets put mild pressure on blackleg workers or on suppliers to the works concerned. But in the early 1970s, new tactics developed in several strikes, culminating in the disputes in the mining and building industries of 1972, when picketing was intensified to make blackleg working or the delivery of supplies to industries involved in industrial action impossible. Large numbers of pickets would be deployed, in some cases being moved rapidly from site to site to anticipate moves by employers. It is particularly noteworthy that in the miners' strike the picketing was directed not so much at the coal industry itself, but at one of its main consuming (and rival) industries, electricity generation. Supplies of both coal and oil were prevented from entering power stations, enabling the miners to have a major effect much more quickly than would have been possible had they simply ceased to mine coal, since it had become clear that the Government had prepared itself for a long battle of attrition.

The dispute in the building industry was made particularly severe by the presence of 'lump labour'—spuriously self-employed, non-unionised workers. There were violent clashes between them and the strikers, leading to the imprisonment of some of the latter for unusually long sentences of three years. A campaign on behalf of the imprisoned men, by the official trade union movement and various unofficial groups and Labour MPs, continued until 1976.

FACTORY OCCUPATIONS

In some senses the occupation of a factory by workers can be considered an extension of the strike, and some recent examples of its use can be seen as simply reinforcing workers' resources during a conflict (Hemingway and Keyser, 1975: Ch. 4). But, as in other countries, it has developed in Britain over the past few years in a context where strike action would hardly be relevant: as a means of preventing mass redundancies.

For many years there has been no tradition of factory occupations in Britain, and the few groups of workers who have undertaken these actions have explored new ground. The first occupation occurred at Upper Clyde Shipbuilders in 1970 (Thompson and Hart, 1972). The company had been the recipient of considerable state support, and when its closure was threatened it was widely suspected that this was part of the incoming Conservative Government's policy of withholding support from companies in difficulty. The workers occupied the shipyard and demanded state action to maintain employment. The incident was therefore thoroughly implicated in wider politics. The occupation continued for several weeks, with the eventual result that the Government arranged attractive terms for an American company to take over the yard, retaining most but not all the employees.

Since then there has been an increasing use of the occupation in such contexts, though instances where the workers attempt to carry on production during the action are less frequent (Hemingway and Keyser, 1975: Ch. 3). The first important use of the sit-in as a general industrial relations tactic was in 1971, when engineering workers in Manchester used it during the unsuccessful attempt by the engineering unions to replace national negotiations by a series of district actions. Since then it has become increasingly frequent (*ibid*: Ch. 4), to the extent that in 1976 the British Institute of Management issued a guide for company directors on how to deal with occupations.

POLITICAL ACTION

Political strikes are considered to be very rare in Britain, though precise knowledge is not available since official statistics do not count political strikes among the figures for industrial disputes. There has certainly been no tradition of large-scale one-day strikes protesting against various government policies, as has occurred in France. However, distinct changes have occurred since 1970, most of the instances being concerned with the industrial relations policies of the Conservative Government. Agitation for strike action against the Industrial Relations Bill led to a one-day unofficial strike in December, involving between 350,000 and 600,000 workers, primarily from the motor and printing industries. In February a march against the Bill attracted 130,000 people, and by March some unions had given official support to a further one-day strike and day of demonstrations. Between 1½ and 2 million workers stopped work. Later in the same year the TUC organised a big demonstration in London on the issue of unemployment, which was growing at that time, and in November 1972 it held a lobby of Parliament to call for an increase in old-age pensions. (In September 1973 the TUC Congress voted for a one-day strike if pensions were not increased by the spring; after the February 1974 election the Labour Government increased pensions, so this resolution was not put to the test.) In March 1973 an emergency Congress rejected the Government's incomes policy and, despite the reluctance of the General Council, called for a 'day of national protest' on May Day. Several unions interpreted this as meaning a strike. Finally, the AUEW called a strike of the whole engineering industry in 1974 to resist implementation of a heavy fine imposed on it by the National Industrial Relations Court. (The recently elected Labour Government had declared its intention to abolish the Court, and the fine of the AUEW was generally regarded as its last 'fling'. In the event the fine was mysteriously paid by an anonymous group of businessmen and the strike lasted only one day.)

Most if not all these actions were defensive ones against state interference in collective bargaining, and can therefore be considered as attempts to maintain rather than break the traditional division between political and industrial action. The strikes occurred, not because workers were taking their militancy into wider areas of government policy, but because the state was taking its activities deep into industrial relations. The same point can be made concerning what is frequently regarded as having been a political strike, the miners' strike of 1974 which led to the resignation of the Heath Government. The issue involved in the strike was not general government policy, but a straightforward wage claim; it became political primarily because the Government was now operating in that area and had chosen to take a stand, though several union leaders were happy to help defeat the Conservative Government.

A more directly and unambiguously political strike was that by Protestant workers in Northern Ireland against Catholic participation in the administration of that province. This complex and entirely successful action, which brought down the provincial constitution as well as its government, is discussed in Section 5. Finally, there has been some evidence in very recent years of smaller, often unofficial strikes of a political nature. Though these constitute a minor element in the spectrum of industrial conflict in Britain, they are significant for their novelty.[8]

THE IMPORTANCE OF THE WORK-GROUP IN CONFLICT

One central question for an interpretation of the resurgence of conflict concerns the identity and specificity of groups which form the units of action among workers. The question arises as a result of the fragmentation of bargaining and conflict. Should this be understood to mean that industrial action is a matter of disparate and unrelated groups of workers and isolated incidents? Or can underlying factors be identified which provide an overall unity and coherence? What is the unit of action in industrial conflict? By the mid-1960s the decline in the relative importance of official union action had led to a new concentration on the work-group as a unit, while the re-emergence of official action requires a reassessment of this.

The Rise of the Work-Group

British unions established strong central organisations in the inter-war years as the economic recession destroyed local points of strength and made necessary defensive institutions at national level in an attempt to prevent competitive reductions in wages. Employers and the Government were not at that time particularly interested in establishing strong bargaining institutions and, if anything, tried to undermine the national structures. It was not until the Second World War, when the state sought the co-operation of the unions in regulating labour relations, that official encouragement was given to industry-level bargaining. During the war and the post-war Labour Government the leaders of these centralised unions became heavily involved in national policy-making, and hence in the restraint of their members' demands under changed economic circumstances. This period reached its climax during the incomes policy of 1948–50, when the restraint on wage demands exercised by union leaderships was broken by shop-floor agitation (Panitch, 1976: Ch. 1). The structure of national-level bargaining which had been established continued to form the main basis for unions' and employers associations' industrial relations activity throughout the 1950s and early

1960s, but increasingly a second level of bargaining was developed alongside it at the plant or work-group (Clegg, 1972: ch. 1).

This phenomenon has become the most frequently studied aspect of British industrial relations, not only because of its importance as an element of social change, but also for it's political significance. 'Official' industrial relations tended to be carried on with predictability and regularity: claims would be made at advertised intervals; there was rarely strike action; failure to agree was likely to result in conciliation and mediation by an external agency, often from the Ministry of Labour, which had established a reputation for conciliation and 'neutrality'; and managers and union leaders developed amicable relations. It was almost an ideal-typical example of the institutionalisation of conflict. By contrast, unofficial activity was unpredictable; a claim for an increase or a protest about conditions of work or managerial orders could erupt suddenly, and it would frequently be resolved by a stoppage of work which might last only a few hours but might continue for several days. Although the actual time lost by unofficial strikes continued to be low, viewed as a proportion of total working time or in relation to time lost through accidents and sickness, the unpredictability of stoppages was particularly resented by management. Furthermore, this kind of unofficial action challenged managerial prerogatives in a way that formal union activity, remote from the individual company and concerned solely with a narrow range of issues, had rarely attempted. Unofficial strikes, shop-floor negotiated pay increases and the new role of shop stewards therefore became major targets for criticism.

A striking characteristic of work-place activity has been its preoccupation with immediate and local concerns within a very limited perspective. This provides its strength in that it stays close to workers' immediate life experience and does not become separated from them by bureaucratic structures. But this same characteristic also gravely inhibits any tendencies to adopt a more political perspective or to organise on a wider basis.[9] Attempts have certainly been made to generate movements with wide perspectives. There have been several instances of shop stewards' committees spanning the different factories of a large firm, or co-ordinating some groups of workers across the whole industry (Lerner and Bescoby, 1966[10]). These act as filters of information about pay rates and management practices, and can sometimes co-ordinate action with considerable success. In both the mining and engineering industries and in the docks, large-scale unofficial strikes have been organised. These shop stewards' movements experience considerable harassment from the official unions, which see them as rival organisations as well as likely foci of left-wing activity (TUC, 1960). Shop stewards' movements are frequently linked to various leftist organisations or to the Communist Party. In some unions stewards involved in such movements risk losing their union credentials, though they may still be accepted as work-place representatives by fellow workers.

If attempts at establishing broad bases of action by unofficial movements have had only intermittent success, it would also be a mistake to see the work-group, strictly defined, as the main nucleus of all militant action. Students of industrial relations have seized on the work-group as a conveniently explicable unit of action, and in doing so they have been affected by the preoccupation of British research in this field with piecework bargaining in the engineering industry. Many examples of unofficial action take place on a wider basis than this. For example, the unit of action in a claim for parity in pay with workers in other parts of the country is the plant as a whole; there is some evidence that disputes of this kind increased in importance following the wave of mergers in British industry since the late 1960s. Similarly, strikes taken to prevent redundancies will affect large groups of workers, and action (official or unofficial) which is based on industry-level negotiations also transcends the work-group. These are all areas which have been increasingly important in Britain in recent years.

Several aspects of this issue have been explored by Hill (1974) in a study of the unit of action in conflict. He points out that the existing literature tends to use the term 'work-group' to describe virtually any unit of action smaller than an official union. On the basis of his own research on dock workers, he says that they (p. 216):

> . . . resist attempts to divide the labour force into gangs as far as industrial action is concerned, in order that the gains of specific groups should immediately be shared by all. Activity tends to be company-wide or occupation-wide (across company boundaries), despite the fact that it does usually take place within the union framework. Stewards are not work-group representatives, since they are elected by all the workers in a firm and not by specific groups. Consequently, gangs constitute work units but not industrial action units.

Hill goes on to refer to the evidence of Turner's study (1967) of the motor industry which suggested that the size of group involved varied with the issue at stake, pay issues involving a smaller unit than, say, redundancy. One might also mention the evidence from a recent study of Ford workers (Beynon, 1973) that action there is increasingly taking place on a company-wide basis, and contrast that with the findings of Brown's study (1973) of piecework bargaining, which described very small, sometimes individual, units of action.

Hill has proposed (p. 217) a framework of analysis for the study of variations in the basis of action, rooted in an interactionist perspective. Some analysis of this kind is clearly needed: to what extent does the unit of action vary systematically with the kind of issue at stake? Do some payment systems generate units of a particular size and kind? What role is played by technology? Do craft and professional groups have typical modes of orientation to action which are distinct from those of workers less closely identified with their employment? Some existing literature makes it possible to suggest tentative hypotheses on some of these questions, but systematic research would be needed to test these properly. Some of these points will be considered further after a discussion of the changing role in conflict of official unions.

Official Unions and Unofficial Militants

With the exception of their opposition to shop stewards' combines, for several years most unions pursued a policy of 'benign neglect' towards shop-floor action. They maintained the position that, however unwelcome they sometimes found unofficial action, they would not accept any legal measures by the state to curb it, nor would they accept a responsibility on unions to go beyond persuasion in their attempts to reduce unofficial strikes. This latter became the main sticking point in the confrontation between the TUC and the Labour Government in 1969; during the following period of Conservative Government the unions opposed legislation which imposed various curbs on unofficial activity. Both these confrontations are discussed in Section 4. With increasing frequency during the late 1960s and early 1970s government actions required unions to adopt a position on unofficial action. Would they support it, or co-operate in state attempts to control it? They certainly renewed their contacts with the shop floor. For example, national discussion of the 'two systems' (Donovan Report, 1968) of industrial relations resulted in several unions delegating more of their work to shop-floor level and giving stewards a more formal role in bargaining (TUC, 1968), though it is a matter for detailed analysis whether (a) the intention and (b) the consequences of such measures were increasing union support for shop-floor action or its incorporation and limitation.[11] There are several instances of unions' official negotiating positions being overtaken by the militancy of the workers (the docks in 1968 and 1969; Ford in 1969; Vauxhall in 1970; refuse collection workers in 1969 and 1970; miners in 1969 and 1970; and the strikes over the Industrial Relations Bill in 1970–1).

The most spectacular instance of a union decentralising its activity in order to strengthen contacts with shop-floor workers came in 1971 when the AUEW, having failed to renegotiate the engineering industry's national bargaining system, instructed all its 4,000 local branches to negotiate plant-level settlements according to targets set down by union headquarters (Roberts and Rothwell, 1974). The venture was not a success; only a minority of branches was able to negotiate settlements, and in these instances they were no higher than the offer which had been made by the employers before the national machinery collapsed. The following year the AUEW returned to a national claim. The incident suggests that important structural features underlie the kind of issue which it is possible to negotiate at various levels. As noted earlier, shop-floor action in the engineering industry has made its great gains by negotiating detailed bargains based on local factors within the framework of a national agreement. This leads to speculation about the likely consequences of developments in payment and negotiation systems which seek to transcend the division between formal national bargaining and local action. Conceived by employer interests as means of restoring 'order' into bargaining, these may in fact strengthen the links between unions and militant shop-floor action. This factor may indeed be an element in the rise in official strikes in recent years.

Two processes described elsewhere in this paper facilitated the re-engagement of the national unions with shop-floor action. Some, especially the TGWU, used productivity bargaining as a means of decentralising bargaining activity to local officials and shop stewards. In this way the union not only gave support to shop-floor activity, but helped it furthermore to extend its scope and ambitions. Secondly, the TUC took various initiatives which brought unions and the TUC itself out from their narrow concern with a few issues. The TUC took up a more political stance, as described on page 217, and in the wake of the Donovan Report it encouraged several unions to re-examine their relationships with shop stewards and the rank and file (TUC, 1968).

The nature of this re-engagement is, as suggested above, highly ambiguous. In some ways it has brought union leaderships and unofficial leaders closer together; there is little doubt that most national unions in Britain were following more militant policies towards both government and employers in the early 1970s than had been the case in the 1960s. But in some instances the strategy of leaving it to local initiative which was followed sporadically by both the AUEW and the TGWU between 1968 and 1972 left local groups in a weak position, not knowing what to do. Further, the re-engagement of national unions can well mean a process of regaining control of shop-floor action in order to institutionalise it.

Most ambiguous of all is the relationship between national unions, local militants and political action. Although many leaders of militant action among workers have contacts with political movements (usually on the left) with wide political perspectives, shop-floor militancy is usually dependent for wide support on issues which are of immediate importance to the workers involved. It is doubtful, for example, if many workers would take strike action over wider political issues, though there have been occasional exceptions, such as the boycott by engineering workers of military equipment being produced for the Chilean Junta after the overthrow of the Allende government. By and large a wider political perspective is not relevant to shop-floor action, while at national level unions are increasingly becoming involved in wider politics. Unions are likely therefore to face renewed tension with the shop-floor movement should they try to use its strength in the work-place in the interests of wider political issues. This problem will exist whether the unions' political task consists of seeking to mobilise support for more militant political demands or the very different objective of accepting government definitions of a national interest and seeking to control workers' actions in line with that definition (Crouch, 1975).

The re-engagement of official unions in industrial conflict may also be seen in the context of conflicting pressures of centralisation and decentralisation, which Turner identified several years before the current crisis (Turner, 1962). The institutionalisation of bargaining in Britain took place at the level of trade union organisations and employers' associations – what is often called the 'industrial' level, though without the precision which that concept entails elsewhere. On one side of these negotiations, the state (the national level) withdrew to a background role, while on the other side the shop-floor was virtually ignored. All the pressures of recent years have been at these two levels, which had been neglected in the existing arrangements, resulting in the re-engagement of the state and the resurgence of shop-floor militancy. Changes in union behaviour can be seen as reactions to these new pressures, though their interpretation is complex. As this section and the discussion on pages 218–20 have shown, unions' responses to state pressures (primarily pressures for the TUC to adopt a more dominant relationship towards its member unions) have ranged from an acceptance of incorporation to an attempt to maintain the old system despite the changes, and again to a new official militancy. These different responses have been partly shaped by the effect on unions of 'pressure from below'. This latter is itself not simply a pressure from workers, but also from the response to that pressure of employers and the state. Productivity bargaining, new payment and negotiating systems, incomes policy and officially backed measures of institutional reform in the wake of the Donovan Commission, have all made demands on unions. Again, therefore, the union response has varied from attempts to re-institutionalise shop-floor activity to measures for articulating its concern.

One element in this complex and as yet not fully studied question is the probable emergence of an analytically distinct fourth level – that of the company. The preoccupation with the distinction between official and shop-floor bargaining, starting with the Donovan Report itself, has led to the assimilation of everything below the 'industry' to the shop-floor level; a similar process in the treatment of the work-group was noted in the previous section. But the distinction between company and plant bargaining may be important. For example, most of the attempts by management to regain the initiative from shop-floor workers in bargaining have involved the formulation of company-level strategies. At the same time, the growth of company-wide negotiations furthers the possibility of a wider base for workers' action, transcending the limitations of the work-group, as noted on page 235.

4 THE INDUSTRIAL RELATIONS SYSTEM

THE BREAKDOWN OF THE POST-WAR CONSENSUS

The developments described in previous sections have had important implications for the British industrial relations system, which after the Second World War seemed to have settled into a pattern of heavily institutionalised relations between employers and unions, with the state playing a role largely restricted to conciliation and peace-making rather than detailed intervention (the tradition of 'voluntarism'). This tradition had its origins in an earlier period, when a high level of unemployment made it unnecessary for capital to resort to overt state action to subordinate labour. The post-war commitment to full employment distorted this, shifting power to the workers. Within the structure of capitalist relations the consequence of this was not a simple transfer of economic power to workers but a succession of inflationary crises.

From early on, therefore, the state became involved in a search for new means of restraining labour; as early as 1948 the Labour Government secured a temporary incomes policy in agreement with the TUC. However, governments were reluctant to become deeply involved because of the importance to the institutionalisation of conflict of the division between political and industrial issues. For most of the period of post-war recovery they avoided the need for major action; partly because the new prosperity provided a margin of resources which could accommodate workers' expectations; partly because official union demands remained modest; partly because the authorities tolerated a certain level of inflation; and partly because they had occasional recourse to deflation and increased unemployment. But as years passed the declining economic position of Britain in particular and the problems of the world economy in general rendered this pattern increasingly inadequate. Inflation became less tolerable and the Government became increasingly involved in general economic management, which included a more detailed role in income determination and industrial relations. From the early 1960s there has been an uninterrupted sequence of official measures, few of which have met with any lasting success, though the overall consequence has been an important change in the structure of industrial relations institutions.[12] Central to the policy developments has been dissatisfaction on the part of the state and employers with the role of unions and workers in allegedly hindering economic progress by their restrictive practices, their disruption of production and their contribution to inflation.

This does not mean that the 'attack' on unions and workers has been pursued in a consistent and concerted way. Although one might expect a close degree of solidarity between employers and the Government, this has only been the case on occasions. Both consider a reduction in the power of workers to be one of the pressing problems facing them in increasingly difficult economic circumstances, but they have different alternative pressures as well. An individual employer, or group of employers, particularly those operating in a domestic market or where labour costs are a small proportion of total costs, may well prefer to concede pay increases and raise prices rather than risk a lengthy strike and deteriorating industrial relations. They may even prefer a temporary reduction in profits to such problems. To the Government, however, the overall rate of inflation and profitability of the economy cannot be so readily evaded.

On the other hand, employers do not face the electoral problems of governments, and at times governments may be more sensitive than employers to the overall level of unrest. Therefore, the different positions of the Government and employers have tended to vary as each has asserted different priorities. Thus, in 1956 the Government exhorted employers to stand firm against pay demands, but when the engineering employers took this advice in 1957 they were eventually deserted by the Government, which was not willing to contemplate a major engineering strike (Clegg and Adams, 1957). In 1961 and 1965 employers in general were prepared to support the Government's incomes restraint, but individual employers later defied the Government by making pay agreements outside the limits of the policy. In the late 1960s important groups of employers advocated new legal controls over workers and unions, but when such controls were established in the Industrial Relations Act of 1971 most employers went along with the demands of unions which sought to ignore the Act, eventually embarrassing the Government which had introduced it (Weekes *et al*, 1975).

Not surprisingly, therefore, the record of state intervention in industrial relations institutions has not been consistent, and although some of the important changes of policy have occurred with political changes of government, they have also occurred within the life-span of individual governments. Waves of intervention have been followed by returns to 'voluntarism', though there has been a distinct tendency for each successive wave to be stronger than the last, involving the rejection of more and more of the tenets of voluntarism. The first pay pause in 1962, though largely voluntary, was seen as a controversial step; the first major ministerial attack on an official strike (in 1966) was a similar landmark; the statutory nature of the pay pause of 1966 marked a major development over 1962; in 1969 a government tried to worsen the legal framework of unions' activities for the first time since 1927; the Conservative Government of 1970–4 was the first to see political *advantage* rather than disaster in major and prolonged national strikes; and the present Labour Government has developed more fully than in the past the strategy of involving union leaders in economic policy discussions in the hope that they would themselves accept the main burden of administering restraint. Each of these actions can be seen to have been a precedent for subsequent bouts of intervention, resulting in the process of intensification mentioned above.

The practical reactions of the unions to these developments have in part been discussed in preceding sections, but for many years their response within the political debate was mainly to argue for a retention of the existing institutional system.[13] They resisted state intervention of all kinds and sought the preservation of both a voluntarist pattern of industrial relations and *ad hoc* criteria in bargaining. Given the continuity of full employment and certain minor adjustments in their legal position, British unions felt strong enough to bargain with employers without seeking any major state involvement on their behalf. This position, articulated by unions with varying degrees of emphasis before the Donovan Commission, acquired an even greater prominence during the great disputes between the Conservative Government and the unions: the Industrial Relations Act and the series of struggles culminating in the miners' strike. By the early 1970s the unions and their supporters were the only major group left supporting the model of voluntarism which had represented the area of consensus between them, employers, the state and the political parties during the 1950s.

Matters became slightly more complex with the adoption of the social contract policy under the Labour Government of 1974, since this involved a closer degree of mutual involvement by state and unions. A series of Acts of Parliament[14] has given the unions a more powerful and legally established position within British society than ever before. The unions' desire for statutory guarantees itself marks a significant change; whether the newly entrenched power of union organisations will become predominantly an instrument for representing workers' interests or for restraining them must await developments over the next few years.

The growth of state intervention may usefully be considered in terms of three major and related areas: institutional reform, incomes policy and changes in the legal framework of industrial relations.

INSTITUTIONAL REFORM

With the exception of certain provisions of the 1971 Act, policies for institutional reform have normally been persuasive rather than coercive. As such, proposals for institutional change have usually been pursued by advocates of 'voluntarism' as alternatives to statutory intervention (Flanders, 1967). The strategy has been used to cover all three aspects of government concern, but especially restrictive practices and the disruption of production. The Donovan Commission represents the high-water mark of this approach. There were in fact considerable divisions among the members of the Commission, several seeking certain forms of legal intervention, but overall its Report was a classic example of the doctrine of the institutionalisation of conflict. Starting from the assumption that conflict was inevitable in industrial relations, it rejected attempts to control its expression by statutory means. Rather, it argued, those conflicts would be more liable to non-disruptive resolution if the institutions which governed collective bargaining were reformed in certain ways. The Report, and the research papers which supported it, therefore drew attention to procedures in certain industries (predominantly in engineering) which could be considered to hinder the peaceful resolution of conflict. At a wider level of generalisation, the Report placed massive emphasis on the division between the realities of shop-floor bargaining and the institutions of national-level negotiations. The Report's proposals were therefore predominantly aimed at voluntaristic means for reforming institutions.

The official encouragement of productivity bargaining may also be considered among the elements of institutional reform; it did in fact form part of the battery of developments commended by the Donovan Commission, into whose philosophy it fitted easily. One of the great attractions for the Government of productivity bargaining was that it provided a non-coercive and constructive means of dealing with both 'restrictive practices' and inflation.

INCOMES POLICY

The Labour Government, 1964–70

From 1965 the Labour Government operated a stronger and more detailed form of control over pay than previous post-war attempts. It operated through the National Board for Prices and Incomes, to which a total of 170 prices and incomes references were made.[15] It was originally intended that the policy be voluntary, and employers' organisations and trade unions were committed to it. However, by 1966 the Government had begun to impart statutory elements (Panitch, 1976: Ch. 5). In the crisis of July 1966 a complete statutory freeze was imposed on pay and price increases. This was succeeded by a series of measures giving ministers the power to delay the implementation of individual pay agreements for various periods while they were investigated by the NBPI. In the event of an adverse report from the Board, further delaying powers could be employed. The Government exercised flexibility in the use of its powers, generally avoiding confrontations with determined unions which could cause considerable disruption through strike action. In the early stages of the statutory policy, most unions co-operated with its implementation, and even after they had ceased to give active support very few sought direct confrontation, preferring to find ways round the policy.[16]

The changes in union policy, together with the implications of incomes policy for their overall bargaining strategy and relations with Government, have already been discussed on pages 207 and 217. By 1969 several unions were refusing to co-operate, while employers had ceased to believe in its usefulness. The Conservative Opposition, which had initially supported incomes policy, had been opposing it since 1966 in favour of a plan for the reform of trade union law. By 1969 the Government itself began to abandon most of the statutory apparatus and rely again on voluntary agreement alone. In part it was motivated in this by the approach of a general election, and in part by the fact that, like the Conservatives, it was beginning to look in the direction of industrial relations law reform.

The Conservative Government, 1970–4

When elected in 1970 the Conservatives entirely rejected the concept of an incomes policy and abolished the NBPI. They intended to rely on an increased level of unemployment, greater resistance to public-sector pay claims and the planned Industrial Relations Act. But from early on the strategy was not successful. For reasons still not fully understood the relationship between the rate of unemployment and the pace of wage increases had shifted; several major compromises had to be reached with public-sector unions, and the Government's thesis that the public sector had been the major source of pay pressure had in any case rested on insubstantial evidence; finally, the Industrial Relations Act was successfully boycotted by the unions.

By 1972 the Government had formally returned to incomes policy, with stronger statutory controls than even under the Labour Government.

Dramatically reversing their strategy of avoiding relations with the unions, the Conservatives tried to reach agreement with the TUC and the CBI on wage restraint by inviting those bodies to share in the determination of a whole range of economic and social policy issues. However, when the TUC took the Government at its word and opened a series of policy debates with it, Mr Heath abruptly ended the talks and introduced a unilateral and statutorily supported policy, though renewed attempts at dialogue were made at the various phases of renewal of the policy.

The first stage, as with previous exercises, was a complete freeze. This was followed by a two-stage relaxation of controls, under which increases were strictly limited. The policy did not incorporate the various exceptions of Labour's policy; neither did ministers retain discretion in its administration. A Pay Board implemented its provisions, and established the very limited ground on which exceptions could be permitted. The final stage of the policy tied pay increases to rises in the cost of living, incorporating the threshold increases described on page 210, which eventually became the source of large rises rather than restraint. Until the eventual confrontation with the miners, there were no frontal breaches of the law.

The Labour Government since 1974

The minority Labour Government of March 1974 accepted the unions' rejection of incomes policy and declared its intention to rely on the social contract and a planned new Advisory, Conciliation and Arbitration Service for the resolution of disputes. However, in the short term it kept the Pay Board machinery in operation, maintaining the criteria of the Conservatives' policy but operating them flexibly. When these powers expired the Government had no formal policy at all, relying heavily on the TUC's efforts to preach restraint under the social contract and on a general spirit of loyalty to the Labour Government among the unions.

By June 1975 the continuing high level of inflation was resulting in massive pressure on sterling, and in the context of a general withdrawal from the left-wing policies which it had been pursuing since its election the Government negotiated a more specific agreement on pay restraint with the TUC and CBI. A flat-rate limit £6 a week for pay increases over the coming year was agreed, with nothing at all for those earning £8,500 a year. Although the Government clearly threatened that it would use legal measures to support the policy if necessary, it was able for the year in question to rely on strong union support together with constant official propaganda over the dangers of continuing high inflation. The policy 'worked', partly because the high level of unemployment was weakening the power of organised labour anyway, partly because of popular and union fears of inflation, and partly because union leaders at all levels were far more anxious to prevent the return of a Conservative Government than they had been when they challenged the Labour Government in 1969.

Early in 1976 agreement was reached on a similar package for the following year, as part of which the Chancellor of the Exchequer announced that income tax concessions could be introduced if restraint were successfully pursued.

These developments have finally led to a position where, in contrast with the earlier British tradition of 'voluntarism', the level of overall wage increases is becoming a matter for negotiation between the Government, the TUC and the CBI, with the unions demanding a range of policy concessions in exchange for pay restraint. In 1972 they refused to reach agreement with the Conservative Government because it would make no compromises on its overall economic and social strategy. In 1974 a commitment by the Labour Government to a programme of public ownership, the redistribution of wealth and improved social as well as specific measures favourable to union interests, was important in securing the social contract. However, the worsening economic and employment position and the loyalty of the unions to the Labour Party have gradually tipped the scales against the unions, so that they have accepted tighter measures of pay restraint in exchange for fewer wider policy commitments from the Government.

INDUSTRIAL RELATIONS LAW

The Situation Before the 1971 Act

Until 1971 there was no statute defining the legality of major forms of industrial action. The presumption of English common law has always been that many forms of strike action would be illegal, but various Acts of Parliament over the past century have excluded withdrawal of labour in pursuance of a trade dispute from the scope of common law.[17] In other words, there has been no legally defined 'right to strike' in English law; rather, statute law has provided *immunity* from what would otherwise be implied by common law. The conflict between statute (passed by Parliament) and common law (defined in particular cases by judges) has been a continuing one. Throughout the late nineteenth century and the early years of this century there were several instances where judges sought to redefine the scope of statutory immunity in order to render strikes vulnerable to the operation of the common law; each major case was followed by agitation (usually successful) for new legislation redefining the immunity and thus nullifying the effect of the judgement. From 1906 to the early 1960s the situation became more stable, judges not challenging a wide interpretation of the statutory immunity. However, since 1962 there has been a renewal of the process as judicial opinion has moved against trade unions. Associated with this were demands for reducing unions' rights at law. However, Conservative governments continued to follow a policy of friendly relations with the unions until 1963, when an important legal decision brought the issue into prominence again. The Government took the opportunity to announce a Royal Commission on trade union law, though by the time it came to the actual appointment of a commission – the Donovan Commission – Labour was in office and held to the plan.

There were considerable divisions among the groups which submitted evidence to the Commission (Crouch, 1977: Ch. 7). Generally, trade unions, academic witnesses and some employers advocated the retention and strengthening of voluntarism, opposing any basic change in the role of the law in industrial relations. As stated above (page 241), the Commission itself concentrated on proposals for non-statutory institutional reform, but an important minor theme of the evidence, and certain expressions of minority thinking among the Commission members, advocated new legal limitations on strikes and other aspects of union action. The main employer representatives, however, called for extensive new controls over unions, in particular for legal requirements that unions should discipline unofficial strikers. Shortly before the Commission reported the Conservative Party issued a policy document, *Fair Deal at Work*, which advocated very similar policies.

The initial response of the Labour Government was to follow the policies of voluntaristic institutional reform favoured by the Donovan majority. However, by the end of 1968 the Government claimed that continuing economic difficulties and mounting unofficial industrial unrest made stronger action necessary. An Industrial Relations Bill[18] was proposed which would embody several of Donovan's proposals (several of which gave increased rights to unions and workers), but which also included limited legal controls on the rights of unions and strikers. The TUC was not prepared to accept the possibility of fines on workers or unions for industrial action. In a typical move it produced counter-proposals for voluntary action by unions to achieve similar results to those sought by the Government. These would give an unprecedented role to the TUC itself in dictating policy to member unions (TUC, 1969; Panitch, 1976: Ch. 7). Meanwhile the unions put strong pressure on the Government *via* the Labour Party. There were fears that some unions would question their financial support to the party, and that union-sponsored MPs would vote against the Government, bringing it down. The Prime Minister tried to negotiate a strengthening of the terms of the TUC's proposals. The sticking point was whether the TUC would require its member unions to guarantee to take disciplinary action against unofficial strikers. They refused, but offered a 'solemn and binding' undertaking to take all possible action to restrict unofficial disputes. In practice this meant that the TUC would intervene in unofficial strikes, sometimes in order to put pressure on the workers involved, but it would not accept *a priori* that unofficial strikers should be seen as in breach of trade union disicpline.

From that time (June 1969) until the general election twelve months later, the Government's policy on both incomes policy and industrial relations swung sharply away from the confrontation with unions which had progressively characterised relations since 1966. The TUC operated its conciliation plan, with somewhat reluctant support from the CBI.

The 1971 Act

The Conservative Party had made legislation to restrain industrial action a central plank of its platform since the publication of *Fair Deal at Work*, and when returned to power in 1970 introduced an Industrial Relations Bill to implement its main provisions. During this period relations between the Government and the TUC were virtually non-existent, and the Government did not encourage the TUC's conciliation plan. This marked a sharp though temporary reversal of the post-war tendency for the TUC to become increasingly closely involved with Government discussions on a wide range of policies. The unions organised various forms of protest demonstrations and stoppages to oppose the Bill, but it was passed in August 1971.

For the purpose of the present analysis, one may categorise the relevant contents of the Industrial Relations Act as follows: (i) certain measures to improve the rights of unions or of indivdual workers against the power of employers; (ii) measures to protect the individual non-militant worker against the power of his union leadership; (iii) measures to increase the responsibilities of the union leadership to discipline militant members; (iv) measures to enable the state or an individual employer to weaken the power of organised labour (whether official or unofficial) when used against employers.

Some of the measures under (i) can be considered as part of a *quid pro quo* arrangement, though others were primarily included to provide a 'balance' against a more potent 'equivalent' constraint imposed on unions; further, some of the advantages could only be secured by unions willing to be 'registered' (see below), and should therefore be seen as an inducement to register rather than as a *quid pro quo*. Apart from certain measures concerned with internal union affairs, the primary aim of measures under (ii), such as prohibition of the closed shop, was to weaken the bargaining strength of unions.

The measures under (iii) were also primarily devised to weaken the power of organised labour, but two different kinds of measure were included. Some proposals, such as the removal of immunity from unofficial strikers, constitute a straightforward change in the balance of advantage at law between employer and employee, reflecting the general view of employers and others that legal immunities granted workers when they were 'weak' were no longer 'needed' now that unions were 'strong'. But other proposals imposed a positive legal duty on union leaderships to control and discipline unofficial strikers among their members. This was mainly secured through the device of registration. To render themselves eligible to retain the statutory immunities from legal action against striking and to enjoy certain other benefits (some new but some which they had held before), the unions were required to register. The conditions of registration included an acceptance of legal liability for controlling the actions of any representative of the union inducing men to strike outside the scope left for strike action under the Act. This was a change of major importance in British industrial relations, since it involved the state placing a legal responsibility on unions to assist employers in maintaining industrial discipline.

The TUC decided to boycott the operation of the new Act; the few unions which registered were eventually expelled from the TUC (Weekes *et al*:

Appendix V). Boycott involved refusing to register (thereby laying the unions open to a wide range of potential legal action, as well as turning down various benefits), and refusing to recognise the newly established National Industrial Relations Court (thereby passing up the opportunity to make use of much existing legislation for employee protection, since such matters as redundancy tribunals were incorporated into the court's machinery in an attempt by the Government to ensure its establishment as an institution). The boycott was effectively maintained. The AUEW went even further than TUC policy by refusing to appear before the Court to defend itself; this involved the union in several expensive legal penalties for contempt of court. Most of the major cases brought to the Court were from individual workers resisting compulsory unionism or from small firms seeking to resist union membership. The TGWU was fined heavily for refusing to restrain a dock strike (*ibid*: Ch. 4).

The Government itself sought to make use of the Court or the Act on few occasions. In 1972 it secured a conciliation pause of two weeks in a national official rail strike; the strike resumed as soon as the pause lapsed. The Government then secured a Court order for a strike ballot; the railwaymen voted by a ratio of six to one in favour of the strike. After this experience the Government, which was by now in any case trying to persuade the unions to participate in a voluntary incomes policy, did not make further use of the Act. The great majority of employers ignored it, allowing unions to operate compulsory unionism, not prosecuting unofficial strikers, and making agreements which were specifically marked as being not legally enforceable. By 1974 the Government had accepted a need for re-examination of the Act, though this implied a combination of both ameliorative and toughening changes.

The Acts of 1974–6

The package of legislation successfully demanded of the new Labour Government by the unions did not, significantly, mean a return to the earlier voluntary system. The Industrial Relations Act was abolished, but other measures were introduced. The rights of individual workers against their employers were considerably strengthened, as were rights to belong to and work for (but not to refuse to belong to) an 'independent' trade union. An Advisory, Conciliation and Arbitration Service was established on a statutory but independent basis under the joint control of the Government, the TUC and CBI. This took over the work previously done by the Ministry of Labour (later the Department of Employment), but it also acquired some important new tasks. It had the responsibility for deciding which unions could be accepted as independent of employers, and was involved in the appointment of a Central Arbitration Committee which was empowered to make binding decisions in case of appeals by unions for recognition (including instances of rival claims by different unions). This emerging system of tripartite supervision of industrial relations has been paralleled in other areas of policy. A tripartite Health and Safety Commission had replaced the Ministry's responsibilities in that area, while a similarly tripartite Manpower Services

Commission had taken over industrial training and the operation of employment exchanges.

An important cause of this development had been union suspicion of the Ministry during the years in which it had become increasingly involved in incomes policy; hence the demand for a conciliation service independent of government. Furthermore, the major initial cause of legislation so favourable to union and worker interests was the increased power of the unions within the Labour Party in the early 1970s. However, while it is early days yet to assess how these policies and new institutions will operate in practice, certain ironic possibilities (though only that) may be noted. At the same time that tripartite institutions have developed to escape the involvement of a Ministry of Labour in incomes policy, so (as discussed on page 244) incomes policy itself has become a tripartite issue. If incomes policy of this kind, with the unions playing a major role in restraining workers' demands, becomes entrenched, what will become the role of the tripartite ACAS? Furthermore, the new legislation provides powerful reinforcement for the rights of established unions against employers, dissident workers and rival unions. These have been conceived as supporting workers' countervailing power; but how will their application develop if unions within the TUC (and hence those acceptable to ACAS) increasingly become agents in the operation of incomes policy, particularly if groups of workers try to escape that policy by forming new autonomous unions (Crouch, 1977: Ch. 10)?

A final area of policy where the Labour Government plans legislation is that of workers' participation. At present, however, the issue is being studied by a Government Committee (the Bullock Committee) and there is no established policy. The position of the TUC on the issue and the ambiguities of recent developments were discussed on page 216.

5 CONCLUSIONS

INDUSTRIAL MILITANCY AND POLITICAL MOVEMENTS

The principal political relation of British unions for many years has of course been that with the Labour Party. The relationship has always been ambivalent, as was noted on page 217. At some levels it has been close, but at others it is a highly marginal one. It did, however, survive major strains during the Labour Government of 1964–70. This was a period when the mutual loyalty of the two institutions was strained to the full, but no union broke off its affiliation, and the voices within the party calling for an end to the relationship have always been in a minority. The Labour Government made major demands on the loyalty of the unions in calling for wage restraint, offering in exchange the somewhat non-political commitment to technological change which characterised that episode in the party's history. For some union leaders, particularly those on the right of the movement, the bonds of loyalty to the party were temporarily effective. From those on the left, and also for those unions not affiliated to the party, there was less response.

But more recently there have been major changes in union-party relations. During the years of Labour opposition of 1970–74 the unions assumed an unprecedented role of political involvement with the party. The Conservative Government was engaged in policies hostile to the unions which the unions wanted a future Labour Government to repeal. Furthermore, both party and unions now realised that the neat separation of industrial and political issues which had characterised much of their former history was no longer tenable in a society where the state was increasingly involved in industrial relations. The immediate outcome of this new relationship was the 'social contract'. Increasingly it has come to mean an intensification of the traditional loyalty of union leaders to the Party, especially as the economic crisis has deepened. At the same time, in recent years several major unions have taken a renewed interest in sponsoring Labour MPs (Ellis and Johnson, 1974), and at local level union activists have become more involved in the affairs of constituency Labour parties.

The Labour Party remains the main institution through which unions and their activists relate to wider political issues, and the weakening of that link between 1966 and 1970 has at least temporarily been reversed. However, among trade union officers, shop stewards and at shop-floor level other bodies are also active.[19] There is a national organisation of Conservative Trade Unionists, but this has not yet succeeded in establishing itself as an independent voice in either the Conservative Party or the unions. The Communist Party has for a long time had important contacts both at shop-floor level and throughout union hierarchies, though it has very rarely been able to mobilise workers in distinctive Communist campaigns; it has had to join its forces to existing expressions of discontent. For example, Communists have been significant in the recent resurgence of conflict in coal-mining, but it is not a new development for Communists to be active in the NUM; for many years there have regularly been Communists among the union's national officers. During the years when conflict in the mines was declining, they accepted that situation: and now that it is increasing they are identified with the increase. At shop-floor level, the involvement of the Communist Party in several industries probably began to increase in the late 1960s, alongside that of various Marxist and Trotskyist groups. These were either creations of, or received major boosts to their membership and prestige during, the student revolts of 1967–70. From this base they then extended their membership to include a number of industrial workers for the first time, though little is known of their precise membership situation, and by the mid-1970s it had passed its peak.

These groups have in turn been involved in some of the other conflicts of the period: squatters, claimants' unions, tenants' associations, and in the emergence of important if small left-wing groups within certain professional occupations – for example, teaching (at all levels), social work, planning and architecture, and acting. However, the extent to which this spread of involvement by radicals has entailed an inter-relationship between industrial action and the other conflict areas in less clear. There is little research on the question, but that which does exist suggests that the level of involvement is not high. For example, during the early 1970s a major issue was the introduction of a new Housing Finance Act by the Conservative Government which involved major increases in the rents of council-house tenants. In several areas important campaigns were waged against the Act by tenants' organisations, Labour councillors and the various leftist groups (Sklair, 1975), but there is little evidence of any major involvement by shop-floor activists as such.

At the other extreme, there have been some examples of the involvement of industrial militants in reactionary causes, alongside which there are cases of the National Front (a Fascist organisation) successfully putting up candidates for election as shop stewards in some industries. During the late 1960s workers in the London docks, the Smithfield meat market and a few other areas demonstrated in support of racialist policies being promulgated by the Conservative MP, Enoch Powell. None of these actions involved strikes, but there were marches on Parliament and some physical attacks on black people. The official unions have always opposed actions of this kind.

Finally, there is one isolated instance of a successful revolutionary political strike by workers in the United Kingdom: the strike of Protestant workers in Northern Ireland in May 1974. Since 1969 there has been considerable violence between the Protestant and Catholic communities in Northern Ireland following demands by the Catholic minority for an end to religious discrimination and for participation in political power. By 1974 the British Government had gained the agreement of established political leaders of both communities on a new constitution for Northern Ireland whereby power would be shared with Catholic representatives. The agreement also involved the eventual establishment of a Council of Ireland which would bring together representatives of the British, Eire and Northern Ireland governments to consider certain issues relating to the government of Northern Ireland. Militant Protestant leaders had opposed power-sharing from the beginning, fearing that it would lead eventually to the unification of the north with the rest of Ireland, which is predominantly Catholic. After the politicians had finally approved the new plans the militants called a general strike of Protestant workers in the province, especially by the strategically placed electricity generation workers. The strikers called for an end to power-sharing with Catholics, no Council of Ireland, the resignation of the Executive (the regional government of the province) and new elections for the regional Assembly. Within a few days the province was totally without electrical power. The Executive resigned, and the British Government dissolved the Assembly and the existing reform plans, though it remains committed to power-sharing. The strike therefore ranks alongside the miners' strike of 1974 in being the only strike in Britain to have ended with the resignation of a government.

Politically, the Protestants of Ulster have been connected with the right of British politics and the Conservative Party. The Catholics have not been unequivocally leftist, though the major party which represents them now is the only effective Labour Party in Northern Ireland. However, there is evidence that some of the main organisers of the strike itself were trade union activists with experience of unofficial disputes in Britain.

SYSTEM CHANGES AND THE NEW MILITANCY

The developments in institutional reform, incomes policy and legal changes demonstrate certain important points concerning the British situation. Firstly, it can be seen, as was suggested in earlier sections, that much of the sudden increase in workers' and unions' militancy can be interpreted as a reaction against the sharply increased militancy of the state. The state itself was reacting, not so much to a sudden sharp challenge, but to a situation which was gradually growing more difficult for several reasons. The emergence of several unions from their complacency over collective bargaining, and their re-engagement with shop-floor concerns, can be seen as a response, partly to the rising militancy of their members, and partly to official institutional interventions.

This process has been noted at several points in this paper: for example, the TUC's collective bargaining committee, which began as a defensive means for imposing voluntary restraint and ended as a mechanism for improving, strengthening and co-ordinating bargaining strategies. The low-pay campaign and the TGWU's pensions campaign can be seen in part as the unions' retort to Government claims that the poor and the old could only be helped through state incomes policy and not through collective bargaining. The renewal of political demands by unions can be traced to their being thrown into the political arena by incomes policy and industrial relations policy. The relationship of the wage explosion to a complex series of government actions was discussed on pages 209–12.

The strengthening of the TUC over its individual members was frequently seen as a panacea by those advocating more order and control in industrial relations; the TUC was seen as moderate and 'responsible', participating as it did in national economic policy discussions with Government and employers. The fullest expression of this belief can be seen in the Government's attempt to persuade the TUC to adopt important disciplinary powers over member unions tolerating unofficial action in June 1969. More generally, the intensified pace of government involvement in national-level discussions with unions and employers gave the TUC an unprecedented prominence throughout the 1960s and early 1970s. But the eventual consequence of this was the use by the TUC of its new prominence to co-ordinate a new degree of militancy between unions, which received *its* fullest expression in the successful boycott of the 1971 Act.

A second conclusion concerns the massive and unresolved tensions between opposed forces within contemporary British industrial relations institutions. 'Voluntarism', whether it is seen in terms of unions' resistance to any degree of encroachment on free collective bargaining, or whether it is interpreted in the 'Donovan' sense of seeking to 'reform' industrial relations and reduce manifest conflict through judicious institutional innovations, remains a very powerful force. Each attempt at a stronger degree of state intervention in incomes policy has ended in failure and disillusionment as the traditional institutions of bargaining, conciliation, compromise and strike have broken the constraints of the policy. Attempts at legal changes to restrain workers' powers have similarly failed against the sheer ability of organised labour to resist.

At the same time, the opposing force, the repeated unwillingness of governments and employers to be content with the consequences of voluntarism, has also been powerful. Periods of state withdrawal from incomes policy have alternated with periods of intervention, and each new wave of interventionism has been more detailed, more coercive and more fraught with conflict than the previous one. Similarly, governments of both major parties moved towards policies of changing the legal framework of industrial relations, and the major organisations of employers were committed to such a strategy from 1966 to 1974. At the present time the Labour Party is opposed to legal limitations on organised labour, and it is doubtful whether a Conservative government in the near future would wish to reintroduce much of the Industrial Relations Act. But in the light of the oscillating history of the past decade it cannot be assumed that 'voluntarism' will ever fully regain its former prominence.

The traditional model of British industrial relations has been considerably eroded by all these developments. According to that model, autonomous groups of employers, unions and government related to one another by bargaining and various forms of conciliation, which were seen as extensions of bargaining. Instead, by the early 1970s government and employers were seeking to substitute for this model one of an over-riding national purpose, in the pursuit of which the three parties must collaborate, under the guidance of the state and according to rules of managerial order. There is at present a relaxation of the process of encroaching legal intervention, but it cannot be seen as a simple 'return' to the pre-existing state of institutions, as though nothing had happened to disturb them. Within the social contract the TUC is much more closely involved in policy-making than ever before, and although it tries continually to extend unions' typical 'bargaining' approach to this forum, its success in so doing is very dependent on the state of the economy and the demands of the holders of sterling.

However, a final factor which will affect the success of and the position of the different interests within the new tripartite machinery is the complex relationship between shop-floor militancy and traditional trade union methods on the one hand, and heightened political concerns and the new economic context on the other. The localism and narrowness of even highly militant shop-floor action was noted at several points in Section 3. However, it was also noted there that these demands and the actions which accompany them increasingly have implications which extend well beyond the local. This also suggests a point of central importance to a study of industrial conflict in Britain: the mutual interaction of changes in workers' demands and action

('Section 3' issues) with changes in state policy and formal institutions ('Section 4' issues). In particular it is interesting to note how in the 'pre-Donovan' period, and before the extended attempts at state incomes policy, the pressure of workers' demands was evident in the 'two systems' of bargaining. At the time this was seen as a fragmentation and as a threat to the institutionalisation of conflict. However, it also served to contain conflict, precisely by separating the area in which workers' demands operated from the wider and politically more salient level of national institutions. In part it has been the very reforms designed to re-institutionalise local action – incomes policy, reforms to bargaining structures and payment systems, productivity bargaining, and industrial relations reform – which have broken the local isolation of militant action and given it wider repercussions both economically and politically. The growth of shop-floor militancy initially produced a government response which forced industrial relations to become intensely politicised, even though political motives were rarely relevant to such shop-floor action. Political re-engagement brought the official unions into a new prominence; they have been willing to embark on a limited degree of political action, though whether they can wield power here, given the nature of their base, is doubtful. Government action also stimulated other sections of the work-force into militancy, and in the rapidly worsening economic environment of the mid-1970s the barriers which for so long protected British industrial conflict from escalation and politicisation seem weaker than at any time in the past half-century.

NOTES

1. For a detailed discussion of these and other conflicts surrounding the policy, see Panitch, 1976: Chs. 4–6.
2. The first of these, *Economic Policy and the Cost of Living* (TUC/Labour Party, 1973) became retrospectively known as the document which constituted the 'social contract'.
3. M. Shalev, 'Lies, Damned Lies and Strike Statistics: the Measurement of Trends in Industrial Conflict'.
4. This section draws heavily on Silver (now Shalev), 1973; Durcan and McCarthy, 1972; and on statistics published in *Department of Employment Gazette* (monthly). Incidentally, it should be noted that M. Shalev used to be known as M. Silver and some of his work has been published under the latter name.
5. For a detailed study of sit-ins in Britain, see Hemingway and Keyser, 1975.
6. For a criticism of this tendency, see Turner, 1968.
7. See the written evidence to the Donovan Commission of the EEF.
8. For a more detailed discussion of political strikes, see *International Socialism*, March 1975.
9. Direct evidence of this narrowness of perspectives will be found in Turner *et al*, 1967. Discussions of the implications of this phenomenon will be found in: Mann, 1970; and Crouch, 1975.
10. This review of the available evidence also demonstrates the importance of concrete factors relating to workers' immediate interests in the success of these combines. For example, specific issues such as automation or redundancy affecting several plants or firms may prompt links between the various shop steward groups, and mergers between companies are likely to have a similar effect.

11. For example, the TUC's pamphlet, *Good Industrial Relations* (1971), written during the high-point of official union militancy, advocated the expulsion from union membership of workers persistently breaking agreements.
12. For an analysis and interpretation of these developments, see Crouch, 1977; and for a detailed account of how they have affected the Labour Party and unions in particular, see Panitch, 1976.
13. See the evidence of most unions to the Donovan Commission; and the response of the TUC to the Conservatives' Industrial Relations Bill (TUC, 1970).
14. The Trade Union and Labour Relations Act, 1974; the Employment Protection Act, 1975; and the Trade Union and Labour Relations (Amendment) Act, 1976.
15. For analysis of the work of the NBPI see Fels, 1972; Crouch, 1974; and Mitchell, 1972.
16. Two important examples occurred in 1968. The TGWU threatened a strike for a pay increase for municipal busmen while the issue was being investigated by the NBPI, rendering such a strike illegal; in the event the union avoided the issue of a strike by negotiating separate productivity deals with individual authorities (which was still possible during the NBPI scrutiny). In the same year the National Federation of Building Trades Operatives threatened strike action against a Government attempt to force a pay *reduction* of 1d an hour following an adverse report on a recent increase by the NBPI. However, a Government order rendered such a strike illegal and the unions (and workers) acquiesced in the wage cut.
17. For general guidance on the role of law in British industrial relations, see K. W. Wedderburn, 1971.
18. Outlined in the White Paper *In Place of Strife*, Cmnd 3888, 1969.
19. Parker (1968) indicates that shop stewards and, especially, trade union officers have a far higher index of membership of political parties than the population as a whole, but says nothing of the distribution of that membership among the various parties.

LIST OF WORKS CITED

Allen, V. L. (1960), *Trade Unions and the Government* (London: Longmans).

—— (1966), *Militant Trade Unionism* (London: Merlin).

Bain, G. S. (1970), *The Growth of White-Collar Unionism* (Oxford: Clarendon Press).

—— and Price, R. (1976), 'Union Growth Revisited: 1948–1974 in Perspective', *BJIR*, XIV, 3.

Banks, J. A. (1970), *Marxist Sociology in Action* (London: Faber and Faber).

Beynon, H. (1973), *Working for Ford* (Harmondsworth: Penguin).

Blackburn, R. M. (1967), *Union Character and Social Class* (London: Batsford).

Brown, W. (1972), 'A Consideration of 'Custom and Practice', *BJIR*, X, 1.

—— (1973) *Piecework Bargaining* (London: Heinemann).

Cameron, G. C. and Eldridge, J. E. T., (1968), 'Unofficial Strikes: some Objections Considered', in J. E. T. Eldridge, *Industrial Disputes* (London: Routledge and Kegan Paul).

Child, J. (ed.) (1973), *Man and Organisation* (London: Allen and Unwin).

Clack, G. (1967), *Industrial Relations in a British Car Factory* (Cambridge: University Press).

Clegg, H. A. (1972), *The System of Industrial Relations in Great Britain*, 2nd (enlarged) ed. (Oxford: Blackwell).

—— and Adams, R. (1957), *The Employers' Challenge* (Oxford: Blackwell).

Cliff, T. (1970), *The Employers' Offensive: Productivity Deals and How to fight Them* (London: Pluto).

CCO (1974), *Putting Britain First* (London: CCO).

Cotgrove, S., Dunham, J., and Vamplew, C. (1971), *The Nylon Spinners* (London: Allen and Unwin).

Crouch, C. J. (1974), 'The Ideology of a Managerial Elite: The Work of the National

Board for Prices and Incomes', in I. Crewe (ed.), *The British Political Sociology Yearbook*. Vol. I (London: Croom Helm).
—— (1975), 'The Drive for Equality', in L. Lindberg *et al.* (eds), *Stress and Contradiction in Modern Capitalism* (Lexington: D. C. Heath).
—— (1977) *Class Conflict and the Industrial Relations Crisis* (London: Heinemann).
Donovan Commission (Royal Commission on Trade Unions and Employers Associations), (1965–68), *Written Evidence* and *Report* (London: HMSO).
Dorfman, G. A. (1973), *Wage Politics in Britain 1945–1967: Government versus the TUC* (Ames: Iowa University Press).
Durcan, J. and McCarthy, W. E. J. (1972), 'What is Happening to Strikes?, *New Society* (2 Nov.).
Ellis, J. and Johnson W. (1974), *Members from the Unions* (London: Fabian Society).
Fels, A. (1972), *The British Prices and Incomes Board* (London: Cambridge U.P.).
Flanders, A. (1964), *The Fawley Productivity Agreements* (London: Faber).
—— (1967), *Collective Bargaining: Prescription for Change* (London: Faber).
Fox, A. (1974), *Beyond Contract: Work, Power and Trust Relations* (London: Faber).
Glyn, A. and Sutcliffe B. (1972), *British Capitalism, Workers and the Profits Squeeze* (Harmondsworth: Penguin).
Goldthorpe, J. H., Lockwood D. *et al.* (1968a), *The Affluent Worker: Industrial Attitudes and Behaviour* (Cambridge: University Press).
—— (1968b), *The Affluent Worker: Political Attitudes and Behaviour* (Cambridge U.P.).
—— (1969), *The Affluent Worker in the Class Structure* (Cambridge: University Press).
Goodman, J. F. B. and Thomson, G. M. (1973), 'Cost of Living Indexation Agreements in Post-War British Collective Bargaining', *BJIR*, XI, 2.
Hemingway, J. and Keyser, W. (1975), *Who's in Charge?* (Oxford: Metra).
Heffer, E. (1971), *The Class Struggle in Parliament* (London: Gollancz).
Hill, S. (1974), 'Norms, Groups and Power: the Sociology of Work-place Industrial Relations', *BJIR*, XII, 2.
Hughes, J. (1972), 'The Low Paid', in Townsend, P. and Bosanquet, N. (eds), *Labour and Inequality* (London: Fabian Society).
Hyman, R. (1972a), *Strikes* (London: Fontana).
—— (1972b), *Marxism and the Sociology of Trade Unionism* (London: Pluto).
—— (1974), 'Industrial Conflict and Political Economy', in Miliband, R. and Saville, J., *The Socialist Register 1973* (London: Merlin).
—— and Brough, I. (1975), *Social Values and Industrial Relations* (Oxford: Blackwell).
Jenkins, P. (1969), *The Battle of Downing Street* (London: Knight).
Labour Party (1974), *Britain Will Win with Labour* (London: Labour Party).
Layton, D. (1973), 'Low Pay and Collective Bargaining', in Field, F. (ed.), *Low Pay* (London: Acton Society Trust).
Lerner, S. *et al.* (1969), *Workshop Wage Determination* (Oxford: Pergamon).
—— and Bescoby, J. (1966), 'Shop Stewards' Combine Committees in the British Engineering Industry', *BJIR*, IV, 2.
Mann, M. (1970), 'The Social Cohesion of Liberal Democracy', *Amer. Soc. Rev.*
Marsh, A. I. (1965), *Industrial Relations in Engineering* (Oxford: Blackwell).
Mitchell, J. (1972), *The National Board for Prices and Incomes* (London: Secker and Warburg).
McCarthy, W. E. J. and Clifford, B. A. (1966), 'The Work of Industrial Courts of Inquiry', *BJIR*, IV, 1.
—— and Marsh, A. I. (1965), *Disputes Procedures in Britain*, Research Paper 5 of Donovan Commission (*q.v.*).

—— and Parker, S. (1965), *Shop Stewards and Workshop Relations*, Research Paper 10 of Donovan Commission (*q.v.*).

McKersie, R. B. and Hunter, L. C. (1973), *Pay, Productivity and Collective Bargaining* (London: Macmillan).

Parker, S. R. (1968), *Work-Place Industrial Relations* (London: HMSO).

—— *et al.* (1974), *Work-place Industrial Relations 1972* (London: HMSO).

National Board for Prices and Incomes (1965), *Payment by Results*, Report No. 65 (London: HMSO).

Panitch, L. (1976), *Social Democracy and Industrial Militancy* (Cambridge U.P.).

Phelps Brown, E. H. with Browne, M. (1968), *A Century of Pay: 1860–1960* (London: Macmillan).

Richter, I. (1973), *Political Purpose in Trade Unions* (London: Allen and Unwin).

Roberts, B. C. and Rothwell, S. (1974), 'Recent Developments in Collective Bargaining in the United Kingdom', *International Labour Review*, Vol. 106.

Routh, G. (1965), *Occupation and Pay in Great Britain: 1906–1960* (Cambridge: University Press).

Silver, M. (or Shalev, M.) (1973), 'Recent British Strike Trends: a Factual Analysis', *BJIR*, XI, 1.

—— (1974), 'Trends in Labour Disputes: 1950–1972' (Paris: OECD, unpublished).

Sklair, L. (1975), 'The Struggle against the Housing Finance Act', in R. Miliband and J. Saville (eds), *The Socialist Register 1975* (London: Merlin).

Thompson, W. and Hart, F. (1972), *The UCS Work-In* (London: Lawrence and Wishart).

TUC (1960), *Disputes and Workshop Representation* (London: TUC).

—— (1967), Written Evidence to Donovan Commission, *q. v.*

—— (1968), *Training Shop Stewards* (London: TUC).

—— (1969), *Programme for Action* (London: TUC).

—— (1970), *Reason* (London: TUC).

—— (1971), *Good Industrial Relations* (London: TUC).

—— (1973, and 1974), Interim and Final Reports on Industrial Democracy (London: TUC).

—— (1975), *Congress Report 1974* (London: TUC).

TUC and Labour Party (1973), *Economic Policy and the Cost of Living* (London).

Turner, H. A. (1962), *Trade Union Structure, Policy and Growth* (London: Allen and Unwin).

—— (1968), 'The Royal Commission's Research Papers', *BJIR*, VI, 3.

——, Clack, G. and Roberts, G. (1967), *Labour Relations in the Motor Industry* (London: Allen and Unwin).

Wedderburn, D. and Crompton, R. (1972), *Workers' Attitudes and Technology*, (Cambridge: University Press).

Wedderburn, K. W. (1971), *The Worker and the Law*, 2nd ed. (Harmondsworth: Penguin).

Weekes, B., Mellish, M., Dickens, L. and Lloyd, J. (1975), *Industrial Relations and the Limits of Law* (Oxford: Blackwell).

Wilberforce, Lord (1971), Report of Court of Inquiry into Dispute in the Electricity Industry (London: HMSO).

Wilkinson, F. and Turner, H. A. (1972), 'The Wage-Tax Spiral and Labour Militancy', in D. Jackson *et al.*, *Do Trade Unions Cause Inflation?* (Cambridge: University Press).

7 *Economic Development, Labour Conflicts and the Industrial Relations System in West Germany*

WALTHER MÜLLER-JENTSCH
and HANS-JOACHIM SPERLING

1 THE ECONOMIC AND POLITICAL CONTEXT

AN OUTLINE OF ECONOMIC DEVELOPMENT IN THE FEDERAL REPUBLIC OF GERMANY

In the following outline of economic development in the Federal Republic of Germany, we shall discuss the changes in conditions for the reproduction and exploitation of labour under West German capitalism, and the effect these have had on the growth of capital and the situation of the workers. Unfortunately, this description must remain sketchy and limited to a few indicators on the macro-economic level; it neither refers to differences between specific industrial sectors nor deals with cyclical fluctuations of economic development in detail. The description is based on three periods that can be more or less clearly identified with regard to the conditions which existed during them.

The first phase (1949–57/8) was centred round reconstruction, in accordance with the political aim of restoring capitalist relations of production in the years immediately after the Second World War. The general need for recovery after the war, the expansion of the domestic consumer market, and expanding demand on the world market created favourable conditions for industrial production, which increased considerably between 1951 and 1957, at an average annual rate of 10.6 per cent.

As far as production processes are concerned, these increases were above all made possible by the re-establishment of long-idle productive capacities and, at the same time, by the re-integration (veterans returning from the war) and integration (refugees) of additional labour into the production process.

Again, with a relatively limited number of innovations being introduced,[1] work productivity was already being greatly increased by an average of 5.6 per cent. During this phase, in which the bargaining power of workers and their unions was relatively weak due to high unemployment,[2] average pay rises already slightly exceeded increases in productivity; however, the firms could easily make such concessions, since they could push through comparatively large price increases due to the post-war boom. On the whole, this period is therefore characterised by growing profit-rates for capital (Altvater *et al*, 1974; Baethge *et al*, 1974) as well as a noticeable increase in real income for wage earners, amounting to an average of 5.6 per cent annually.

At the end of the fifties, the economic situation in West Germany clearly began to change when compared to the previous period of reconstruction. As the post-war recovery was achieved and foreign competition became stronger with the increase in the volume of world trade, the growth of industrial production diminished sharply in the ensuing period (1958–65). The average increase only amounted to 6.2 per cent annually; despite the easing-off in the growth-rate, bottlenecks in production became increasingly apparent, since available production capacities were generally employed, and the influx of labour began to dry up. The unemployment rate continued to decrease; in 1961 it fell below the 1 per cent mark for the first time, remaining there until 1966, while the number of those employed in industry increased only insignificantly between 1958 and 1965 by an average of about 2 per cent per year. This increase was based to a large extent on the introduction of foreign labour, whose percentage of the total number of workers increased to more than 5 per cent by 1965.

On the other hand, the growing labour shortage strengthened the bargaining position of the unions during contract negotiations (*Tarifverhandlungen*): workers' hourly wages rose on average 9.4 per cent per year between 1958 and 1965–a substantially higher rate than in the previous period.

The lack of reserve capacity, the shortage of available labour, and the enforcement by the unions of higher wages and shorter working hours forced the employers into widespread investments, the introduction of new, labour-saving technologies, and the pursuit of changes in the organisation of work, the aim of which was the intensification of the work effort. Statistically, this fact is expressed in the increase in capital intensity, which rose between 1958 and 1965 by an average rate of 7.4 per cent annually.

As a result of these measures, productivity rose by an annual average of 7 per cent, and therefore, by a great deal more than in the previous period; however, it did not manage to off-set the wage increases completely. While the working class still managed to achieve a notable rise in its real wages, which increased by an average of 4.5 per cent during this period, the profit-rate now sank a good deal and by 1965 was well below that of 1950.

The contradictions generated by these developments came into the open in the economic crisis of 1966–7. Due to heavy investment in the late fifties and early sixties, an obvious surplus capacity had already developed by 1962, when the growth of production had tended to slacken off; as the growth of industrial production stagnated further in the course of 1966, the extent to which capital investments were utilised continued to sink, forcing down already shrinking profit-rates still further. The crisis made it even more difficult for capital to be realised; yet at the same time the crisis made its own solution possible by the destruction of capital, increasing concentration and centralisation and the regimentation of the workforce through unemployment and shorter hours. In 1967, during the low point of the recession, industrial production with a utilisation of capacity of only 79.5 per cent decreased (by 2.8 per cent) for the first time in the history of West Germany. The average yearly unemployment rate totalled 2.1 per cent in 1967; for a time, the number of unemployed was close to the million mark, while at 4.2 per cent on average for industry, the growth-rate for hourly wage-rates reached a low that had not been experienced since the early fifties.

The recession of 1966–7 was relatively quickly overcome by a favourable trend in exports, the selective implementation of government contract orders in accordance with anti-cyclical financial policy, and a 'wage stop'. Nevertheless, it still represents perhaps the most important turning-point in West Germany's economic development, since it marked the return of its economy to the capitalist cycle of crises after a long period of prosperity.

Although the recession was followed by a distinct recovery, with growth-rates for industrial production of 11.7 per cent (1968) and 12.7 per cent (1969), the boom quickly proved to be short-lived. In 1971 there was once again a serious interruption of growth, with a growth-rate of only 1.8 per cent, and industrial production practically stagnant. This was followed by a moderate, intermittent up-swing, which was then followed by the crisis of 1974–5 which, as regards the decrease in production and the scope of unemployment, has greatly exceeded the 1966–7 recession in intensity. As a result, between 1966 and 1974 the average annual growth-rate of industrial production was only 4.5 per cent.

Although the proportion of immigrants in the work-force has doubled—from 5.1 per cent (1965) to 11 per cent (1973/4)—the number of those employed in industry has remained essentially constant since 1966. Thus, industrial growth was founded solely upon the employment of labour-saving technology and more intense utilisation of labour; this is expressed in the intensity of capital, which once again rose sharply (by 7.6 per cent annually), and sharply rising work productivity (6.5 per cent on average).

On the strength of technological changes in production, rationalisation gained in importance; this was indicated by an intensification of the work process. Despite great efforts at rationalisation, the amount of leeway capital can allow itself in concessions on wage increases has greatly diminished in the last few years. Although the wages of industrial workers rose nominally by 10.5 per cent annually during 1966–74, this merely reflects an intensified struggle over the distribution of wages which was also accompanied by an accelerating rate of inflation. It indicates the continually deteriorating opportunities for the utilisation of capital, as well as the possible consequences of this situation, namely that even in the area of the realisation of profits the problem can be transferred to the workers. The boom of 1968–9 could only momentarily halt the fall in the rate of profit, and the process of concentration continued at an accelerated rate even after 1966–7. Simultaneously, businesses particularly increased their efforts to relocate labour-intensive manufacturing processes in 'low-wage countries'.

Thus, not only is the West German working class faced by a work load which has been increasing for some time, and by dequalification as a result of changes in technical organisation, but also, in the seventies, its material welfare is endangered. On the one hand, one must reckon on a relatively high base of structural unemployment in the future. On the other hand, following the already meagre increases in real wages of the past years, and the decrease in real wages for a growing number of workers, everything indicated that in 1976 there would be a real loss of workers' consumer power even by those who were not yet threatened by unemployment or short-time working. This accompanied the simultaneous reduction of previously granted social security measures by the SPD/FDP government.

THE PRINCIPAL ASPECTS OF POLITICAL DEVELOPMENT IN WEST GERMANY

The post-war conservative governments followed a policy of 'moral persuasion' and public defamation towards trade unions. In public appeals for moderation, they invoked popular fears about inflation and directed them against the wage policies of the unions. When such appeals did not succeed, the Federal Chancellor and the Minister of the Economy denounced the unions as a 'state within the state', as egotistical power structures which undermined the free market economy and thus endangered democracy.

The first post-war recession, that of 1966–7, which was accompanied by a crisis in state finances, shook the political establishment. The ruling conservative coalition (*Bürgerkoalition*) could no longer be sustained in the crisis situation; its base had become too narrow. The successful entrance on the political scene of a neo-Nazi party, the NPD, which received up to 10 per cent of the votes in the elections to the *Länder* parliaments, alarmed the public. Although the establishment of a coalition government by the CDU and SPD in 1966 was more broadly based, it resulted in there being no parliamentary opposition. In the years which followed, this encouraged the establishment of an extra-parliamentary opposition (*ausserparlamentarische Opposition*, or 'Apo' for short) which particularly attacked the passage of the Emergency Laws which were passed by Parliament in 1968. With the publicly influential (cultural revolutionary) activity of the extra-parliamentary opposition the political climate in the BRD changed decisively.

Besides the protest movement against the Vietnam war and the 'authoritarian state', which was essentially supported by students, the most apparent indications of the changed political situation were:

(a) the development of a left-wing within the SPD Young Socialists (*Jungsozialisten*);
(b) the re-establishment of a Communist Party (DKP) in 1968;
(c) the development of citizens' initiatives against land speculation and the destruction of housing in the urban centres, as well as alliances of groups of parents who actively worked to eliminate deplorable conditions in pre-school and school systems;
(d) the actions and activities of many political groups with various concrete goals, such as women's liberation, resocialisation of prisoners, support for liberation movements in developing countries.

Following a Social Democratic election victory in the boom year of 1969, the Grand Coalition was replaced by a small coalition (the SPD/FDP government of Willy Brandt). This change in government further encouraged the establishment of a New Left. With the 'new East European policy' (*Neue Ostpolitik*), which aimed at the diplomatic recognition of socialist countries, the climate of anti-communism was relaxed. The domestic reforms anticipated by the government's programme also partially took into consideration the ideas of leftist movements about the need to reform existing social and political institutions.

The partially successful revival of socialist thought and the increased study of Marxism in West Germany – above all among intellectuals and politically organized youth – led to a campaign of repression by the state against the West German Left in the seventies. Following the replacement of the 'Reform Chancellor', Willy Brandt, by Helmut Schmidt, the pragmatist, political repression was intensified. In the context of the world-wide economic crisis of 1974–5, it now threatens to develop into a 'second era of restoration' in the Federal Republic of Germany.

2 THE MAIN CHARACTERISTICS OF THE CONFLICTS

THE PHASES OF DEVELOPMENT OF STRIKE ACTIVITY

Three phases of strike activity can be identified in the period 1950–74 (see Figure 7.1). After relatively intensive strike activity during 1950–8, the period 1959–65 was one of quiescence which made possible the widespread interpretation of West German industrial relations as a system of 'social peace'. Since then, however, there has been a period of obvious, though irregular, increase in strike activity. This phase is characterised by an increase in both union and unofficial strikes, and also by the inclusion of new groups of workers in the conflicts. The strike movement of this period stands in a close relationship to cyclical developments.

The workers' experiences during the economic recession of 1966–7 were important elements in the outbreak of a series of spontaneous strikes. This is particularly true of the strikes in the metal industry, which were basically

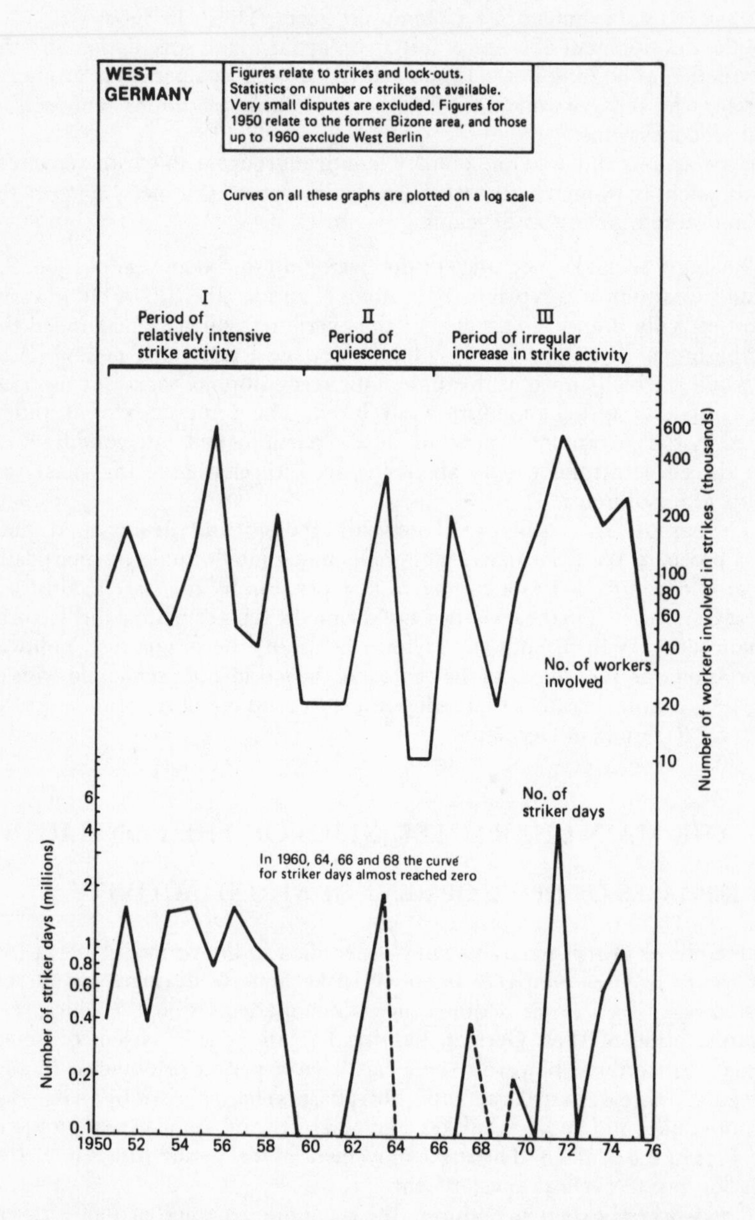

FIGURE 7.1: Industrial conflict in West Germany, 1950–75 (log scales)

directed against cuts in non-contractual bonuses and company benefits. The work-force's shop-floor resistance against the effects of the crisis was usually supported by the unions, and in the autumn of 1967 workshop conflicts in the rubber industry in Hesse were even incorporated into a union contract strike. And under the jurisdiction of IG Bau-Steine-Erden (the union for construction workers and workers in associate industries), a nine-week-long union strike was undertaken by tile-layers to prevent a reduction in piecework.

The policy of wage restraint, which the unions practised even in the years of economic recovery (1968–9) led to a widely-based strike movement in September 1969, during the high-point of the boom. In a single period of little more than three weeks, approximately 140,000 workers from about seventy workshops participated in spontaneous shop-floor strikes; the wage demands which were established aimed at correcting inadequate contract agreements. The focal points of industrial activity were the iron and steel and the metal manufacturing industries, as well as in the mines of the Saar; scattered work stoppages also took place in the civil service sector.

Workshop strikes continued throughout 1970. Once again, they were centred on the metal industry; in the autumn of 1970, a wave of token and protest strikes took place in workshops in support of the unions' stance in the current contract negotiations. About half a million employees participated in the strikes.

During the succeeding period the focal point of labour struggles shifted to strikes which had been initiated and organised by the unions. Thus, in 1971, several workshops in the textile industry of North Rhein-Westphalia, went out on a two-week-long strike. Similarly, in the early summer of 1971, the first union strike in fifty years took place in the chemical industry; within a period of four weeks, there were several different strike actions, particularly in middle-sized workshops in Hesse, North-Rhein-Westphalia and Hamburg.

The selective strike of 120,000 employees begun by IG Metall in Baden-Württemberg in the autumn of 1971 was countered by the industrialists with a widespread, regional lock-out, and ended after a three-week-long labour conflict. The number of working days lost was the highest since 1950.

In 1971, union strike activities also took place in sectors outside the industrial labour force. These included strikes by members of Lufthansa Airline ground crews and the union-organised journalists of a news agency, as well as actions similar to strikes undertaken by doctors employed by hospitals.

In 1972, there was only one selective strike—within the jurisdiction of IG Chemie—in a few workshops in the polishing-tools industry. Next year there was a limited, two-day-long strike in the printing industry, the first in twenty years.

By 1973, however, bargaining over contracts was characterised by demands and settlements which were attuned to the requirements of economic stability (*stabilitätsgerecht*). But against the background of a high rate of inflation, this only intensified the dissatisfaction of the workers with union contract policy. Once again they expressed their discontent in a wave of spontaneous workshop strikes, a movement which lasted for nearly a whole year in several focal-points separated both in time and by region. Approximately 275,000 blue- and white-collar workers from at least 335 workshops participated in this activity. The industrial activity was again centred on iron and steel and metal manufacturing, as well as in the mines of the Saar; scattered work stoppages also took place in the civil service. In most cases, the demands were for supplementation of contract settlements by cost-of-living bonuses. In a few cases the demands were also directed against an intensification of working conditions.

Throughout 1974 and 1975, both years of crisis, there were scattered workshop strikes by workforces to resist wage cuts. Protest actions against dismissals and factory closures also took place. On the whole, the activity in this period was once again basically centred around IG Metall—in other words, the iron and steel industries and the metal manufacturing industry. Strike actions were regionally concentrated in the industrial areas of North Rhein-Westphalia and Baden-Württemberg.

These branches of industry and regions are also traditional centres of the union movement. Nevertheless, strike activities of recent years have also come to include other industrial sectors, middle-sized and small workshops, as well as new groups within the working class, such as foreigners and women, as well as salaried employees, particularly those in the civil service (Steinhaus, 1975).

In the following section, the characteristic features of this new phase in labour struggles will be described from the point of view of the content of demands and of the forms of conflict.[3]

3 THE CONTENTS OF DEMANDS AND FORMS OF STRUGGLE (1966–74)

ASPECTS OF THE DEVELOPMENT OF WORKING-CLASS DEMANDS

The economic and social conditions of the working class under capitalism are structured by the socio-economic relations of paid labour, and are collectively expressed in the workers' conception of their interests. These interests find their concrete expression in the form and content of workers' demands. As an expression of the workers' basic interests, the demands are mainly concerned with the level of the price of labour, and with working conditions as well as with job security.

Wage Demands

In general, the workers and their unions have emphasised wage demands during this period; this is true for the centrally and regionally established wage demands for contract negotiations carried out by the unions, as well as for the main demands drawn up during spontaneous shop-floor labour activity.

While these demands express the price of labour as a commodity under capitalism, it should also be recognised 'that wage demands can more easily be articulated than other conditions for conflict, and that wage demands, under existing conditions, are more able to allow a rational analysis of the activity' (Pöhler, no date: p. 12).

In addition, one must remember that the establishment, specification and enforcement of wage demands are generally formalised by the system of contract negotiations, conducted by the unions. Until the sixties, the development of contract negotiations had been essentially characterised by a 'contract automatism' whereby wage agreements were agreed without the participation of the union membership. Although this form of negotiation secured a continual increase in employees' actual income, union contract negotiating policy began to change by the end of the sixties. This has been accompanied by changes in the size, form and legitimation of wage demands, which have led to occasional discrepancies between union wage policy and the interests of the union membership. In each situation those demands and interests which were influenced by the particular state of the economy were expressed in a different manner through the formulation and specification of wage demands.

During the 1966–7 recession, union wage policy aimed at the preservation of effective earnings although it was unable effectively to secure non-contractual wage components such as bonuses, premiums and benefits; however, workforces who struck to resist reductions in non-contractual bonuses were aiming at the withdrawal of cuts in—or the preservation of—the effective level of income. The self-imposed limitation on unions' wage demands in 1968 and 1969 – with the goal of not endangering economic recovery – made the lagging of wages behind company earnings apparent during the boom of 1969. This discrepancy formed a point of reference for the wage demands which were formulated on the shop floor in the September strikes of September 1969. These demands laid claim to a share for the worker in economic recovery, and took the form of a critique of the results of union wage policy.

A further discrepancy between union wage policy and the interests of union members was manifested by the spontaneous strike movement of 1973. The increases in income which had been achieved through relatively low wage agreements, and had been declared by the unions to be contributions to economic stability, were overtaken by the rising cost of living. The demands of employees for cost of living bonuses in the form of increases in hourly wages, company bonuses, holiday pay, etc., were aimed at adjusting incomes which had been devalued by inflation. This should make it clear that the standards and criteria for the wage interest of the employees have changed during the course of economic development.

While the wage demands of the September strikes focussed on the above-average increase in profits and were justified by the adjustment of the wage-lag, as research studies and opinion polls among workers having participated in the strikes clearly indicate, rising prices and, therefore, the inflationary devaluation of incomes formed the basis for demands in the strike movement of 1973.

A reduction in the 'money illusion' of the workers is reflected in both these demands and in union wage demands which, since about 1969, have referred to the growing rates of inflation: a fixation about price stability has disappeared in favour of wage demands which include factual and prospective price increases as part of their basic strategy. By contrast, preserving the level of real wages became of the utmost importance for the specification of demands during the 1966–7 recession and the crisis of 1974–5. The demands were usually aimed defensively at preventing direct cuts in wages; the pressure behind the demands was weaker, and the wage interests of the employees were clearly over-shadowed by their interest in job security. For this reason, the low wage demands of the unions did not meet with any essential resistance among their members.

During the course of the disagreements within the unions over wages since 1970, active groups of union-organised workers have taken a greater role than in the past in establishing demands, and have thus brought the unions to include their members – even though on a limited basis – in the contract negotiations. The comparatively greater degree of mobilisation of employees for union wage demands may also be attributed to the increased resistance of companies to wage demands, given the more limited economic leeway for conceding wage improvements over the last few years.

A further central characteristic of wage demands since 1969 is the trend towards unified demands. For the first time, flat-rate wage increases for all employees were demanded in the September strikes of 1969. While across-the-board demands are usually an essential prerequisite for a general mobilisation in workshop conflicts, they are also directed – even if usually implicitly – against the capitalist system of wage payment, which tends to intensify competition among the workers through its extensive differentiation.

Demands for cost of living bonuses are also usually formulated by the strikers in lump sums. The effects of inflation on the cost of living plays an important role in the justification of these demands, which are expressed in the dictum: 'An increase in the price of bread is the same for everybody' ('*Das Brot kostet für alle gleich viel mehr*').

A unifying factor is also contained in those demands which call for the abolition of lower wage groups (usually 'light' wage groups for women). These demands have become the subject of workshop as well as union wage-scale demands. Linear demands, which have been established more frequently since the September strikes, have been incorporated during workshop strikes into the unions' policy of demands in such a way that, increasingly, percentage rises in contractual wages are no longer demanded. Instead, 'mixed demands' have often been formulated – for example, a linear lump-sum plus a percentage demand or a percentage demand with a minimum sum for lower wage groups.

Linear and 'mixed' demands were established above all in those enterprises and sectors of industry that have a high percentage of lower wage groups, such as the textile and clothing industry, as well as in the civil service, because under percentage increase the position of the lower wage groups deteriorates relative to that of the higher groups. However, linear demands have also been established in the chemical and metal industries. In these industries, it was often active union members among the workers who specified the levelling of wage differences for reasons of political solidarity. As a result, these workers came into conflict with the traditional wage policy of the union leaderships.[4]

Demands Regarding Working Conditions

Disputes in the work-place and the factory which concern shop-floor working conditions often take such forms as high rates of fluctuation in the workforce, absenteeism and sabotage; they less frequently reach the level of collective forms of conflict. However, recently demands which were expressly aimed at changing working conditions have been more frequently raised during spontaneous and official union strikes. Nevertheless, a strict division between so-called quantitative and qualitative demands is partially misleading: issues which concern working conditions are also at least indirectly implied in conflicts over wage problems. Besides the wage problems, shop-floor demands relating to the conditions for piecework always concern the burden and pace of work as well. In this manner, the spontaneous strikes in the iron and steel industry in 1969 were essentially brought about by the intensification of work due to overtime, by a heat wave, etc., though these conditions were not mentioned in the demand for a general pay rise in which the workers' expression of their dissatisfaction had been basically formulated. Generally, these events followed a pattern which until recently has dominated the expression of demands: as a rule, West German industrial workers have reacted to the deterioration of working conditions (high level of noise, filth, 'graveyard' shifts and day-work) by demanding financial compensation for the increased burden, while the working conditions themselves rarely become the subject of demands.

By contrast, in the spontaneous strike activities of 1973, it was the unskilled groups of workers, mainly male and female foreign workers, who most frequently put forward demands about the conditions under which they were forced to work, as well as wage demands (Kern, 1974: 25).

Thus, assembly-line workers in the car industry primarily raised demands for paid special holidays to compensate for working extra shifts, for paid rest-breaks, for a decrease in the speed of the assembly line and for the better regulation of relief. More frequently, demands were made—mainly by foreign workers—for the withdrawal of an increase in daily production and for alterations in the piece-work system. These demands directly express the restrictive working situation experienced by lower wage groups, characterised by fragmented, monotonous forms of work which have, in addition, clearly been intensified by increases in the pace and content of the work.

The possible compensations for such working conditions are limited by the living conditions which the foreign workers are expected to accept (housing conditions, health care, etc.); these are, to some extent, included among the objectives of workers' demands—for example, demands for an extension of the annual holiday in order to have enough time to visit their native countries, and demands for decreases in the high rents paid, as formulated in 'rent strikes', particularly in the large cities.

In recent years working conditions have been increasingly determined by the steps taken by capital towards technical rationalisation and rationalisation in the organisation of work, the result of which has been a greater restriction and intensification of work. That this development has created a potential for conflict, is expressed in the union demands which were formulated in connection with action for the enforcement of a new union pay scale agreement in North-Württemberg/North-Baden at the end of 1973. The demands were for rest periods of 6 minutes per hour, minimum wage guarantees for pieceworkers, and the prohibition of pace-rates under 1.5 minutes, as well as for income guarantees and protection against dismissal for older workers.

During the contract disputes in Baden-Württemberg, a change in the logic behind union demands was indicated for first time; the demands were more strongly related to workshop conditions for the employment and utilisation of labour. Even though the demands could not be fully enforced, the conflict itself made it clear that the demands for an alteration of working conditions covered major areas of the workers' own experiences and interests. Not limited to those from the lower social groups within the working class, they also tended to include the experiences and interests of skilled workers whose occupations have been subjugated to the principles of capitalist rationalisation.

In addition, working conditions and the development of demands concerning these conditions are gradually attracting more attention due to a relatively broad discussion which has taken place within the unions under the title of 'the humanisation of the working world' (*Die Humanisierung der Arbeitswelt*).[5] This discussion was held at the beginning of the seventies, but since the further development of the crisis the subject has lost its urgency.

Demands for Job Security

Although the unemployment rate has remained low since the end of the fifties, the threat to job security is still experienced by parts of the working class in the course of cyclical development, especially during general cyclical crises, as in 1966–7 and 1974–5, in sectors of industry experiencing structural crises (as in the mining and textile industries) and during the process of concentration and of rationalisation at corporate and company levels. Demonstrations and demands for political intervention have been made by both workers and unions. There have, however, been few successes in such campaigns, and union strategies have been largely defensive.

Political Demands

Although in the early fifties some working class activities took the form of demands to political bodies and the government, political strikes have seldom taken place since then.

For the first time since the fifties, large-scale political protest actions were taken against the passage of the emergency laws by the Grand Coalition of the CDU and SPD in 1968; however, these actions were essentially conducted by the extra-parliamentary opposition of the student movement. Only a few work-forces participated. Demands that the DGB should call a general strike remained limited to opposition groups within the unions.

At the end of April 1972 the attempt by the CDU/CSU opposition to oust the government of Willy Brandt and Walter Scheel led to widespread mobilisation of the public, with marches and demonstrations and a wave of spontaneous political strikes in the workshops. The strikes were usually organised by Social Democratic works councils and were directed against the possible establishment of a government led by Franz Josef Strauss and Rainer Barzel (CDU/CSU). They also demanded the continuation of the SPD/FDP coalition and the ratification of the East European treaties. Over 100,000 workers, salaried employees and civil servants participated in token strikes. The focal point of the workshop strikes was in North Rhein-Westphalia, where large sections of the work-forces went out on short spontaneous strikes in nearly all factories in the iron and steel industry. Wildcat strikes also took place in the automobile, ship-building and the metal manufacturing industries throughout the country. A series of protest strikes was also held in West Berlin (Schmidt, 1973: 41).

SOME ASPECTS OF THE DEVELOPMENT OF FORMS OF ACTION

The forms of conflict adopted by the working-class movement collectively express the extent of its organisation and consciousness; in its concrete stages, this development can help us to understand movements and trends in the development of labour conflicts, its supporters and its organisational forms.

One obvious aspect of strike activities during the last few years has been the dominance of spontaneous strikes, continuing a general trend in strike development, whereby the percentage of spontaneous strikes in the total volume of strikes has increased since the war. The percentage of spontaneous strikes doubled during the period 1949–68;[6] this trend has continued in the years since 1968, during which there occurred – in 1969 and 1973 – comparatively widespread, lengthy spontaneous strike movements above the workshop level.

Although 'differences between union-organised and wildcat strikes . . . do not [result from] theoretical, organisational or similar pressures, [but] are expressive of existing, political power relations' (Matthöfer, 1971: 174), and reflect the legal regulation of strikes by labour law jurisdiction, a few aspects of the development of labour conflicts in the last years can still be described with the help of this differentiation.

Union Strikes

The increase in union strikes over the enforcement of wage demands, with the aim of improving employees' pay as well as their working conditions, has not altered the dominant union belief that labour conflicts represent 'the last resort'. The strikes themselves are also usually preceded by bargaining rounds, attempts at mediation and union contract votes; in a departure from this policy, IG Chemie introduced a provision into its statutes in 1963, according to which the central executive can call a strike after the failure of arbitration even without taking a strike vote; in the civil service sector, an arbitration agreement was signed only after the strike in 1974.

The organisational form of the strikes followed the union strategy of the 'programmed' strike, the organisational prerequisite of which was control of the strike's progress by the union leadership.

Therefore, the unions' strategy of labour conflict is aimed at avoiding strikes over a large area, favouring the selective strike which remains limited either regionally or to one contract district; alternatively the strike can be based on selected workshops and administrations within a contract district, such as the strikes in sectors of the civil service (the post office and the railways). In the course of these strikes an expansion of the conflict into other workshops and groups of employees often took place.

As a departure from the traditional type of union selective strike the 1971 strike in the chemical industry—the first wage strike in this branch of industry for the last fifty years—was characterised by several original factors. The strike inexperience of the chemical workers and their comparatively low degree of organisation, above all in the heavy chemical industry, allowed the union executive to pursue the concept of an 'active contractless state of affairs'. The call to strike was made without a vote and included a series of different strike forms which took workshop and organisational conditions into account and, thus, created room for manoeuvre for the union's base. In this way, lightning strikes and strikes of different sectors of the workforce, departmental and total strikes, token strikes, rotation strikes, as well as strikes of limited and unlimited length, demonstrations and speeches could be conducted in nearly all districts. Strike activity lasted for four weeks, focussing around the middle-sized chemical workshop in which the disputes became severe at times (blockades of factory entrances, fights with strike breakers, police actions). Nevertheless, the conflict potential which had been mobilised by the strike action could not be developed further, and the strike could not be extended since the inclusion of the large corporations in the strike front was not achieved.

Decisions about the organisation and development of union strikes are essentially concentrated on the central or regional strike leaders, whose composition is determined by the union leaderships alone. This predetermination within their organisation limits the authority of local and workshop strike leaders and also the strikers' potential for influencing the course of the strikes. The strikers themselves participate as pickets, but the pickets make up only a small proportion of the strikers. The low number of strike-breakers usually frees the union strike helpers for organisational duties of striker registration.

Due to the payment of strike support, which is approximately equal to their usual net income, the majority of organised workers can regard strike days as holidays, especially when expressions of solidarity are limited by strike leaders who only rarely hold meetings or demonstrations.

Nevertheless, independent initiatives by strikers, mainly shop stewards, have led to an intensification of conflicts. Thus, within the framework of union strikes, demonstrations and expansions of strike actions occurred which had been organised independently by strikers and were subsequently legitimated by the union. During the metal-workers' strike in the Lower Weser region in the spring of 1974, strikers organised the reinforcement of pickets in front of workshops that were less strongly union-organised (Eisegg, 1974: p. 116); and during the strike in the printing industry in 1973, the compositors and printers in a few workshops that were on strike refused to set or to print commentaries which tried to deny that the workers were supporting the strike: the newspapers appeared with empty columns.

Despite the increase in union-organised strikes in the sixties, helped by the strengthening of union organisation during the strikes, the strikers' claim for total enforcement of their demands has often conflicted with the union negotiators' attitude of compromise. This conflict has been expressed in disputes within the union which have followed many strikes and in the results of the second contract votes, during which bargaining compromises were often rejected by more than half the strikers.

Spontaneous 'Union' Strikes

The restrictions on the legality of strikes, as defined by judgements in the labour courts and by the peace obligation laid down in labour contracts, are accepted by union leaders as a self-imposed obligation, and help to justify the rejection of spontaneous, non-union strikes. The dividing line between unionist and non-unionist spontaneous strikes is, nevertheless, fluid in the case of spontaneous strikes which are conducted during union contract bargaining in support of union demands, and show a relatively high strike participation.

Thus, for example, half a million metal workers went on strike in the course of IG Metall contract activity in 1970, without a union contract strike taking place; in the period before the official strike in 1974, 100 000 blue- and white-collar workers from branches of the civil service and postal and railway workers participated in short token strikes.

These token and protest strikes have been interpreted by the union leaderships as legitimate support for union bargaining conduct (*Der Gewerkschafter*, 1966). For this reason one can correctly speak of the 'ritual of limited token strikes' (Schmidt, 1973: p. 31).

Spontaneous Strikes

The union monopoly on representation and strikes was practically abolished in those strikes – usually at the workshop level – which tried to enforce work-forces' own demands without organisational or legal support from the unions.

These autonomous actions by workers have clearly increased during recent years, and culminated in two broad strike movements in 1969 and 1973. Although these activities were aimed at the improvement of inadequate union contract settlements, spontaneous strike actions are frequently caused by shop-floor conflicts over pay and working conditions, such as cuts in wage components and large increases in the work effort, as well as total or partial factory closures. Even if they are not officially supported by the unions, spontaneous strikes still keep essentially to the pattern and logic of union measures for labour conflict, although they often go beyond the established forms for the settlement of conflicts.

Organisationally, the strike's spontaneity depends, as a rule, on informal, shop-floor networks of communication maintained by groups of workers who are particularly conscious of conditions in the workshop and usually exercise workshop or union representative functions. Above all, shop stewards provide the organisational structure for many wildcat strikes; in addition, the works councils are often the initiators and active supporters of shop-floor actions, despite their legal obligation to maintain industrial peace.

At the same time these union and workshop representatives are usually a type of worker – the German skilled worker – whose position in the production process makes it possible for him to maintain broad contact within the workshop.[7] While this type of worker generally determined the course of the 1969 September strikes and other wildcat workshop strikes, an important new factor appeared in the spontaneous strike activity of 1973: the initiators and active supporters of the spontaneous strikes were—relatively more frequently, and usually for the first time—groups of relatively unskilled workers. Above all, assembly-line workers, foreign workers and women workers struck in 1973, mainly in large and middle-sized workshops in the motor industry and its suppliers (Hildebrandt and Olle, 1975).

White-collar workers have only rarely been involved in the spontaneous strikes of the last few years: they have usually supported general workshop demands by hesitant participation, and seldom enforced their own demands by active measures. In a series of strikes, the salaried employees operated as active strike breakers; and in a few workshop strikes in 1973, they participated in the active suppression of the strike.

The spontaneous strike is essentially characterised by its short duration; as a rule, it lasts less than a day. Nevertheless, during the strike activities of 1969 and 1973 a few strikes continued over a period of almost two weeks.

The short, spontaneous workshop strike usually takes the following form. Particular groups of workers or union cadres within the workshop often initiate the strike, gradually expanding its base by means of marches through the workshops and departments. After the stoppage of work, the strikers then gather on company land. The assembly of strikers is usually attended by the works council and the company management; the conflict is brought out into the open, and the demands which have been formulated are emphatically expressed. The brevity of many spontaneous strikes lends them the character of extraordinary workshop assemblies. The workers often insist upon the immediate fulfilment of their demands, and protract the strike according to the company's reaction; nevertheless, after the return to work, the representation of work-force demands is frequently delegated to the works council, and the demands are pushed through within the channels of workshop negotiation, even though they are often only partially enforced.

By comparison, spontaneous strikes of longer duration are more often characterised by forms of strikers' self-organisation. By their continuous presence in the workshop, by frequent demonstrations on company land, and by regular or permanent strike assemblies, the strikers often manage to keep control over events within the workshop.

In a series of larger, spontaneous workshop strikes, autonomous strike committees were created which had been elected by the strikers and were under their control. In a few strikes, the committees were informally run by workshop or union officials; in other strikes, the election of an autonomous strike committee was expressly directed against the passivity of the works council or against its policy of representation, which was geared to the interests of company management. The strike committee's objective was clearest in those strikes in which foreign workers played a dominant role; in such cases, the establishment of a committee was a direct expression of the fact that foreign workers' interests are not represented by workshop and union bodies whose policy is orientated towards German workers. Generally, the strikes of 1973 in which foreign workers were predominantly involved were characterised by more militant forms of action. In some cases, strikes were conducted by foreign workers alone; the involvement of German workers was achieved in only a few cases. The reluctance of Germans to unite with foreign co-workers led to a shop-floor schism in the workforce and made it easier for the company management to suppress the strikes with the support of reports in the mass media which were hostile to foreigners. Generally, in the course of the development of labour conflict during recent years, forms of open confrontation between industrialists and workers have been intensified. While in 1969 the police were involved in only one of the workshop strikes, the conduct and settlement of spontaneous strikes in 1973 were more frequently characterised by the employment on a massive scale of workshop 'shock troops' recruited from white-collar workers and police employees.[8] In addition, companies employed other repressive measures more frequently – such as immediate dismissals and the reprimand of striking workers.

The strikers tried to create their own publicity, through which to articulate their own experiences and demands, in autonomous organisational forms such as demonstrations and assemblies; but such attempts were relatively impotent against the power of the bourgeois publicity media. This situation was further emphasised by the fact that the publicity achieved by the strikers was carried primarily by the mass media, while the strikers themselves did not develop any forms of communication or co-ordination above the workshop level. Strike organisation in the wildcat workshop strikes of 1973 was primarily determined by the fact that they remained limited to individual workshops. In a few rare cases, contact between striking work-forces in the same local area or region was achieved; there was practically no case in which the strikers made contact between workshops within a branch of a corporation. For this reason, the 1973 strike activity in the iron, steel, and metal-manufacturing industries was characterised by a high degree of fragmentation.

During the spontaneous workshop strikes, hardly any demands and forms of action were developed which threatened the prerogative of the capitalists over the production process. The strikers frequently blocked or occupied company administration buildings by sit-down strikes, but the production installations were less frequently affected. So far it would be hard to deduce from the workers' presence in the workshops during the strikes that 'nearly every single strike took on the form of a practical occupation of the workshop'.[9]

By contrast, the 150 employees of a cement factory in Westphalia occupied their workshop in the spring of 1975 to support their struggle against mass dismissals. This was the first time that a more lengthy occupation had taken place in West Germany. The workers' struggle to preserve their jobs was also widely publicised. The occupation of the workshop ended after eight weeks; the struggle was at first continued in the form of a strike and then shifted to the level of labour court decisions (Duhm, 1975: p. 18).

Similar to other spontaneous forms of workers' resistance, this strike was supported by the union at the local level, at least unofficially; however, this subjected the workers to attempts by the union to channel their actions into traditional forms for the settlement of conflicts. This exemplifies a general characteristic of union leaderships' attitudes towards spontaneous strike actions which have neither been initiated nor controlled by them. As a rule, the leaderships try to end spontaneous strike actions and solve the basic conflict through negotiations, and thus re-instate their claim to worker representation.

4 THE STRESSES ON THE INDUSTRIAL RELATIONS SYSTEM AND ITS CHANGES

THE SEARCH FOR A NEW CLASS COMPROMISE

The latest phase of socio-economic development has been characterised by various efforts by the state and organised social groups to renew, through new forms of class co-operation, the post-war class compromise which has become much weaker since the 1966–7 recession. The material basis of the socially peaceful post-war development was a long period of prosperity accompanied by a fairly wide scope for concessions (high growth-rates and a high level of employment). This brought material successes for union policies, and since the mid-fifties these had, as a rule, been achieved in a socially peaceful manner. As current experience has shown, the diminution of the socio-economic conditions for success cannot be compensated for simply by new institutional arrangements.

Since the mid-sixties, the unions have come under double pressure—from the state and from the membership—and these pressures have threatened to jeopardise the co-operative wage policy. Pressure from the state had been expanded in such a way that it was expected of and demanded from the unions that they should respect the altered conditions for growth in the West German economy and should consciously attune their wage policy to the demands of an economy that was growing ever more susceptible to crises. This pressure has found its main institutional expression in the establishment of institutions for the execution of an incomes policy. Pressure from union members has increased with the tendency towards active representation of interests at the same rate at which the unions have acquiesced in the instrumentalisation of their wage policy for purposes of state economic policy. Accustomed to full employment and rises in real wages during the years of prosperity, the workers have acknowledged the unions' *Realpolitik* with obvious dissatisfaction at the bargaining results and outspoken criticism within the union of its conduct.

In the general political debate as well as in academic discussion, increased attention has been directed at the role and purpose of the unions. Their importance for social peace in West Germany had not been fully recognised until the present period of change—in other words, until this role seemed to be threatened. During the Erhard era, the unions were still an object of frequent public defamation. The unions' co-operation has since become increasingly important for the state's crisis management, because it can only effectively practise its 'new economic policy' (macro-economic regulation in the interest of an undisturbed capital accumulation and a high level of employment) with the voluntary co-operation of the relevant social groups and organisations. Nevertheless, such co-operation has proved to be uncertain, since it has led to a gap between the union leadership and active membership. This became evident for the first time during the wave of spontaneous strikes in the autumn of 1969.

At the workshop level the state has also been forced to accommodate itself to changed socio-economic conditions. In the amended Betr. VG (Works Council Law) not only were partial concessions made to the workers, who had become increasingly aware of their interests, but the institution that was designed to secure peace in the shop was refined. But not even these measures could prevent a new outbreak of dissatisfaction with working conditions during the wave of strikes in 1973.

The measures and concessions described above have not as yet managed to create a new compromise for social peace which could be described as stable. It seems that laws and new institutions hardly compensate for reduced material rewards for pacification. Only since unemployment reached a high level has crisis management apparently found an adequate disciplinary tool against workers' demands. Nevertheless, it is uncertain how long West

German workers, who have been accustomed to full employment, will allow themselves to be restrained by the development of the crisis.

THE BASIC CHARACTERISTICS OF THE INDUSTRIAL RELATIONS SYSTEM

Before going into the latest changes in the system of industrial relations and union policy, the most important characteristics of the system will be described, in order to ensure a better understanding of the question. The following section will be limited to a description of the form that the system acquired in the mid-sixties. Important changes that occurred following this period—the introduction of a state incomes policy and the amendment of the Betr. VG will be discussed in the succeeding sections.

Legal Standardisation and the Dual System of Interest Representation

Unlike in the Anglo-Saxon countries, industrial relations in the Federal Republic of Germany are subject to a high degree of legal regulation. In this manner, the issues of industrial conflict are restricted and the forms for their settlement legally defined. This applies to relations between the bargaining parties as well as to those between the management and employee representatives on the works council.

In this manner, the legal structural conditions and principles for negotiations, arbitration and labour conflicts between the bargaining parties have been laid down. They were partially laid down in the Union Contract Law (Tarifvertragsgesetz 1949), but for the most part are the result of labour law jurisdiction (Arbeitsrechtsprechung), and are thus legal creations of the courts. These creations are concerned primarily with strike law, which has developed strict criteria for the legality of strikes. According to these, labour conflicts can only be led by parties legally qualified to bargain (unions or employers' associations) and may be initiated only after the end of the 'peace obligation' (the exhaustion of all bargaining possibilities and arbitration procedures), and can only be carried out according to the principles of 'fair play' and over contractually regulated issues. According to these provisions, the following are illegal: strikes not organised by the union, strikes with political aims, sympathy or solidarity strikes.

The representation of workers' interests by the unions has been further limited by two important decisions of the Federal Labour Court (Bundesarbeitsgericht) in the area of wage contract law:

(a) Wage contracts that differentiate between union-organised and non-organised employees are invalid (prohibition of clauses regulating contract exclusions). This means that every improvement enforced by the unions in accordance with their wage policies is also automatically valid for non-members. Although the employers had previously considered that contract settlements established minimum wage standards for all employees,[10] the legally binding decision against contractual privileges for union members has now given legal recognition to this. The unions have also lost an important argument for the recruitment of new members.

(b) Contractual agreements with provisions for adding negotiated pay rises to the wages that the companies actually pay (effective wages), are illegal (prohibition of clauses regulating effective wages). This means that pay rises stipulated by contract agreements can (in part or in full) be ascribed to wage components not covered by union contract. This decision has given management a free hand in establishing an autonomous wage policy on the workshop level.

The legal establishment of the works council as an autonomous body of employee representation – formally independent of the unions – in the Betr. VG (1952; amended in 1972) has resulted in a further serious limitation of the unions' potential scope of activity. The regulation of workshop conflicts falls essentially under the competence of the works council, so that union activity remains limited to the area of wage and contract negotiations above the workshop level. For the representation of workshop interests, the unions can at the most act as consultants to the works councils. This lays the foundation for the specific dual character of the representation of interests within the system of industrial relations.

The Organisation of the Official Bargaining Parties

THE UNIONS

The reconstruction of the German unions after 1945 was based on two principles: that of a unitary organisation and that of industrial unionism. The common resistance of Christian, Social Democratic and Communist trade unionists against the Nazi regime had laid the foundation for the establishment of a unitary union independent of political and religious affiliations to replace the previously dominant form of affiliated trade unions (*Richtungsgewerkschaften*). The founding congress of the German Trade Union Federation (DGB) took place in Munich in October 1949. Over one hundred trade unions were represented at the congress, and these were consolidated into sixteen new industrial unions as constituents of the new union federation. Occupation and social status were no longer accepted as criteria for membership in a union. All occupations and groups of employees (blue- and white-collar workers as well as civil servants) were organised in the same union according to the dictum 'one workshop – one union'.

At the end of 1974, the DGB consisted of sixteen unions with a membership of about 7.5 million employees; this amounts to over 80 per cent of all union-organised employees in the Federal Republic of Germany. The German Federation of Civil Servants (DBB) with 720,000 members (1974), and the German Salaried Employees Union (DAG) with 470,000 members (1974), do not belong to the DGB. In addition, a few other smaller unions for civil servants and salaried employees still exist, but they exert as little influence on the collective bargaining process as the Christian Federation of Trade

Unions. Discussions about a possible merger have been carried on by the DAG and the DBB for some time, as the two unions generally agree with one another on their economic and socio-political objectives.

The sixteen DGB unions differ quite a bit in size; the absolute numbers of members range from 36,000 to 2.6 million. Although the absolute membership of DGB unions has tended to rise slightly, the degree of union organisation (the ratio of union members to the total number of employees) tended to decline continuously up to 1970. But since then it has been increased by the greater organisation of foreign workers, women workers, and salaried employees.

The DGB fulfils its functions as representative of the common interests of its sixteen constituent unions particularly in relationship to the political system. It represents union interests in numerous official bodies and institutions and is their representative to the councils of the European Community. In accordance with its function as a centre for co-ordination and arbitration between the member organisations, it exercises little authority over their decisions. For example, it only has the power to establish guidelines for wage policy; individual unions remain completely autonomous in this important sphere of their activity.

The concept of the unions' formal organisational structure as a democratic system of delegation according to the principles of 'democratic centralism' is distorted in daily practice by strong tendencies towards bureaucratic administration and centralised leadership. This is particularly evident in the manner in which wage policy is carried out. According to the union statutes, the formal right to make binding decisions regarding wage policies at every level of organisation rests with the executive committees. The negotiating committees which are responsible for the execution of wage policy on the district level possess only the right to present 'position papers' and 'recommendations' to the executives. Wage policy is carried out in co-operation between the executives and the district leaderships. During the post-war years the centralised establishment and co-ordination of wage policy have generally been enforced. This form of execution of wage policy leaves the members and officials in the lower echelons little chance of influencing the size and form of union demands. The authority of the executive committees is limited only in regard to strike decisions, when the membership must be called out to vote on a strike referendum; however, whether a vote to strike is held or not is also decided solely by the executive committees.

Besides their authority over decisions on wage policy, the executive committees possess other effective means for enforcing their views: they control the available share of membership funds as well as the large financial reserves of the organisation.

According to a conservative estimate made by Hirsche, who worked for the DGB for many years, the income from the membership funds of the sixteen unions in the DGB amounted to over 500 million DM in 1970. In the same year, the total nominal assets of the DGB amounted to around 1.5 milliard DM (Hirsche, 1972: p. 141, 375).

These assets make it possible for the executives to establish a centralised board of experts who present arguments in support of the policies of the executive committee to the lower echelons of the union. In addition, the executive committees direct the training and recruitment of cadres of officials by means of their control over the central training institutions of the union. Besides this, by controlling the official newspaper of the federation, whose editors are selected by the executives and whose political stance is defined by them, the executive committees possess the most effective means of influencing opinion within the mass organisation. Finally, the most important activities of the local branches are carried out in accordance with guidelines and orders that the executive and advisory committees formulate and adopt—in particular, guidelines for local educational activity, the nomination of candidates for works council elections and the activity of the shop-stewards.

Although the congresses form the highest governing body within the union hierarchies, experience has shown that they do not effectively counterbalance the authority of the executive committees. Their ability to check the powers of the executive committees is limited, and their directives for future policy usually remain within the framework of previously practised policies. This has resulted in a tendency to ratify present policy and re-elect the executive committees during congresses, even when strong criticism had been expressed during the preceding discussions.

THE EMPLOYERS' ASSOCIATIONS

For a few years after the war, the occupying forces attempted to obstruct any alliances between German industrialists; however, once this resistance let up, the employers in the Federal Republic of Germany allied themselves in two central organisations: the Federal Association of German Industry (BDI) and the Federal Union of German Employers' Associations (BDA). While the BDI mainly represents the common economic interests of the industrialists, especially before the executive and legislative branches of the Federal and Länder governments, the BDA attends to the employers' interests concerning social and wage policies.

According to the latest estimates, approximately 80 per cent of all private enterprises are organized in the BDA through their industrial associations; these companies employ about 90 per cent of all employees in private industry.[11] Thus, West German industrialists are organised to a much greater extent than their employees. The coalition of employers is a federation of actual and potential competitors who have formed a cartel against their common adversary, the unions, and a pressure group on Parliament and the state bureaucracy.

One analysis of the decision-making process in the employers' associations during central bargaining in the metal industry (Noé, 1970: p. 198) concludes that, during central negotiations, the decisions on bargaining concepts, strategies and settlements are made by fifty people occupying positions of leadership in both 'Gesamtmetall' and big industry. As representatives of the employers, these fifty people make decisions concerning contract agreements that will affect over 4 million employees.

The System of Collective Bargaining

The wage policies of the unions and the employers' associations are put into practice within a large and barely surveyable system of contracts. Between 7000 and 8000 wage contracts, affecting about 20 million employees, are registered each year in the contract register kept by the Federal Minister of Labour (*Die Quelle*, 1974: p. 258).

There are three forms of union contracts for the regulation of wages and working conditions:

(*a*) *Wage- and salary-rate contracts* are negotiated during periodical bargaining rounds and are usually valid for twelve months. They establish the nominal gross income for the various wage groups, and are usually valid either for an entire sector of industry or for the regional union districts of one industrial sector.
(*b*) *Wage-hierarchy contracts* regulate the characteristic activity of the various wage groups, and the basic principle for their classification and pay as well as the general principles for time- and piecework.
(*c*) *General contracts* regulate general working conditions (working-hours, bonuses for overtime and the length of holidays).

In addition, there are many separate agreements on specific issues (protection against rationalisation, methods of arbitration). The wage-hierarchy and general contracts cover an entire sector of industry and are usually valid for several years.

Among the special agreements, the arbitration arrangements are of great importance. Through these agreements, arbitration has become an integral part of the bargaining system. In comparison with the Weimar Republic, in which mandatory arbitration was enforced by the state, the arbitration process in the BRD is based on voluntary arrangements between the bargaining partners. Although it often happens that the governments of the *Länder* or the Federal Government try to mediate between the parties during impending or current conflicts, these interventions are carried out *ad hoc* without any formal obligation on the part of the bargaining partners. On the other hand, the establishment of voluntary arrangements has been based in part upon repeated threats by the state that it would if necessary create its own arbitration powers.

The arbitration process to which the bargaining partners have agreed typically calls for a 'neutral' or 'impartial' chairman, who generally has a vote. In prevailing practice, the chairmen are usually civil servants who are also qualified lawyers (Keller, 1975: p. 126). Other arbitration arrangements call for a two-phased negotiating process carried out solely by the bargaining partners. This shifts the level of bargaining up to the national level and is supposed to make possible an agreement between the central organisations. All arbitrations enforce the extension of the 'peace obligation'; the arrangements often provide for the automatic start of arbitration following unsuccessful negotiations. Before they can take effect, the arbitrated settlements must be approved by both bargaining parties.

The Representation of Employees' Interests in the Workshop

The representation of the workforce's interests at workshop level is formally independent of the unions. The basic components of shop-floor representation are the works councils and co-determination.[12] In many branches of industry there is an additional form of representation—the shop stewards of the unions.

THE WORKS COUNCILS

In workshops with five or more employees, the election of a works council is stipulated by law, although there are still many small and medium-sized workshops without works councils. In 1975, about 200,000 works council members were elected in 30,000 workshops (*Die Quelle*, 1975: p. 441). The works council is elected by the entire workforce. Its size increases in proportion to the number of employees in the workshop. For example, in workshops with 100 employees there are 5 works council members, in workshops with 500 employees 9 members and in those with over 1000 employees 15 members. A maximum size has been deleted in the amended Betr. VG. In workshops with over 9000 employees, 2 additional works council members are elected for every 3000 employees in addition to the prescribed 31 members. Some of the works council members receive work-leave and can, therefore, perform their duties within the works councils on a fulltime basis.

The works council possesses co-determination and co-operation rights for the regulation of social, economic and personnel matters. The specific rights allotted to it in the amended Betr. VG will be discussed in a later section of this paper (page 288). Its general duties include the enforcement and observance of laws protecting the workers' rights and interests, and of ordinances, safety regulations, union contracts and workshop agreements. The works councils are also supposed to present the complaints, suggestions and demands of the workers to company management.

Characteristically, the works council has no effective bargaining power within the system of workshop negotiations. During talks with management, the works council is bound to the 'peace obligation'. Even if an agreement cannot be reached, it still cannot initiate strike actions; it can at most call upon the labour court.

Nevertheless, the works council's importance as a representative of shop-floor interests should not be underestimated. Especially in large workshops where economic leeway allows for an autonomous workshop wage policy, the works council exerts substantial influence on the size and distribution of wage components not stipulated in union contracts. Its influence stems from its role as the bargaining opponent of management – based upon its legally established right of co-determination. Workshop wage policy allows the works council to establish its own basis of loyalty within the work-force, parallel to and outside of the unions. The works council must maintain this local loyalty, since re-election is dependent upon it. That this succeeds, is evidenced by the frequent re-elections which are especially common in the larger workshops.

While their legal status and their basis of loyalty independent of the unions lend the works councils a relative autonomy in relationship to the union, the great majority of works councils actually consist of loyal union members. These people know that their position as representatives of shop-floor interests is dependent on the support of the unions as a source of training and upon the expert knowledge of union officials as well as upon the activity of union members on the shop-floor. More than three quarters of the works councils are elected from lists of official union candidates compiled by the union shop stewards in the workshop in co-operation with the executives of the unions' local branches. The percentage of works council members organised in the DGB is about 80 per cent.[13]

The works councils play a dominant role within the union organisations. Due to their legal status and their privilege of negotiating directly with management, they determine the importance and influence of the union within the workshop as well as the scope of union activity in such areas as the activity of the shop stewards, the admission of union officials to the workshop, the recruitment of union members, the distribution of the union newspaper, etc. The works councils can organise and sustain the recruitment of union members and the collection of union dues more effectively than any other group within the union, including shop stewards and union officials. For ensuring the essential elements of the maintenance of the organisation, the works councils are indispensable. These duties are absolutely necessary for union organisation, with the result that works councils develop an enormous influence on the local level that is carried over (through the system of general elections) by the system of delegation into the higher echelons of union hierarchy. Consequently, their members constitute at least a relative, often an absolute majority, not only in the local branches, but also in the negotiating committees and in the regional executive committees, as well as very often at union congresses.

THE SHOP STEWARDS

Unlike the works councils, the shop stewards form a body of representation within the workshop that falls totally under the jurisdiction of the unions. This is reflected by the fact that they are elected exclusively by union members. A few are appointed by local union executives. Individual stewards are elected by a department, section of a workshop or a work-group, and represent as the case may be between thirty and fifty colleagues from their work-places.

During the last elections, over 120,000 shop stewards were elected in close on 6000 workshops organized within IG Metall;[14] in 850 workshops organised by IG Chemie, more than 40,000 shop stewards were elected.[15] The agreements recently adopted into contract settlements by a few unions (IG Metall, Gewerkschaft Textil-Bekleidung and the Deutsche Postgewerkschaft) for the protection of shop stewards, indicate the growing importance of these union functionaries. According to these settlements, the shop stewards may not be penalised by company management for their activities within the workshop. IG Metall is trying to enforce an improved union contract that would provide for paid leaves from work for a limited number of hours along with other improvements.

The functions of stewards are limited. As a rule they are stipulated in guidelines established by the national executive of the union. Only IG Chemie grants statutory rights to its shop stewards. Their duties include above all odd jobs for union organising activities: information about and explanation of union decisions and contract negotiations to the members, recruitment of new members and the distribution of union information materials. In addition, they are expected to support the activity of the works councils; in many workshops this has led to the domination and regimentation of the works council by the shop stewards. At the time of their establishment in the fifties and early sixties, the stewards had been expected, especially by the unions' left-wing, to keep control of the works councils and to work against their tendencies towards alienation from the union and its members. Instead of fulfilling these expectations, the shop stewards have basically become an extended arm of the works councils. A poll conducted by IG Metall of the chairmen of the shop steward groups in 2,300 metal workshops has shown that steward elections are usually organised and led by the works councils and that stewards' scope for activity on the shop-floor is also determined essentially by the councils since they supply them with the necessary information about the workshop and technical resources and also procure leaves from work for them so that they can attend union training sessions.[16]

In the area of wage policy, the duties of the shop stewards are restrictively defined. On the one hand, they are expected to discuss union demands and the form of future contracts with union members and to support the local union executives during bargaining rounds. On the other hand, their chances of influencing the decision-making process in matters of wage policy are very limited. They limit themselves to discussions, gathering information and making suggestions.

Nevertheless, during the last few years, it has become apparent that, in many large workshops in the metal and chemical industries—following the growing militancy of the workers – the shop stewards have begun to outgrow their subordinate position and become more autonomous of union bureaucracy and the works councils (see page 292).

Sectoral and Workshop Wage Policy

The wage structure in the BRD is characterised by the particularly large difference between union-negotiated and effective wages (wage gap). Since the mid-fifties at the latest, the rise of effective wages has regularly exceeded the increase in union wage-rates. In 1970 the hourly wages paid within the workshops exceeded those stipulated by union contract in the metal industry by 24 per cent, and by 20 per cent in the chemical industry.[17] This discrepancy between union contract and effective wages is based on the dual system of wage policy.

The broad and economically heterogeneous bargaining areas lead necessarily to pay-rate agreements that are geared to the average level of profits and not to the profitability of the more productivie, big enterprises. Leeway for company pay rises that were not exhausted in the union contracts, creates the basis for an independent workshop wage policy. Generally, company bargaining follows official union bargaining. During workshop negotiations, management and the works council negotiate additional wage increases by adapting union pay rises to the specific conditions and wage hierarchies of the workshop or by transposing the union contract agreements into specialised workshop wage systems. Unlike the sectoral wage negotiations between the national bargaining partners, which are settled during each bargaining round within a limited period of time, the process of adaptation in the workshop is kept going continuously by the many initiatives on wage policy undertaken by individual groups of workers (wage-wage spiral) and by the reaction of management to changes on the labour market and the state of the economy. So far as the results of negotiations are not unilateral decisions made by management, they are usually set down in workshop agreements.

Until the mid-sixties, this dual system of wage policy managed to meet both the demands of the economic system and the interests of union members with relatively few problems. For the stability and growth of the West German economy, this form of institutionalised wage conflict brought nearly optimal results. While standard wages were established by the sectoral wage policy in proportion to the average rate of increase of productivity (including the rate of price increase), the workshop wage policy reacted flexibly—as the movements of wage drift indicated—to short-term changes in the labour market in the course of cyclical trends. And high growth-rates allowed enough room for acceptable contract agreements during autonomous collective bargaining that resulted increasingly rarely in strikes.

Upon this material base, the unions' wage policy and, later, their programme took on an increasingly conformist character. Since the mid-fifties, the unions' tendency to gear their wage policy to economic guidelines has been enforced, and as a result of the centralised union policy, decisions of the union executive committees on wage policy made according to these guidelines could be enforced upon the lower echelons with relatively few conflicts within the organisation.

Thus, the social peace of the late fifties and early sixties was based on the substantial leeway for wage concessions which was made possible by a prosperous economy and the institutions and mechanisms of the dual system of industrial relations. Under these economic conditions, this system possessed a relatively high degree of flexibility and the ability to absorb industrial conflict, and not until the recession of 1966–7 did the West German system of industrial relations prove to be in need of amendment.

STATE INCOMES POLICY

Incomes policy was not introduced into the Federal Republic of Germany as a new instrument of economic policy – as it was in other Western countries – for reasons of continuously high inflation rates or chronic balance-of-payment deficits. Instead, it was a result of the recession of 1966–7, which led to a general re-orientation in economic policy. Its immediate goal was the commitment of the unions to a temporary restraint on wages in order to induce a new boom by means of developing over-proportional profits. The general intention was to adapt future union wage policy to the specific conditions of the business cycle—in fact, to make use of the unions as a component of planning and an instrument for securing growth and stability. The instruments of incomes policy, which are supposed to ensure that union policy conforms with the system, consist of 'concerted action' and 'guidelines for wages' (*Orientierungsdaten*). The co-operation between the state, unions and employers' associations that has been termed 'concerted action', resulted from initiatives on the part of the Council of Experts. The 'concerted stabilisation action' proposed in their second annual report (1965) envisaged a 'co-ordinated adjustment of conduct' towards the gradual containment of inflation. Unions and employers' associations announced that they were prepared to co-operate, but the scheme failed when the ruling CDU Government refused to allow its economic policy aims to be quantified. Only after the reorganisation of the Government (the Grand Coalition of the CDU and the SPD) was the proposal for 'Concerted Action' accepted into the formulation of the final version of the 'Law for Promoting the Stability and Growth of the Economy' that was drawn up by the Keynesian Social Democratic Minister of the Economy, Karl Schiller.

In Paragraph 3 of this law, it is intended that 'in the case of a threat' to the goals of economic policy (price-level stability, high employment rates, balance of payments surplus together with a constant and adequate growth rate) the Federal Government could make 'guidelines available for the simultaneously co-ordinated conduct (Concerted Action) of the regional bodies, unions and employers' associations'. While these guidelines, according to the text of the law, include 'a description of the macro-economic interdependencies', they still serve basically to indicate the possible growth of wage earnings in line with the specific conditions of economic development. With the establishment of a state incomes policy, the previous form of institutionalised wage conflict has been expanded by two important elements: firstly, the state now participates in the process of wage-establishment as an independent, continually intervening 'third party'; secondly, its participation aims at influencing the quantitative results of distribution solely in the interest of the general regulation of the national economy and not as a distributive goal for its own sake. With the introduction of this policy, wage negotiations which had been carried out between two parties were explicitly related to the conditions for overall economic development. In addition, state intervention brought new areas of activity into consideration – namely legal means of sanction – which impede the implementation of traditional means of social pressure, particularly by the unions. Although, according to both the text of the law and prevailing practice, 'concerted action' remains a means of information and consultation through which no binding decisions are made, the publicly influential guidelines for wage increases form a potential limitation on free collective bargaining. The guidelines have an unfavourable influence during collective bargaining itself, since they magnify the importance of macro-economic arguments. The actual aim for which 'concerted action' was created has already made the unions' structural handicap obvious. It consisted of securing the programme of economic expansion – which had been established during the low-water mark of the recession – within union wage policy. The earnings expectations of private employers, which had been improved by two investment budgets totalling 11 milliard DM and other state financial measures, were to be respected by the unions and not be undermined by any wage demands. To compensate for wage restraint, the possibility of a planned future adjustment of wage lag was promised.

The union leadership agreed to this programme for several reasons. Firstly, they were interested in rapidly overcoming the recession; secondly, they could expect greater consideration for their interests with the SPD's participation in the new Government; thirdly, there was the promise that their concessions on wage policy would be adjusted during the expected boom ('social symmetry'); fourthly, they were dealing for the first time with a Federal Minister of the Economy who recognised the justification and necessity of limited pay rises; and fifthly, they had demanded elements of this 'new economic policy' in their own Düsseldorf Programme (1963).

That the unions adhered to the Minister's guidelines during the first two years is shown in the following table:

TABLE 7.1

Year	Guidelines in percentage terms	Union wage increases in percentage terms
1967	3.5	3.3
1968	4.0–5.0	4.2
1969	5.5–6.5	6.0– 7.1 (Jan.–Aug.)
		8.5–12.5 (Sept.–Dec.)

Source: H. -D. Hardes, 1974: p. 94

The deviation of union wage increases from the guidelines in the second half of 1969 (and also in the succeeding years) originated in the wave of unofficial strikes in September 1969. These strikes freed the unions from the fetters of the incomes policy. After restraint in union wage policy had brought about a rapid economic upswing, the unions—having continued to bargain cautiously—were still incapable of action due to the long duration of their contracts, even though the grounds for restraint had long disappeared. The increasingly obvious discrepancy between the development of wages and earnings during the entire period of the boom and the increasing demands for work efficiency (without adequate compensation) created a potential for dissatisfaction which exploded at the height of the boom when the promise of 'social symmetry' remained unfulfilled, while the unions were still bound by the 'peace obligation'.

Following this strike activity, which was totally unusual for the Federal Republic, the unions and the employers' associations quickly agreed to early contract negotiations, in which much larger settlements were reached than in the collective bargaining of the first half of the year. The sudden revision of the unions' restrained wage policy due to their dissatisfaction on the part of their members was a decisive turning point for the state incomes policy. Since this revision, 'concerted action' and the guidelines have had only limited influence on actual wage policy (see page 291).

Nevertheless, this does not mean that the state institutions of economic policy have abandoned their attempts to exert a mitigating influence upon union wage demands. In a sense, they have returned to the earlier policy of 'moral suasion'. Although the participants in 'concerted action' continued to be invited every few months by the Minister of the Economy to discuss the economic situation (a total of thirty-five meetings had taken place by August 1975), the effect of these on the conduct of the bargaining partners must in fact be considered limited. For these reasons, suggestions of statutory incomes policy have become more frequent within public and academic discussion, and such policy could lead to the *de facto* abolition of free contract bargaining. These technocratic concepts generally overlook the fact that unions are members' associations and that, as a result, union leaderships cannot direct their membership's interests on wage policy by force nor by manipulating them according to the needs of anti-cyclical policy without evoking major internal crises. These suggestions will probably become as entangled in their own contradictions as the previously practised policy.

One decisive cause of the failure of the incomes policy can be found in the concept of the policy itself. The 'concerted action' has restricted itself to general and functional aims, while those of the unions concerning the distribution of incomes and wealth have been totally ignored. In the end, this has led the unions' wage policy to perform the part of a stop gap, given the increasing inability of economic policy to control and regulate the economy. It is evident that distribution based on social justice cannot form an integral part of the incomes policy of the BRD—or of any other capitalist country. This certainly does not mean that an incomes policy does not need to take into consideration ideas of equity. Every incomes policy that demands at least a temporary wage restraint is dependent upon mass loyalty; union restraint is necessary if incomes policy is to succeed, and the unions must legitimate this in the eyes of their membership. The formula of 'social symmetry' had this central function of legitimation. Because of its broad capacity for interpretation, it was particularly suited for the unwritten compromise. While the employers' associations understood the formula as nothing more than the simultaneous realisation of the four general aims of economic policy, the Minister of the Economy used it to create the belief that the one-sided effects on distribution would be adjusted after the crisis. At the same time, the unions' ideas implied a change in the *status quo* of distribution that went further than an adjustment. The formula of 'social symmetry' created expectations on the part of the unions and the workers, and helped to legitimate claims that transcended what was feasible and possible within the narrow margins of economic policy. Some union members saw the instrumentalisation of union wage policy for the regulation of the economy under these conditions as representing the alienation of the unions from their members and from the membership's wage interests. This situation was tolerated only as long as the aim of full employment had first priority.

THE AMENDMENT OF THE WORKS COUNCIL LAW

The relations within the company between management and the work-force were comprehensively regulated in the Works Council Law (Betriebsverfassungsgesetz). The Betr. VG was passed in 1952 against the votes of the SPD and against the resistance of the DGB. Its prototype was the Works Council Law of 1920, which legally set down the dual character of industrial relations as well as the foundation for peaceful co-operation between employers and works councils. AT the end of 1971, the Betr. VG 1952 was amended by the SPD/FDP coalition without encroaching upon the general concept of the existing law. In comparison with the earlier law, the participatory rights of the works council (information, consultation and co-determination rights) were broadened, though the 'partnership' obligation was not diminished.

The amendment of the Betr. VG took account of the changed conditions for the representation of shop-floor interests. Thus, with the development of larger industrial units resulting from concentration, the previous limitation of the number of works council members to a maximum of thirty-five had proved to obstruct the effective representation of interest in the gigantic corporations. In the new Betr. VG this maximum size has been deleted. Similarly, the establishment of both central councils and councils on the corporate level in enterprises with several workshops or subsidiaries has been made mandatory. In this manner, the centralisation of corporate decisions has been faced with the concentration of the representation of employees' interests at the same organisational level.

West German legislators also reacted to the growing proportion of foreign workers by deleting the restrictive regulations concerning the eligibility of foreign workers for membership of works councils. In the first election after the amendment of the Betr. VG this change led to an increase in the proportion of foreign works council members. In the workshops organised by IG Metall, the proportion of foreign members rose from 0.3 per cent (1968) to 2.2 per cent (1972), although this is far from representing a proportionate share of works council mandates. In the latest works council election (1975) this figure rose only marginally. In the workshops organised by IG Metall the proportion of foreign workers in the councils rose to merely 2.9 per cent, whereas their share of the work-force amounts to about 16 per cent.

Finally, a series of amendments to the Betr. VG were undertaken in view of the continual increase in the duties of the works councils. This is especially true of agreements concerning payment for work proficiency. The old law had attempted to limit the function of the works council in respect to wage policy to the formal side of the establishment of workshop wages – a limitation that, in reality, was scarely observed. The new Betr. VG stipulates that the works councils must agree to the establishment of piecework and bonus rates, including their wage factors. The increasing demands made on the works councils are echoed by their members asking for leave from work in order to participate in training and educational sessions, which increase their knowledge of the problems with which the councils are confronted. Every member of a council is now entitled to a three-week paid sabbatical during his period of office.

According to the Betr. VG, the works council possesses co-determination and co-operation rights in the regulation of social and personnel affairs. Its most important rights concern:

(a) The establishment of payment principles, especially the implementation of new pay methods, as well as the establishment of work compensations based on productivity (piecework and bonus rates).
(b) The regulation of valid working hours and holiday arrangements, as well as the organization of overtime and short-time work.
(c) The formulation of personnel questionnaires, principles of work evaluation and guidelines for recruitment.
(d) The hiring, classification, transfer and lay-off of employees.

The works councils are entitled to be informed and consulted about the arrangement of the work-place, the process of work and the work-place environment; the right of co-determination only takes effect if an alteration in the work-place results in an increased work-load for the workers. As to economic decisions, the works council possesses only information rights; management's freedom of decision is not limited. In the case of a cut-back in production or a company closure, the works council can only demand regulations to ensure the compensation of redundant employees to a limited extent (the firm's social plan). The most important rights, since they concern the workforce's material interests, are the co-determination rights in the regulation of wage incentive systems and workshop benefits not covered by union contract. As a rule, they are the subject of workshop agreements that – like union contracts – possess immediate and compulsory validity; however, they can be unilaterally terminated.

The other side to the expansion of participatory rights was a large number of provisions which impede the decisive representation of workers' interests by the works council. The works council's co-determination rights, which are certainly numerous and not ineffective, are subject to the general clause concerning 'responsible co-operation' with company managment 'for the welfare of the employee and of the company' (Paragraph 2). This means that the works council is fundamentally bound to the 'peace obligation'; it is explicitly stiuplated in the Betr. VG that the works council may in no event call for 'measures of labour conflict' (Paragraph 74, 2)—i.e. strikes or protest actions.

Closely connected with the 'peace obligation' is the institution of the 'settlement board', which is comparable to obligatory workshop arbitration. While on the one hand the law considers the possibility of workshop conflicts and, on the other, binds the employee representation to the 'peaceful' arbitration of the conflict, it still has to establish a regulation should peaceful settlement fail. The solution has been found in the 'settlement board', whose judgment can supersede an agreement between the two bargaining parties. Equal numbers of representatives from both parties belong to this board and it has a neutral chairman to whose appointment both parties must agree; otherwise he is installed by the labour court. A further characteristic of the attempt to contain workshop conflicts is the absolute prohibition on political activity (the distribution of leaflets, political agitation).

That the works councils inadequately fulfil their legally stipulated purpose as a form of workforce representation was expressed by the wildcat strikes of Autumn 1969, and still more clearly during the many unofficial work-place strikes in 1973. It became more difficult for the works councils to pay adequate attention to workers' interests for two reasons. Firstly, the councils (especially in large workshops) tend towards bureaucratisation and professionalisation; in other words, they tend to become alienated from the interests of the work-force. However, this occurs not only because the activity of a works councillor is full-time—involving long terms of office, the necessary specialisation in particular problems (wage incentive systems, job evaluation, labour law, company social benefits, etc.), and expert knowledge—but equally because of the works councils' obligations to the 'welfare of the company' and to the explicit observance of management interests. Secondly, the councils are not legally in a position to mobilise pressure (including strike threats) to enforce the workers' interests. As a result of the unions' remoteness from the shop-floor and their centralised wage policy, the numbers of wage problems that are regulated on the workshop level and workplace problems have increased. It is difficult enough for the works councils to manage this mass of problems alone, but with the additional change in economic conditions, their chances of success have diminished. As long as labour was scarce, and management's capacity for making concessions was large, the works councils could achieve successes for the workforce even within the limits of negotiation – by reference to the dissatisfaction of the workforce, high absenteeism, fluctuations and poor work results. The lack of an institutionalised negotiating system on the workshop level which could settle conflicts has led to a situation in which active and dissatisfied groups of workers have resorted to self-help—to the enforcement or defence of non-contractual wage components and to 'illegal' strikes against deteriorating working conditions. The fact that these strikes could not be brought under union control and often took on unusually militant forms, has caused labour law experts to consider the limited legalisation of workshop strikes in the hope of channelling them.

UNION POLICY AND CHANGES WITHIN UNION ORGANISATION

Union Wage Policy (1967–75)

Union wage policy between 1967 and 1975 has reflected changed economic conditions, the decrease in and greater instability of economic growth. The policy has been characterised by inconsistency and rapid adaptation to the varying socio-economic and political constraints placed upon it. Periods in which wage policy is subjugated to the demands of economic policy and necessity follow periods of active wage policy geared to the interests of the workers.

One can identify the following phases of wage policy:

(a) *1967–9*. During the cyclical recession of 1967, the unions voluntarily accepted the state incomes policy and held back on their wage guidelines for 'concerted action' until the culmination of the economic boom of 1969 (*cf.* page 284). As a whole, wage demands remained below the rate of increase of total industrial productivity. The unions' participation in 'concerted action', and the tendency toward the centralisation of wage policy which accompanied it, provoked controversies within the unions concerning incomes policy and union wage policy. The wave of spontaneous strikes during the boom year of 1969 made it clear that criticism within the unions over wage policy was supported by widespread dissatisfaction with the results of this wage policy among the membership.

(b) *1969–71*. Following the spontaneous strikes, the bargaining rounds during the boom and the downturn that followed it were characterised by a phase of active wage policy, with a partial retreat from central contract bargaining. The contractual wage increases clearly exceeded the guidelines set by the incomes policy. Not until the economic downturn of 1971 could the size of these increases be forced down to the level suggested by the guidelines, and this was achieved only against the militant resistance of the unions. This resistance was expressed in two lengthy conflicts in the chemical and metal industries. On the whole, the rises in effective wages were above the rate of increase of productivity.

(c) *1972–3*. With the start of the economic boom, the rates of inflation began to rise at an unprecedented rate, and so the restrictive measures adopted by the Federal Government and the Federal Bank (Bundesbank) received top economic priority. Union wage policy was brought into line with these policies, which were aimed at stabilisation: the negotiated wage increases barely kept up with the rise of the cost of living, while the inflationary increase of prices continued uninterruptedly. This development in wage and price policies resulted in great dissatisfaction within the work-force, which led to a new wave of wildcat strikes during the boom year of 1973. The majority of these strikes were aimed at winning cost of living bonuses. The wage improvements enforced by the strikes were able to halt stagnation in the growth of real wages.

(d) *1974*. The boom, which was soon 'brought to heel' by a rigorously restrictive economic policy, was followed by a phase in which the economy grew ever more susceptible to crisis. This tendency first became noticeable in the simultaneous increase of inflationary tendencies and deterioration of the situation on the labour market. The experiences with the spontaneous strikes of the previous year and the continuing trend of price increases forced the unions to execute an aggressive nominal-wage policy. This could be achieved only with the aid of official strikes in the civil service and the metal industry. The wage increases that were achieved were clearly larger than those recommended in the guidelines established by the incomes policy.
(e) *1975*. The economic crisis was intensified by conditions on the world market (the price increase of raw materials and the shrinking demand for West German exports), and in the winter of 1974–5 the number of unemployed rose above a million. The union wage policy once again acquiesced to the recommendations of the Federal Government and its Council of Experts. Contractual wage increases were kept within the guidelines of the incomes policy, which provided only for an adjustment of wages to price increases and also planned a redistribution favourable to corporate earnings. The fear that spread throughout the work-force due to the altered situation on the labour market had helped to subordinate wage interests to interests of job security, so that hardly any manifest dissatisfaction arose over the unions' policy of adaptation.

In the bargaining rounds since 1967, as described above, a typical pattern of wage policy becomes obvious:

(a) During situations of cyclical crisis (economic low-water marks, recession), the unions can be moved relatively easily to co-operate with incomes policy. The situation on the labour market and the existential fears of the workers make it feasible for the unions to adapt their wage policies to the guidelines of incomes policy – in the interest of initiating a new boom. This usually means that productivity and corporate earnings rise faster than income from wages.
(b) When the situation on the labour market improves, the unions' stand on wage policy is offset during the boom by workers' actions that place the unions under pressure to legitimate their policy practices. Impelled by their members' increased expectations, the unions initiate an active wage policy during the beginning of the downturn, and no longer allow themselves to be bound by state incomes policy. With the support of official strikes, wage increases are enforced that usually exceed the rate of increase of productivity and place corporate earnings under pressure. On the whole, the unions' wage policy probably not only reflects the cyclical development of the economy; it may also have intensified this development.

The Beginnings of Opposition within the Unions.
The contract policy practised by the unions since 1967 has led to conflicts within their organisations – particularly in IG Metall and IG Chemie.

Particular controversy has been provoked by the issues of centralisation and 'concerted action'.

Until the mid-fifties, the influence of the central executives on wage policy had been of an informal nature. The largest West German union (IG Metall) is a good example of this. The earliest bargaining activities and labour conflicts in the metal industry took place without any obvious co-ordination: neither the demands nor the settlements were co-ordinated with one another. Only after the failure in 1954 of a large labour conflict in Bavaria – due among other things to the lack of co-ordination – and subsequent demands for cuts in working hours, did IG Metall develop a strong tendency to centralise contract policy. The negotiations over reduced working hours were conducted centrally, because the employers' associations insisted on negotiating these at the same time as pay raises, so that they could be balanced against one another. IG Metall expressed its willingness to do so, since a federally unified regulation of working hours also corresponded with union aims. With this decision, however, contract initiative and decisions on bargaining tactics were transferred to the central executive. The most important settlements on working-hours were made in the second half of the fifties, and were tied to centrally negotiated wage and salary increases that were simply formally incorporated into regional pay-rate contracts. Although the main reason for central contract negotiations disappeared after this, central bargaining between the heads of the bargaining parties remained the rule during the sixties. This later proved to be particularly convenient for the 'concerted action' programme. Between 1956 and 1969, IG Metall carried out seven central bargaining talks and only three regional talks. While the centralisation of union contract policy and the unions' participation in the 'concerted action' were met with widespread approval among members of the employers' associations, these actions created grave organisational problems within the unions.

The open subjugation of union wage policy to state incomes policy made it difficult for union leaders to legitimate their activities to active union members. As a result of centralisation and a resulting decrease in membership participation, members' altered potential for expressing their interests could not be recognised early enough and could not be adequately analysed. Union participation in 'concerted action' led to controversial discussions within the active membership and among union functionaries. During conferences of union representatives and at union congresses, strong opposing minorities attacked the executives for undertaking policies which had become alienated from the unions' membership, and demanded withdrawal from 'concerted action'. These criticisms were accompanied by the argument that the unions should consider themselves as democratic mass organisations and militant leagues for the workers.

The militant core of opposition within the unions is recruited mainly from officials of the lower and middle echelons of the union hierarchy. Shop stewards form the most relevant group: due to their specific role within the internal process of organisation, stewards—and especially those who lead bodies of shop stewards—tend to become active in a manner that exceeds the limits of membership participation established by the unions.

During critical phases of contract activity, when referenda and strikes are imminent, the shop stewards have a key function. They must inform passive members, convince them of the legitimacy and effectiveness of union demands and induce them actively to support union strategy. These duties demand not only that shop stewards generally identify with union policy, but that they become personally engaged and convinced that their activities are not without effect upon the policies practised by the union. Since a co-operative union wage policy only rarely employs the activated potential of the unions' power to back up negotiations and enforce demands in full, the cuts made in union demands during bargaining must appear to the stewards as 'lame compromises'. On top of this, the stewards may feel compelled to present to a group of equally disappointed union members a contract settlement which they have not approved but which has been legitimated by the formally democratic decision of the negotiating committee. This can intensify the dissatisfaction with wage policy among the militant unpaid officials of the unions, and can quickly produce criticism of the unions' disregard of chances to enforce demands as well as substantial doubt about the concept of a 'democratic process of opinion forming' within the organisation. This situation has developed many times during the last few years.

Due to the shop stewards' close contact with union members and their knowledge of the situation on the shop-floor, their criticism also reflects the mood among relevant groups within the unions' membership. This became obvious during the waves of spontaneous strikes in 1969 and 1973 that surprised the union bureaucracies – due to their having either no or purely formal contact with the members – just as much as the general public. The stewards' position is also expressed by the results of a series of strike votes during the sixties, in which often more than half the members entitled to vote rejected the bargaining settlements that had been negotiated and recommended by the union executives. In five strike votes held between 1972 and 1974, between 38 and 57 per cent of the voting membership rejected contract compromises negotiated by the executive committees in order to end strike activity. In three strike votes, more than 50 per cent of those who voted rejected the contract settlements of the executives (Bergmann *et al*, 1976: p. 425, n. 14).

Militant union officials within the workshops (shop stewards as well as critical works councils) have also initiated and led many unofficial strikes, especially those in September 1969, and have often publicly called for the rejection of the executives' compromise settlements during strike referenda. The activities of the union opposition have also affected the representation of workers' interests on the workshop level. The 'natural' allies of the executive committees, the works councils, have also been caught up in the criticism. Conflicts within workshops between shop stewards and works councils have also had an effect on the entire union organisation. These conflicts have broken out frequently during the last few years, and have been caused by the often close co-operation of the works councils with management in matters concerning workshop wage policy. Their co-operative attitude has often led to accusations of corruption against 'established' works councils. During the works council elections in 1972 and 1975, open conflicts erupted between the shop stewards and incumbent works councils. In the large workshops in the centres of industry the stewards made use of their right to influence decisively the selection of lists of candidates and positions on these lists. In several cases this meant that the incumbent members were not automatically given positions that would ensure their re-election. In several large workshops in the automobile and chemical industries this led to their ejection from office, militant shop stewards being elected in their stead.

In the last few years the union leaderships and incumbent works councils have been confronted by the greater dissatisfaction and opposition of certain sections of the working class, especially of foreign workers and organised women workers. These groups are usually employed as unskilled workers and are paid for the work of the lowest wage groups. They feel that their wage and job interests are not being represented as well as those of the German skilled workers. In comparison with their size these groups are clearly inadequately represented within union election committees and bodies of union officials. This not only explains why their interests are inadequately represented, but also the fact that they sometimes attempt to enforce their own demands during the height of workshop conflicts without the support or approval of the union or workshop representatives, and sometimes even against the resistance of the representatives, as happened during several wildcat strikes in 1973.

Changes in Union Leadership's Policy

So far, the union leadership has reacted in a contradictory manner to the developing legitimacy crisis and to changes in its members' potential and among its functionaries. On the one hand, it has tried to reduce the members' increasingly manifest dissatisfaction by partially taking up previously neglected issues and by enforcing their interests more strongly. On the other hand, it has confronted its critics with expulsion or the threat of expulsion. Its reactions to the spontaneous strikes in 1969 and 1973 indicate that the leadership rejected a self-critical debate on their origins and consequences. Although the executives of both the most strongly affected unions – IG Metall and IG Bergbau – took different lines towards the unofficial strikes, both looked outside their own organisations for the causes. Their defensive reactions to the strikes' serious implications for the unions indicate that they cannot draw the necessary conclusions for the union and its wage policy without making fundamental changes in their organisation. On the other hand, pressure from the rank-and-file is apparently not yet strong enough to force them to undertake these changes. Its organisational and contract practices have still not gone beyond tactical concession and partial submission to the activated and dissatisfied members.

IG Metall's attitude following the September strikes provides an example of tactical concession. The union departed from its practice of many years of central contract bargaining, and has once again allowed its districts greater autonomy in wage policy. It should be noted that in 1975 (a crisis year) central bargaining was once again carried out. The union also made partial allowances for increased militancy at its base. The strikes, which have clearly increased since the beginning of the seventies, were not limited to IG Metall. Six other unions in the DGB called large official strikes between 1971 and 1974.

The altered situation within the unions and the attitudes of the workers—who have become more aware of their interests—have defined the discussions within the unions. The stronger emphasis on socio-political questions and the attention paid to new areas of demands (working conditions, savings inducement, economic co-determination, investment planning, reform of occupational training) only partially reflect the qualitative demands articulated by the unions' base. The 'socio-political turn' taken by the DGB also certainly expresses the recent politicisation of West German society, and the main subject of this spreading political interest is the system's need for reform. On the other hand, it can hardly be denied that the tacit acceptance of the systematic limits of union wage policy is reflected within this politicisation process. In recent years, unions have repeatedly had to realise that successes in wage policy, if they have any effect upon distribution, can be countermanded by unemployment and further price increases; nevertheless, they have decided against discussing these relationships openly within the organisation and have drawn no conclusions for union strategies from the discussions which have taken place. Instead, they try to compensate for the self-imposed limitations on wage policy or to conceal the impossibility of a redistributive wage policy by paying lip-service to socio-political goals such as 'the humanisation of work' and 'the quality of life' that enjoy popularity because of their great symbolical content.

Concessions to the interests of the members have been offset by increased restrictions within the organisation against potential initiators and supporters of movements at the grass roots and alternative union strategies. Alterations made by IG Metall to their guidelines on the activities of shop-stewards are an example of such restrictions; these amendments were aimed at further limiting shop stewards' activity and at making them more dependent on the formal organisational structure. This can be understood as a reaction against the recent activities of shop stewards, who had escaped from their subordinate positions within the union hierarchy in many large workshops in the metal industry, in steel manufacturing and in the automobile industry. Their antagonistic attitude during the last contract activities, their active role in wildcat strikes and their criticism of the works councils' social partnership, have met with disapproval within the union bureaucracy.

Criticism and opposition – in so far as they are mounted – must at present face up to massive disciplinary measures such as exclusion, the dissolution of elected committees, or the dismissal or removal of troublesome functionaries or secretaries. The 'incompatibility decisions' enforced by DGB unions, which deem membership of radical leftist organisations incompatible with union membership, are not only employed against known Maoist and radical Communist circles. Due to the broad interpretive possibilities of the clauses, they also enable union leaders to accuse of unfriendly activity those groups which threaten to develop into an opposition within the union.

The ambiguity of official union reactions to the changes within its rank and file and among union officials makes it apparent that the unions may be able to assimilate the pressure from below in one way or another, but that they still cannot adequately control the developing crisis of legitimacy. The unions' practice of co-operation has given them an autonomous influence which is still effective, even though its foundations – prosperity and apathy – are dwindling. This is partly a result of their orientation towards the stability and growth of the late-capitalist economy and partly of political loyalty to the governing Social-Democratic party.

5 CONCLUSIONS

The strike movements and protest actions carried out by the West German workforce in the late sixties emphatically repudiated the theory—spread by the bourgeois social sciences during the period of restoration and economic prosperity—that the working class in the Federal Republic of Germany was socially contented and integrated into bourgeois society (Deppe, 1971). After more than ten years of relatively peaceful labour relations, the conflicts and disagreements between capital and labour began to flare up to an ever-increasing degree. This 'new militancy' within the West German workforce needs to be explained in terms of social science, even though it might seem relatively undeveloped in comparison with that reached by the class struggles in Great Britain, France and Italy.

Empirical studies of the causes, course and consequences of the recent struggles of the West German workers are available only to a limited extent. In this paper, it has not been possible to discuss the politico-economic analyses which relate the economic factors responsible for the resurgence of the workers' struggles to the altered conditions for the accumulation of capital following the attainment of full employment (1959–60) and, above all, the 1966–7 recession (page 258) (Altvater *et al.*, 1974).

The following section will be restricted instead to the rather limited analytical level of 'sociological' explanation. The available works on the subject present three main theses about the causes and consequences of the new militancy:

(a) The workers' levels of material expectations have risen; more specifically, the thesis of a 'new wage consciousness' (*neues Lohnbewusstsein*).
(b) As a result of the intensified introduction of technical innovations and the rationalisation of the organisation of the work process, the structure of qualifications within the labour force has altered, and increased work-loads have been enforced.

(c) The forms and contents of the unions' policy of representation which had been developed in the years of prosperity, did not meet the altered objective and subjective demands of the workers. For this reason, a crisis has taken place in the 'co-operative' union policy.

We will now examine these theses in rather more detail.

(a) Empirical studies undertaken after the September strikes have suggested that changes in the demands and expectations of the workers help to explain them. These studies are particularly concerned with the relevance of these demands and expectations to the conduct of the strike actions. They have also introduced the thesis of a 'new wage consciousness' into their analysis (Schumann *et al*, 1971; Bergmann, 1972; Bergmann and Müller-Jentsch, 1977).

According to this thesis, the workers' demands for wage increases have been interpreted as components of a dynamic system of reference: 'the economic process is perceived as a process of growth, and the wage demands which are made with reference to it, are understood as claims to an appropriate share of the growing social product'. (Bergmann, 1972: p. 173).

These claims were put into practice during the new economic boom which followed the recession of 1966–7, when the apparently rapid economic recovery led to an above average increase in profits coupled with a delayed growth in wages. The workers felt that this situation violated their claim to a 'just' share in economic recovery. This attitude was one of the factors which produced the strikes, while the experience of the generally successful strike movement strengthened the collective confidence of the workers—and was even shared by those workers who were not directly involved in the strikes. One empirical study of the September strikes observes (Schumann, 1971: pp. 136–7):

> In the opinion of the majority of all workers interviewed, not only had an immediately obvious success been achieved in the September strikes; in addition, the strikes have favourably affected the confidence of the workforce. 60 per cent of those interviewed spoke of the 'increased courage of the workers for future conflicts' as a consequence of the strikes. Only 27 per cent consider the strike movement to have been an incident 'which passed over the workers more or less without leaving a trace'.

During the succeeding strike actions, from 1970 to 1973, this increased confidence continued to be of actual importance. The successful strikes organised within the workshops as well as by the unions generated an awareness of the unions' importance (*gewerkschaftliches Bewusstsein*) among the workers and salaried employees which can be deduced from the growth of union membership and the improvement in the extent of union organisation. Thus, one cannot speak of a general loss of legitimacy for the unions in relation to their members, even though the willingness of union members to enforce their own demands, if need be even without the unions, increased.

Nevertheless, the expectations and demands that were encompassed by the 'new wage consciousness' remained within the limits of 'the process of the distribution of wealth, and did not touch the relations of power upon which this distribution is based' (Bergmann, 1972: p. 175).

While political interpretations of the strike activities as well as direct intervention by political groups were repudiated by the participants in the September strikes and later conflicts, the changes in the political majority in Parliament in 1969 did influence the workers' struggles. The Grand Coalition of Christian and Social Democrats, which had been formed during the crisis of 1966, was replaced by a social-liberal coalition (liberal Free Democrats and Social Democrats). This change in government under the leadership of the Social Democrats was not immaterial to the rise in labour conflicts. The election campaign of 1969 was an important factor in the development of the workers' political awareness of the unions (and coincided with the September strikes). In this campaign, the problems of social inequality and discrimination (unequal distribution of wealth, shortcomings in the system of public health, unequal opportunity in education, etc.) were brought out into the open.

In 1972 the political mobilisation of large sections of the industrial workforce following the vote of no-confidence by the opposition (CDU/CSU) in Parliament, as well as the mobilisation of workers' votes during the election campaign which followed, made it additionally clear that the Social Democrats had managed to create a point of reference for political activity through mobilisation of the workforce's expectations of reform (the quality of life, co-determination, tax reform, educational reform). Although the student movement, which had developed since 1967, claimed to constitute an extra-parliamentary opposition, by comparison with those of France and Italy it did not manage to establish any practical political relationship with the workers' struggles, other than occasional co-operation.[18] The same applies to the German Communist Party (DKP) which was newly founded in 1968, though the activities of DKP members on the shop-floor modifies this assessment. The party is represented within groups on the shop-floor especially in the 'traditional' sectors of West German industry (the iron and steel industry, mining, the metal industry). These groups make themselves noticed by regularly publishing workshop newsletters and performing important publicity functions during strikes. Their members are usually active union functionaries, although their political importance is usually limited.

Thus, the workers' awareness of the unions' importance, as expressed in the increase in labour conflicts, was most closely associated with expectations of the Social Democrats reform programmes and economic policy; however, the limits of these programmes became obvious when, from 1973 onwards, the possibilities of aggressively enforcing the workers' economic interests began to decline as a result of the economic crisis. The spontaneous strikes of 1973 as well as those led by the unions in the metal industry in 1973 and 1974 and in the civil service in 1974 represent not only the high-point, but also the beginning of the end of a particular phase in West German labour conflicts.

Although no conclusions based on sociological studies are available for the strikes which succeeded the September strikes, it can be assumed that they cannot be unconditionally interpreted in terms of the 'new wage consciousness'. The major demand in these conflicts was for cost of living bonuses—in other words, for the adjustment of strikers' incomes, which had been devalued by inflation. This reflects different motivations to those which applied during the strikes of 1969. The effects of accelerating inflation—resulting from the developing crisis—shifted the emphasis of demands towards the maintenance of previously achieved levels of pay.[19]

The relatively high and persistent unemployment that followed and which stood in sharp contrast to the workers' experience of the sixties, forms an essential factor in the present stage of strike activity and seems to have affected the work-force's awareness of the importance of union activity and its willingness to act in its own interests. High unemployment contributes to the uncertainty underlying those demands which had earlier formed part of the 'new wage consciousness' during the September strikes, and provided the basis for the new militancy among the workers.[20]

The politico-economic regimentation of the workers by the crisis has at the same time weakened elements of collective confidence which had been developed during and expressed by the workers' struggles of 1969–73. The intensification of competition among workers has tended to favour individualistic modes of behaviour and has made collective action that much more difficult to achieve.

At the level of socio-political development, this trend corresponds to declining expectations of and demands for reform and their subordination to the necessities of a capitalist solution to the crisis, as dictated by the Social Democrats and union leaders. As a result those positions which had formed the political point of reference for the workers' struggles after 1969 were demolished without there appearing to be any political alternative to them. This has led to shifts in the political majority on the parliamentary level, but has left the workforce without assistance in finding a new political orientation.

(b) So far we have attempted to describe the workers' political awareness of the unions' importance in terms of motives, of aspects of the subjective conditions for militancy. Some aspects of the more objective conditions for militancy must also be described. Although the form and intensity of labour conflicts must be related to these subjective and objective conditions, another essential factor is still to be considered, and is reflected in the scope for historical inconsistency. While certain groups of workers—such as the steelworkers and the workers in the metal industry – could refer to experiences with and traditions of previous conflicts both in and above workshop level, other groups—such as those in the chemical industry as well as civil service employees – participated in strike activity for the first time.

The material basis of this historical inconsistency is essentially determined by the structure and development of the economic process. Economic and technological changes not only structure the branches of production and the sectors of industry, but also the distribution of labour in general. The course of these changes will be sketched here in so far as they are related to the development of labour conflicts in West Germany during recent years.

In this context it is apparently important to note that since the crisis of 1966–7, firms have increasingly reacted to the deteriorating conditions for the utilisation of capital by introducing technical innovations and, still more, measures of rationalisation which affect the organisation of labour. This is not only true of private industry; greater rationalisation has also occurred in the civil service (Armanski, *et al*, 1975).

These developments have led, on the one hand, to lay-offs which have particularly affected individual groups within industry, such as mining and the textile industry. On the other hand, they have led to changes in the structure of the qualification of labour and the demands of the work process, which have resulted in increased work loads as well as in the threat of dequalification. The effects of these changes have reached into the ranks of the previously privileged skilled workers (Baethgc *et al*, 1974; Mergner *et al*, 1975).

The actual development of these trends was much more diffuse than is indicated by this generalised description; however, they can still help us to gain an understanding of the form and content of labour conflicts in two ways.

Since the early sixties, the workers have become increasingly aware of the increased work load due to the division and acceleration of the process of work as well as higher proficiency standards, the introduction of new systems of work evaluation and payment, etc. As a result, the potential for dissatisfaction among certain groups has increased, causing a growing sensitivity to intolerable work conditions. This potential for conflict was expressed by spontaneous strikes during 1973 including the union-led conflict of the metal workers in Baden-Württemberg in the autumn.

But the contents of these conflicts were developed during a comparatively favourable economic situation. Even though the crisis has led to work conditions being intensified through companies' rationalization measures, the experience of the crisis has reduced workers' willingness to speak out against increases in the work load. Job security alone seems to have become the workers' primary concern, pushing their concern for working conditions into the shade.

Technical innovations and greater rationalisation have increased the importance of less qualified work groups due to the lower levels of qualification required. In relation to the labour market situation, this trend is expressed by a large increase in the proportion of foreign workers within the total work-force, concentrated principally in the iron and metal industries.

At the same time, these lower-paid groups of wage earners in particular – above all, male and female foreign workers – often took the initiative and played a leading role in the spontaneous strike activity of 1973. Shifts in the structure of labour within workshops and branches of industry as well as the intensification of work conditions help to explain the militancy of shop-floor conflicts led by unskilled workers. In political discussions on this subject, a version of the theory of the mass worker has been presented which hypothesised certain aspects of these conflicts (Brand, 1974; Roth, 1974). The supposed break in the development of the workers' struggles marked by the shop-floor conflicts of 1973 fails to recognise that traditional workshop and union organs continue the truly effective representation and enforcement of workers' interests. Their members are still primarily skilled workers. This becomes apparent not only from the role of these skilled workers in the September strikes, but also in union strikes and, in many cases, the spontaneous strikes of 1973.

(c) While the subjective and objective conditions mentioned above encouraged the rise of labour conflicts in West Germany, one must remember that, as far as the organisational prerequisities for these conflicts are concerned, the workers' organisations tended to obstruct their struggles rather than to support them effectively. Due to their fixation with the guidelines and patterns action laid down in the years of prosperity, under the new economic conditions the union organisations have neither taken the new wage consciousness of their members into account, nor have they fought against those company strategies which subjugate labour to increased economies and intensification of the work effort in order to raise productivity. This union attitude resulted in the self-help activities of the workers outside the official union framework. According to a recent, detailed study of organisational and political developments within the West German unions since 1945, these actions indicate a 'crisis in the unions' co-operative policy' (Bergmann *et al*, 1976).

Within the union organisations the militancy which has become manifest outside official patterns of action implies, on the one hand, a reduced role for and confidence in the official organisations; and, on the other hand, a potential for conflict with which the union leadership must reckon in its future contract policy (*ibid*; p. 325).

Nevertheless, in their conclusions, the authors have not taken the 'pacifying' effects of mass unemployment and reduced hours into consideration. These manifestations of the present economic crisis have revived existential fears among the West German workers and have given greater importance to the problem of job security than to questions of wage increases and improvements in working conditions. Since spontaneous actions are fraught with greater dangers during the crisis than under conditions of full employment, resistance to the various attacks by capital on the social situation of the workers makes union organisation more necessary than ever.

The fact that a union-organised defence against capitalist anti-cyclical policies has not yet been developed and that, instead, the union bureaucracies have even continued to legitimate their passivity as a contribution to the reattainment of full employment, has not made the thesis of a crisis in the unions' co-operative policy invalid. This crisis is at present not as manifest in conflicts within the unions as it is in the disconcerted state of union policy which has found neither a theoretically nor a strategically adequate answer to the present crisis. Instead, union policy has for the present waived its right to defend the workers' vital interests for the sake of an uncertain economic recovery in the future.

The likely consequence of this is for rank-and-file union members and officers to become disoriented, with the result that the union movement itself is weakened. For, in the last resort, the unions' ability to act and to enforce their goals depends to a very considerable extent on the political consciousness and active involvement of members and unpaid officers. If these conditions no longer apply owing to the lack of effective membership representation during a time of acute crisis, the union movement not only loses its very substance but also deprives itself of its political scope for action.

NOTES

1. One rough indicator of the degree of innovation in technical organisation, so far as it is aimed at the relative economising of labour, is furnished by the intensity of capital, which rose only slightly by an average of 2.8 per cent of annually in this period.
2. The unemployment rate, which stood at 11 per cent in 1950, decreased continually, but still stood at 3.7 per cent as late as 1957.
3. This description is based only to a limited extent on available scientific literature, since the historical and theoretical study of labour struggles in the Federal Republic of Germany is still too undeveloped. Thus, the description is mainly based on the secondary evaluation of union publications, newspaper reports, political periodicals, leaflets and strike reports. As a rule, these sources are not cited individually.
4. For example, Hans Mayr, the member of the executive committee of IG Metall who is responsible for contract questions, rejected the demand for 'equal amounts of money for all employees' at the beginning of the round of bargaining of 1970, with the argument: 'this would represent a change in the existing policy of IG Metall that our wage and salary policy should be based on work proficiency.' (Quoted in *Der Gewerkschafter*, No. 2a, Feb. 1970).
5. 'Humanisierung der Arbeit als gesellschaftspolitische und gewerkschaftliche Aufgabe', Protokoll der DGB-Konferenz vom 16. und 17. Mai 1974 in München, Frankfurt-Cologne 1974.
6. This trend is portrayed by Kalbitz (1972: 95) in its quantitative aspects: in relation to total strike activity in the Federal Republic of Germany, 1949–1968, the spontaneous strikes' share of the total number of strikes has changed between the periods 1949–53 and 1964–8 as follows: the share of spontaneous strikes has risen from 42 per cent to 83 per cent, the percentage of employees involved in spontaneous strikes from 12 per cent to 66 per cent, the percentage of working days lost from 5 per cent to 30 per cent, and the number of workshops affected from 12 per cent to 32 per cent.
7. With reference to the September strikes of 1969, the Institut für Marxistische Studien und Forschung (IMSF) (1974: 240) makes the following assessment: 'Under the form of specific occupations, groups of skilled workers have been the supporting and motive force behind the strikes in the majority of workshops. A relatively important role was also often played by those groups of workers who possessed, due to their key positions in the production process, a particularly good view of the situation in the whole workshop and contacts in many departments of the workshop (employees in shop-floor maintenance and transportation). These groups produced the movement's speakers and organisers.'
8. *Cf.* the strike reports in: Redaktionskollektiv *Express*, 1974: 53 ff.
9. IMSF, 1974: 245 (Also: Schmidt, 1971: 117). This thesis has been correctly contradicted: 'The militant element in the September strikes was too weak; the attempts to combine presence in the workshop with the practical seizure of the means of production were too rare; the simple need for information and co-ordination were too much in the foreground' (Schumann *et al*, 1971: p. 10).

10. The bargaining parties have only occasionally made use of the possibility, foreseen in the *Tarifvertragsgesetz*, of allowing the Minister of Labour to declare wage contracts to be generally binding: 'Of the 43,500 wage contracts that have been registered since 1965, only about 500 have been declared generally binding.' (*Materialien zum Bericht zur Lage der Nation 1972*: p. 178.)
11. Figures from *Welt der Arbeit*, 8 June 1973, p. 5.
12. Co-determination in the enterprises in the iron-and steel-manufacturing industries and mining (*Montanindustrie*) will not be discussed in this paper. This form of co-determination affects about sixty large companies with a work-force of around 600,000. Cf. *Bericht der Sachverständigenkommission zur Auswertung der bisherigen Erfahrungen bei der Mitbestimmung*, pp. 11, 13.
13. 83.3 per cent in 1965; 83.1 per cent in 1968; 77.6 per cent in 1972; 78.7 per cent in 1975.
14. IG Metall, *Ergebnis der Vertrauensleutewahlen 1973*, p. 7.
15. IG Chemie-Papier-Keramik, *Geschäftsbericht 1969–1971*, p. 265f.
16. IG Metall, *Ergebnis einer Befragung zur Vertrauensleutearbeit*, 1975.
17. These figures are the result of a study made by the Institut für Sozialforschung in seven large workshops in the metal industry and five large workshops in the chemical industry. Due to their limited size, they are not necessarily representative. *Cf.* Institut für Sozialforschung, 1973: p. 22.
18. Thus, the SOFI study of the September strikes notes the following results: 'Only a few of the workers interviewed relate the spontaneous strikes and the student movement to one another. Most of the workers tend to observe the students and their action with a certain ambivalence in which one can recognize at the most an indirect relationship to the strikes' (*ibid*: p. 144).
19. More recent sociological studies by SOFI indicate that crisis situations lead to demands for improvement being abandoned and the worker's primary concern becomes the maintenance of his existing standards. (Schumann, 1974: p. 12)
20. According to the results of an empirical investigation of 1970, job security in particular had become a fixed demand in the opinion of the workers: 'Full-employment, and with it the certainty of finding an appropriate job at all times, was established as a legitimate and realisable claim to job security'. (Bergmann, 1972: p. 176).

LIST OF WORKS CITED

Altvater, E. *et al.* (1974), 'Entwicklungsphasen und – tendenzen des Kapitalismus in Westdeutschland', in *Probleme des Klassenkampfes*, Nos. 13 and16.

Armanski, G., Penth, B. and Pohlmann, H. (1975), *Staatsdiener im Klassenkampf: Soziale Lage und Kämpfe Staatlicher Lohnarbeiter in der BRD* (Gaiganz: Politladen).

Autorenkollektiv Bochum (1974), *Die Tarifspolitik der IG Metall 1969–1971* (Frankfurt a/M: Roter Stern).

Baethge, M. *et al.* (1974), *Produktion und Qualifikation* (Hanover).

Bergmann, J. (1972), 'Neues Lohnbewusstsein und Septemberstreiks', in Jacobi *et al.* (*q.v.*).

——, Jacobi, O. and Müller-Jentsch, W. (1976), *Gewerkschaften in der Bundesrepublik*; Vol. I: *Gewerkschaftliche Lohnpolitik zwischen Mitgliederinteressen und Ökonomischen Systemzwangen* (Frankfurt a/M: Aspekte).

—— and Müller-Jentsch, W. (1977), *Gewerkschaften in der Bundesrepublik*; Vol. II: *Gewerkschaftliche Lohnpolitik in Bewusstsein der Funktionäre* (Frankfurt a/M: Aspekte).

Betriebszelle Ford der Gruppe Arbeiterkampf (1973), *Streik bei Ford Köln* (Cologne: Rosa Luxemburg Verlag).

Blechschmidt, A. (1974), *Lohne, Preise und Gewinne* (1967–1973) (Lampertheim: Kubler).

Brand, F. (1974), *Die Lage der Arbeitenden Klasse in Deutschland* (Hamburg).

Deppe, F. (1971), *Das Bewusstsein der Arbeiter* (Cologne).
Duhm, R. (1975), 'Betriebsbesetzung des Zementwerkes Seibel & Söhne in Erwitte', in Jacobi *et al.* (*q.v.*).
Hildebrandt, E. and Olle, W. (1975), *Ihr Kampf ist Unser Kampf: Ursachen, Verlauf und Perspektiven der Auslanderstreiks 1973 in der Bundesrepublik* (Offenbach: Verlag 2000).
Hirsche, K. (1972), *Die Finanzen der Gewerkschaften* (Düsseldorf, Vienna).
Hohne, G. (1974), *Wir gehen nach vorn! Erfahrungsbericht über die Arbeitskämpfe bei Mannesmann* (Berlin: Rotbuch).
Hoffmann, P. and Langweiler, P. (1974), *Noch sind wir da!* (Reinbek: Rowohlt).
Hoss, D. (1974), *Die Krise des 'Institutionalisierten Klassenkampfes': Metallarbeiterstreik in Baden-Württemberg* (Frankfurt, Cologne: Europäische Verlagsanstalt).
IMSF (1969), *Die Septemberstreiks 1969* (Frankfurt: Eigenverlag).
—— (1972), *Über die Streiks in der Chemischen Industrie im Juni/Juli 1971 in einigen Zentren der Tarifbewegung in Hessen und Rheinland* (Frankfurt: Eigenverlag).
Institut für Sozialforschung (1973), *Aspekte Betrieblicher Lohnpolitik* (Frankfurt: mimeo).
Jacobi, O., Müller-Jentsch, W. and Schmidt, E. (eds) (1972–76), *Gewerkschaften und Klassenkampf: Kritisches Jahrbuch* (Frankfurt: Fischer).
Kalbitz, R. (1972), *Die Arbeitskämpfe in der BRD – Aussperrung und Streik 1949–1968* (Bochum: mimeo.).
Keller, B. (1975), 'Determinanten des Schlichtungsprozesses: Konfliktmanagement durch Intervention Dritter', *Kyklos*, Vol. 28.
Kern, H. (1974), 'Die Bedeutung der Arbeitsbedingungen in den Streiks 1973', in Jacobi *et al.* (*q.v.*).
Kittner, M. (ed) (1974), *Streik und Aussperrung, Protokoll der Wissenschaftlichen Veranstaltung der IG Metall vom 13.–15. 9. 73 in München* (Otto-Brenner-Stiftung).
Leminsky, G. B. and Otto (1975), *Politik und Programmatik des Deutschen Gewerkschaftsbund* (Cologne: Bund Verlag).
Limmer, H. (1973), *Die Deutsche Gewerkschaftsbewegung* (Munich: Olzog).
Lotta Continua (1974), *Arbeiterautonomie in Westdeutschland* (Gaiganz: Politladen).
Matthöfer, H. (1971), 'Streiks und streikähnliche Formen des Kampfes der Arbeitnehmer in Kapitalismus', in Schneider (*q.v.*).
Mergner, U. *et al.* (1975), *Arbeitsbedingungen im Wandel* (Göttingen).
Nickel, W. (1972), *Zum Verhältnis von Arbeiterschaft und Gewerkschaft* (Cologne: Bundverlag).
Noé, C. (1970), *Gebändigter Klassenkampf, Tarifautonomie in der Bundesrepublik Deutschland. Der Konflikt zwischen Gesamtmetall und IG Metall vom Frühjahr 1963* (Berlin: Duncker und Humblot).
Osterland, M. *et al.* (1973), *Materialien zur Lebens- und Arbeitssituation der Industriearbeiter in der Bundesrepublik* (Frankfurt: Europäische Verlagsanstalt).
Pöhler, W. (no date), 'Arbeitspapier zur Analyse spontaner Streiks' (mimeo).
Redaktionskollektiv 'express' (1974), *Spontane Streiks 1973 – Krise der Gewerkschaftspolitik* (Offenbach: Verlag 2000).
Redaktionskollektiv der Projektgruppe Ruhrgebietsanalyse (1973), *Opel Streikt* (Bochum).
Roth, K. H. (1974), *Die 'andere' Arbeiterbewegung* (Munich: Trikont).
Schmidt, E. (1971), *Ordnungsfaktor oder Gegenmacht: die Politische Rolle der Gewerkschaften* (Frankfurt: Suhrkamp).
—— (1973), 'Spontane Streiks 1972/73', in Jacobi *et al.* (*q.v.*).
Schneider, D. (ed.) (1971), *Zur Theorie und Praxis des Streiks* (Frankfurt: Suhrkamp).

Schumann, M. *et al.* (1971), *Am Beispiel der Septemberstreiks – Anfang Rekonstruktionsperiode der Arbeiterklasse* (Frankfurt: Europäische Verlagsanstalt).

—— (1974), *Report to the Colloquium of the Institut für Sozialforschung, Frankfurt, 12. – 13. 10. 74.* (mimeo).

Sozialforschungsstelle Dortmund (1973 onwards), *Berichte zur Untersuchung offener Konflikte im Bereich der Chemischen Industrie*, 6 vols. (Dortmund: mimeo).

Steinhaus, K. (1975), *Streiks in der Bundesrepublik 1966–1974* (Frankfurt: Marxistische Blätter).

APPENDIX I: SELECTED ECONOMIC AND OTHER STATISTICAL DATA

Note: In these tables the names of the six countries are abbreviated as follows: *B*=Belgium, *F*=France, *I*=Italy, *NL*=Netherlands, *UK*=United Kingdom, *WG*=West Germany

TABLE 1: *Persons employed in Main Divisions of Economic Activity (Thousands)*

Sector	*Year*	*B*	*F*	*I*	*NL*	*UK*[c]	*WG*
Agriculture, forestry and fishing	1960	257	4,189	6,567	465	—[g]	3,623
	1965	230	3,468	4,898	388	846	2,876
	1970	174	2,907	3,613	329	784	2,262
	1975	136	2,350	2,964	299	667	1,822
Mining and quarrying	1960	131	345	159	58	—[g]	808
	1965	95	287	280[a]	50	628	450
	1970	52	232	292[a]	21	411	336
	1975	37	179	333[a]	8	350[e]	359[d]
Electricity, gas and water supply	1960	30	177	138	37	—[g]	199
	1965	30	154	[a]	42	418	256
	1970	31	165	[a]	43	391	191
	1975	33	178	[a]	45	347[e]	239[d]
Manufacturing	1960	1,172	5,240	5,316	1,241	—[g]	9,544
	1965	1,278	5,405	5,435	1,331	9,133	10,392
	1970	1,199	5,670	5,868	1,203	8,462	10,309
	1975	1,128	5,785	6,132	1,089	7,994[e]	8,900[d]
Construction	1960	243	1,551	1,775	379	—[g]	2,193
	1965	297	1,846	1,944	464	1,913	2,206
	1970	302	1,999	1,957	505	1,649	2,066
	1975	295	1,881	1,840	436	1,766[e]	1,923[d]
Transport, storage and communication	1960	240	1,039	815	296	—[g]	1,496
	1965	264	1,175	998	304	1,702	1,580
	1970	238	1,113	989	305	1,641	1,480
	1975	269	1,171	1,058	304	1,594[e]	1,486[d]
Finance, insurance, real estate, business services	1960[b]	—	—			—	—
	1965	85	713		—[b]	—[g]	945
	1970	185	954		258	1,003[f]	1,100
	1975	222	1,194		295	1,168[ef]	1,316[d]
Trade, restaurants, hotels	1960[b]	—	—	—	—	—	—
	1965	592	2,870	5,448	757	3,505[f]	3,838
	1970	678	3,233	5,974	827	3,154[f]	3,844
	1975	697	3,438	6,669	814	3,205[f]	3,599[d]
Community, social and personal services	1960[b]	—	—		—	—	—
	1965	748	3,626		1,050	6,512[f]	3,875
	1970	806	4,121		1,063	6,879[f]	4,581
	1975	926	4,588		1,213	7,618[f]	5,184[d]

(Italy figures for Finance, Trade and Community services are bracketed together as a single combined entry.)

TABLE 1: *Continued*

Sector	*Year*	*B*	*F*	*I*	*NL*	*UK*[c]	*WG*
TOTALS	1960	3,385	18,712	20,136	4,019	24,258	25,954
	1965	3,619	19,544	19,003	4,349	25,324	26,418
	1970	3,665	20,394	18,693	4,554	24,373	26,169
	1975	3,744	20,764	18,996	4,506	24,576	24,828

Notes: Caution needs to be exercised in the use of these data, both in comparisons between countries and in tracing developments over time. There are important differences in the definitions used in different countries, and over the years there have been changes in the systems of classifications used. The table can therefore be used for general guidance only. Details of some of the qualifications which are needed will be found in the source material; others are listed in the specific notes below.

[a] Combined figures for mining and quarrying and electricity, gas and water supply.
[b] Figures collected on a non-comparable basis.
[c] The UK system of classification was revised in 1964.
[d] The German system of industrial classification was revised in 1972.
[e] Figures for 1974.
[f] In the UK restaurants, hotels, accounting and legal services are included under community, social and personal services.
[g] UK figures in 1960 were calculated on a non-comparable basis.

Source: ILO, *Yearbook of Labour Statistics*.

TABLE 2: *Gross domestic product by kind of economic activity (at 1970 prices)*

Sector	*Year*	*B (billion BF)*	*F (billion FF)*	*I*[a] *(billion lira)*	*NL (index of volume)*	*UK (index of volume)*	*WG (billion DM)*
Agriculture, hunting, forestry and fishing	1962	47.7	–	4,367		82.0	18.56
	1965	44.4	–	4,782	79[f]	91.0	18.67
	1970	46.0	49.43	5,284	100	100.0	21.53
	1974	50.7	52.95	5,340	128	116.0	25.47
Mining and quarrying	1962	15.5		271		126.5	10.33
	1965	14.9		276		122.3	10.23
	1970	12.0		374		100.0	10.15
	1974	10.8		375		83.0	9.34[a]
Manufacturing	1962	245.8	–	8,729	–	75.2	182.60
	1965	292.5	–	9,903	74[f]	87.6	222.87
	1970	411.5	282.09	14,933	100	100.0	293.28
	1974	519.0	345.54	17,063	119	108.0	325.68
Electricity, gas and water supply	1962	14.4		650	–	65.9	9.32
	1965	19.4		859	59[f]	78.6	11.35
	1970	29.4		1,274	100	100.0	15.80
	1974	47.1		1,587	148	119.7	19.68[a]
Construction	1962	65.5	–	3,561	–	83.3	39.99
	1965	76.2	–	3,592	83[f]	95.0	47.14
	1970	88.6	77.74	4,412	100	100.0	55.90
	1974	100.8	92.68	4,291	97	98.2	57.44

TABLE 2: *Continued*

Sector	*Year*	*B* (*billion BF*)	*F* (*billion FF*)	*I*[a] (*billion lira*)	*NL* (*index of volume*)	*UK* (*index of volume*)	*WG* (*billion DM*)
Trade	1962	147.1	–	4,353[b]	–	84.0	69.81
	1965	176.0	–	5,167[b]	80[f]	91.0	79.25
	1970	222.9	129.97	7,221[b]	100	100.0	95.31
	1974	266.6	155.55	8,429[b]	118	113.0	95.03
Transport, storage and communication	1962	61.8	–	2,394	–	76.0	26.25
	1965	73.3	–	2,515	79[f]	85.0	29.72
	1970	92.6	39.86	3,475	100	100.0	38.04
	1974	110.1	52.76	4,077	115	114.0	42.87
Finance, insurance real estate and business services	1962	97.6	–	3,794	–	[c]	27.37
	1965	109.9	–	4,410	81[f]	[c]	32.19
	1970	137.4	147.86	5,526	100	[c]	43.72
	1974	167.1	190.54	6,169	117	[c]	53.47
Non-governmental community, social and personal services	1962	72.0				–	32.92
	1965	80.9				97.0	38.17
	1970	98.4				100.0	45.84
	1974	117.5				107.0	64.45
Government community, social and personal services	1962	31.0	–	2,430[d]	–	78.0	46.08
	1965	41.6	–	2,687[d]	88[f]	86.0	52.48
	1970	56.5	76.56	3,767[d]	100	100.0	63.28
	1974	73.2	88.58	4,239[d]	109	118.0	75.66
Public administration and defence	1962	55.4		4,447		94.0	
	1965	66.0		4,912		97.0	
	1970	78.5		5,623		100.0	
	1974	94.5		6,118		102.0	
Gross domestic product at purchasers values (total)[e]	1962	873.0	–	38,729	–	79.5	467.61
	1965	1,011.9	–	43,456	78[f]	89.3	545.48
	1970	1,280.9	783.02	57,940	100	100.0	686.96
	1974	1,555.7	956.50	64,596	117	109.7	772.43

Notes: The figures for Belgium and West Germany are computed on a somewhat different classification system from the other countries. Other notes in the tables are as follows:

[a] These figures refer to 1973 and not 1974
[b] Includes restaurants and hotels
[c] Figures relevant to this sector are given as follows in the UK data:

owner-occupied dwellings	1962	68.0
	1965	87.0
	1970	100.0
	1974	109.0
other	1962	68.0
	1965	80.0
	1970	100.0
	1974	128.0

TABLE: 2: *Notes Continued*

[d] Excludes restaurants and hotels

[e] The sectoral data in the original source include certain non-market services to private households, including domestic service. These figures, which are very small, have been excluded from the detailed breakdown given here, though they are included in the overall totals.

[f] These figures refer to 1966 and not 1965.

Source: National Accounts of OECD Countries, OECD, Paris.

TABLE 3: *Annual Rate of Growth in per capita GDP by volume (per cent)*

Year	*B*	*F*	*I*	*NL*	*UK*	*WG*
1965	2.8	3.2	2.4	3.9	1.4	4.5
1966	2.4	5.6	5.1	1.5	1.5	2.0
1967	3.4	2.8	6.3	4.2	2.1	−0.5
1968	3.9	3.8	5.7	5.6	3.1	6.7
1969	6.3	6.5	5.0	5.6	1.0	7.1
1970	6.1	6.1	4.3	5.6	2.0	4.9
1971	3.6	4.3	0.9	3.1	2.2	1.8
1972	5.1	4.8	2.4	2.9	2.3	2.7
1973	6.0	4.5	5.8	5.0	5.7	4.6
1974	3.7	2.2	2.5	1.6	0.2	0.6
1975	−2.3	−1.5	−4.4	−1.9	−1.3	−2.8

Source: National Accounts of OECD Countries, OECD, Paris

TABLE 4: *Annual Rate of Growth by Volume (per cent) in (1) private final consumption, (2) government final consumption and (3) gross fixed capital formation.*

Year	B			F			I			NL			UK			WG		
	1	2	3	1	2	3	1	2	3	1	2	3	1	2	3	1	2	3
1965	4.2	5.8	4.0	4.5	3.0	6.7	2.9	4.2	−8.4	7.5	1.5	5.2	1.3	2.7	4.7	6.7	4.7	4.6
1966	2.8	4.5	6.9	4.8	2.2	8.3	7.0	3.6	4.3	3.2	1.7	8.2	1.8	2.8	2.5	3.7	2.3	0.9
1967	2.9	5.8	2.8	5.3	3.4	5.3	7.3	3.3	11.7	5.4	2.4	8.1	2.1	5.7	8.4	0.9	3.2	−8.4
1968	5.4	3.6	−1.5	4.5	6.4	5.7	4.8	4.4	10.9	6.6	2.2	11.1	2.5	0.3	4.6	3.8	0.0	7.9
1969	5.2	6.1	5.6	6.0	4.2	9.3	6.1	2.6	7.4	7.7	4.5	−2.1	0.7	−1.8	0.4	7.7	4.8	11.9
1970	4.4	3.3	8.8	4.6	4.7	8.8	7.4	1.4	2.7	7.6	5.9	10.1	2.6	1.5	2.6	7.0	4.9	11.4
1971	4.9	5.8	−1.8	6.6	3.4	7.1	2.9	5.4	−3.1	3.3	3.2	3.3	2.7	2.9	2.6	5.5	7.2	4.5
1972	6.1	5.8	3.1	5.8	2.8	7.1	3.4	5.0	1.0	3.6	2.2	−3.5	5.8	4.3	2.1	4.1	4.0	2.8
1973	7.8	4.8	7.1	5.5	3.3	6.7	6.1	2.6	8.4	4.1	0.2	5.5	4.5	4.1	4.0	2.8	4.2	0.6
1974	2.6	3.6	8.0	2.5	2.7	1.3	2.4	2.1	3.7	2.3	1.4	−4.2	−1.0	2.5	−2.4	0.2	4.6	−8.1
1975	0.9	7.2	−3.3	3.5	2.8	−4.4	−2.1	0.8	−12.7	3.0	2.6	−3.9	−0.7	4.9	−1.3	2.6	3.8	−4.2

Source: *National Accounts of OECD Countries*, OECD, Paris.

TABLE 5: *Indices of labour productivity (1970 = 100) (1) national economy; (2) industrial sector*

Year	*B*		*F*		*I*		*NL*		*UK*		*WG*	
	1	2	1	2	1	2	1	2	1	2	1	2
1966	83	75	80	76	81	79	81	67	89	86	81	81
1967	86	78	84	80	85	84	86	73	92	89	84	84
1968	90	85	90	89	91	91	90	83	96	96	90	91
1969	95	92	95	94	96	95	95	92	98	98	96	98
1970	100	100	100	100	100	100a	100	100a	100	100	100	100
1971	102	103	105	106	102	101	104	107	103	104	103	102
1972	108	111	112	113	106	106	109	116	106	109	106	108
1973	—	—	117	121	113	115	114	126	109	115	112	115
1974	—	—	120	126	115	118	118	132	108	111	114	116
1975	—	—	120	125	111	107	—	129	107	109	114	116

Notes: Caution needs to be exercised in the use of these data, since both differences of classification and calculation between countries and changes of method over time by individual countries are involved. For details of some of these variations, see the original source. In particular, UK data are alone in including construction within the industrial sector, while West Germany is alone in excluding gas, electricity and water supply from it.

With the exception of France data in columns (1) refer to GNP or GDP per person employed; those in columns (2) to net production (or contribution to NDP or GDP) per employed person. In France before 1970 data refer to final gross production per man hour; since 1970 to final gross production per employed person.

a Series replacing former series

Source: ILO, *Yearbook of Statistics*.

TABLE 6 (a): *Unemployment (as given by individual governments)* (N = thousands)

Year	*B*		*F*[a]	*I*		*NL*[b]		*UK*[c]		*WG*	
	N	%	N	N	%	N	%	N	%	N	%
1960	114.3	5.4	130.1	836	4.2	30.1	0.9	377.2	1.6	271.7	1.5
1961	89.1	4.2	111.1	710	3.5	22.4	0.7	346.5	1.5	180.9	1.0
1962	70.9	3.3	122.6	611	3.0	22.7	0.7	467.4	2.0	154.6	0.8
1963	59.1	2.7	140.3	504	2.5	25.0	0.8	558.0	2.4	185.7	0.9
1964	50.4	2.2	114.1	549	2.7	22.1	0.6	404.4	1.8	169.1	0.7
1965	55.4	2.4	142.1	714	3.6	26.7	0.7	347.1	1.5	147.4	0.6
1966	61.5	2.7	147.7	759	3.9	37.3	1.0	361.0	1.5	161.1	0.7
1967	85.3	3.7	196.0	679	3.5	78.5	2.0	558.8	2.3	459.5	2.1
1968	102.7	4.5	253.8	684	3.5	71.8	1.9	586.0	2.5	323.5	1.5
1969	85.3	3.6	223.0	655	3.4	52.9	1.4	580.9	2.5	178.6	0.9
1970	71.3	2.9	262.1	609	3.2	46.4	1.1	618.0	2.6	148.8	0.7
1971	70.9	2.9	338.2	609	3.2	62.0	1.6	799.1	3.5	185.1	0.8
1972	86.8	3.4	383.5	697	3.7	107.9	2.7	875.5	3.8	246.4	1.1
1973	91.7	3.6	393.9	668	3.5	109.9	2.7	618.8	2.7	273.5	1.2
1974	104.7	4.0	497.7	560	2.9	134.9	3.3	614.9	2.6	582.5	2.6
1975	177.4	6.7	839.7	654	3.3	195.3	4.7	977.6	4.2	1,074.2	4.7
1976 (June)	215.1	8.1	813.0	693	3.5	194.1	4.7	1331.8	5.7	921.0	4.0

Notes: Comparison between countries on the basis of these figures is almost impossible, since they vary widely in the means of data collection and definitions. For an attempt at providing data on a comparable basis, see Table 6(b).

[a] No percentage data available. Since June 1972 certain categories of unemployed persons over 60 years old have been excluded from the figures.

[b] Since 1968 married women who are not breadwinners have also been eligible for inclusion.

[c] Since 1972 adult students registering for vacation employment have been excluded.

Source: ILO, *Yearbook of Labour Statistics*.

TABLE 6 (b): *Unemployment (as calculated by the US Department of Labor)*

The US Department of Labor publishes periodically a calculation of unemployment data in selected countries, applying the criteria used in US unemployment statistics. This makes possible some inter-country comparison. Data relating to those countries covered in the US material which are also the concern of the current project are as follows (N = thousands):

Year	*F*		*I*		*UK*		*WG*	
	N	%	N	%	N	%	N	%
1960	430	2.2	880	4.3	540	2.3	200	0.8
1961	370	1.9	750	3.7	500	2.1	120	0.5
1962	360	1.9	640	3.2	720	3.0	100	0.4
1963	370	1.9	530	2.7	910	3.8	120	0.5
1964	310	1.6	590	3.0	630	2.6	90	0.3
1965	360	1.8	780	4.0	550	2.3	80	0.3
1966	360	1.8	830	4.3	600	2.4	70	0.3
1967	460	2.3	740	3.8	930	3.8	260	1.0
1968	550	2.7	750	3.8	910	3.7	300	1.2
1969	430	2.1	720	3.7	890	3.7	220	0.8
1970	460	2.2	660	3.4	960	4.0	140	0.5
1971	580	2.7	660	3.4	1,290	5.3	180	0.7
1972	630	2.9	760	4.0	1,490	6.2	240	0.9

Source: *Monthly Labor Review*, June 1972 and January 1974, US Dept of Labor, Bureau of Labor Statistics.

TABLE 7: *Changes in indices of (1) consumer prices and (2) hourly earnings in manufacturing industry. (1963 and 1970 = 100).*

Year	*B*		*F*		*I*		*NL*		*UK*		*WG*	
	1[c]	2[h]	1	2[j]	1[d]	2[j]	1	2[jk]	1[f]	2[m]	1[g]	2
1960	95.6	83	88.1	78.8	87.1	75.4	93.8	80	90.9	—	92.1	75.2
1961	96.5	86	91.0	84.9	88.9	78.7	94.7	85	94.0	—	94.3	83.2
1962	97.9	92	95.4	92.1	93.1	87.2	96.6	93	98.0	—	97.1	93.2
1963	100	100	100	100	100	100	100	100	100	100	100	100
1964	104.2	111	103.4	106.9	105.9	114.0	105.7	116	103.3	107.6	102.3	108.4
1965	108.4	122	106.0	113.1	110.7	123.6	111.0	128	108.2	115.1	105.8	118.6
1966	112.9	134	108.9	119.8	113.3	128.4	117.4	141	112.4	122.1	109.5	127.2
1967	116.2	143	111.8	127.0	116.9	135.0	121.4	150	115.2	126.2	111.1	132.3
1968	119.3	150	116.9	142.7	118.5	139.9	125.9	161	120.6	136.9	113.1	137.9
1969	123.8	162	124.4	158.8	121.6	150.4	135.3[e]	177	127.2	147.8	116.1	150.4
1970[a]	128.6	181	131.2	175.5	127.6	183.1	141.3	196	135.3	166.5	120.5	170.9
1970[b]	100	100	100	100	100	100	100	100	100	100	100	100
1971	104.3	112	105.5	111.1	105	113.5	107.5	112	109.5	111.3	105.3	111
1972	110.0	128	111.7	123.7	110.9	125.3	115.9	127	117.0	125.6	111.1	121
1973	117.0	149	119.9	141.0	122.4	155.7	125.2	143	126.7	141.5	118.8	134
1974	132.6	180	136.3	169.1	146.2	190.6	137.2	169	147.0	165.7	127.1	148
1975	149.5	216	152.2	198.3	171.3	241.4	151.3	192	182.5	209.3	134.7	160

Notes: The differences in the bases of calculation in the different countries are such as to render comparisons between countries highly misleading; the data are best used to give an indication of trends over time within individual countries.

[a] old index
[b] new index
[c] index excludes housing rents
[d] index covers wage and salary earners only
[e] there was a big rise in indirect taxes in this year
[f] index excludes large seasonal fluctuations
[g] before 1968 index only covers families with four persons
[h] includes mining and transport
[j] index covers rates, not earnings
[k] before 1970 index only covers males; includes mining and construction
[m] excludes Northern Ireland

Source: *OECD Main Economic Indicators: Historical Statistics, 1955–71; OECD Main Economic Indicators*, July 1976 (Paris: OECD).

TABLE 8: *Trade-union membership*

The significance of union membership varies widely between countries, as does the kind and adequacy of the data available. The following details should therefore be used with caution and are of use in considering developments within a country rather than in comparing countries:

Belgium

Membership of main federations

CSC: 1,139,061 (1974)
FGTB: 968,590 (1973)
CGSLB: 123,210 (1970)
Total is about 68% of labour force: 82% of manual and 38% of non-manual workers

Share of seats gained in elections to conseils d'entreprise (%)

Confederation	Year	Manuals	Non-manuals	Young workers	Total
CSC	1950	33·39	48.86	–	36.41
	1954	33·56	50.46	–	36.65
	1958	40.09	51·36	–	42·27
	1963	43·72	57·36	58.04	47·96
	1967	42.32	53·06	50.64	45·61
	1971	44·51	53·05	52·70	47·61
	1975	47·37	57·26	52.00	51·17
FGTB	1950	64.86	47·23	–	61.42
	1954	64.08	45·03	–	60.60
	1958	57·79	44·62	–	55·24
	1963	53·63	37·21	40·32	48.88
	1967	54·83	40.69	47·73	50.85
	1971	52·59	42.13	46.09	49·10
	1975	49·83	38.03	45·64	45·40
CGSLB	1950	1.73	3·89	–	2.15
	1954	2·35	4·49	–	2·75
	1958	2.11	4.01	–	2·47
	1963	2.64	5·41	1.63	3·14
	1967	2.85	6.25	1.63	3·54
	1971	2.90	4.81	1.21	3·28
	1975	2.80	4·71	2.36	3·43

Source: 'Le taux de syndicalisation en Belgique 1970', CRISP Ch No 595, 9 March 1973 and 724–5, 18 June 1976.

France

Membership of main confederations, 1950–74 (approximate estimates)

Year	CGT	CFDT	FO	CFTC	CGC	Others
1950	3,993,800	330,000	?	–	?	?
1954		323,000				
1955	1,479,919		?	–	?	?
1960		422,000				
1961	1,606,404		?	–	?	?
1963		500,000				
1965	1,791,238		?	?	?	?
1974	2,000,000	900,000	650,000	?	?	?

In 1974 it was estimated that 20% of the labour force was in union membership

Sources: various, including Caire, G., 1971, *Les Syndicats Ouvriers* (Paris: PUF); Adam, G., 1964, 'La CFTC', *Collection Etudes Syndicals*, No 1, September 1964.

Share of vote in elections to comités d'entreprise, 1973 (%)

Confederation	Manuals	Non-manuals	Total
CGT	48.1	16.5	40.8
CFDT	20.3	17.2	19.6
FO	7.7	7.8	7.7
CFTC	2.5	3.1	2.6
CGC	–	22.2	5.1
Other	4.6	7.9	5.2
Non-union	16.8	25.3	19.0

Source: Ministère du Travail.

Italy

Membership of main confederations, 1968–74

Year	CGIL	CISL	UIL
1968	2,461,297	1,622,158	–
1969	2,625,442	1,641,591	–
1970	2,943,314	1,809,028	–
1971	3,136,345	1,973,499	–
1972	3,214,827	2,184,279	–
1973	3,435,405	2,214,199	900,000
1974	3,827,175	2,372,701	1,050,000

Note: The UIL did not make statistics of its membership available until 1973.

Density of CGIL membership (members per 100 employees), 1962–74

Year	Density	Year	Density
1962	20.8	1969	20.8
1963	20.6	1970	22.9
1964	21.5	1971	24.2
1965	20.9	1972	24.7
1966	20.4	1973	25.9
1967	19.7	1974	28.1
1968	19.8		

Source: *Quaderni di Rassegna Sindacale*, Nos 50 and 51, September–October and November–December, 1974.

Netherlands

Percentage of members affiliated to the main federations, 1950–73

Year	Total union members	NVV	CNV	NKV (KAB)	EVC	Others
1950	1,161,000	33.0	13.0	26.0	14.0	14.0
1964	1,434,500	35.7	15.8	29.1	–	19.3
1967	1,534,400	36.3	15.5	27.7		20.4
1969	1,530,500	36.3	15.7	26.8	–	21.1
1971	1,577,900	38.8	15.1	25.6	–	20.5
1973	1,654,200	39.7	14.2	24.0	–	22.1

Union density (proportion of work-force who are members of unions) has increased from 30% in 1947 to 38% in 1974, having touched 40% in the late 1960s.

Source: G. J. M. Conen, *Censusmonografie OBW* (Centraal Bureau voor de Statistiek).

United Kingdom

Union membership and density (members per 100 employees), 1950–74

Year	Members (000)	Density (%)	Year	Members (000)	Density (%)
1950	9,289	44.1	1967	10,190	42.8
1955	9,741	44.5	1968	10,193	43.1
1960	9,835	43.1	1969	10,472	44.4
1961	9,916	42.9	1970	11,179	47.7
1962	10,014	42.7	1971	11,127	47.9
1963	10,067	42.7	1972	11,349	48.7
1964	10,218	43.1	1973	11,444	48.5
1965	10,325	43.2	1974	11,755	49.6
1966	10,262	42.6			

Union membership and density by type and sex of worker, 1948–74

	White-collar		Manual		Total	
	(000)	(%)	(000)	(%)	(000)	(%)
1948						
Male	1,267	33.8	6,410	59.5	7,677	52.9
Female	697	25.4	988	26.0	1,685	25.7
Total	1,964	30.2	7,398	50.7	9,362	45.0
1964						
Male	1,681	33.4	6,329	60.0	8,010	51.4
Female	1,003	24.9	1,206	32.6	2,209	28.6
Total	2,684	29.6	7,534	52.9	10,218	43.1
1970						
Male	2,143	40.0	6,123	63.3	8,266	55.0
Female	1,447	30.7	1,364	35.2	2,811	32.7
Total	3,592	35.2	7,587	56.0	11,179	47.7
1974						
Male	2,593	44.5	5,972	64.7	8,565	56.9
Female	1,629	32.6	1,561	42.1	3,190	36.7
Total	4,263	39.4	7,491	57.9	11,755	49.6

Source: G. S. Bain and R. Price, 'Union Growth Revisited: 1948–1974 in perspective', BJIR, November 1976, XIV, 3.

West Germany

Union membership and density (DGB-affiliated unions only), 1950–74

Year	Members	Density (%)
1950	5,449,990	35.7
1955	6,104,872	34.4
1960	6,378,820	31.0
1965	6,574,491	30.0
1970	6,712,547	30.0
1971	6,868,662	30.4
1972	6,985,548	30.9
1973	7,167,523	31.5
1974	7,405,760	32.6

Source: Geschäftsberichte des DGB von 1950–1974; J. Bergmann, O. Jacobi, W. Müller-Jentsch, *Gewerkschaften in der Bundesrepublik* (Frankfurt: Aspekte, 1976).

APPENDIX II: PROBLEMS OF STRIKE MEASUREMENT

Michael Shalev

Most deficiencies of strike statistics concern questions of *validity* – in othei words, do they actually measure what they set out to measure? Confusion arises, first of all, over exactly what it is that the figures are *supposed to measure*. Are all forms of labour dispute to be counted, or only those which lead to a stoppage of work? Are all groups of workers and sectors of the economy to be surveyed, or only those which are allowed to strike, or where it is regarded as politically acceptable to strike? Are strikes to be defined as purely 'domestic' events (i.e. conflicts between employees/unions and employers), or are protests enacted on the 'political' stage also to be considered as 'industrial disputes'? Our concern here is not with suggesting the 'correct' answers to these kinds of questions, but in pointing out that the answers given differ within countries, between countries, and over time.[1] The practices formally laid down in the six countries of most immediate interest are indicated below (pages 326 – 30), from which it will be obvious that even before the actual process of measurement begins, the statistics are incompatible. Setting aside this problem for the moment, and looking only at 'operational' measurement error, what exactly is it that imparts validity to statistics?

The first criterion of validity must be that of *completeness* – whether, in this instance, data on strikes (however defined) cover all those instances which actually occurred. This is manifestly not the case, and in any reasonably open society never could be, if only because of limitations on observational resources. Thus in all countries, the smaller, shorter, more localised, and less publicised a dispute is, the less likely it is to receive statistical recognition. Nevertheless, both the size of this unrecognised margin and the efficacy of data collection in general does vary considerably. Partly this is a matter of the sources of information which are utilised. Most countries exploit only a fraction of their potential informational input on the occurrence of disputes: The available channels might include local employment offices, social welfare agencies, mediation and arbitration services, newspaper reports, the police, and of course the parties directly involved and their representatives (Durcan, 1975: p. 23). In particular, there is a regrettable tendency to rely exclusively on one or the other of the 'social partners' (usually employers) as an informational source. This of course intensifies another of the problems, namely that 'The social nature of the process of defining and classifying strikes means that the statistics provided by those parties directly involved are linked in a systematic way to their goals, strategies and relative positions of power' (Ingham, 1974: p. 27).

Charges of manipulation and suppression of information have been raised in nearly every country, even (or especially) in the minority in which the reporting of strikes constitutes a legal obligation. Governments themselves are occasionally laid open to such charges. Unauthorised or illegal strikes and political protests tend to be especially singled out for neglect, irrespective of whether or not they are formally supposed to be counted. In one country, the authorities even went so far as to declare the day of a massive protest strike a national holiday in order to banish it from the stoppage statistics. In another case, officials acted over-conscientiously in following up a series of 'strikes' which consisted of workers all over the country slipping off the premises for a few hours in order to witness a major sporting event.

Successful strike-watching depends not only on the quality (i.e. accuracy and impartiality) of *sources* of information, but also on the amount and type of *resources* devoted to the task of information-gathering. There is some evidence of Parkinson's Law operating here, in the sense that the more (or less) officials whose job it is to count strikes, the more (or less) strikes will be recorded. When looking at those countries, such as Sweden and the Netherlands, which have particularly 'good' strike records, one cannot help being struck by their meagre allocations of staff to the task of compiling stoppage statistics, and wondering which of the two factors (few recorded strikes, or few strike-watchers) has caused the other.[2] Of course, over-devotion to the task may have equally confusing results, as is the case in one country whose statistics are regarded especially highly, but where a recent staff expansion in the office responsible for strike surveillance was followed by a directly proportional increase in the number of strikes recorded! Frequently, however, the problem is not so much a lack of staff, but that the persons concerned have their attention divided between filing strike reports and far more pressing tasks – such as running a labour exchange, a police force, a conciliation service, or whatever. These problems are aggravated when, as is often the case, the agency responsible for gathering information and that responsible for compiling it are under the wings of different (and rival) government departments.

Most serious of all, however, is the problem that: 'Public agencies are very keen on amassing statistics – they collect them, add them, raise them to the nth power, take the cube root and prepare wonderful diagrams. But what you must never forget is that every one of these figures comes in the first instance from the village watchman, who just puts down what he damn well pleases.'[3] In the course of investigating the way in which data-collection takes place at the grass roots of the system, the present author has come across numerous instances of arbitrary, even erratic practices. One of the most piquant of these[4] was the case of a stoppage report filed by a German labour exchange upon which was noted: 'This dispute was not actually a strike because lost production was made up when the workers returned to work.' Perhaps it would be reasonable to expect quirks like these to cancel eachother out, but this can hardly be so in relation to the kinds of local reporting practices which *systematically* bias the statistical record (e.g. the adoption of unofficial 'thresholds' in deciding whether or not to record disputes).[5]

The official adoption in a number of countries (two out of the six under consideration here) of thresholds below which stoppages are statistically ignored, puts a very obvious limit on the completeness of strike reportage. It also creates equally obvious problems of international comparison, although it is doubtful that such disparities should always be taken at face value since, as we have already indicated, many stoppages 'slip through the net' whether they are eligible for recording or not.[6] In the UK, for example, where a complex and relatively restrictive threshold is in operation, and where Turner (1969) and McCarthy (1970) once bickered at length over its precise impact on the strike record, it appears that some of the arguments may have been in vain. On the one hand, only a very small percentage of all stoppage reports (under 7 per cent in 1972) are in fact eliminated as a result of the operation of this threshold. On the other hand, a recent interview survey of nearly 300 work-places indicates that one element of the threshold – the minimum of a day's duration – would have eliminated as many as a quarter of the strikes most recently experienced (Parker, 1974: 66).[7] In other words, in the British case the loss of *available* data as a result of the operation of a formal threshold is inferior by far to the loss which results from stoppages simply not coming to the attention of the responsible officials.

On balance, we would suggest that it is the *joint* effect of both the relative efficiency of the reporting system and the relative restrictiveness of formal thresholds which determines the completeness of the statistical coverage of strikes in any given country. Since it is obvious however that there is no country in which the official statistics constitute a *complete* sample of the entire universe of work stoppages, in questioning the validity of this sample we must also examine how *representative* it is. In other words, is the likelihood of being missed out subject to random, or systematic influences? We have already indicated that systematic distortions play a disturbingly extensive role, for example in the case of quantitatively insignificant stoppages or politically embarrassing disputes, which are particuarly likely to escape attention. Another source of built-in bias, not yet mentioned, arises from the differing arrangements which may be in effect for recording disputes in different branches of the economy. It is, for example, common to find that publicly-operated and/or highly centralised industries, such as mining and the docks, tend to keep their own very comprehensive records of work stoppages and to relay them directly to the statistical authorities. It is perhaps no coincidence that these same industries are invariably inordinately 'strike-prone'.

The third and final criterion for assessing the validity of strike statistics is their *homogeneity* – i.e., the degree of equivalence of individual observations, which is of course an essential prerequisite for legitimately counting anything. At this point we encounter a very serious problem, summed up in Ross and Hartman's famous dictum that: 'To consider all strikes as homogeneous occurrences stands in the way of enlightenment' (1960: p. 24). Quite apart from the considerable variation between both times and places in the *functions* of strikes and their *meaning* for the 'actors' concerned, there are also obvious differences of a *quantitative* sort which relate to strike 'shapes' (their size and length).[8] In what sense can it be argued that a half-hour 'downer' by a few dozen men in a single workshop is equivalent to a six-week all-out strike at General Motors? The descriptive characteristics of the two events are very far apart; yet they do possess analytical similarities. Both are individually identifiable acts of conflict, and each of them arose from a separate and distinguishable strike decision. In reality, as we shall see, the boundaries between individual conflicts are by no means as unambiguous or clear-cut as this formulation might imply, yet for the moment it is safe to assume that in the abstract strikes do possess *conceptual* equivalence. In this sense, two strikes are definitely *more* than one, although differences in size and length prevent us from saying *how much* more (hence, two strikes cannot be 'twice as many' as one, arithmetically speaking.) If this means that strikes are measured on an ordinal (not interval or ratio) scale, this raises serious doubts as to the legitimacy of using techniques of statistical analysis (such as multiple regression) which necessarily assume otherwise. Yet here comes a major paradox, for the very econometric studies which make quite the wrong assumptions about strikes do in fact succeed in 'explaining' a good deal about them. This kind of evidence suggests, as we have pointed out elsewhere, that strike figures 'evince a degree of patterning and regularity which is suggestive of unitary characteristics which embrace the diverse components of the aggregate statistics' (Silver, 1973: p. 68). In other words, there *is* a certain theoretical justification for trying to describe strikes statistically – although, as we shall shortly see, the precise *limits* of the extent to which aggregation is feasible can only be determined empirically.

Thus far we have been considering criteria – completeness, representativeness, and homogeneity – relevant to assessing the validity of stoppage statistics as a measure of labour-management disputes. Another problem which must be considered is that of the *reliability* of strike statistics. Here our concern is with whether the 'measuring instrument' we are using performs the same way on different occasions, and it will already be clear to the reader that the answer is that it does not. Different levels of resource allocation and efficiency, and different operating standards on the part of strike-watchers in different regions or in respect of different branches of activity certainly introduce unreliability into strike reports. Still, if such distorting influences could be assumed to be constant, or to have a random impact on the final result, we might at least be justified in considering time series of strike activity to be reliable. Although this may indeed be a reasonable (and necessary) working assumption, its drawbacks must be recognised.

A few examples from the French context should serve to illustrate the kind of long-term unreliability which can enter into strike statistics. In France, as in a number of other European countries, the post-war years saw a drastic reorganisation of the system of stoppage reporting, the task in this case being shifted from Departmental prefects under the supervision of the Ministry of

Commerce to local inspectors of the Ministry of Labour (Shorter and Tilly, 1974: p. 352). Territorial adjustments are another source of unreliability; in France, this is because of the inclusion of Algeria in the official statistics for certain years (1921–35). Finally, over the years different solutions may be adopted for the problem of fixing the boundaries of a single 'unit of conflict' for the purposes of the statistics. The possibility of changes in the *minimal* definition of a strike or lockout does not arise in France because there has never been any official threshold in operation. However, there is also the problem of setting *upper limits*, which basically means deciding whether the appropriate unit of conflict is an individual stoppage of work, or else is defined by the broader concept of 'dispute': the latter may comprise a number of separate (but linked) stoppages at different places and/or different times. At one time the practice of French statisticians was to register as a single *conflict* all strikes which occurred simultaneously in the same region/industry. With the recent decentralisation of the responsibility for collating stoppage statistics to the Departmental level, individual disputes have undoubtedly been duplicated in the nationwide statistics.[9]

Another contemporary source of duplication has arisen as a result of changes in the forms of strike action – to wit, the rise in *multiple stoppages* (grèves tournantes and *débrayages*) connected with the *same dispute*. The French authorities have solved this problem in a bureaucratic rather than sociological fashion, having decreed (since 1971) that any break of forty-eight hours or more between individual stoppages signals the beginning of a new *conflit*. By recalculating the 1971 statistics on the basis of *motifs* (disputes) rather than forms of action (stoppages), Durand and Harff (1973) reduced the total number of conflicts by 40 per cent. They also succeeded in showing that what seemed to be a decline in the duration of conflicts in recent years was in fact an optical illusion due to the tendency for a greater number of briefer stoppages to occur in the course of each dispute, while the overall length of disputes remained roughly the same.

So much for reliability inside individual countries and over time; what of *cross-country* reliability? It goes without saying that each of the problem-areas in strike measurement which we have identified in the context of a single nation are amplified almost beyond redemption in an internationally comparative context, due to the fact that each country answers the same methodological questions in a different fashion. The most essential of these differences are outlined on pages 326 – 30, although it is a disturbing reflection on the whole problem of uncertainty in strike measurement that even the apparently straightforward task of determining how work stoppages are counted in different countries could not be accomplished with certainty.[10]

One very simple way around these methodological differences is, once again, to introduce the assumption that measurement error within countries remains either constant or random over time. If this is assumed, then although *levels* of strike activity in different countries are not amenable to comparison, *trends* – i.e. relative changes over time – may be compared. Thus, although it is difficult to say with any precision whether one country experiences more or less strikes than another, we can certainly make an informed judgement as to the country in which strike activity has been increasing fastest over a specified period. Essentially, the basis of such a strategy is the realisation that the problem of validity is far more serious than the problem of reliability. In comparing levels, we would have to be quite sure of what was being compared. But in comparing trends, so long as the statistics all measure work stoppages in some fashion, and have done so fairly consistently in the course of time, we are reasonably safe in making deductions from them.

The problem of validity does not affect all direct comparisons equally. The most problematic index is of course the number of stoppages, which is the hardest to define and keep track of The other two primary indices – involvements and man-days – are more easily operationalised, and are also less problematic because they are composites of individual elements and are little influenced by the kinds of minor disputes which tend to go unnoticed by statisticians. At the *interpretative* level, however, the 'broader' the measure, the more ambiguous it is. If, for example, the volume of strikes (number of man-days) increases, is this because stoppages have become more frequent, more extensive (larger), or more intense (longer)?[11] The most sensitive index to the climate of employment relations and to economic and political conditions is still the number of strike decisions – i.e. the frequency of strikes. Furthermore, it is impossible to get any clear idea of the 'shape' of strikes (their size and length) without the help of frequency distributions, which clearly make it possible to learn much more than global averages can tell us.

This brings us to a further crucial barrier to reliable comparative analysis. Even assuming that, for reasons of invalidity or ambiguity, we are prepared to rule out the use of national statistics for making direct comparisons, in favour of an analysis of relative trends, we still have to face the question of what these trends mean. Such a question arises because of the enormous aggregation which is involved in the use of nation-wide strike indices. To return to the subject of strike 'shapes', it will be obvious that trends in the size and length of strikes in any particular country might well differ between different industries, different forms of conflict (strike/lock-out, official/unofficial, wage/non-wage, etc.), and different parts of the size or duration spectrum. In most instances, we simply do not have the cross-tabulations of data which would be needed in order to disentangle these various effects. An example of the kinds of complexities revealed when the necessary figures can be analysed is furnished by the possibility of differentiating stoppages in Italy according to their scope. Looking back over the last few decades, it emerges that nearly all the overall increase in the number of strikes is attributable to the type of conflict which does not extend beyond a single firm. At the same time, however, major global changes in the size and duration of stoppages have hardly any counterpart in what has been happening to the single-firm strike, and this is so despite the fact that numerically it constitutes by far the most important form of conflict.

It is of course a general rule that particularly 'monstrous' (large and/or long) strikes inevitably have a vastly disproportionate and distorting influence on the characteristics of strike activity at the nationwide level of analysis (Silver, 1973: pp. 83–85). The importance of disaggregation has also been remarked upon by researchers struck by regional and industrial variation in conflict behaviour. In certain countries – for example, Australia (Gordon, 1968) and Canada (Jamieson, 1968) – geographical variability is so strong as 'to make a "national" system or pattern a rather meaningless abstraction' (Jamieson, 1968: p. 43). At the industry-specific level, difficulties are often caused by 'deviant' industries whose employment relations are under the influence of quite different forces to those operating in the rest of the economy, with the result that the trend in a 'deviant' case is likely to be at odds with, and even completely to distort, a genuine national pattern. The classic case here is the coal-mining industry, whose once pivotal role in total strike activity has been diminishing drastically over just the same period that conflict elsewhere has been on the rise.[12]

Consideration of the significance of inter-industry differentials in strike activity raises the possibility of these being systematic in nature and holding good across international boundaries. The classic enumeration of such a thesis is Kerr and Siegel's (1954) famous paper on 'The Inter-Industry Propensity to Strike'. There is, however, a quietly accumulating body of research which flatly contradicts these authors' static and highly structuralist conception of the causes of employment conflict.[13] To some extent the very idea of internationally immutable inter-industry differentials is absurd when one considers that the technical definitions, and indeed the entire meaning of given divisions of economic activity, are subject to considerable cross-country variability. The same industrially defined boundaries may have different implications in different countries for factors like: the structure of collective bargaining; infrastructural characteristics (type of ownership, scale, concentration); technology; characteristics of the workforce; or geographical locations. Thus we suggest that the main benefit of industry-specific analysis of strikes data is to aid our understanding of *intra*-national patterns and trends, rather than directly to compare inter-industry strike behaviour on a cross-national basis. Naturally, it cannot be denied that the industrial composition of a particular country's economy – along with many other factors affecting the organisation of production and the nature of work – is likely to have *some* systematic influence on its overall national strike propensity. However, this is quite different from endorsing the unqualified use of industrially-disaggregated strike statistics as a means of pinning down the causes of strikes at a world-wide level of analysis.

These, then, are the major deficiencies of work-stoppage statistics:

(1) Their formal *subject-matter* – what they are supposed to be measuring – varies significantly between countries, within countries, and over time.

(2) Similar variability characterises the degree to which the figures afford a *complete coverage* of the entire area of work stoppages which they set out to depict. The nature and quality of informational sources, and of the resources

which are set aside for the task of strike surveillance, constitute the most important limiting factors in this respect.

(3) Much of the variability in how and how well strikes are measured, being unsystematic in nature, implies that the statistics are not only an incomplete but also an *unrepresentative* and *unreliable* sample.

(4) The legitimacy of counting strikes at all depends on whether they may legitimately be aggregated, which is in turn a function of the *homogeneity* of the individual units of analysis. Labour conflicts were shown to possess more analytical than descriptive equivalence. Their comparability may not be assumed but must be tested empirically. The characteristics of stoppages in any given country may well vary systematically between different points on the size or duration spectra, different regions or industries, and so on.

SELECTED INFORMATION ON THE METHODOLOGY OF STRIKE MEASUREMENT IN THE SIX COUNTRIES

INTRODUCTION

1 (a) None of the countries count 'partial' forms of strike action – i.e. 'on-site' sanctions during which work does not actually cease.

(b) Late starts or early departures may or may not be counted as work stoppages. In the UK they are said to be eligible provided their volume exceeds 100 man-days; in the Netherlands they would in principle be counted; in Belgium they would be counted provided the time 'lost' was not paid for. In France, Italy and Germany they are definitely excluded.

2 Each of the six countries recognises some phenomena above and beyond the narrow concept of the economically-motivated strike as work stoppages. Hence none of them exclude inter- or intra-union disputes, sympathetic strikes, or lockouts. Only Italy and the UK definitely exclude 'political' strikes.

3 (a) The number of workers involved is always inclusive of employees 'involuntarily idled' by a dispute concerning fellow-workers *in the same establishment*.

(b) Generally speaking, if an individual worker is involved in more than one stoppage in a year, he is multiply counted in the total number of involvements for that year. The exceptions are France and the UK, which counted 'strikers' and 'involvements' separately until 1968. Since then the UK has reverted to standard practice (number of 'involvements'), while France publishes only the number of individual strikers.

Belgium

DEFINITION OF THE CONFLICT-UNIT

(a) Threshold: None

(b) Exclusions: None

(c) Scope: The establishment is the basic reporting unit, but figures on the number of conflicts in effect describe the number of *disputes*.

SOURCES OF INFORMATION

The Ministry of Labour and Employment collates (and passes on to the National Statistical Institute) reports from the nineteen officers of its conciliation service who also serve as presidents of 'parity committees'. These conciliators only have direct knowledge of disputes in cases where their intervention is sought by one or more of the parties concerned. However, information from nearly a dozen newspapers, and reports submitted by the police (who are routinely informed of impending stoppages by employers) constitute important secondary sources.

France

DEFINITION OF THE CONFLICT-UNIT

(a) Threshold: None

(b) Exclusions:

1 There is no record of disputes in agriculture since 1962. 'Administration publique' is also excluded, but generally this does not apply to public utilities and state-owned enterprises or commercial operations. The most significant 'unknowns' are teachers and postal and communications workers.

2 Although 'political' strikes are in theory included, it is probable that France's brief but massive demonstration strikes have not been regularly reported. In any event, data concerning any kind of multi-industry and/or multi-regional stoppage are obviously highly inaccurate guesses (and not only in France).

3 Strikes in protest against redundancies are excluded, on the grounds that the participants are unemployed and therefore incapable of participating in a temporary stoppage of work.

(c) Scope: Each *conflit* is in effect a discrete stoppage of work. In particular, since 1971 a single stoppage is considered to have been terminated if interrupted for forty-eight hours or more. The appropriate physical boundary of each *conflit* is not rigidly defined. However, since 1971 strike reports concerning the private sector have been collated independently in each Department, instead of at the national level, which has probably led to more duplication than in the past.

A further problem concerns the numbers of workers involved in strikes, which since 1967 has been measured only in terms of the number of *individuals* involved in the course of a year, irrespective of whether some of these individuals participated in strikes more than once during the period. However, measurement of the number of individual strikers only began in 1954. Before then, figures on the total number of *involvements* were published, and continued to be collected alongside those for 'strikers' until 1967.

SOURCES OF INFORMATION

Except in the case of public enterprises or services (which report directly to their respective Ministries, and thence to the Ministry of Labour *if* non-'civil-servants' were involved), stoppage data are transmitted by local *inspecteurs du travail*. The inspectors rely primarily upon *délégués du personnel* for their information, but they may also approach management or the strike leaders for details. The inspectors are usually alerted to the existence of a dispute in the course of their informal activity as conciliators, but they are also notified by the Ministry of Labour of stoppages reported in the newspapers.

Italy

DEFINITION OF THE CONFLICT-UNIT

(a) Threshold: None

(b) Exclusions: 'Political' strikes – defined as protests against or attempts to influence legislation or governmental policy – are not included in the statistics.

(c) Scope: Officially the basic unit of stoppage registration is the enterprise, but in practice individual stoppages are delineated in terms os the cause of the dispute, not the place in which it occurs. Similarly, multiple actions *in time* (e.g. rolling strikes) are considered to constitute a single stoppage if connected with a single dispute.

SOURCES OF INFORMATION

Reports are submitted to the Central Institute of Statistics by police headquarters in each of Italy's ninety-four provinces. The police are alerted to the existence of stoppages mainly by applications from workers or unions planning a strike and requiring a permit to carry out a public demonstration. However, newspaper reports, which come directly to the attention of the police or else were transmitted via ISTAT, may prompt an enquiry to the employer concerned.

Netherlands

DEFINITION OF THE CONFLICT-UNIT

(a) Threshold: None

(b) Exclusions: None. (In practice, however, strikes by public employees – admittedly few and far between – tend to be ignored.)

(c) Scope: The basic reporting unit is the *enterprise*, but figures on the number of conflicts in effect describe the number of *disputes*. The temporal scope of a single conflict includes cases where 'several intermittent actions take place in the same establishment'.

SOURCES OF INFORMATION

The district employment offices of the Ministry of Labour are supposed to report on disputes which come to their attention or which they are made aware of by the Central Statistical Office (on the basis of its surveillance of newspaper reports). The labour exchanges request the relevant details from employers. The CSO may occasionally seek additional information from the unions.

United Kingdom

DEFINITION OF THE CONFLICT-UNIT

(a) Threshold: Only a stoppage involving at least ten workers *and* lasting at least one day is counted, *unless* its volume exceeds 100 man-days.

(b) Exclusions: 'Political' stoppages are not included in the aggregated statistics. Significant cases may however be noted separately.

(c) Scope: Any number of separate stoppages, regardless of their physical dispersion, will be defined as a single 'stoppage' if they concern the same issue and are carried out under the same auspices. However, only if they occur at 'about the same time' are such stoppages considered to constitute a single dispute. In case of 'fragmentation', the lapse of more than a month is considered to signal the start of an entirely new dispute.

SOURCES OF INFORMATION

Certain nationalised industries and statutory authorities (most notably in coal-mining and the docks) transmit information directly to the Department of Employment. In other sectors the main source is local employment exchanges, which get to hear of strikes primarily from local newspapers or as a result of strikers applying for unemployment benefit. The details are sought directly from employers. Regional manpower advisors are an additional source of information. In the case of major disputes the DE may itself apply to the employer concerned to obtain information. Very occasionally, information is also sought from trade unions.

West Germany

DEFINITION OF THE CONFLICT-UNIT

(a) Threshold: Only a stoppage involving at least ten workers *and* lasting at least one day is counted, *unless* its volume exceeds 100 man-days.

(b) Exclusions: None. (In practice, however, in relation to lock-outs it appears that only those deemed to have been provoked by strike action are included in the statistics.)

(c) Scope: The reporting unit is the individual *establishment*, and no data are furnished on the number of *disputes*.

SOURCES OF INFORMATION

Local employment exchanges file reports to statistical offices at the regional (*Land*) level, from whence they are transmitted to the Federal Statistical Office. (It appears that significant amounts of data are 'lost' at each stage of this journey). Employers are under a legal obligation to report stoppages to the local Labour Offices, but in practice the only sure recipients of such information are employers' associations, and they keep it to themselves.

NOTES

1. Fisher (1973) will be found valuable as a source both of information on actual practices and of well-considered judgements as to their utility. On the question of what forms of conflict are worthy of measurement, we may note that in at least two countries (New Zealand and Israel), there is an attempt to count 'on-site sanctions' which do not involve a stoppage of work, while in Japan statistics are even available concerning differences of opinion which are not accompanied by *any* outward acts of dispute. On the vexed question of what constitutes a 'political' strike, readers are referred to Gubbels (1968), Shorter and Tilly (1974), and Perrot (1973).
2. In Sweden, for example, non-governmental strike data indicate that stoppages are actually far more common than has been supposed (cf Fulcher, 1973).
3. For this delightful quotation, attributed to Sir Josiah Stamp, we are indebted to Lind (1973: p. 204).
4. Drawn to my attention by Dr Rainer Kalbitz of Bochum University.
5. There is one country, for example, which formally has one of the most liberal definitions of 'industrial dispute' in the world, but where, in one particular region – which happens to be the source of a majority of stoppages – the responsible officials have decided that any dispute in which work is not stopped for at least four hours will not be reported.
6. It must be admitted, however, that if dispute-recording is efficient, the threshold can make a big difference. In Israel, for example, several factors – the small size of the country, the newspapers' preoccupation with strikes, and the existence of positive incentives to report them – combine to enhance the coverage of the statistics. Hence it is not surprising that when, in 1960, the minimum duration of recordable disputes was altered from one day to only two hours, the number of stoppages shot up nearly threefold.
7. This is actually an oversimplification, because under certain circumstances stoppages lasting under a day *are* counted officially – see page 329 for details. Perhaps a more clear-cut

example of the incompleteness of statistics governed by thresholds would be Italy, where A. Pizzorno has estimated that 90 per cent of recorded strikes last for only a few hours, and where in recent years well over a quarter of the stoppages which are officially registered would have been excluded by the operation of a UK-type minimum volume of 100 man-days.

8. Surprisingly, it is only in recent years that the *individuality* of each quantitative dimension of the strike has been fully recognised in studies which attempt to explain strike behaviour. See e.g. Britt and Galle (1972).
9. The two sources of unreliability mentioned so far – territorial changes and the regional/industrial boundaries of disputes – are not mere methodological niceties. As a result of having adopted different criteria on these matters to those used by official statisticians, Shorter and Tilly (1974: p. 383) come up with vastly different results when calculating correlations between strike frequency and various economic-explanatory variables.
10. The single most useful source of information is Fisher (1973: pp. 97–132), but inaccuracies or at least contradictions do emerge when comparisons are made with our other sources – which were mainly interviews and correspondence with officials and national experts, and the methodological notes accompanying tables in national or international statistical publications. We warn the reader that despite every attempt to be accurate, the information we convey is only tentative, and would not necessarily be approved by the authorities concerned.
11. The precise nature of these relationships was first spelled out by Forchheimer (1948: p. 10), who pointed out that Volume is the product of Frequency, Average Size and Average Duration.

    Thus Volume = Frequency × Size × Duration

    $$\textit{or}\ \text{Man-days} = \cancel{\text{Strikes}} \times \frac{\cancel{\text{Strikers}}}{\cancel{\text{Strikes}}} \times \frac{\text{Man-days}}{\cancel{\text{Strikers}}}$$

12. In Britain, for example, the inclusion of coal-mining in aggregate data on strike frequency actually *reverses* the trends in other industries (Silver, 1973: pp. 71–9).
13. This is not the place to quote chapter and verse for the above assertion, but for one study which brilliantly illustrates the poverty of a rigid Kerr-Siegel type of hierarchisation of 'strike-proneness', see Rimlinger (1959).

LIST OF WORKS CITED

Britt, D. and Galle, O. R.(1972), 'Industrial conflict and unionisation', *American Sociological Review* 37, 1, 46–57.

Durand, M. and Harff, Y. (1973), 'Panorama statistique des grèves', *Sociologie du Travail*, 15, 4, 356–75.

Durcan, J. W. (1975), 'Report of the OECD working party on industrial dispute statistics' (Paris: OECD, Social Affairs and Industrial Relations Division, mimeo.

Fisher, M. (1973), Measurement of Labour Disputes and their Economic Effects (Paris: OECD).

Fulcher, J. (1973), 'Class conflict in Sweden', *Sociology*, 7, 1, 49–70.

Gordon, B. J. (1968), 'A classification of regional and sectoral dispute patterns in Australian industry, 1945–64', *Journal of Industrial Relations* 10, 3, 233–2.

Gubbels, R. (1968), 'The strike: A sociological analysis', in B. C. Roberts (ed.), *Industrial Relations: Contemporary Issues* (London: Macmillan).

Ingham, G. K. (1974), *Strikes and Industrial Conflict: Britain and Scandinavia* (London: Macmillan).

Jamieson, S. M. (1968), *Times of Trouble: Labour Unrest and Industrial Conflict in Canada, 1900–66*, Study No. 22, Task Force on Labour Relation (Ottawa: Queen's Printer).

Kerr, C. and Siegel, A. (1954), 'The inter-industry propensity to strike: an international comparison', in A. Kornhauser, R. Dubin and A. M. Ross (eds), *Industrial Conflict* (New York: McGraw-Hill).

Lind, J. A. D. (1973), 'Foreign and Domestic Conflict: The British and Swedish Labour Movements, 1900–1950' (Ph.D. thesis, University of Michigan).

McCarthy, W. E. J. (1970), 'The nature of Britain's strike problem', *British Journal of Industrial Relations*, 8, 2, 224–36.

Parker, S. R. (1974), *Workplace Industrial Relations 1972* (London: HMSO).

Perrot, M. (1973), 'Débat' on Tilly and Shorter, 'Les vagues de grèves', *Annales*, 35, 4, 88–91.

Rimlinger, G. V. (1959), 'International differences in the strike propensity of coal miners: experience in four countries', *Industrial and Labor Relations Review*, 12, 3, 389–405.

Ross, A. M. and Hartman, P. T. (1960), *Changing Patterns of Industrial Conflict* (New York: Wiley).

Shorter, E. and Tilly, C. (1974), *Strikes in France, 1830–1968* (Cambridge: University Press).

Silver, M. (or Shalev, M.) (1973), 'Recent British Strike Trends: A Factual Analysis' *BJIR*, xi, i.

Turner, H. A. (1969), *Is Britain Really Strike-Prone? A Review of the Incidence, Character and Costs of Industrial Conflict*, Occasional Paper No. 20 (University of Cambridge, Department of Applied Economics).

Subject Index

Letters in brackets refer to the names of the six countries: B = Belgium, F = France, I = Italy, NL = Netherlands, UK = United Kingdom, WG = West Germany.

Institutions included in the List of Abbreviations on pp. xix–xxiv are listed here in their abbreviated form.

References to disputes, workers, etc within a particular industry are included in the general references to that industry.

absenteeism, 68, 150, 267
ABVA (NL), 166, 181
ACAS (UK), 243, 247, 248
accords d'intéressement, 99n
acting, 249
action, direct, 82, 83, 98, 118
administration publique, 327
Agence Nationale pour l'Emploi (F), 78
agreements, collective, 72, 78–81; *see also* bargaining; c.a.o. agreements; *and conventions collectives*
  long-term, 72
  national, 145, 151, 153
  plant-level, 142, 156n
agriculture, 5, 6, 102, 104, 107, 127, 128, 137, 153, 186, 329
  small-holders in, 111
  workers in, farmers, 85, 107, 139; *see also braccianti*
airline flight-control staff, 180
  ground crews, 263
  pilots, 121, 223
AKZO, 174
Alfa-Romeo, 119, 122
Algeria, 325
  war in, 94
alienation, 63–7, 91, 129
Ampex, 39, 44
Amsterdam (NL), 178
anarcho-syndicalism, 118
ANBM (NL), 167
Arbeitsrechtsprechung, 276
arbitration, 81, 224, 270,276, 280, 290
architecture, 249
aspirations, *see* expectations
asset-stripping, 195
AUEW (UK), 198, 216, 218, 230, 232, 236, 237, 247
ausserparlementarische Opposition, 260
Australia, 15, 327
authorities, public, 74, 83, 84, 133; *see also* public sector
autogestion, 26, 63, 91, 98; *see also* self-management
automobile industry, *see* car industry
autoriduzione, 118, 119, 135

Baden-Württemberg (WG), 263, 264, 301
balance of payments, 191–4, 197, 208, 212, 285
banks, 23, 40, 87, 90, 180, 224
Banque Nationale (B), 28
bargaining, negotiations, 65, 71, 74–87, 133, 148, 149, 153, 169, 173, 187, 199, 204–6, 218, 219, 233, 241, 251–3, 263–5, 274, 276, 280, 281, 291–6; *see also Tarifverhandlungen*
  articulated, 140
  levels, 225–9, 234–8, 241
    company, 238, 284
    industry, 28, 30, 74, 76, 104, 235–8, 295, 296
    interprofessionnel, inter-industry national, 28, 29, 74–80, 84–7
    national, 73–80, 86, 87, 106, 149, 213, 227, 228, 233–8, 241, 264
    plant, shop, 28, 30, 76, 77, 80–3, 127, 129, 141–9, 206–9, 234–8, 241, 251, 252, 264, 289
    regional, 30, 264
  strategies, 81–6, 99n, 103, 122, 123, 136

Batignolles, 73
Bavaria (WG), 293
BBA (NL), 161, 164
BDA (WG), 279
BDI (WG), 279
Beek en Donk (NL), 174
Belgium, 3–8, 12–18, 21–51 *passim*, 307–16, 328
Bell, 39
Berlin, West (WG), 269
Betr. VG (WG), 275–7, 281, 288–90
black-legs, 112, 115, 231
braccianti, 128
Breda (NL), 173
Britain, Great, 12n, 13n, 69, 297, 333n; *see also* United Kingdom
Brittany (F), 98
British Institute of Management (UK), 232
broadcasting, 67, 69
Brussels (B), 21, 23, 49n
BSN, 39
BSP (B), 49; *see also* PSB
Bullock Report (UK), 248
Bundesarbeitsgericht, 276
Bundesbank (WG), 291
Bureau de Plan (B), 31
  de Programmation (B), 31
Bürgerkoalition (WG), 260
bus-drivers, tram-drivers, 132, 178, 254n
building industry, *see* construction industry
BVA (NL), 166

Cabinet (UK), 197
Canada, 15
Candy (I), 122
c.a.o. agreements, negotiations, 164, 170–2, 178, 181, 187n
capital, 56, 57, 84, 101, 257–60, 297, 303n
capitalism, capitalist, 48, 66, 71, 72, 84–90, 94, 101, 103, 133, 134, 159, 206, 211, 212, 239, 264–6, 274, 302
  neo-, 46, 185
car industry, automobile, motor industry 114, 116, 119, 122, 221, 222, 226, 228, 232, 235, 267, 269, 272, 296
Cassa Integrazione Guadagni, 156n
Catholic Church, Catholics, 22, 88, 89, 108, 111, 129, 162, 163, 167, 199, 203, 233, 250
  Bishops of (NL), 167
CBI (UK), 220, 243–7
CBS (NL), 160, 174, 187n, 331
CCO (UK), 254n
CCSP (B), 24
CDU (WG), 260, 269, 285, 299
cement industry, 179, 274
Central Arbitration Committee (UK), 247
  Bank (NL), 171
Centrale Générale des Services Publics (B), 24
CFDT (F), 53, 63–8, 71–3, 78, 79, 86–98 *passim*, 99n
CFT (F), 75, 76
CFTC (F), 71, 87, 90, 94, 99n
CGC (F), 88
CGIL (I), 108–11, 121, 124–8, 137–9, 144, 148–52, 156n, 157n
CGSI (F), 74, 76
CGSLB (B), 22, 23
CGT (F), 53, 63–6, 71–3, 78, 79, 86–97 *passim*
Chancellor, Federal (WG), 260, 261
  of the Exchequer (UK), 243
Charte d'Amiens (F), 91
  du Patronat Français (F), 98n
chemical industry, 48, 88, 98n, 111–14, 122, 124, 127, 132, 145, 173, 174, 186, 263, 267, 270, 283, 291, 300, 304n
Chile, disputes over, 177, 237
Christian(s), 25, 26, 87–90, 166, 277
  Democratic Parties, Governments (B), 26
    (I), 138, 147
    (WG) *see* CDU
  Federation of Trade Unions (WG), 277
  -Liberal Government (NL), 170, 185
Church schools, 35, 50n
cigar industry, 162, 173
CISL (I), 111, 126, 38–40, 144–51, 156n, 157n
Citroën, 39, 40
civil service, servants, 107–10, 120, 121, 168, 206, 223–5, 263, 264, 267–71, 277, 280, 292, 299–301
claimants' unions, 249
class(es), 160, 274
  bourgeois, 40, 48
  entrepreneurial, 138, 139
  middle, 48
  political, 134
  ruling, 22, 35, 133, 139
  working, 26, 66, 67, 88, 103–6, 109, 111, 115, 117, 121, 124–32, 138, 139, 142, 258–60, 264, 268, 269, 295, 297
class struggle, 65, 67, 89, 90, 95, 160
clerks, *see* workers, office
closed shop, 138, 246; *see also* trade unions, membership, compulsory
closures, shutdowns, 21, 38, 44, 45, 55, 180, 205, 216, 289
CNPF (F), 74–8, 85, 89, 98n
CNPS (B), 48, 50n
CNV (NL), 161, 162, 167–9, 173, 183
  Werkende Jeugd, 180

coal-mining, miners, 5, 6, 12n, 13n, 16, 17, 23, 35–44, 48, 55, 87, 166, 186, 194–203, 211, 219, 221, 227–36, 240, 243, 249, 263, 264, 299, 304n, 323, 331, 333n
Cockerill, 42
co-determination, 168, 169, 281, 289, 299, 304n; *see also* demands
Cold War, 102, 161
College van Rijksbemiddelaars (NL), 161, 164
Comité National d'Expansion Economique (B), 28
de Développement (F), 71
comités d'entreprise, 57, 70, 80
de sécurité et d'hygiène 23, 27, 70
commerce, trade, 5, 6, 110, 120, 180
Commission du Plan (F), 71, 76
Supérieure des Conventions Collectives (F), 74, 76
commissioni interne, internal commissions, 102, 139, 142–6, 150, 155n
committees of inquiry, 206
Common Market, *see* EEC
Communists, Communist Parties (B), 29, 31
(F), 89, 92, 97
(I), 102, 108, 131, 138, 142, 144, 147, 156n
(NL), 161
(UK), 203, 234, 249
(WG), 261, 277, 297, 299
comparability, 206
comparisions, 106, 108, 206–9
concentration of industry 57, 59, 84, 195, 259, 260
'concerted action' 285, 287, 291, 293
conciliation, 72, 80, 81, 153, 225, 229, 234, 252
Confagricoltura (I), 139
Confcommercio (I), 139
Conférence Nationale de l'Emploi (B), 28, 30, 33
Confindustria (I), 138–41, 150, 151, 154, 157n
Confintesa (I), 139
consciousness, 86, 96, 297–302
Conseil Economique et Social (F), 71, 76
Général de l'Economie (B), 28
National de la Formation Professionnelle (F), 78
du Travail (B), 28
conseils d'entreprise, 23, 27, 29; *see also* works councils
professionnels, 29
Conservative Party, Governments (UK), 192–200, 211, 218, 220, 224, 228, 231–3, 236, 240–5, 249–52, 254n
consigli di fabbrica, factory councils, 120, 145, 146, 150, 154, 155n; *see also* works councils
di zona 154
Constitution, Republican (I), 140
construction industry, building industry, 6, 24, 168, 173, 174, 179, 228, 231, 263
containerisation, 221, 222
contingenza, 103, 155n
contrats de progrès, 99
conventions collectives, 33; *see also* agreements
Conversation of Leidschendam (NL), 170
co-operatives, 212, 216
corporatism, corporate state, *corporativo*, 107, 151, 159–61, 185–7
cost of living, 39, 64, 111, 135, 155n, 211; *see also* demands, pay
Council of Experts (WG), 285, 292
CREDOC (F), 99n
CRESST (F.), 72
crises, economic, 39, 63, 115, 117, 131, 134–6, 153, 154, 191–200, 212, 266
CSC (B), 22–7, 50n
CSU (WG), 269, 299
CUB (I), 142
culture, cultural system, 47, 55, 66, 86, 91, 159, 203
customs staffs, 110, 121
CVP (B), 49

DAG (WG), 277, 278
DATA (UK), 230
DBB (WG), 277, 278
DC, *see* Christian Democrats (I)
débrayages, 323
décrets d'application, 76
delegati, 113, 120, 130, 133, 142–6, 150, 156n
délégations syndicales; délégués syndicaux, 27, 29, 37, 43, 70
délégués du personnel, plant stewards, 70, 73, 80, 99n, 328
syndicaux, see délégations syndicales
demands, 66, 80, 93, 122–36 *passim*, 155n, 175–8, 205–20 *passim*, 252, 264–9, 296, 304n
co-determination, 296
control (of jobs, production, work organisation), 64, 98n, 122, 124, 129–32, 176, 176, 177, 214–17, 267, 268
economic policy, 134–6, 148, 155n, 171, 220
education policy, 171, 178, 180
employment protection, job protection, 61, 64, 68, 73, 79, 136, 177, 207, 264–8, 272, 302, 304n
grading, hierarchy, upgrading, 42, 64–9, 122, 125, 130, 132
health, 267
holidays, 63, 68, 73, 207, 267, 268

house-building, housing policy, 170, 171, 178, 180, 220, 267
Investment, 156n, 161, 296
pay, wages, 10, 42, 61, 64, 65, 68, 73, 79, 111, 122, 131, 135, 153, 171–6, 187n, 205–14, 264–7, 272, 291, 302
cost-of living bonus, 206, 264–6, 291, 300
differentials, maintenance of, 214
egalitarian, levelling, 43, 64, 124–8, 166, 170, 171, 175, 176, 182
equal, for women, 43, 176, 214, 266
flat-rate, lump-sum, 10, 64, 106, 122–7, 176, 213, 266, 267
guarantees, 68, 135, 176, 268
minimum, 171
parity, 209, 235
percentage, 13n, 64, 68, 266
standard of living, maintenance of; purchasing (spending) power, maintenance of , 63, 79, 135, 136, 173, 175
'tapered', 213
pensions, 79, 135, 153, 207, 213, 232, 251
political, 43, 65, 177, 178, 205, 213, 217–20, 251, 268, 269
profits, controls over, 170, 178
public ownership, 220
retirement, age of, 63, 68, 73, 79
social reforms; welfare, 33, 79, 131–6, 147–9, 155n, 156n, 171, 178
subsidies, 220
trade-union rights, 61, 73, 79, 98n, 124, 131, 132, 155n
training, 296
transport policy, 220
working conditions, environment, 10, 42, 43, 61–5, 68, 69, 73, 111, 112, 129–32, 155n, 180, 187n, 267, 268, 272, 296, 302
hours, 61–4, 68, 73, 79, 106, 124, 129, 178, 205, 214, 267
rates, speeds, 42, 64, 122, 129, 130, 267, 268, 272
democracy, industrial, 216
trade unions, in, 96, 142
demonstrations, 68, 117, 121, 178, 179, 224, 232, 269–71
Denmark, 15
Department of Employment (UK), 247, 331
of Industry (UK), 212
Deutsche Postgewerkschaft (WG), 282
devaluation, 192, 193, 196, 197, 209, 212
DGB (WG), 269, 277, 278, 282, 288, 296
differentials, 48, 108, 110, 123, 125, 180, 206, 225; *see also* demands, pay
disarmament, nuclear, 218
dismissals, sackings, 76, 150, 273
distributive trades, 23, 124, 127, 196; *see also* shops *and* supermarkets
docks, 41, 168, 170, 173, 177, 187n, 221, 222, 228, 229, 234–6, 247, 250, 323, 331
doctors, 111, 222, 224, 263
Donovan Commission, *see* Royal Commission on Trade Unions
draughtsmen, 223, 227, 230
droit syndical, 98n; *see also* trade unions, rights
DS – 70 (NL), 171
Düsseldorf Programme (WG), 286

economy (B), 21, 22, 47–9
(F), 53–8
(I), 101–3
(UK), 191–6
(WG), 257–60, 275, 292
statistical details of, 307–15
education, 133, 153, 171, 299; *see also* demands
EEC, 84, 155, 186, 200, 216, 220, 278
EEF (UK), 253n
Eire, *see* Ireland, Republic of
elections, national (F), 85, 86
(I), 109
(UK), 197, 199, 200, 219, 224, 229, 232, 245
electrical appliance industry, 114
engineering industry, 186
power generating industry, 23, 28, 31, 33, 44, 127, 194, 228–31, 250
electronics industry, 39
Emergency Laws (WG), 260, 269
employers, 29, 30, 38, 39, 48, 53, 59, 60, 65, 70, 71, 78–87, 93, 98n, 128, 132, 135, 138–40, 150, 154, 160–4, 169–74, 177, 181–6, 194, 205, 206, 211, 222–5, 229, 233, 238–40, 245–7, 252, 286, 329, 331
associations, organisations, 26, 27, 32, 33, 73, 137–41, 150–2, 181, 183, 204, 233, 237, 242, 276, 279, 280, 285, 287
employment, 43, 74, 75, 78, 85, 87, 102, 103, 131, 136, 151, 155n, 172, 186, 191–6, 208, 212, 220, 231, 239, 240, 274, 275, 285, 297, 302
exchanges, 248, 331
statistics of, 307, 308
Employment Protection Act (UK), 254n
Enabling Act (NL), 169–72
encyclicals, Papal, 162
engineering industry, engineers, 5, 7, 24, 25, 48, 66, 72, 88, 221, 228, 232–6, 240, 241; *see also* metal-working industries
England (UK), 73
ENKA, 173, 177, 180
Esso Oil Refinery, 215

EVC (NL), 161
exchange, foreign, 191–4, 200
expectations, aspirations, 183, 211, 212

fascism, 135–8, 150, 250
Fawley (UK), 215
FDP (WG), 261, 269
Federal Statistical Office (WG), 330
Federation of CGIL-CISL-UIL (I), 145, 148
Federmeccanica (I), 151, 152
FEN (F), 88
FGTB (B), 22–77, 33, 50n
Fiat, 109, 115, 118, 122, 130, 131, 140, 156n
Fifth Republic (F), 82, 83
FIM-CISL (I), 126, 156n, 157n
financial markets, services, 57, 196
Finland, 15
FIOM-CGIL (I), 126, 156n
firemen, 110
First Plan (F), 91
fiscal policy, 191, 192, 212
Flanders, Flemish (B), 21–7, 35, 37, 43, 48, 49n
flight-control staff, *see* airline
FME (NL), 172
FNV (NL), 167
Fondation National de l'Emploi (F), 77
food industry, 23, 166
footwear industry, 55
Force Ouvrière (F), 71
Ford Motor Company, 39, 228, 235, 236
foreign workers, 258, 259, 264, 267, 272, 273, 278, 288, 295, 301; *see also* immigrant workers
foremen, 115
France, French, 2–8, 12n, 13–18, 35, 53–100 *passim*, 108, 192, 197, 232, 297, 299, 307–15, 317, 324, 325, 328, 329

gas industry, 23, 28, 127, 223
Gaullism, 57, 93
General Motors, 39
Germany, West, 3, 8–18 *passim*, 54, 69, 73, 102, 206, 257–306 *passim*, 307–15, 319, 322, 328, 332
Gesamtmetall (WG), 279
Gewerkschaft Textil-Bekleidung (WG), 282
glass-making, 23, 48
Glaverbel, 39, 44
go-slows, 65, 68, 111–18, 230
governments, 27, 29, 59, 60, 65, 71, 84–6, 92, 101, 102, 107, 118, 122, 133–6, 139, 148–51, 154, 169–73, 180–5, 191–201 *passim*, 205, 206, 209–25 *passim*, 228–33, 236, 239–53 *passim*, 260, 261, 269, 285, 286, 291, 292
employees of (central and local), 110, 196, 206, 222–5, 228, 230
grading, 155n; *see also* demands
Grand Coalition (WG), 261, 269, 285, 299
Grenelle (F), 65, 75
Grès de Bouffioulx, 44
grèves tournantes, 323
Groningen (NL), 173, 176, 179
growth, economic, 53–8, 75, 151, 154, 191, 192, 196, 218, 259, 274, 285, 291, 310 311
guidelines, 285, 286; *see also Orientierungsdaten*
guerre scolaire, 35

hairdressing, 39
Hamburg (WG), 263
Health and Safety Commission (UK), 247
health services, 133, 205, 228
Hesse (WG), 263
holidays, 280, 289; *see also* demands
Holland (NL), 9
hospital workers, 107, 121, 124, 178, 223, 263
'hot autumn', 1969 (I), 109, 113, 114, 118, 130, 143, 144, 148
hotels and restaurants, 110, 120, 127, 196
Housing Finance Act (UK), 250
housing policy, 48, 133, 171, 194, 250, 261; *see also* demands

ideology, 91, 187
IG Bau-Steine-Erden (WG), 263
IG Berbau (WG), 295
IG Chemie (WG), 263, 270, 282, 283, 292, 304n
IG Metall (WG), 263, 264, 271, 282, 283, 288, 292–6, 303n, 304n
ILO, 2, 3, 15, 36, 62, 105, 165, 202, 262, 308, 312, 313
immigrant workers, migrant workers, 39–42, 64, 68, 79, 85, 88, 109, 113, 115, 180; *see also* foreign workers
IMSF (WG), 303n, 305n
incomes, *see* wages
policy 178, 186, 192–4, 197–200, 209–15, 218, 219, 222, 223, 230–3, 238, 239, 242–5, 248, 251–3, 275, 284–8, 291–3; *see also* wages, policy
incorporation, 159, 183
Industrial Relations Act, 1971; Bill (UK), 198, 200, 203, 217–19, 229, 232, 236, 240, 242, 245–7, 251, 252, 254n
Bill, 1969 (UK), 218, 245
Industrial Reorganisation Corporation (UK), 195
industrialisation, 21, 84
Industriebond-NVV (NL), 166, 167, 174, 179, 188n

industry, industrial, 104, 106, 137, 139, 155, 194–6, 257, 259, 279
structure of, 56, 57, 163, 195, 196
inflation, 39, 45, 101, 103, 131, 135, 169–71, 192–5, 199, 200, 210–13, 239–43, 259, 260, 263, 265, 291, 292
Inquadramento Unico, 106, 126–8, 131
inspecteurs du travail, labour inspectors, 61, 83, 330
Institut für Sozialforschung (WG), 304n, 305n
institutionalisation, 32–4, 45–9, 72, 116, 160, 161, 182, 204, 234, 237–41, 253
insurance companies, 23, 120
integration, 159, 183, 185
internal commissions, *see commissioni interni*
Intersind (I), 139–41
investment, 35, 136, 154, 172, 194, 195, 211–13, 258, 259; *see also* demands
foreign, 21, 33, 48
private, 48, 56, 151, 212
public, 43, 56–8, 135
Ireland, Northern (UK), 199, 233, 250, 251
Republic of, 15, 250
iron industry, *see* steel and iron industries
Israel, 332n
ISTAT (I), 330
Italy, 2–9, 13–18, 54, 101–58 *passim*, 297, 299, 307–15, 317, 318, 328, 330, 333n
Mezzogiorno, south, 106, 135, 136, 153, 154
north 106, 108, 136, 137, 140
ITT, 39

Japan, 15, 332n
job enrichment, 131, 155n
evaluation, 127, 215
security, 111, 120, 301
JOC (F), 88
Joint Français, 55
Joint Left (F), *see* Union de la Gauche
journalists, 263
journées d'action, 63, 73, 79, 97
judges, 111, 244
Jungsozialisten (WG), 261

KAB (NL), 162, 167
KEN (NL), 179, 188n
kernen, 161, 169
Keynesianism, 101, 285
Korean War, 102
KWJ (NL), 180

labour inspectors; *see inspecteurs du travail*
market, 54, 60, 85, 103, 123, 164, 206, 284, 292
movement, 49, 64, 98, 128, 131, 205
Labour Party (UK), 192–200, 210–13, 216–20, 225, 228, 231–3, 236, 239–52 *passim*, 254n, 255n
National Executive of, 217
law; legal framework, 74–6, 79–84, 152, 153, 181, 193, 197, 198, 244–8, 251–3, 254n, 276, 277; *see also* strikes, legislation
courts of, 116, 182, 271, 276; *see also* National Industrial Relations Court
law of 11 February 1950 (F), 80, 99n
December 1968 (F), 88
27 December 1973 (F), 75
lawyers, 111, 280
left-wing groups, 43, 101, 107, 115, 118, 142, 172, 234, 249, 250, 296
Leidschendam (NL), 170
Leninism, 89, 91
Leyland-Innocenti, 119
Liberals, Liberal Party (B), 22, 23
(UK), 199, 200
Liège (B), 27
Limbourg (B), 27, 41, 42
Limburg (NL), 180
Lip, 55
local government employees, *see* governments
lock-outs, 150, 182, 325, 332
Lohnbewusstsein, neues, 297; *see also* consciousness
London (UK), 250
Loonwet, Wages Act, Bill (NL), 169, 170, 177
lorry-drivers, long-distance, 98
Lotta Continua (I), 143
Lower Weser (WG), 271
low-income groups, low-paid, 135, 153, 172, 176, 210, 213, 214, 222, 223, 251, 266, 267
Lufthansa Airline, 263
'lump labour', 231

mai rampant (I), 108
management, managers, 38, 40, 88, 102, 112, 115, 116, 145, 151, 180, 181, 205, 209, 215, 223, 227, 230, 234, 272, 273, 277, 283, 284, 289, 290, 295
Manchester (UK), 232
Manpower Services Commission (UK), 247
manufacturing industry, 102–4, 155n, 163, 196
Maoism, Maoists, 297
Marchand, 44
Marches, 112, 115, 250, 269
marginal workers, 93, 103
Marxism, Marxists, 63, 88–92, 128, 249, 261
May 1968 (F), 58–67, 94, 97, 98
measured day work, 209, 215
media, mass, workers in, 111, 273

mediation, 80, 81, 153
mergers, reorganisations, takeovers, 58, 84, 187n, 195, 235, 253n
metal (-working) industries, 5–8, 12n, 35, 104, 106, 113, 114, 122, 124, 127, 129, 135, 143, 145, 148–51, 155n, 156n, 162, 168, 173, 174, 179, 203, 261–4, 267–71, 274, 279, 283, 291–3, 296, 299–301; *see also* engineering
Michelin, 40, 42
migration, 55, 103; *see also* immigrant workers
mining, *see* coal-mining
Minister of the Economy (WG), 260, 285–7
  Labour (I), 153
    (WG), 280, 304n
  Social Affairs (NL), 169, 170
  Technology (UK), 197
Ministry of Commerce (F), 322
  Labour (F), 70, 317, 325, 330
    (I), 153
    (NL), 331
    (UK), 14, 234, 247, 248
    (WG), 14
    and Employment (B), 329
monetary policy, 102, 191, 192
'money illusion', 207, 266
motor industry, *see* car industry
multi-nationals, 38, 39, 57, 60, 163
Munich (WG), 277

National Coal Board (UK), 224
  Federation of Building Trades Operatives (UK), 254n
  Front (UK), 250
  Health Service (UK), 224
  Industrial Relations Court (UK), 198, 232, 246, 247
  Plan (UK), 192
  Statistical Institute (B), 329
  Union of Teachers (UK), 224
nationalisation, nationalised industries, 38, 53, 57, 69, 86, 90, 93, 94, 218, 223, 228, 331; *see also* state ownership
Nationalist Parties (UK), 199, 200
Nazis (WG), 260, 277
NBPI (UK), 208, 215, 224, 242, 254n, 256n
NCW (NL), 163, 171, 182
negotiations, *see* bargaining
Netherlands, 3, 4, 8–18 *passim*, 159–89 *passim*, 307–15, 318, 322, 328, 330
  east, 180
  north, 174
  south, 180
  west, 179
Neue Ostpolitik, 261
New Left, 143, 261
New Zealand, 15, 332n
newspapers, 263, 329, 331
Nieuwe Noord Nederlandse Scheepswerven, 176
NKV (NL), 166–73, 177, 180, 183
Noord-Brabant (NL), 173, 174, 180
North Rhein Westphalia (WG), 263, 264, 269
North Württemberg/North Baden (WG), 268
Norway, 15
NPD (WG), 260
NUBE (UK), 224
NUM (UK), 194, 227, 230, 249
nurses, 223
NVV (NL), 161, 162, 166–73, 177, 183, 184
  Jongerenkontakt, 180

occupations, 41, 44, 68, 114, 119, 173, 174, 179, 180, 205, 216, 231, 232, 274
OECD, 1n, 3, 10, 11n, 14, 310, 311, 315
Office de Sécurité Sociale (B), 28
  Nationale de l'Emploi (B), 28
  of Industrial Employers (NL), 182
office workers, *see* workers, office
oil industry, 40, 44; *see also* petroleum
  crisis, 171, 172, 194, 211
Olivetti, 130, 131, 140
Orientierungsdaten, 285; *see also* guidelines
ORTF (F), 69
Oude Pekela (NL), 173
out-workers, home-workers, 103, 110, 132, 155n
ouvriers spécialisés (F), 55, 64, 65, 68, 98n
overtime, 205, 215, 230, 280, 289
  bans on, 178, 179, 230

parliaments, 27, 170, 180, 197, 198, 232, 244, 250, 260, 279, 299
Parodi system (F), 99n
participation, 25–8, 31, 35, 71, 130, 183; *see also* workers' participation
parties, political, 26, 27, 32, 33, 67, 89, 91, 94, 95, 101, 109, 111, 133–7, 147, 149, 156n, 178, 187, 203, 254n
paternalism, 108, 110
patronati, 138
pay, *see* wages
Pay Board (UK), 243
payment systems, 222, 235, 252, 289
PBO (NL), 161, 168
peace obligation, 271, 276, 280, 281, 287–90
peasants, 107
pensions, 155n, 205; *see also* demands
petroleum industry, 23, 28, 48; *see also* oil
Philips, 163
pickets, picketing, 112, 231, 270
  'flying', 205, 231

mass, 112, 114, 205, 231
piecework, 113, 208, 209, 215, 221, 222, 227, 228, 235, 263, 280, 289
Pirelli, 109, 122
Report (I), 151, 158n
planning, economic, 33, 56, 91, 94, 153, 154, 192, 193, 196, 197, 220
physical, 249
plant stewards, 167; *see also délégués du personnel*
work, 167, 168, 182–6, 187n
police, 102, 115, 270, 273, 329, 330
polishing-tools industry, 263
politicisation, political action, 133, 154, 220, 234, 237, 253
politics, 85, 86, 117, 196–201, 248–51, 260, 261, 290; *see also* demands
postal services, 110, 121, 223, 228–30, 270, 271, 329
potato flour industry, 173
pound, *see* sterling
power industry, *see* electrical power generating
President (F), 57
prices, commodities, 193, 194, 209, 211, 213
policy 172, 194, 200, 212, 220
Prime Minister (UK), 197, 198n, 245
printing industry, 108, 162, 232, 263, 271
prisoners, 261
private sector, 23, 195, 201, 212, 223, 301
production, decentralisation of, 131, 132
means of, 91
mode of, 59
relations of, 128
productivity, 55–9, 102, 123, 193, 195, 206, 207, 217, 258, 259, 284, 289–92, 302, 312
agreements; bargaining, 72, 207, 215, 217, 237, 238, 241, 252
professions, 196, 235, 249
'professionalism, new' (I), 126, 127, 131, 155n
profit, rate of, 194, 211, 258–60, 284
programmation sociale, 28, 29, 33–8, 41
programme Commun (F), 91, 93
promotion, 69, 123
Protestants, 161, 163, 166, 199, 203, 233, 250
PSB (B), 26, 27, 31, 49
PSC (B), 26, 27, 31, 49
PSIUP (I), 142
public administration, 110, 111, 120–2, 132
employees, 24, 88, 124, 125, 166, 178, 180, 213, 222–5, 228, 329
expenditure, spending, 102, 169–72, 193, 210
sector, services, 6, 23, 51, 67, 69, 77, 80, 83, 86, 107–10, 132, 135, 137, 138, 148, 150, 153, 193, 194, 203–9, 228, 242, 323
utilities, 5, 6, 196, 203, 329
PvdA (NL), 160, 171

Quadragesimo Anno, 162
qualifications, 66
'quality of life', 296, 299

Raad van Overleg (NL), 167
racialism, 250
railways, 121–4, 132, 194, 222, 229, 230, 247, 270, 271
rank-and-file, 30, 46, 64, 72, 73, 89, 96, 107, 117, 123–34 *passim*, 137, 138, 142–9, 154, 162, 185, 216, 237, 295, 303; *see also* trade unions, membership
committees 110, 142; *see also* CUB
rationalisation of industry, 39, 44, 45, 60, 109, 133, 134, 195, 259, 268, 280, 297, 301
reconstruction, post-war, 101, 163, 257, 258
redundancy, lay-offs, 132, 156n, 180, 195, 205, 215, 216, 221, 231, 235, 253n, 301, 329
refuse collection, 236
Reggio Calabria (I), 135
Renault, 65, 98
rents, 118, 220, 268
re-organisation, *see* mergers
Republican Party (I), 138, 147
Rerum Novarum, 162
Resistance, the, 28, 108
restrictive practices, 217, 239, 241
retirement, 78, 79, 85
retraining, 98n
Richtungsgewerkschaften, 277
RMHP (NL), 166, 167
Rotterdam (NL), 168, 173, 174, 187n
Royal Commission on Trade Unions and Employers Associations; Donovan Commission (UK), 218, 221, 227, 236–41, 244, 245, 253n–255n
rubber industry, 116, 263

Saar (WG), 263, 264
sabotage, 116, 267
sackings, *see* dismissals
schappen, 161
Schiphol airport (NL), 180
schools, 107, 110, 121, 224, 261
church, 35, 50n
teachers, 121, 150, 223, 224, 249, 329
science, workers in, 111, 196
Scotland (UK), 174, 199
SDAP (NL), 160
seamen, 196
Second World War, 3, 21, 119, 160–3, 178, 233, 238, 257
Secretary of State for Industry (UK), 212

section syndicale, 70
secularisation, 166
self-management, 66, 90, 91, 95, 119, 168; *see also autogestion*
sequestration, 82, 83
SER (NL), 161, 169, 170, 182, 189n
services sector, 5, 6, 85, 88, 98, 104, 107–10, 120, 124, 137, 196; *see also* tertiary sector *and* public services
shareholding, workers', 72, 76, 77, 84, 85
ship-building, 174, 176, 203, 221, 269
shops, shop-keepers, 85, 98, 110; *see also* distributive trades *and* supermarkets
shop-stewards, 143, 182, 204, 226–8, 234–7, 249, 250, 253n, 254n, 271, 272, 279–83, 293–6
  committees of, 234
shutdowns, *see* closures
'sit-ins', 232, 253n; *see also* occupations
Sixth Plan (F), 84
SMIC (F), 66, 75, 79
Smithfield Meat Market (UK), 250
social compact, social contract, 151, 171, 195, 200, 220, 241–4, 252, 253n
Social Democratic Parties (I), 138, 147
  (WG), 277, 300; *see also* SPD
'social-justice bargaining', 213
social policy, services, 45, 135, 154, 178, 196, 231, 244, 249
  reforms, 150, 151
  symmetry, 286–8
Social Solidarity Pact (B), 28, 29
Socialism, Socialist Parties (B), 22, 23, 26, 31
  (F), 66, 89, 90, 94, 95
  (I), 108, 138–42
  (NL), 161
  (UK), 197, 203, 205, 212
SPD (WG), 260, 261, 269, 285–8, 297, 299
squatters, 249
staff associations, 224
  workers, *see* workers, staff
'stagflation', 193
state, the, 34, 35, 43, 48, 71, 74–9, 83, 85, 90, 93, 137, 140, 141, 152, 153, 160–4, 183–7, 198–201, 205, 212, 217, 220, 233, 238–41, 246, 251–3, 274, 275, 279, 284–8
  ownership, public ownership, 195, 200, 212, 217, 220, 244, 329; *see also* nationalisation
State of Emergency (UK), 229
Statuto dei Lavoratori (I), 116, 141, 143, 152, 153
steel and iron industries, 23, 28, 35, 40–2, 48, 112, 116, 263, 264, 267, 269, 274, 296, 299–301, 304n
sterling (UK), 191–6, 200, 208, 212, 243, 252
Stichting van de Arbeid (NL), 161–4, 169–72
straw-board industry, 173, 178
street sweepers, 121
strikes, 35–45 *passim*, 46, 60, 67–9, 79–83, 104–22, 155n, 168, 171–4, 178–84, 193, 199, 201–5, 210, 220–33 *passim*, 242, 261–76 *passim*, 284, 290–302 *passim*
  ballots, referenda, 73, 227, 247, 278, 294
  committees, 43, 273
  general, 35, 48, 133
  legislation, 164, 244–7, 276, 277; *see also* law
  May 1968 (F), *see* May 1968
  national, industry-wide, 119
  notices, 72, 82, 83
  official, union, 8, 9, 12n, 13n, 41, 64, 174, 179, 187n, 201–4, 221–9, 237, 240, 261–4, 292, 296, 301
  pay, funds, 97, 138, 179, 223, 226, 227, 230, 231, 271
  plant-level, workshop, 63, 73, 111–16, 129, 134, 141–3, 146, 154, 226, 263, 264, 271–4, 290, 302
  political, 67, 68, 177, 178, 203, 232, 233, 253n, 269, 276, 328–30, 332n
  regional distribution of, 7, 8, 18
  right to, 155n, 181, 244
  September 1969 (WG), 263–7, 272, 286, 295, 298–300, 303n, 304n
  spontaneous, 'wildcat', 8, 73, 113, 263–75 *passim*, 291, 292, 295, 299–302, 303n, 304n
  statistics of 1–18 *passim*, 36, 61–3, 105, 160, 164, 165, 174, 187n, 201–3, 232, 262, 303n, 321–34 *passim*
  types of:
    articulated, 111–13
    'confetti', 113
    internal, 111
    'lightning', 111, 270
    one-day, 229, 232; *see also journées d'action*
    registration, 113
    'reverse', 119
    'rolling', 111–13, 116, 117, 330; *see also grèves tournantes*
    rotation, 270
    selective, 179, 230, 270
    'spot', 111–13, 116
    sudden, 116, 121
    token, 270, 271
    'to the finish', 120, 121
  unconstitutional, 204, 226
  unofficial, 9, 12, 35, 37, 40–3, 64, 73, 164, 172–7, 181–4, 187n, 201, 204, 221–8, 234–6, 245–7, 261, 286, 290
Strikes Bill (NL), 177

students movement, 43, 97, 98, 109–12, 115, 142, 197, 249, 260, 269, 299, 304n
subsidies, 200, 220
supermarkets, 124
supervisors, 68, 223
Sweden, 15, 322, 332n
Switzerland, 15
SWOV (NL), 177, 189n

takeovers, *see* mergers
Tarifverhandlungen (WG), 258
Tarifvertragsgesetz (WG), 276, 304n
taxation, 133, 192–4, 197–200, 210, 211, 217, 244, 299
taxis, taxi-drivers, 173, 176
Taylorianism, 129, 131
teachers, *see* schools
technicians, *see* workers, technical
technology, 59, 64, 85, 125–9, 228, 235
tenants' associations, 249, 250
tertiary sector, 4, 6, 103, 174, 186; *see also* services sector
textiles industry, 5, 6, 23, 24, 35, 55, 108, 127, 132, 166, 201, 263, 267, 301
TGWU (UK), 197, 198, 213, 218, 230, 237, 247, 251, 254n
three-day week (UK), 194
threshold agreements, 171, 210, 211, 243
tile-layers, 263
Tilsitt (F), 75
tourism, 48
trade, *see* commerce
Trade Union and Labour Relations Act (UK), 254n
  (Amendment) Act (UK), 254n
trade unions, 22–42 *passim*, 46–9, 53, 55, 63–6, 69–82 *passim*, 85–97 *passim*, 98n, 102–54 *passim*, 156n, 159–87 *passim*, 192–209 *passim*, 213–53 *passim*, 254n, 258, 260, 263–71, 275–303 *passim*, 329
  'autonomous', independent, 121, 149, 150, 184
  branches, 73, 217; *see also section syndical*
  'category', 162
  craft, 214
  industry-level, 120, 124, 133–7, 144, 145, 148, 156n, 170, 180, 184
  leaders, officers, 73, 130, 142–4, 154, 162, 183, 204, 220, 223, 233, 234, 237, 240, 246–9, 254n, 267, 270, 271, 278, 282, 286, 287, 293–7, 300, 302
  membership, unionisation, 22, 23, 39, 40, 87, 88, 110, 138, 140, 149, 150, 156n, 159, 162, 166, 177, 184, 204, 222, 223, 254n, 265–7, 275–8, 282, 283, 287, 288, 291, 294, 295, 298, 303; *see also* rank-and-file
    compulsory, 162, 247
    statistics of, 23, 316–19
  plant-level, 119, 120, 150, 167, 177
  rights, 39, 61, 64, 76, 79, 85–7, 98n, 199; *see also* demands *and droit syndical*
  subscriptions, 162
  unification of, 135, 137, 147, 148, 166, 167, 183
  white-collar, 214, 223, 225
  work-place representatives, 64, 73, 113–15, 142, 145, 147, 181, 295, 299, 303; *see also* shop stewards
Trafalgar Square (UK), 224
training, 55, 66, 69, 74–8, 84, 87, 155n, 248; *see also* demands
transport 6, 98, 107, 121, 133, 166, 174, 196, 203; *see also* demands
  equipment industry, 174, 203
  fares, 118, 172
  goods, 176
tripartitism, tripartite, 35, 75, 198, 247, 248, 252
troops, 122
Trotskyists, 249
TUC (UK), 192–200, 213–20, 224, 225, 232–9, 243–8, 251, 252, 254n, 256n
  General Council of, 232
tug-boats, 181
Turin Labour Chamber, 144
typre industry, 114

UIL (I), 138, 144–51, 156n
UILM (I), 156n
underemployment 102, 103
unemployment, unemployed, 21, 30, 55, 101–3, 139, 151, 155n, 159, 164, 170, 180, 184, 191–5, 210, 220, 232, 239, 242, 243, 258–60, 275, 292, 296, 300, 302, 303n, 313, 314
  benefit, 74, 75, 162
Unie-BLHP (NL), 166
Union de la Gauche, Joint Left (F), 91, 93
unionisation, *see* trade unions, membership
Unionist Party (UK), 199
United Kingdom, 3–9, 14–18, 54, 191–256 *passim*, 307–15, 318, 319, 323, 328, 331, 333n
United States of America, 15, 39, 54, 102
Upper Clyde Shipbuilders, 174, 216, 231
urban protests, 98, 117
urbanisation, 103

Val Saint Lambert, 44
value-added tax, 169, 170
Van Thiels United, 174

Vauxhall, 236
Vietnam War, 260
vine-growers, 98
violence, 115, 199
VNO (NL), 163, 170, 171, 182
voluntarism, 238–41, 244, 251, 252

'wage explosion', 205, 209, 211, 251
wages, wage increases, pay, incomes, 60, 75, 77, 102, 103, 140, 170–2, 193–6, 200, 207–13, 228, 242, 258–60, 277, 286, 291, 292, 315; *see also* demands, pay
  contracts, 280
  controls, restraint; incomes controls, restraint, 170, 171, 192, 194, 198, 243, 244, 263, 285
  drift, 163, 204, 208, 284
  guaranteed, 132
  policy, 163, 164, 169–72, 178, 278, 283, 284, 291–6; *see also* incomes policy
Wages Act, *see* Loonwet
Wales (UK), 199
Wallonia (B), 21–7, 37, 48, 49n
Weimar Republic, 280
welfare (state), 159, 162, 198, 217
Westphalia (WG), 274
women, female workers, 39, 45, 47, 64, 68, 69, 88, 106, 110, 176–80, 261, 264, 272, 278, 295
  movements, feminism, 40, 47
workers:
  craft, 68, 108, 215, 221, 235
  manual, blue-collar, 22, 25, 40, 88, 109, 122, 126, 138, 155n, 180, 203, 210, 222, 228, 264, 277
  marginal, 67, 93, 103
  non-manual, 87, 203
  office, 69, 109, 110, 115, 117, 166
  production-line, assembly-line, 67–9, 98n, 108, 119, 122–6, 180, 267, 272
  rural, 98
  salaried, 113, 264, 269, 278
  self-employed, 111
  semi-skilled, 109, 115, 117, 122–6, 155n; *see also ouvriers spécialisés*
  skilled, 40, 44, 64, 68, 88, 96, 109, 114, 123, 126, 155n, 268, 272, 295, 301, 302
  staff, 23, 66, 180, 184, 223
  technical, 23, 68, 69, 96, 109
  unskilled, 40, 44, 67, 68, 113–16, 122, 125, 126, 267, 272, 295
  white-collar, 22–5, 39, 40, 88, 96, 106, 109, 126, 127, 138, 155n, 162, 180, 204, 223–5, 264, 273, 277
workers' control, 26, 38, 43, 44, 64, 87, 143, 204, 205; *see also* demands
  directors, 216
  participation, 78, 85, 217; *see also* participation
work-group, 64, 233–8
working conditions, 39, 74–8, 85, 87, 129, 169, 275, 280, 301 *see also* demands
  hours, 54, 75, 118, 280, 289, 293; *see also* demands
works councils, 161, 168, 169, 183, 186, 187n, 216, 269, 272, 273, 276–84, 288–90, 294, 295; *see also conseils d'entreprise and consigli di fabbrica*
Works Councils Act (NL), 161, 168, 184
  Law (WG), *see* Betr. VG
work-to-rule, 114, 121, 178, 179, 230

young workers, 39, 42, 67, 88, 109, 110, 113–17, 176–80
Yugoslavia, 168

Name Index

n=an entry in the Notes or in the List of Works Cited

Accornero, A., 155n, 156n, 157n
Adam, G., 87, 96, 99n, 317
Adams, R., 209, 240, 254n
Aglieta, R., 156n, 157n
Agosti, A., 157n
Akkermans, T., 159–89 *passim*
Albanese, L., 156n, 157n
Albeda, W., 160, 183, 188n
Allen, V. L., 192, 214, 254n
Allende, S., 237
Altvater, E., 258, 297, 304n
Amoretti, A., 149, 157n
Armanski, G., 301, 304n
Augusti, A., 143

Bachy, J. P., 63, 70, 99n
Baethge, M., 258, 301, 304n
Bain, G. S., 223, 254n, 319
Bakker, B. de, 37, 38, 50n
Banks, J. A., 218, 254n
Barzel, R., 269
Baudoin, P., 187n, 188n
Baumfelder, E., 55, 99n
Beccalli, B., 101n, 155n, 157n
Beckers, M., 38, 50
Beekfeld, C. van, 168, 177, 188n
Benetti, B., 155n, 158n
Benn, T., 212
Benschop, A., 177, 188n
Berg, H. van der, 187n, 188n
Bergmann, J., 298–302, 304n, 319
Berlinguer, E., 155n
Bescoby, J., 234, 255n
Beynon, H., 235, 254n
Bianchi, G., 155n, 156n, 157n
Bianchi, S., 157n
Biesheuvel, B., 185
Blackburn, R. M., 224, 254n
Blechschmidt, A., 304n
Bolzani, P., 155n, 157n
Bonifazi, A., 156n, 158n
Bos, W., 169, 188n
Bosanquet, N., 255n
Bosc, S., 73, 99n
Brand, F., 302, 304n
Brandt, W., 261, 269
Brej, B., 188n
Britt, D., 333n
Brough, I., 205, 206, 255n
Brown, W., 206, 208, 215, 226, 227, 235, 254n
Browne, M., 205, 206, 256n
Buiter, J., 167, 188n
Bulcke, D., van den, 51n
Bullock, Lord, 248

Caire, G., 317
Cameron, G. C., 221, 254n
Carabelli, G., 155n, 157n
Cardulli, C., 155n, 157n
Carré, J. J., 56, 99n
Carton de Wiart, A., 50n
Castellina, L., 143, 157n
Cazzola, G., 152, 157n
Censi, G., 157n
Chiaberge, R., 156n, 157n
Child, J., 212, 254n
Cini, D., 150, 158n
Clack, G., 19n, 226, 254n, 256n
Claeys, P. H., 23, 28, 50n
Clegg, H. A., 208, 209, 221, 234, 240, 254n
Cliff, T., 212, 254n
Clifford, J., 206, 255n
Conen, G. J. M., 318
Cornelissen, I., 160, 188n
Cotgrove, S., 214, 254n
Cousins, F., 197
Crewe, I., 255n
Crompton, R., 215, 228, 256n
Crouch, C. J., 191–256 *passim*

d'Agostini, F., 157n
d'Antonio, M., 157n
Dassa, J., 100n
Debuyst, F., 26, 27, 50n

Declercq, G., 90, 99n
Delamotte, Y., 99n
Deppe, F., 297, 305
Depuy, F., 99n
Desseigne, G., 66, 99n
d'Estaing, G., 57
Dickens, L., 256n
Dickson, D., 99n
Dina, A., 156n, 157n
Disraeli, B., 1n
Donovan, Lord, 221, 227, 236–41, 244, 245, 251, 253, 254n, 255n
Dorfman, G. A., 192, 255n
Drenth, H., 187n, 188n
Dubin, R., 334n
Dubois, P., 53–100 *passim*
Duhm, R., 274, 305n
Dulong, R., 98, 100n
Dunham, J., 254n
Dunlop, F., 2
Durand, C., 13n, 19n, 53–100 *passim*
Durand, M., 13n, 19n, 61, 99n, 325, 333n
Durcan, J. W., 253n, 255n, 321, 333n

Eisegg, E., 271
Eldridge, J. E. T., 221, 254n
Ellis, J., 197, 249, 255n
Erbès-Seguin, S., 53–100 *passim*
Erhard, L., 275

Fels, A., 254n, 255n
Field, F., 255n
Fisher, M., 332n, 333n
Flanders, A., 215, 255n
Foa, V., 139, 155n, 156n, 157n
Forbice, A., 156n, 157n
Forchheimer, F., 333n
Fortuyn, P., 187n, 188n
Fox, A., 215, 255n
Frere, J. P., 50n
Frey, L., 157n
Fuà, G., 102, 157n
Fulcher, J., 332n, 333n

Galle, O. R., 333n
Garavini, A., 144, 157n
Garavini, S., 155, 156n, 157n
Gaulle, C. de, 94
Giambarba, E., 139, 157n
Glyn, A., 211, 212, 255n
Goldthorpe, J. H., 212, 214, 226, 228, 255n
Goodman, J. F. B., 255n
Gordon, B. J., 327, 333n
Groenevelt, A., 179, 188n
Grootings, P., 159–89 *passim*
Gubbels, R., 332n, 333n
Guidi, E., 155n, 158n
Guilbert, B., 56, 100n

Halevi, J., 155n, 158n
Hardes, H.-D., 286
Harff, Y., 13n, 19n, 61, 99n, 325, 333n
Hart, F., 231, 256n
Hartmann, P. T., 3, 4, 19n, 323, 334n
Heath, E., 198, 199, 233, 243
Heemskerk, C., 180, 188n
Heffer, E., 198, 255n
Hemingway, J., 231, 232, 253n, 255n
Hen, P. de, 181, 188n
Heyvaert, H., 50n
Hildebrandt, E., 272, 305n
Hill, S., 235, 255n
Hirsche, K., 305n
Hoeven, P. ter, 160, 183, 187, 188n
Hoffman, P., 305n
Hohne, G., 305n
Hoss, D., 305n
Hostalier, F., 66, 100n
Hughes, J., 213, 255n
Hunter, L. C., 215, 216, 256n
Hyman, R., 205, 206, 209, 212, 214, 222, 226, 229, 255n

Ingham, G. K., 322, 333n

Jackson, D., 256n
Jacobi, O., 189n, 304n, 305n, 306n, 319
Jacob-Ory, A., 100n
Jacops, J., 187n, 188n
Jamieson, S. M., 327, 333n
Jenkins, P., 197, 255n
Johnson, W., 197, 249, 255n
Jong, J. de, 170, 179, 180, 186, 187, 188n

Kalbitz, R., 9, 19n, 303n, 305n, 332n
Kee, T., 177, 188n
Keller, B., 280
Kelsall, E. P., 219n
Kerckhove, J. van de, 37, 51n
Kergoat, D., 73, 100n
Kern, H., 267, 305n, 333n
Kerr, C., 327, 333n, 334n
Keyser, W., 231, 232, 253n, 255n
Kittner, M., 305n
Kleerekoper, S., 160, 188n
Knowles, K. G. J. C., 4, 12n, 19n
Kornhauser, A., 334n
Krasucki, H., 92, 100n
Krijnen, G., 179, 188n
Krumnov, F., 65, 100n

Laloire, M., 28, 50n

Lammers, C., 164, 188n
Langweiler, P., 305n
Layton, D., 209, 213, 255n
Leemans, 50n
Leijnse, F., 160, 168, 177–81, 187n, 188n, 189n
Lelli, M., 155n, 158n
Leminski, G. B., 305n
Leon, P., 158n
Lerner, S., 206, 208, 234, 255n
Limmer, H., 305n
Lind, J. A. D., 332n
Lindberg, L., 255n
Lloyd, J., 256n
Lockwood, D., 255n
Lorwin, V. R., 23, 26–8, 32, 33, 49n, 50n
Lupton, T., 99n

McCarthy, W. E. J., 206, 221, 227, 253n, 254n, 255n, 256n, 323, 334n
McKersie, R. B., 215, 216, 256n
Macloug, P., 100n
Malinvaud, E., 99
Mallet, S., 64, 100n
Mann, M., 253n, 255n
Marchese, C., 155n, 158n
Marochi, M., 158n
Marsh, A. I., 221, 255n
Martin, D., 99n
Masi, G. de, 155n, 156n, 157n
Matthöfer, M., 269, 305n
Mayr, H., 303n
Mellish, M., 256n
Mergner, U., 301, 305n
Miliband, R., 255n, 256n
Mitchell, J., 254n, 255n
Molitor, M., 21–51 *passim*
Müller-Jentsch, W., 257–305 *passim*, 319

Neuville, J., 22, 23, 50n
Nickel, W., 305n
Nieuwstadt, M. van, 179, 188n
Noé, N., 279, 305n

Olle, W., 272, 305n
Oppenheim, J.-P., 90, 94, 100n
Orazi, A. M., 155n, 158n
Osterland, M., 305n
Otto, O., 306n
Outrive, L. van, 25, 28, 50n, 51n

Paci, M., 158n
Panitch, L., 192, 197, 198, 218, 233, 242, 245, 253n, 254n, 255n, 256n
Parker, S. R., 206, 226, 227, 254n, 256n, 323, 334n
Pauli, H., 160, 189n
Penth, B., 304n
Peper, B., 184–7, 189n
Perrot, M., 72, 100n, 332n, 334n
Phelps Brown, E. H., 205, 206, 256n
Piehl, E., 187n, 189n
Piret, C., 38, 46, 50n
Pizzorno, A., 101n, 122, 139, 158n, 333n
Pöhler, W., 265, 305n
Pohlmann, H., 304n
Poppe, C., 168, 188n, 189n
Powell, E., 250
Prestat, C., 99n
Price, R., 223, 254n, 319
Proudhon, P. J., 90

Quere, L., 98, 100n

Ramondt, J., 179, 181, 189n
Razzano, R., 150, 158n
Regalia, I., 101–58 *passim*
Regini, M., 101–58 *passim*
Renard, A., 24
Reynaud, J.-D., 99n, 100n
Reyneri, E., 101–58 *passim*
Richter, I., 218, 256n
Rieser, V., 122, 158n
Rimlinger, G. V., 333n, 334n
Roberts, B. C., 207, 236, 256n
Roberts, G., 19n, 256n
Roethlisberger, R., 99n
Romagnoli, G., 156n, 158n
Ronge, A. de, 35, 50n
Rositi, F., 152, 158n
Ross, A. M., 3, 19n, 323, 334n
Roth, K. H., 302, 305n
Rothwell, S., 207, 236, 256n
Routh, G., 205, 256n
Roy, D., 99n

Salvarani, G., 156n, 158n
Salvati, M., 101n, 155n, 158n
Saucier, R., 50n
Saville, J., 255n, 256n
Scardigli, V., 60, 100n
Scheel, W., 269
Schiffres, M., 90, 100n
Schiller, K., 285
Schmidt, E., 269, 271, 303n, 304n, 305n
Schmidt, H., 261
Schneider, D., 305n
Schumann, M., 298, 303n, 304n, 306n
Sclavi, S., 122, 155n
Sellier, F., 99n, 100n
Shalev, M., 1–19 *passim*, 201, 203, 227, 253n, 256n, 321–34 *passim*

Shorter, E., 72, 100n, 325, 332n, 334n
Siegel, A., 327, 333n, 334n
Silver, M., *see* Shalev, M.
Simiand, F., 64, 100n
Sklair, L., 250, 256n
Smolders, Y., 160, 178, 179, 189n
Snels, G., 179, 188n
Sperling, H.-J., 257–305 *passim*
Spitaels, G., 38, 51n
Stamp, Sir J., 332n
Stearns, P. N., 2, 19n
Steinhaus, K., 264, 306n
Storms, B., 51n
Strauss, F. J., 269
Sutcliffe, B., 211, 212, 255n

Terpstra, G. H., 163, 169, 189n
Teulings, A., 160, 179, 181, 186, 187n, 189n
Thompson, W., 231, 256n
Tilly, C., 72, 100n, 325, 332n, 334
Torrisi, G., 50n
Townsend, P., 255n
Trentin, B., 139, 156n, 157n
Treu, T., 139, 152, 156n, 158n
Turner, H. A., 10, 19n, 208, 210, 213, 222, 226, 235, 237, 253n, 256n, 323, 334n
Turone, S., 155n, 156n, 157n, 158n

Vachets, A., 100n
Vall, M. van der, 163, 164, 189n
Vamplew, C., 254n
Vandewalle, J. F., 28–30, 51n
Ven, F. van de, 187n
Veneziani, B., 153, 158n
Verdès-Leroux, J., 98, 100n
Verdier, J. M., 99n
Verly, J., 51n
Vroeman, J., 179, 189n
Vroey, M. de, 50n

Walker, K. F., 1, 19n
Wallenburg, H., 188n
Wedderburn, D., 215, 228, 256n
Wedderburn, K. W., 254n, 256n
Weekes, B., 240, 246, 256n
Wilberforce, Lord, 229, 256n
Wilkinson, F., 208, 210, 213, 256n
Willener, A., 99n
Windmuller, J., 160–70, 185, 186, 189n